Law of Export Credit Insurance and Guarantees

Examining the law of export credit insurance and export credit guarantees, this book clarifies the legal nature of ECI and ECGs as insurance and guarantees, respectively, by comparing their legal characteristics regarding the contract formation process, terms and conditions, duty of fair presentation, claim handling process and subrogation and recoveries. It further explores why some export credit agencies provide export credit guarantees in addition to export credit insurance, notwithstanding that an ECG is a more client-friendly product and easier than ECI for banks to use.

Analysing the legal principles applicable to export credit insurance and export credit guarantees reflected by English case authorities and statutory law, the book is a doctrinal study informed by substantive empirical research. It studies a large number of export credit insurance and export credit guarantee contractual terms in order to propose several model clauses and scrutinise the influences of the Insurance Act 2015 on ECI.

This book is an important reference for students, academics and practitioners in the field of commercial and insurance law. In particular, it seeks to provide guidelines for all potential parties who wish to arrange an ECI/ECG transaction, including export credit agencies, private credit insurers, brokers, banks, exporters and buyers, to correctly identify and choose the suitable cover.

Law of Export Credit Insurance and Guarantees

Cheng Lin

Routledge
Taylor & Francis Group
LONDON AND NEW YORK

First published 2023
by Routledge
4 Park Square, Milton Park, Abingdon, Oxon OX14 4RN

and by Routledge
605 Third Avenue, New York, NY 10158

Routledge is an imprint of the Taylor & Francis Group, an informa business

British Library Cataloguing-in-Publication Data
A catalogue record for this book is available from the British Library

Library of Congress Cataloging-in-Publication Data
A catalogue record has been requested for this book

ISBN: 978-1-032-26293-2 (hbk)
ISBN: 978-1-032-26294-9 (pbk)
ISBN: 978-1-003-28755-1 (ebk)

DOI: 10.4324/b22864

Typeset in Times New Roman
by Deanta Global Publishing Services, Chennai, India

Contents

Detailed Contents

Preface

Export credit insurance (ECI) and export credit guarantees (ECGs) are important financial instruments to support international trade. Although ECI and ECGs have long been used in the industry, whether and how they are legally distinguished from each other does not seem to be well comprehended, since the terms "insurance" and "guarantee" are often used interchangeably by export credit agencies (ECAs) to label their products.

This research aims to demonstrate that the true legal nature of an export credit facility depends on its substantial terms and that ECI is a contract of insurance and an ECG a contract of guarantee, respectively. It compares their legal characteristics from a contractual perspective and demonstrates that an ECG is a client-friendlier product and easier than ECI for banks to use: (a) the formation process of an ECG is more straightforward than ECI; (b) an ECI policy imposes more substantial obligations on banks than an ECG contract; (c) banks are subject to the duty of fair presentation only under ECI; (d) the claim handling process under ECI could be prolonged, whereas, under an ECG, ECAs normally pay banks straight away. In the meantime, this research also reveals that there is no significant difference between an ECG and ECI in terms of subrogation and recoveries.

Based on the observations above, this research seeks to further explore why some ECAs provide ECGs in addition to ECI, despite the fact that ECI is the mainstream product in the market: an ECG is generally more costly than ECI, which, among other practical reasons, makes it a less popular product. However, because of its legal characteristics, it still plays an essential role in supporting certain tailored supplier/buyer credit transactions. Protected by an ECG, banks will be most encouraged to finance exporters.

This book is primarily a doctrinal study that analyses all reported ECI and ECG cases in the UK. The recent case of *ABN AMRO Bank NV v Royal and Sun Alliance Insurance Plc* [2021] EWCA Civ 1789, where credit risk was placed in the marine cargo insurance market, will be examined in detail. This work also involves substantive empirical research on the basis of the author's previous internship research project at the International Association of Credit & Investment Insurers (Berne Union) on the legal nature of buyer credit insurance and buyer credit guarantee in 2019–20 (the Berne Union Academic Survey), which collected 26 questionnaire responses, eight interview responses, 15 copies of standard ECI policies and two standard ECG contracts from members of the Berne Union. All those materials enabled the author to study a large number of contractual terms of ECI and ECGs and propose several model clauses accordingly. In particular, the Insurance Act 2015 and its influences on ECI policies will be explored throughout this work.

This book aims to serve as a helpful reference for students, academics and practitioners in the field of commercial and insurance law. In particular, it seeks to provide guidelines for all potential parties who wish to arrange an ECI/ECG transaction, including ECAs, private credit insurers, brokers, banks, exporters, buyers and law firms, to correctly identify and choose the suitable cover and draft the ECI/ECG contract.

The law is endeavoured to be stated as of 1 February 2022.

Cheng Lin
February 2022

Acknowledgements

I am immensely indebted to the following people and institutions from whom I received great help and support throughout my PhD research and the preparation of this book.

First and foremost, I would like to express my most sincere gratitude to Prof Özlem Gürses, my first supervisor at King's College London. Her advice, comments and encouragement enabled me to complete my research plan step by step. She has always been a role model for me to learn from as an excellent, cheerful, diligent, self-disciplined and warm-hearted scholar. The same appreciation should go to Prof Eva Lomnicka QC (Hon), my second supervisor, who always encourages me to bridge the gap between academic research and commercial practice. Without her help, I could not have gained so much essential knowledge of the export credit industry. She is such a renowned and respected leading expert in English law, and I feel so lucky to have studied under her supervision.

I feel fortunate to have had the opportunity to carry out an internship research project at the Berne Union in 2019–20. I owe a great debt of thanks to Mr Vinco David, the Secretary-General of the Berne Union, and Mr Laszlo Varnai, the Associate Director of the Berne Union Secretariat. With their kind guidance and support, I was able to conduct the Berne Union Academic Survey which was highly tailored to the theme of my PhD research. I am also very grateful to the individuals who contributed to the survey on behalf of their institutions. They offered insightful answers to my research questions with great patience, and I appreciate the privilege of their time.

My PhD research is funded by the generous King's College London–China Scholarship Council joint PhD scholarship. The Dickson Poon School of Law of King's also offered me various postgraduate research allowances that supported my conference trips abroad, from which I benefited a lot. Special thanks also go to Prof Adolfo Paolini and Dr Kyriaki Noussia, the examiners of my PhD viva panel, for their valuable comments and suggestions. With their kind recommendation, I had the honour to receive the King's College London Outstanding PhD Thesis Award 2021.

I would like to thank Ms Siobhán Poole, Mr Sanjo Joseph Puthumana and Mr Jake Millicheap, my commissioning editor and editorial assistants at Routledge, for all their help with the production of my book. I am also grateful for the anonymous reviewers' comments on my book proposal.

I wish to thank various people in China, too. Thank you, Prof Liying Zhang from China University of Political Science and Law, the supervisor of my LLB and LLM programme, for opening the door for me to the academic career and the fascinating area of maritime and insurance law. Thank you, Prof Xiaoli Shi, for your enlightening international trade law lectures which attracted my interest in ECI and ECGs for the first time. And thank you, Prof Yuqing Zhang and Dr Chenghua Jiang, the prominent experts from the Ministry of Commerce of China, for your endless help and guidance.

Lastly, I owe an endless debt of gratitude to my parents, Ms Yueqiong Chen and Prof Mr Yuanfu Lin. Your affection, guidance and education are always the greatest support throughout every stage of my life. And I am so lucky to have met you, my fiancée, Miss Lifang Gao. I promise that I will be a good husband and father.

Cheng Lin
February 2022

Author biography

Dr Cheng Lin is an Associate Professor at the School of Law, Fujian Normal University, China. He read his PhD at King's College London under the supervision of Prof Özlem Gürses and Prof Eva Lomnicka QC (Hon) after obtaining LLB and LLM degrees from China University of Political Science and Law. He was awarded the King's Outstanding PhD Thesis Prize 2021 after passing the viva without corrections. Dr Lin has published widely in leading law journals such as *Journal of Business Law* and *Lloyd's Maritime and Commercial Law Quarterly*. He has also had extensive legal internships at the International Union of Credit & Investment Insurers (2019–20), China Export & Credit Insurance Corporation (2017), Yuqing Zhang Law Firm Beijing (2016–17) and the Supreme Court of China (2014). Dr Lin passed the Chinese National Bar Exam in 2013 and holds the Chinese legal qualification.

Abbreviations

Berne Union	The International Union of Credit and Investment Insurers
Berne Union Academic Survey	The Berne Union Academic Survey on the Legal Nature of Buyer Credit Insurance and Buyer Credit Guarantees
Directive 98/29/EC	The European Commission Directive 98/29/EC on Harmonisation of the Main Provisions Concerning Export Credit Insurance for Transactions with Medium and Long-Term Cover
ECA	Export Credit Agency
ECG	Export Credit Guarantee
ECGD	Export Credits Guarantee Department
ECI	Export Credit Insurance
Export Finance Buyer Credit Agreement	Loan Market Association's Single Currency Term Facility Agreement for Use in Export Finance Buyer Credit Transactions
GUA	General Underwriters Agreement
IA 2015	The Insurance Act 2015
ICISA	The International Credit Insurance & Surety Association
Lloyd's	Lloyd's of London
LMA	Loan Market Association
LMG	London Market Group
MIA 1906	The Marine Insurance Act 1906
OECD	The Organisation for Economic Co-operation and Development
OECD Agreement	The OECD Agreement on Officially Supported Export Credits
UKEF	UK Export Finance
WTO	World Trade Organisation
WTO SCM Agreement	The WTO Agreement on Subsidies and Countervailing Measures

Table of Cases

A & J Inglis v John Buttery & Co (1878) 3 App Cas 552
A/S Rendal v Arcos [1937] 58 Ll L Rep 287
AB Svensk ExportKredit v New Hampshire Insurance [1988] 3 WLUK 387
ABN AMRO Bank NV v Royal and Sun Alliance Insurance Plc [2021] EWCA Civ 1789
Adare Finance DAC v Yellowstone Capital Management SA [2020] EWHC 2760 (Comm), [2020] 10 WLUK 285
Agapitos v Agnew (The Aegeon) (No 1) [2002] EWCA Civ 247, [2003] QB 556
Alder v Moore (1961) 2 QB 57
Aldrich v Cooper (1803) 8 Ves Jr 382, 34 ER 1050
Allied Maples Group Ltd v Simmons & Simmons [1995] 1 WLR 1602
Anglo-Californian Bank Ltd v London and Provincial Marine and General Insurance Co Ltd (1904) 20 TLR 665
Ankar Pty Ltd v National Westminster Finance (Aust) Ltd (1987) 162 CLR 549
Anson v Anson [1953] 1 QB 636
Aras and others v National Bank of Greece SA [2018] EWHC 1389 (Comm), [2018] 6 WLUK 127
Arnold v Britton [2015] UKSC 36, [2015] AC 1619
Arterial Caravans v Yorkshire Insurance [1973] 1 Lloyd's Rep 169
Aspen Insurance UK Ltd v Pectel Ltd [2008] EWHC 2804 (Comm), [2009] Lloyd's Rep IR 440
Assicurazioni Generali di Trieste v Empress Assurance Co Ltd [1907] 2 KB 814
Axa General Insurance v Gottleib [2005] EWCA Civ 112, [2005] 1 All ER (Comm) 445
Bank of India v Riat [2014] EWHC 1775 (Ch)
Bank of Nova Scotia v Hellenic Mutual War Risks Association (Bermuda) Ltd (The Good Luck) [1982] 2 Ll Rep 540
Bank of Scotland v Henry Butcher & Co [2001] 2 All ER (Comm) 691
Banque Keyser Ullmann SA v Skandia (UK) Insurance Co Ltd and Others [1991] 2 AC 249
Blaaupot v Da Costa (1758) 1 Eden 130
Blest v Brown (1862) 4 De G F & J 367
Blindley Heath Investments Ltd v Bass [2015] EWCA Civ 1023, [2017] Ch 389

Boag v Standard Marine Insurance Co Ltd [1937] 2 KB 113
Bond v Commercial Assurance (1930) 35 Com Cas
BP Exploration Co (Libya) Ltd v Hunt (No.2) [1979] 1 WLR 783
Bridge v Campbell Discount Co (1962) AC 600
Brit Uw Limited v F & B Trenchless Solutions Limited [2015] EWHC 2237 (Comm), [2016] Lloyd's Rep IR 69
British Credit Trust Holdings v UK Insurance Ltd [2003] EWHC 2404 (Comm), [2004] 1 All ER (Comm) 444
Brooks Wharf & Bull Wharf Ltd v Goodman Bros [1937] 1 KB 523
Brotherton v Aseguradora Colseguros SA (No.2) [2003] EWHC 1741 (Comm), [2003] Lloyd's Rep IR 746.
Buckland v Palmer [1984] 1 WLR 1109
Burnand v Rodocanachi (1882) 7 App Cas 333
Buttes Gas & Oil Co v Hammer (No. 3) [1981] QB 223
Callaghan v Dominion Insurance Co [1997] 2 Lloyd's Rep 541
Caparo Industries Plc v Dickman [1990] 2 AC 605
Carlingford Australia General Insurance Ltd v EZ Industries Ltd [1988] VR 349
Carter v Boehm (1766) 3 Burr 1162
Castellain v Preston (1883) 11 QBD 380
Cavendish Square Holding BV v Makdessi [2015] UKSC 67, [2016] AC 1172
Central Insurance Co v Seacalf Shipping Corp [1983] 2 Lloyd's Rep 25
China Export & Credit Insurance Corp v Emerald Energy Resources Ltd [2018] EWHC 1503 (Comm), [2018] 10 WLUK 487
CIA Barca de Panama SA v George Wimpey & Co Ltd [1980] 1 LI Rep 598
Close Invoice Finance Ltd v Watts [2009] EWCA Civ 1182
Clydebank and District Water Trustees v Fidelity & Deposit Co of Maryland (1915) SC 362
Commercial Bank of Australia Ltd v Amadio (1983) 151 CLR 447
Commercial Union Assurance Co v Lister (1874) LR 9 Ch App 483
Compania Colombiana de Seguros v Pacific Steam Navigation Co [1965] 1 QB 101
Craythorne v Swinburne (1807) 16 Ves Jr 160
Credit Lyonnais Bank Nederland NV (now Generale Bank Nederland NV) v Export Credits Guarantee Department [1999] CLC 823
Crown Aluminium Ltd v Northern and Western Insurance Co Ltd [2011] EWHC 1352 (TCC)
Culford Metal Industries Ltd v Export Credits Guarantee Department [1981] CLY 2752
D&J Koskas v Standard Marine Insurance Co Ltd (1927) 27 Ll L Rep 59
Dane v Mortgage Ins Corp Ltd [1894] 1 QB 54
Davies v London and Provincial Marine Insurance Co (1878) 8 Ch D 469
Dering v Earl of Winchelsea (1787) 1 Cox Eq Cas 318
Deutsche Bank v Sebastian Holdings (No2) [2011] 2 All ER 245
Director of the Serious Fraud Office v Airbus SE [2020] 1 WLUK 435
Doe v Canadian Surety Co [1937] SCR 1

Railton v Matthews (1844) 10 Cl & F 934
Rainy Sky SA v Kookmin Bank [2011] UKSC 50, [2012] 1 All ER 1137
Randal v Cockran (1748) 1 Ves Sen 98, 27 ER 916
Rap Industries Pty Ltd v Royal Insurance Australia Ltd (1988) 5 ANZ Insurance Cases 60-876
Rathbone Brothers Plc v Novae Corporate Underwriting [2013] EWHC 3457 (Comm), [2015] Lloyd's Rep IR 95
Rawstone v Parr (1827) 3 Russ 539, 38 ER 678
Re Denton's Estate [1904] 2 Ch 178
Re Howe Ex p. Brett (1871) LR 6 Ch App 838
Re Law Guarantee Trust and Accident Society Ltd, Liverpool Mortgage Insurance Co Ltd's Case [1914] 2 Ch 617
Rickaby v Lewis (1905) 22 TLR 130
Roper v Cox (1882) LR Ir 200
Royal & Sun Alliance Insurance Plc v Dornoch Ltd [2005] EWCA Civ 238, [2005] Lloyd's Rep IR 544
Royal Bank of Scotland v Etridge [2001] UKHL 44, [2002] Lloyd's Rep 343
Santos Ltd v American Home Assurance Co (1987) 4 ANZ Insurance Cases 60-795
Schoolman v Hall [1951] 1 Lloyd's Rep 139
Scottish Amicable Heritable Securities Assn Ltd v Northern Assurance Co (1883) 11 R (Ct Sess) 287
Seaton v Heath [1899] 1 QB 782
Sempra Metals Ltd v Inland Revenue Commissioners [2007] UKHL 34, [2008] 1 AC 561
Simmonds v Cockell [1920] 1 KB 843
Simon Container Machinery Ltd v Emba Machinery AB [1998] 2 Lloyd's Rep 429
Simpson v Thomson (1877) 3 App Cas 279
Standard Life Assurance Ltd v Oak Dedicated Ltd [2008] EWHC 222 (Comm), [2008] 2 All ER (Comm) 916
Stimpson v Smith [1999] 2 WLR 1292
Svenska Handelsbanken v Sun Alliance and London Insurance Plc [1996] CLC 833
Talbot Underwriting Ltd v Nausch Hogan & Murray Inc [2005] EWHC 2359 (Comm), [2005] 2 CLC 868
Tebbets v Mercantile Credit Guarantee Co of New York 73 Fed Rep 95
Thomas v Nottingham Incorporated Football Club Ltd [1972] Ch 596
Toomey v Eagle Star (No. 2) [1995] 2 Lloyd's Rep 88
Trade Indemnity Co Ltd v Workington Harbour & Dock Board (No. 1) (1936) 54 Ll L Rep 103
Tricontinental Corp Ltd v HDFI Ltd (1990) 21 NSWLR 689
US Trading Ltd v AXA Insurance Co Ltd [2010] Lloyd's Rep IR 505
Versloot Dredging BV v HDI Gerling Industrie Versicherung Ag [2016] UKSC 45, [2017] AC 1

Table of statutes and statutory instruments

International statutory materials

WTO Agreement on Subsidies and Countervailing Measures

art 3.1(a)

UK statutes

The Arbitration Act 1996

s 9
s 49

The Bills of Exchange Act 1882

s 24

The Consumer Right Act 2015

s 64

The Enterprise Act 2016

s 13A
s 13A(1)

The Export and Investment Guarantee Act 1991

art 14

The Financial Services and Markets Act 2000 (Regulated Activities) Order 2001

s 3
art 14, Pt I, Sch 1
art 15, Pt I, Sch 1
Pt II, Sch 1

The Fraud Act 2006

s 2
s 3

The Industry and Exports (Financial Support) Act 2009

s 2

The Insurance Act 2015

s 3(3)(b)
s 3(4)(b)
s 3(5)

s 20
s 21
s 22

The Mercantile Law Amendment Act 1856

s 5
s 17

The Senior Courts Act 1981

s 35A

The Small Business, Enterprise and Employment Act 2015

s 12

The Statute of Frauds 1677

s 4

UK statutory instruments

The Civil Procedure Rules 1998 (SI 1998/3132)

Pt 24

The Companies Act 2006 (Amendment of Part 25) Regulations 2013 (SI 2013/600)

s 859A

1 Introduction

This book aims to demonstrate the legal nature of export credit insurance (ECI) and export credit guarantees (ECGs). In the field of international trade and finance, the term "export credit" means that the buyer pays at a later date instead of making an immediate cash payment.[1] By providing credit terms, the exporter can make a more competitive offer, and thus, the transaction deal is more likely to be concluded.[2] However, credit terms also mean greater risks, both commercially and politically.[3] To control the various types of risks and avoid potential losses, the exporter needs extra protection. ECI and ECGs are the exact means for such protection to insure or guarantee against the risks in transactions based on credit terms. While a detailed analysis of the different types of ECI and ECG products will be provided in the following chapters, it is necessary first to introduce the research background of this book.

ECI and ECG covers are primarily provided by export credit agencies (ECAs).[4] Regarded as the "unsung giants" of international trade and finance,[5] ECAs are institutions established or funded by governments worldwide to support national export and investment and thereby boost their national economy.[6] By definition, ECAs are policy-oriented institutions rather than commercial entities. The legal system of ECAs originated after World War I when the governments in Europe felt it important to revitalise the export industry disrupted by the

1 International Credit Insurance & Surety Association (ICISA), *A Guide to Trade Credit Insurance* (Anthem Press 2015) 6.

2 Anders Grath, *The Handbook of International Trade and Finance* (Kogan Page 2008) 109.

3 The definition of commercial risks and political risks will be provided in Chapter 2 of this book.

4 Worldwide, a considerable number of private credit insurers also run ECI businesses, the details of which will be discussed throughout this book.

5 Delio E. Gianturco, *Export Credit Agencies: The Unsung Giants of International Trade and Finance* (Quorum 2001) 1.

6 Zlatko Salcic, *Export Credit Insurance & Guarantees: A Practitioner's Guide* (Palgrave Macmillan 2014) 9–10.

DOI: 10.4324/b22864-1

Great War and promote employment. In 1919, the United Kingdom established the Export Credits Guarantee Department (ECGD), the first ECA in the world, which was followed by many industrialised countries, such as the Netherlands, France, Italy, Germany, Japan and the United States. During World War II, ECAs were particularly committed to helping the military industry, including the rubber and mining sectors, but after the war, they helped restore the whole export industry and assist the post-war reconstruction.[7] Many developing countries also established ECAs after the war. According to the International Union of Credit & Investment Insurers (the Berne Union), the international organisation of ECAs and private credit insurers, its members now consist of 69 national ECAs, 4 regional/multinational ECAs and 13 private credit insurers around the world.[8]

ECAs play a significant role in today's world economy. The export industry not only contributes to employment growth and tax revenue but also introduces new technology and management techniques. By financing the export industry, ECAs essentially help to boost the export country's economy.[9] By the end of 2020, 13 per cent of the world's cross-border trade and investment, which equals USD 2.77 trillion payment risks in total, is protected by the ECI and ECG products provided by the Berne Union members.[10] Moreover, ECAs also benefit the import countries, many of which are developing or mostly undeveloped countries. ECAs make it more possible for buyers in those countries to import advanced commodities, capital equipment and services so that the social welfare, living standard and infrastructure construction in those countries can all be improved.[11]

Different ECAs take different organisational forms, such as (a) governmental departments or agencies; (b) public insurance companies fully owned or controlled by the government; (c) public export–import banks; or (d) private insurance companies supported by governments. Each country's choice of its ECA's organisational type depends on certain geographic, economic and political factors.[12] The UK Export Finance (UKEF), the current operating name of the ECGD, belongs to category (a) under the Export and Investment Guarantees Act 1991 (as amended by the Industry and Exports (Financial Support) Act 2009 and the Small Business Enterprise and Employment Act 2015).

7 Gianturco (n 5) 41.

8 Berne Union, "How credit insurance supports the real economy" (2 February 2022), 13 < https://www.berneunion.org/Articles/Details/529/How-credit-insurance-supports-the-real-economy> accessed 1 February 2022. See also <https://www.berneunion.org/Members> accessed 1 February 2022.

9 Gianturco (n 5) 3.

10 Berne Union, "2020 State of the Industry Report" (8 November 2021), 17 <https://www.berneunion.org/Articles/Details/606/2020-State-of-the-Industry-Report> accessed 1 February 2022.

11 Gianturco (n 5) 3. See also Cheng Lin, "China's Legal Protection of Overseas Investment along One Belt and One Road" [2016] (1) *Journal of Economy and Finance* 45, 45–6.

12 Gianturco, ibid, 63–5. A detailed description of the organisation types of ECAs around the world can be found on the Berne Union website. See n 8 above.

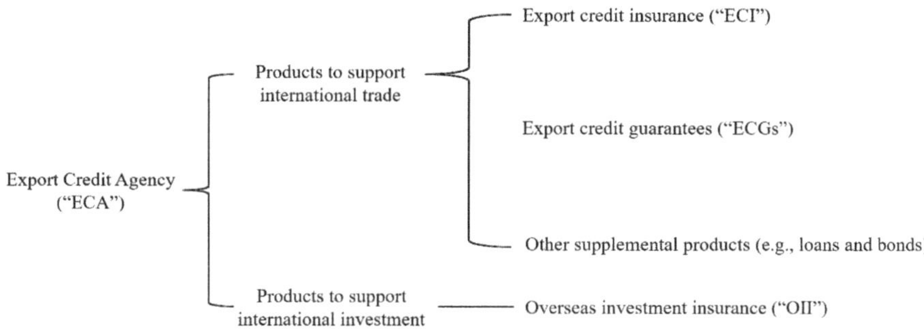

Figure 1.1 The different types of products provided by ECAs.

ECAs provide various products including ECI, ECGs, direct loans, bonds[13] as well as overseas investment insurance (OII) (see Figure 1.1).[14] Loans and bonds are usually provided by commercial banks, and since ECAs tend to avoid competition with them, loans and bonds are normally supplemental products provided by ECAs. OII, on the other hand, also falls outside the scope of this book because it relates to international investment rather than international trade. Therefore, the focus of this book will be on ECI and ECGs, the core programmes ECAs operate to boost international trade.

Exporters can be insured directly under ECI, whereas in many cases, ECI and ECGs can also be granted to banks that finance exporters. Worldwide, ECI is currently the mainstream product in the market, whereas some ECAs also provide ECGs in addition to ECI.[15]

Although ECI and ECGs have long been used by ECAs, whether and how they are legally distinguished from each other does not seem to be well comprehended by the industry. The legal nature of ECI and ECG contracts is somewhat confusing, which is particularly the case as far as English law is concerned. Read literally, ECI seems to refer to insurance and ECGs to guarantees, but in England, the terms "insurance" and "guarantees" are often used interchangeably by the industry to label its products. English courts have considered many cases where

13 In international trade, in order to secure the exporter's obligations under the export contract, the buyer might require that a bond be issued. A bond is in essence a guarantee, which can be issued by the exporter's parent or group company, a financial institution or an ECA. Bonds can be of different types including bid bonds, performance bonds, advanced payment bonds and warranty bonds. Bonds are often "the glue" that "holds a deal together". See Grath (n 2) 69–75; Salcic (n 6) 92–4. As will be demonstrated throughout this book, ECGs are not bonds because ECGs are always issued to secure transactions where a bank finances the exporter or the buyer.

14 See Gianturco (n 5) 76–7, 155; ICISA (n 1) 121–4.

15 Cheng Lin, "Why Export Credit Agencies Provide Guarantees in addition to Insurance: A Contractual Perspective" [2021] (1) LMCLQ 149–65. How ECI and ECGs are used in the industry will be discussed in detail in Chapter 2.

the legal nature of ECI and ECGs is far from clear. Even if the court has confirmed that the ECI or ECG cover is a contract of insurance or guarantee, it remains questionable whether all aspects of the principles of insurance or guarantee law should be applied to ECI or ECG contracts.

Neither the judiciary nor the academic literature in the UK has provided a satisfactory answer to the questions above. Some attempts by the English courts have tried to clarify the legal nature and the applicable law to ECI and ECGs. However, even such attempts do not seem to have provided a comprehensive analysis. Also, academic research is scant. Existing studies analysed ECI and ECG issues from the view of either financial regulations or economics.[16] International organisations, such as the Berne Union, also publish statistical reports, handbooks or working papers on ECI and ECGs, but they do not directly cover insurance law and guarantee law issues either.

Therefore, the purpose of this book is to explore the legal nature of ECI and ECGs from a contractual perspective. It seeks to answer the following questions:

- How are ECI and ECGs used in the current export credit industry?
- Are ECI policies and ECGs contracts[17] of insurance or guarantee in their legal nature? Can principles of insurance law and guarantee law apply to ECI and ECGs, respectively? If so, to what extent?
- What are the differences in the legal characteristics between ECI and ECGs?
- Why do ECAs provide ECGs in addition to ECI despite the fact that ECGs remain a less popular product in the market? Which arrangement, i.e., ECI or ECGs, would be the most ideal for banks and why?
- How should the contractual terms of ECI and ECGs be drafted so as to balance the interest of ECAs, exporters, banks and buyers?

This book is written on the basis of the following studies:

Doctrinal study. This book examines the doctrines and principles applicable to ECI and ECGs, respectively. Primary resources, such as cases and statutes, as well as relevant academic works in the context of English law will all be reviewed. In particular, the Insurance Act 2015 (IA 2015) and its influences on ECI policies, a significant issue that has yet to be explored by the previous literature, will be analysed in detail.

Case study. This book reviews all reported ECI and ECG cases in the UK. There have been at least 35 relevant cases, but very few of them were discussed in the existing leading insurance/guarantee law textbooks (and often in brief paragraphs). This book aims to fill this gap by scrutinising all these cases.

16 See, e.g., Eva Lomnicka, "Export Credit Guarantees", in Michael Bridge (ed.), *Benjamin's Sales of Goods* (11th edn, Sweet & Maxwell 2020); Grath (n 2); Gianturco (n 5).

17 The Berne Union Academic Survey found that ECAs normally do not call their ECG contracts "policies" in the same way as they refer to ECI. Therefore, in this book, the term "ECG contracts" will be used throughout.

Empirical study. This book refers to the outcome of the author's previous internship research project at the Berne Union Secretariat (the Berne Union Academic Survey) in 2019–20 on the legal nature of buyer credit insurance and buyer credit guarantee, a pair of typical products of ECI and ECGs. The author collected 26 questionnaire responses and 8 interview responses from members of the Berne Union, who included both ECAs and private credit insurers, about their understanding of the legal nature and characteristics of ECI and ECGs.[18]

Policy wording study. This book collects and analyses a large number of contractual terms of ECI and ECGs that are used in the global export credit industry. First, it analyses the contractual wordings of ECI and ECGs considered by the English courts in reported cases. Second, it reviews the standard ECI and ECG contracts collected through the Berne Union Academic Survey. Many of them are available on the members' websites, and thus the links to these contracts are attached in Appendix 3 of this work for the readers' convenience. Besides, three anonymous Berne Union members kindly permitted the author, for the purpose of this publication, to use certain extracts from their standard ECI/ECG contracts which are not available online. Third, this work also discusses the user guide and full text of the Loan Market Association's (LMA) "Single Currency Term Facility Agreement for Use in Export Finance Buyer Credit Transactions",[19] a model loan agreement designed for ECA-supported buyer credit transactions. A copy of this document was generously shared by the LMA with the author.[20] Fourth, based on a critical study of all policy wording in the aforementioned extracts, this work proposes several model clauses for ECI and ECGs.

This book aims to serve as a helpful reference for students, academics and practitioners in the field of commercial and insurance law. In particular, it seeks to provide guidelines for all potential parties that wish to arrange an ECI/ECG transaction, including ECAs, private credit insurers, brokers, banks, exporters, buyers and law firms, to correctly identify and choose the suitable cover when drafting an ECI/ECG contract.

18 The outcome of the Berne Union Academic Survey is available on the Berne Union website. See Cheng Lin, "Berne Union Academic Survey: The Legal Nature of Buyer Credit Insurance and Buyer Credit Guarantee", *The BUlletin (The Official Newsletter of the Berne Union)*, January 2020, 24–31 <https://www.berneunion.org/Articles/Details/489/January-BUlletin-Mega-Trends-and-Trade> accessed 1 February 2022.

19 LMA, "Single Currency Term Facility Agreement for Use in Export Finance Buyer Credit Transactions (20/03/2020)", available to LMA members via <www.lma.eu.com>.

20 Disclaimer: *Whilst the Loan Market Association ("LMA") has consented to the quotation of, and referral to, parts of its documents for the purpose of this publication, it assumes no responsibility for any use to which its documents, or any extract from them, may be put. The views and options expressed in the publication are the views of the author and do not necessarily represent those of the LMA. Furthermore, the LMA cannot accept any responsibility or liability for any error or omission. ©2021 Loan Market Association. All rights reserved.*

References

Gianturco, D, *Export Credit Agencies: The Unsung Giants of International Trade and Finance* (Quorum 2001)
Grath, A, *The Handbook of International Trade and Finance* (Kogan Page 2008)
ICISA, *A Guide to Trade Credit Insurance* (Anthem Press 2015)
Lin, C, "Why Export Credit Agencies Provides Guarantees in addition to Insurance: A Contractual Perspective" (2021) 1 LMCLQ 149
Lomnicka, E, "Export Credit Guarantees" in M Bridge (ed) *Benjamin's Sales of Goods* (11th edn, Sweet & Maxwell 2020)
Salcic, Z, *Export Credit Insurance & Guarantees: A Practitioner's Guide* (Palgrave Macmillan 2014)

2 How are ECI and ECGs used in the industry?

This chapter aims to explore how export credit insurance (ECI) and export credit guarantees (ECGs) are used in the export credit industry.

The first part discusses the general distinctions between insurance and guarantees and clarifies the elements that help to distinguish them from each other. It then proposes that despite some peculiarities of ECI and ECGs, many differences between insurance and guarantees also exist between ECI and ECGs – a hypothesis to be examined throughout this work.

The second part identifies all different forms of ECI and ECG products. It demonstrates that the basic ECI cover is the universal product in the global export credit industry and that ECI is generally a more common product than ECGs. It also reveals that there are some export credit agencies (ECAs) that provide ECGs in addition to insurance. The reason behind this state of affairs will also be explored throughout this book.

The focus of this chapter will be on the formation process of ECI and ECGs. The third part analyses two alternative approaches for an ECI contract to be concluded: it examines how to obtain an ECI cover from an ECA and private credit insurers, respectively. In particular, the roles of underwriters and brokers under ECI will be discussed in detail. This part aims to prove that the formation process of ECI can be very similar to that of other types of insurance contracts. On the other hand, the fourth part demonstrates that the formation process of ECGs is similar to that of general guarantee contracts, too. Therefore, ECI and ECGs appear to be contracts of insurance and guarantee, respectively. The fifth part further shows that the formation process of supplier credit insurance could cause difficulties to banks who finance the transaction, whilst the formation process of supplier credit guarantees seems straightforward and flawless, which indicates that an ECG is a friendlier product to banks than ECI in terms of the formation process.

In contrast to Chapters 3–7 of this thesis, this chapter does not seek to directly reveal the legal nature of ECI and ECG contracts from their detailed terms and conditions. Instead, it aims to contribute to the overarching theme of this research by drawing a full picture of how ECI and ECGs are used in the industry. The discussion throughout this chapter will provide an essential foundation for readers to understand the further analysis in Chapters 3–7 of the legal nature of ECI and ECGs.

DOI: 10.4324/b22864-2

General distinctions between insurance and guarantees

Confusion in English ECI and ECG cases

As seen in many English ECI cases, the words "insurance" and "guarantee" are often used interchangeably by the ECA, and either "insurance" or "guarantee" could refer to an ECI cover. For example, in *L Lucas Ltd and another v Export Credits Guarantee Department*,[1] the court confirmed that the ECA issued a policy of insurance although being described as a "guarantee"; similarly, in *Lonrho Exports Ltd v Export Credits Guarantee Department*,[2] the ECA issued two standard form contracts of insurance called "external trade guarantee" and "comprehensive short-term guarantee" respectively; in *Kazakstan Wool Processors (Europe) Ltd v Nederlandsche Credietverzekering Maatschappij NV*,[3] the ECA agreed to pay "a guaranteed percentage" of the insured's loss caused by the default in payment by the buyer, but what the ECA provided was actually an insurance cover; in *Morgan Grenfell & Co Limited v SACE Istituto Per I Servizi Assicurativi Del Commercio*,[4] the term "guarantee" was used throughout the policy instead of "insurance" and even the bank was referred to as "the guaranteed party" under the policy, but the court observed that the contract was in essence an insurance policy; furthermore, in *Formica Ltd v Secretary of State acting by the Export Credits Guarantee Department*,[5] the ECA provided a "comprehensive short-term guarantee" to the exporter, but again, it was a contract of insurance.

However, the term "guarantee" could also refer to an ECG cover. In *Credit Lyonnais Bank Nederland v Export Credits Guarantee Department*,[6] the ECA issued a "comprehensive short-term guarantee" (CST) to the exporter and a "specific bank guarantee" (SBG) to the bank that financed the exporter. The exporter wished to obtain immediate finance, and the bank provided it with a loan. The ECA then issued a guarantee to the bank for the repayment of the loan and issued a separate insurance policy to the exporter against the non-payment by the buyer. Hence, the ECA entered into a contract of guarantee with the bank and a contract of insurance with the exporter, but both were named "guarantee".[7]

It therefore seems difficult to tell the legal nature of ECI and ECGs merely from the terms used. To identify their legal nature, it is necessary first to clarify the general distinctions between contracts of insurance and guarantee and then analyse the legal characteristics of each particular ECI and ECG product.

1 [1973] 1 WLR 914, 914–5.
2 [1999] Ch 158, 168–9.
3 [2000] CLC 822, 823.
4 [2001] EWCA Civ 1932, [2002] CLY 2729, [13].
5 [1994] CLC 1078, 1089–90.
6 [1999] CLC 823, 845.
7 Hobhouse LJ specifically clarified that the CST was in essence a contract of insurance although being "confusingly called a guarantee". See *Credit Lyonnais Bank Nederland v Export Credits Guarantee Department* [1999] CLC 823, 845.

The similarities and differences between general contracts of insurance and guarantee

Generally, a contract of guarantee is similar to a contract of insurance (especially credit insurance or guarantee insurance) as they both contain "a promise to make good a loss".[8] Under s 3 of the Financial Services and Markets Act 2000 (Regulated Activities) Order 2001, "contract of insurance" means any contract of insurance which is a contract of long-term insurance (listed in Pt II, Sch 1) or a contract of general insurance (listed in Pt I, Sch 1). Section 3 clarifies that a contract of general insurance includes "fidelity bonds, performance bonds, administration bonds, bail bonds, customs bonds or similar contracts of guarantee" and, in particular, "credit insurance"[9] and "suretyship"[10] are both classified as a contract of general insurance in Pt I, Sch 1. Therefore, the distinction between insurance and guarantees seems insignificant for regulatory purposes.

However, there are some fundamental distinctions between insurance and guarantees: a surety under a guarantee is "a person who answers for the default of another", whereas an insurer is "a person who guarantees against loss by an event".[11] Such distinctions are important for contractual purposes:

- A contract of guarantee must be in written form,[12] whilst a contract of non-marine insurance can be made orally,[13] and a contract of marine insurance can also be oral (although the assured must hold a policy in order to make a claim).[14]
- A contract of guarantee is accessory to the underlying contract between the creditor and the principal debtor, whereas a contract of insurance is

8 Robert Merkin, *Colinvaux's Law of Insurance* (12th edn, Sweet & Maxwell 2019) [1-030].

9 Art 14 of Pt I, Sch 1 of the Order defines the term "credit insurance" as:

> Contracts of insurance against risks of loss to the persons insured arising from the insolvency of debtors of theirs or from the failure (otherwise than through insolvency) of debtors of theirs to pay their debts when due.

10 Art 15 of Pt I, Sch 1 of the Order defines the term "suretyship" as:

> (1) Contracts of insurance against the risks of loss to the persons insured arising from their having to perform contracts of guarantee entered into by them.
> (2) Fidelity bonds, performance bonds, administration bonds, bail bonds or customs bonds or similar contracts of guarantee, where these are
> (a) effected or carried out by a person not carrying on a banking business;
> (b) not effected merely incidentally to some other business carried on by the person effecting them; and
> (c) effected in return for the payment of one or more premiums.

11 What an insurer is guaranteeing is not the default of a person; he is guaranteeing that no loss shall happen by the event. See *Castellain v Preston* (1883) 11 QBD 380, 403 (Bowen LJ).

12 Under s 4 of the Statute of Frauds 1677, a guarantee must be evidenced by a note or memorandum in writing. See John Birds, Ben Lynch and Simon Paul, *MacGillivray on Insurance Law* (14th edn, Sweet & Maxwell 2018) [3-006].

13 The MIA 1906, s 21.

14 Ibid, s 22.

independent of any underlying contract. For instance, a guarantee is void if the principal debt is void,[15] but a contract of insurance is not automatically void as a result of the creditor-debtor contract being void. Furthermore, the surety's obligation under a guarantee will be discharged if the principal debtor's obligation is discharged, but that is not necessarily the case for the insurer.[16] Conversely, the surety's payment discharges the principal debtor's debt, but the payment by the insurer does not have such an effect.[17] In other words, the obligation of the insurer is direct, whereas the obligation of a guarantor is accessory.[18]

- A contract of insurance is a contract based upon utmost good faith[19] and is subject to the duty of fair representation under the IA 2015 which requires the assured to make full disclosure of the risk and not to misrepresent material facts. On the contrary, the duty of fair representation does not apply to guarantees, and the principal debtor's duty of disclosure is limited.[20]
- After making a payment, the surety has the right of indemnity against the principal debtor[21] and could have the right against the creditor[22] and the co-sureties[23] as well, whilst the insurer is merely entitled to be subrogated to the assured's rights.
- Insurance contracts are construed strictly according to the terms and conditions,[24] but guarantees are construed strictly against the creditor.[25]

15 Birds and others (n 12) [33-040].
16 *Scottish Amicable Heritable Securities Assn Ltd v Northern Assurance Co* (1883) 11 R (Ct Sess) 287, 303; *Dane v Mortgage Ins Corp Ltd* [1894] 1 QB 54, 61.
17 Merkin (n 8) [24-038].
18 Birds and others (n 12) [33-040].
19 The MIA 1906, s 17.
20 *Lee v Jones* (1864) 17 CB (NS) 482; *Phillips v Foxall* (1872) LR 7 QB 666; *Workington Harbour and Dock Board v Trade Indemnity Co Ltd* (1934) 49 Lloyd's Rep 430; *Credit Lyonnais* [1996] CLC 11; *Royal Bank of Scotland v Etridge* [2001] UKHL 44, [2002] Lloyd's Rep 343, 387. See also H.G. Beale, *Chitty on Contracts* (33rd edn, Sweet & Maxwell 2018), [45-037].
21 The surety has the right to an indemnity if he has an express or implied agreement with the principal debtor or has the right of restitution in quasi-contract. See the Hon Mrs Justice Geraldine Andrews & Richard Millett QC, *Law of Guarantees* (7th edn, Sweet & Maxwell 2015) [10-002].
22 See *Anson v Anson* [1953] 1 QB 636, 641–2; *Brooks Wharf & Bull Wharf Ltd v Goodman Bros* [1937] 1 KB 523, 544–5.
23 See *Dering v Earl of Winchelsea* (1787) 1 Cox Eq Cas 318; *Craythorne v Swinburne* (1807) 16 Ves Jr 160; *Wolmershausen v Gullick* [1893] 2 Ch 514; *Dering v Earl of Winchelsea* (1787) 2 Bos & P 270.
24 It has been observed by the commentators that whilst English courts do not regard it an underlying approach to construe insurance contracts in favour of the assured, American courts tend to do so. The author of this book agrees with this view. See Alison Padfield, *Insurance Claims* (2nd edn, Tottel Publishing 2007) 1. See also *Yorkshire Water Service Ltd v Sun Alliance & London Insurance plc* [1997] 2 Lloyd's Rep 21, 28. Meanwhile, some scholarships said that insurance contracts are construed "strictly in favour of the cover", but the author respectfully disagrees: as will be demonstrated throughout this research, courts in English ECI cases construed ECI contracts according to their terms and conditions. See Malcolm A. Clarke, *The Law of Insurance Contracts* (3rd edn, LLP Limited 1997) 11.
25 Clarke (n 24) 11–2. See also *Blest v Brown* (1862) 4 De G F & J 367, 376; *Doe v Canadian Surety Co* [1937] SCR 1, 19.

This research proposes that the abovementioned differences between general contracts of insurance and guarantee apply to ECI and ECGs, a hypothesis that will be examined throughout this book.

The elements to distinguish a general contract of insurance from guarantees

It is often difficult to distinguish insurance from guarantees: English courts have long noted that the distinction cannot be identified by merely reading the words "insurance" and "guarantee".[26] The legal nature of the contract in question depends on "its substantial character and how it came to be effected".[27] Despite the difficulties, some elements can help to distinguish insurance from guarantees. On the one hand, if a contract is called a "policy" and terms such as "insurer" and "insured/assured" are thoroughly used, then it is apparently a contract of insurance. If, on the other hand, a contract is called a "guarantee", it could still be insurance as long as the following elements are considered in identifying the legal nature of the contract in question:

- **The manner of dealing**. To conclude the contract, the insurer usually directly deals with the insured creditor rather than the debtor, whilst the surety is usually approached by the debtor;
- **The motive of the parties**. An insurer provides insurance in consideration of premiums paid by the insured. In other words, an insurer runs its business for money and profits.[28] Meanwhile, whilst a guarantor may provide a guarantee for commercial purposes (e.g., a parent company guarantees its subsidiaries' debt), it may also do so out of the mere motivation of the friendship with the debtor;[29]
- **The means of knowledge**. An insurer is deemed to be unable to know the particular information about the risks and has to rely on the insured's disclosure of material facts, whilst a guarantor is usually fully aware of the risks he guarantees, or is "at least, in as good a position as the creditor to discover the true nature of the risk".[30]

The elements above can be helpful to distinguish ECI from ECGs but are not conclusive. As for the motive of operating business, since the statutory purpose

26 See *Re Denton's Estate* [1904] 2 Ch 178; *Dane v Mortgage Insurance Corp Ltd* [1894] 1 QB 54; *Finlay v Mexican Investment* [1897] 1 QB 517.

27 *Re Law Guarantee Trust and Accident Society Ltd* [1914] 2 Ch 617, 631 (Buckley LJ). See also *Seaton v Heath* [1899] 1 QB 782, 793.

28 *Re Law Guarantee Trust and Accident Society Ltd* [1914] 2 Ch 617, 631 (Buckley LJ); *Parr's Bank Ltd v Albert Mines Syndicate Ltd* (1900) 5 Com Cas 116; *Tebbets v Mercantile Credit Guarantee Co of New York* 73 Fed Rep 95, 97 (1896).

29 *Lee v Jones* (1864) 17 CB (NS) 482, 503 (Blackburn J).

30 Birds and others (n 12), [33-042]. See also *Re Denton's Estate* [1904] 2 Ch 178, 188–9 (Williams LJ).

of all ECAs is invariably to support national export and investment,[31] they receive premiums not to make profits but only to break even, whether under ECI or ECGs;[32] Besides, the means of knowledge of ECAs could be similar in ECI and ECGs, which will be examined in Chapter 4 of this research.

The different types of ECI and ECG products

An overview of ECI and ECG products around the world

Based on the discussion above, this section seeks to identify the different forms of ECI and ECG products. Worldwide, ECI and ECGs are generally used in three different forms: the "basic" cover, supplier credit transactions and buyer credit transactions. First of all, an exporter needs credit risk protection by being insured by the ECA. Such "basic" covers are normally insurance rather than guarantees around the world.[33] In the meantime, the exporter may need a bank to finance the trade, and this can be arranged via either a supplier credit or a buyer credit transaction. In a supplier credit transaction, the bank either provides a loan to the exporter (i.e., the pre-shipment manufacturing finance) or purchases the negotiable instruments (e.g., bills of exchange or promissory notes) from the exporter, and the ECA insures/guarantees the bank in case the loan is not repaid by the exporter or the negotiable instruments are not honoured by the buyer. In a buyer credit transaction, the bank provides a loan to the buyer, and the ECA insures/guarantees the bank in case the loan is not repaid by the buyer.[34] Therefore, the exporter here does not assume the credit risk, the bank does: the exporter "extends the credit" to the buyer.[35]

Therefore, in addition to the "basic" insurance cover for the exporter, theoretically, four different types of products are available to the bank: supplier credit

31 See, e.g., the Export and Investment Guarantee Act 1991, Part II; See also s 2 of the Industry and Exports (Financial Support) Act 2009 and s 12 of the Small Business, Enterprise and Employment Act 2015.

32 Andrews & Millett (n 21), [15-006]. It should be noted that whilst the term "premium" generally refers to the price for an insurance policy only (and that the price for a guarantee is usually called a "fee"), in the export credit industry the prices for ECI and ECG can be both called "premiums". For instance, Annex IX of OECD's Arrangement for Officially Support Export Credits provides different "minimum premium rates" (MPR) for ECI and ECGs, respectively.

33 The rare situation where a "basic ECG cover was placed was considered by the English court in *Crown Aluminium Ltd v Northern and Western Insurance Co Ltd* [2011] EWHC 1352 (TCC), [6]–[15]. It should be noted that in this case a bank was willing to finance the exporter by purchasing the bills of exchange so that the "basic" ECG cover could have become a supplier credit guarantee. However, due to the technical difficulties the surety failed to set up an account for the purpose of trade finance, and thus the bank was never able to actually participate in the transactions. The exporter, therefore, remained the creditor under the "basic" ECG cover.

34 Zlatko Salcic, *Export Credit Insurance & Guarantees: A Practitioner's Guide* (Palgrave Macmillan 2014) 77–8.

35 Eva Lomnicka, "Export Credit Guarantees", in Michael Bridge (ed.), *Benjamin's Sales of Goods* (11th edn, Sweet & Maxwell 2020), [25-002].

Table 2.1 How ECI and ECGs are used by the Berne Union members – summary

Type of cover	*Subtype of cover*	*Categorisation*	*BU members*	*User of the cover*
Basic cover	Insurance	ECI	67	Exporter
	Guarantee	ECG	0	
Supplier credit facility	Insurance	ECI	15	Bank
	Guarantee	ECG	4	
Buyer credit facility	Insurance	ECI	44	Bank
	Guarantee	ECG	5	

insurance, supplier credit guarantees, buyer credit insurance and buyer credit guarantees. The user of ECI could be an exporter or a bank, whereas the user of ECGs is invariably a bank. To better understand how ECI and ECGs are used in today's global export credit industry, this research studied 67 Berne Union members who offer clear and detailed product descriptions at their websites (see Appendix 2 for a full list and Table 2.1 for a summary).[36]

It can thus be seen that ECI is a more common product than ECGs. In terms of the "basic" cover, almost every Berne Union member provides ECI rather than ECGs.[37] With respect to both supplier and buyer credit facilities, ECI also prevails. Whilst no private credit insurers provide ECG products, there are some ECAs who provide ECGs in addition to ECI. It might be questioned whether an ECG has some strengths over ECI. This chapter, together with the rest of the chapters of this book, aims to explore all the possible answers.

The main ECI products in the UK

What is insured under ECI: political risks and commercial risks

It should be noted that the types of facilities which UKEF offers have changed in their nature and scope over the years. Therefore, "in the light of the fairly constant changes and updates", it is unlikely to be helpful or desirable to try to describe all the various facilities currently available at the UKEF in detail.[38] The following paragraphs discuss the main types of the UKEF's ECI and ECG products.

It is first necessary to clarify that, whether in the UK or worldwide, under any ECI cover, when an ECA insures the risk of the non-payment by the foreign buyer,

36 A full list of the websites of the Berne Union members is available at <https://www.berneunion.org/Members> accessed 1 February 2022.

37 The only Berne Union member who does not provide basic ECI is Sovereign, a private credit insurer who specialises in buyer credit insurance. See <https://www.sovereignbermuda.com/our-products> accessed 1 February 2022.

38 Andrews & Millett (n 21), [15-006].

it is actually insuring the risks of such non-payment caused by certain political events and commercial events.[39] In practice, the expressions "political risks" and "commercial risks" are widely used by the industry instead of the terms "commercial events" and "political events".[40] This research therefore follows such usage.

The definition of political risks and commercial risks depends on the wording of each particular ECI policy.[41] In general, political risks include the ban on imports imposed by the buyer's country, the ban on exports imposed by the exporter's country, the prevention or delay in the transfer of money due to the buyer's country, war, civil disturbance, force majeure, expropriation, nationalisation and confiscation.[42] Commercial risks, also known as "credit risks", normally refer to the insolvency of the buyer (or the buyer's guarantor), the protracted payment default by the buyer (or the buyer's guarantor) or the buyer's arbitrary or unjustified repudiation or refusal to pay.[43]

Basic ECI cover

The UKEF currently provides one basic ECI product called the "Export Insurance Policy",[44] which insures the exporter against up to 95% of the loss as a result of certain political and commercial risks. It appears that the "Export Insurance Policy" is a contract of insurance: the attached Export Insurance Policy application form states that the UKEF's ECI policies "take account of" the IA 2015.[45]

Supplier credit insurance

Supplier credit insurance always involves a bank. Where the length of the export contract is more than two years and the payment is made by instalments, the exporter may need the money earlier than the due date of payment in order to keep its business running, and the ECA may provide supplier credit insurance or buyer credit insurance. At this time, a bank can provide financial support to the exporter (i.e., the "supplier") via a loan or other forms of support,[46] and the exporter assigns its right to claim to payment under the underlying contract, together with its right

39 See *Culford Metal Industries Ltd v Export Credits Guarantee Department* [1981] CLY 2752, 2753 (Neill J).

40 Salcic (n 34) 17.

41 A sample of the wording of political and commercial risks will be discussed in Chapter 3 of this work. For an illustrative list of political and commercial risks, see ss 14–22 of The European Commission Directive 98/29/EC on Harmonisation of the Main Provisions concerning Export Credit Insurance for Transactions with Medium and Long-Term Cover.

42 ICISA, *A Guide to Trade Credit Insurance* (Anthem Press 2015) 23–4.

43 Ibid, 22; Lomnicka (n 35), [25-020].

44 See <https://www.gov.uk/guidance/export-insurance-policy> accessed 1 February 2022.

45 Ibid. The same view is shared by Andrews & Millett (n 21), [15-008]; Lomnicka (n 35), [25-016].

46 For example, the bank can purchase the receivables of the foreign buyer from the exporter at a discount. The exporter can also transfer the bill of exchange, drafts or promissory notes issued by the foreign buyer to the bank.

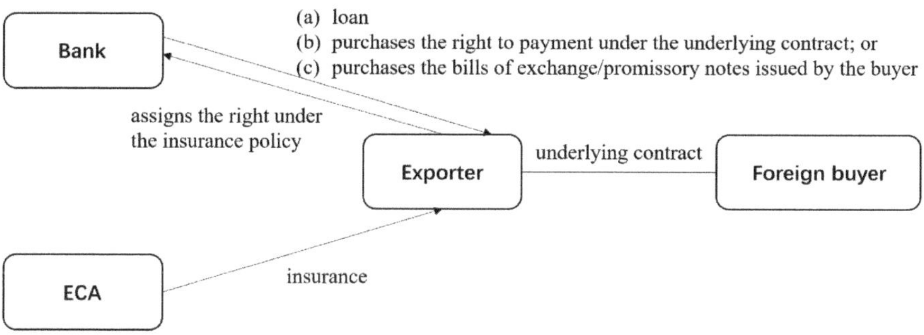

Figure 2.1 Supplier credit insurance transaction.

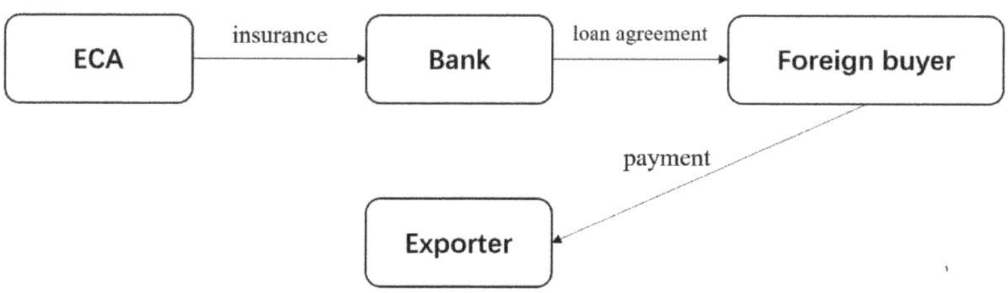

Figure 2.2 Buyer credit insurance transaction.

to claim under the ECI policy to the bank. The bank then becomes the beneficiary of the ECI policy (see Figure 2.1).[47]

Supplier credit insurance is widely used by ECAs around the world.[48] However, the UKEF does not currently provide such supplier credit insurance cover involving a bank. Instead, it provides supplier credit guarantees. The rationale behind this state of affairs will be discussed throughout this work.

Buyer credit insurance

In a buyer credit insurance transaction, the bank provides a loan to the foreign buyer, and the ECA insures the bank against the risk of non-payment of the loan by the buyer (see Figure 2.2).

Buyer credit insurance is also a contract of insurance under which the insured party is the bank. It is widely used by ECAs around the world.[49] The UKEF used

47 Alternatively, in practice, the exporter may also assign the insurance proceeds to the bank. See Delio E. Gianturco, *Export Credit Agencies: The Unsung Giants of International Trade and Finance* (Quorum 2001) 27.

48 Salcic (n 34) 53.

49 Ibid.

to provide buyer credit insurance covers[50] which, however, are now no longer available. The UKEF now provides buyer credit guarantees instead. The underlying reason will also be discussed throughout this work.

The main ECG products in the UK

Supplier credit guarantees

Two typical supplier credit guarantee products are currently provided by the UKEF.

In the "Export Working Capital Scheme", the UKEF issues a guarantee to the bank that provides a loan to the exporter to support its pre- and post-shipment manufacturing. The UKEF guarantees to pay to the bank up to 80% of the loss as a result of non-payment of the loan by the exporter. The purpose of the "Export Working Capital Scheme" is to support the exporter's business: the exporter pays the bank interest on the loan and promises to repay the principal when it receives payment from the foreign buyer, and the bank pays the UKEF a portion of that interest as the premium for the guarantee.[51]

In the "Supplier Credit Financing Facility", the UKEF issues a guarantee to the bank which purchases the bills of exchanges or promissory notes from the exporter. The duration of this facility is 2–5 years, and it can be even shorter or longer on a case-by-case basis.[52]

Those two products above appear to be contracts of guarantee rather than contracts of insurance because, under those covers, the UKEF does not insure the bank against certain political and commercial risks but promises to pay the bank if the exporter fails to repay the loan or if the buyer does not honour the negotiable instruments (see Figure 2.3).[53]

Notably, the UKEF has a Master Guarantee Agreement (MGA) with certain banks that are eligible to participate in supplier credit transactions.[54] The "Export Working Capital Scheme" and the "Supplier Credit Financing Facility" can be accessed either directly through UKEF or via the banks under the MGA. In the latter situation, the exporter may benefit from a "streamlined" approval process.[55]

50 The buyer credit insurance products that the UKEF used to provide can be seen in *Export Credits Guarantee Dept v Turner* 1981 SLT 286 and *Lonrho v ECGD* [1998] 3 WLR 394.

51 See <https://www.gov.uk/guidance/export-working-capital-scheme-overview-and-how-to-apply> accessed 1 February 2022.

52 See <https://www.gov.uk/guidance/supplier-credit-financing-facility> accessed 1 February 2022.

53 The same view is shared by Andrews & Millett (n 21), [15-009]; Lomnicka (n 35), [25-032-033].

54 The MGA is an umbrella agreement which sets out the principal terms and conditions on which the UKEF will guarantee payment to banks that make finance available using the facility. The UKEF sets out the particular terms and conditions of cover for individual transactions when making an offer of support for a particular export contract. See ibid.

55 See n 51 above.

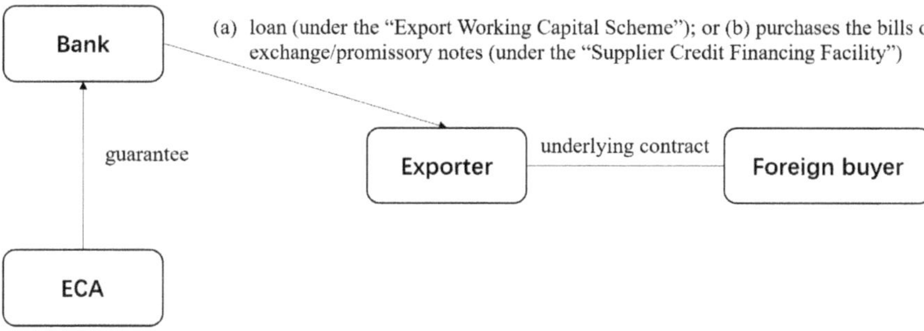

Figure 2.3 Supplier credit guarantee transaction.

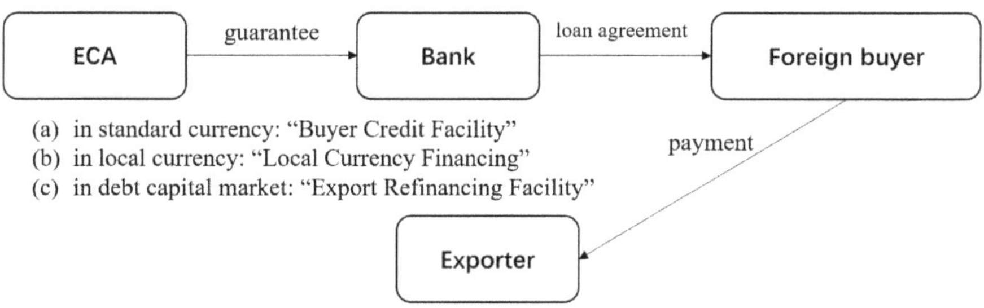

Figure 2.4 Buyer credit guarantee transaction.

Buyer credit guarantees

The "Buyer Credit Facility" is the UKEF's standard buyer credit guarantee product for the bank which provides a loan to the foreign buyer. The UKEF requires that the minimum contract value of the eligible export contract is £5m and that the period for repayment of the loan must be at least two years. The UKEF then guarantees the bank the full payment of the loan plus interest.[56]

There are two add-ons to the "Buyer Credit Facility" (see Figure 2.4). If the export contract is paid in local currency instead of the standard currency (sterling, US dollars and euro), the UKEF can provide a "Local Currency Financing" guarantee[57] to the bank. If the bank is funding non-sterling buyer credit loans typically with values above £50m that are intended to be refinanced through the debt

56 See <https://www.gov.uk/guidance/buyer-credit-facility> accessed 1 February 2022.

57 See <https://www.gov.uk/guidance/buyer-credit-facility-additional-features> accessed 1 February 2022. As the UKEF indicates, "Local Currency Financing" is particularly suited to projects that do not usually generate foreign currency revenue, such as water/gas/electricity utilities, local transport and local municipalities.

capital markets or other commercial loans, then an "Export Refinancing Facility" is available.[58]

The three products above also appear to be contracts of guarantee.[59] The UKEF does not require that the exporter obtain these products by approaching the banks under the MGA agreement as they must under the supplier credit guarantees.

The formation process of ECI

How to obtain an ECI cover from the ECA?

The application process

In England, insurance business generally takes place at the London market (which consists of the Lloyd's market and the company market).[60] However, that is not necessarily the case in the context of ECI. Exporters and banks in the UK can directly obtain ECI from the UKEF, whose website contains detailed steps for applicants.[61] In sum, exporters and banks will always need to read the standard terms and conditions of the ECI policy and then submit a proposal form, based on which the UKEF will decide on whether or not to issue a policy. Due to word limits, this research does not seek to describe the application process in detail, whereas some clarification needs to be made here: a basic ECI cover is always concluded between the ECA (i.e., the UKEF) and the exporter, and a buyer credit insurance policy is always issued by the ECA to the bank. Therefore, the formation process of those two types of products is very straightforward. What remains problematic is the formation of supplier credit insurance, where the ECA usually insures the exporter in the first place rather than directly insuring the bank that finances the exporter. Such a formation process could cause significant difficulties to the bank, which will be analysed at the end of this chapter.

Situations where a single transaction should be insured by more than one ECA

It is sometimes necessary for a single transaction to be insured by more than one ECA. Exporters and banks, therefore, should check if their transaction is comprehensively insured when applying for an ECI cover. Such situations were illustrated by the court in *Culford Metal Industries Ltd v Export Credits Guarantee Department*,[62] where the plaintiff, an English subcontractor, supplied building materials to a German contractor who worked on construction projects for the Saudi Arabian government. As was identified by the court, there were two

58 Ibid. As the UKEF indicates, the "Export Refinancing Facility" is priced competitively as a result of the UKEF's Guarantee of Payments Scheduled Principal and interest due under the bonds.
59 See Andrews & Millett (n 21), [15-011]; Lomnicka (n 35), [25-036].
60 Özlem Gürses, *Marine Insurance Law* (2nd edn, Routledge 2017) 20.
61 See n 44 above. See also Andrews & Millett (n 21), [15-012].
62 [1981] CLY 2752.

interrelated risks regarding the plaintiff's transaction with the contractor: (a) the risk of non-payment by the Saudi Arabian government (i.e., the end buyer) to the contractor (hereinafter referred to as "the Saudi risk") and (b) the risk of non-payment by the contractor to the plaintiff (hereinafter referred to as "the German risk"). The export contract between the plaintiff and the contractor contained a clause which provided that the contractor should pay the subcontractor upon arrival of the materials at the building sites and payment by the end buyer. Such contracts were called "if and when contracts" in the industry, of which the peculiarity was well explained by Neill J: whilst subcontracts for building works in England at that time "almost invariably" imposed an unconditional obligation on the contractor to pay the subcontractor whether or not any payment in respect of the subcontract work was made by the end buyer, "if and when contracts" were common where the end buyer was in the Middle East. Under such contracts, payment by the end buyer was a condition precedent to the contractor's liability to pay the subcontractor.[63] The contractor in *Culford* entered into an ECI policy with Euler Hermes, the German ECA, to cover the Saudi risk (hereinafter referred to as the "Hermes cover"), and the export contract referred to the Hermes cover in the following clause:

> The subcontractor will be charged with a proportion of the costs of the insurance, without transport insurance ... The subcontractor, however, bears the cost of the manufacturing risks with the Hermes.

Accordingly, the contractor told the plaintiff that it would not be automatically included in the Hermes cover unless it paid a proportion of the cost of insurance. However, the plaintiff remained concerned whether the Hermes cover could well protect it against the German risk. It then contacted ECGD (who now uses the operating name "UKEF"), enquiring about whether it should (a) participate in the Hermes cover or (b) insure the German risk with ECGD under a separate ECI policy. ECGD failed to provide clear advice, and the plaintiff chose the former arrangement. Eventually, the Saudi Arabian government paid the money, but the contractor was unable to pay the assured due to financial difficulties. Euler Hermes rejected the plaintiff's claim because the Hermes cover was only covering the Saudi risk rather than the German risk. Neill J held that this was justifiable because there was no direct contractual link between the plaintiff and the end buyer. The court noted that, although "under a scheme devised by the EEC in 1970" it was possible for a subcontractor to be included in the contractor's ECI policy, the contract between the subcontractor and the contractor should be an unconditional contract. The plaintiff's transaction, based on an "if and when" contract, was thus held ineligible for such a scheme.[64]

63 Ibid.
64 Ibid.

The ECA's liability for "bad advice"?

An ECA may carry some extra functions in addition to providing ECI (and ECGs): it often provides "technical advice and, in some cases, credit information and country risk analysis services".[65] Thus, where exporters or banks, as the potential policyholders, consult with the ECA in respect of their transactions, the ECA should seek to provide the correct advice and to help them with the placement of the suitable ECI cover. Failing to do so may render the ECA liable for its "bad advice".

The liability for "bad advice" was confirmed by the House of Lords in *Hedley Byrne & Co Ltd v Heller & Partners Ltd*,[66] which established that in making a statement at the request of another, a duty of care would be owed by the representor to the inquirer if it was plain that, in seeking information or advice from the representor, the inquirer was reasonably trusting him to exercise such a degree of care as the circumstances required and the representor knew or ought to have known that the inquirer was doing so. If in those circumstances the representor gave information or advice which was negligent, he would be liable for any pecuniary or personal damage caused to the inquirer; unless the representor had expressly excluded responsibility for reliance on his statement, no liability arose.

The *Hedley Byrne* principle was applied by the court in the context of ECI in *Culford* above, where the plaintiff contacted ECGD and enquired about the proper ECI cover it should purchase. The plaintiff telephoned the head office of ECGD in the City of London but was instructed to contact ECGD's regional office in north London in the first place. However, officers there felt unable to help because they were not familiar with the transaction to be insured. They had to tell the plaintiff to get back to the head office. After writing to the head office explaining the entire transaction and stating that the matter was of "urgency", the plaintiff received a reply letter, where the head office merely suggested that the plaintiff (a) contact the contractor for advice and (b) if the Euler Hermes cover was not sufficient to cover its risks, then take out an ECI cover with ECGD. Then, as is mentioned above, the plaintiff opted to participate in the Hermes cover rather than placing the German risk with ECGD, and Euler Hermes rejected its claim. The court held that ECGD did not provide clear and useful advice and that as an ECA, ECGD should have advised the plaintiff that the suitable cover for protection against the German risk was the ECGD cover rather than the Hermes cover. Neill J rejected ECGD's argument that the plaintiff in its correspondence implied that it was seeking the particular Hermes cover and the officers misunderstood what the plaintiff wanted: the plaintiff "put sufficient facts before ECGD...to have expected to receive advice to cover against the German risk".[67] The judge reasoned that the plaintiff was merely seeking general advice and ECGD overlooked something which an exporter with the lack of experience of the plaintiff might properly

65 Gianturco (n 47) 78. See also Lomnicka (n 35), [25-010].

66 [1964] AC 465.

67 *Culford* [1981] CLY 2752.

expect. Therefore, ECGD was held in breach of its duty of care and liable for its negligent advice to the plaintiff.

Notably, the court in *Culford* was only concerned with the issue of liability, whereas the issue of damages remained untouched. Nevertheless, it is suggested by the commentators that principles established by *Hedley Byrne* regarding tortious liability for negligent misstatement are perfectly applicable to public bodies such as the ECA.[68] Therefore, the ECA could be liable for any pecuniary damages caused to the inquirer by the negligent advice (for instance, the losses the plaintiff suffered due to the non-payment by the contractor in *Culford*).

How to obtain an ECI cover from private credit insurers?

The early attempt to introduce ECI business at Lloyd's

There was an attempt to introduce ECI business as an admitted line at Lloyd's in the early 20th century, when Mr Cuthbert Heath, a respected Lloyd's underwriter and the first Chairman of the Trade Indemnity Company, a major credit insurance company at that time, proposed "eight principles of credit insurance" as the foundation of professional underwriting of political and credit risks:[69]

1. Credit risks for goods sold and delivered;
2. Losses due to insolvency;
3. No guarantee of payment at due date or payment of disputed items;
4. Insured debts to be self-liquidating;
5. Terms of payment should be short;
6. Coverage of no more than 75% of sums at risk;
7. No cover for existing commitments;
8. No insurance of loans or advances by banks.

However, that attempt failed in 1923 as a result of a fraud case of which the details were discussed in *Industrial Guarantee Corp Ltd v Corporation of Lloyd's*.[70] The assured in that case ran a car hire–purchase business and wished to insure the risk of default of the buyers with underwriters at Lloyd's. Such insurance was, in essence, a domestic credit insurance cover that shared the very identical legal nature with ECI.[71] Mr H, an underwriter at Lloyd's, placed the risks even knowing that the assured did not have sufficient security for its business. Mr H charged

68 Clive Lewis, *Judicial Remedies in Public Law* (10th edn, Sweet & Maxwell 2014), [15-039].

69 Whilst some of those principles seem no longer applicable in today's industry, they were helpful guidelines to establish the underwriting discipline for such risks that were not well understood at that time. See Glenn Sexton, "The English Legal View of Trade Credit Insurance – A Practitioner's View", <http://aida.org.uk/pdf/Glenn%20Sexton%20Credit%20Insurance.pdf> accessed 1 February 2022.

70 (1924) 19 Ll L Rep 78.

71 For a detailed description of the nature of the hire-purchase business, see ibid, 80–1 (Bailhache J).

a premium of £20,000, which was inadequate to meet his liability of over £2m. The assured then suffered from fraudulent bills of exchanges and made a claim amounted to £428,000 in total. Mr H, however, found himself unable to pay: underwriters were required to place deposits at Lloyd's, but if he withdrew his deposits, then Lloyd's would have known that he was in "hopeless difficulty" and stopped his underwriting. Mr H then sought to forge further bills of exchanges to meet his liability. Unsurprisingly, none of them was honoured, and Mr H was only able to carry on his business for a few months longer until Lloyd's was eventually aware of his fraud.

To preserve the reputation of the Lloyd's market, all syndicates and members trading alone agreed, unprecedently, to subscribe a policy of £2m insuring the amount of Mr H's deficiency on his credit insurance account.[72] However, because many of the transactions on which claims were based had been fraudulent, the Committee of Lloyd's paid only such portion as they saw fit. The assured then sued Lloyd's, relying on a pamphlet called "The Story of Lloyd's" which the assured received in purchasing its cover. The pamphlet stated that Lloyd's was a reputable insurance market where each underwriter's account was annually audited to ensure that his assets were sufficient to meet his liabilities. The pamphlet emphasised that the committee of Lloyd's had taken "ample measures to provide for any expected contingencies that could possibly arise". The assured contended that the pamphlet constituted an offer of insurance and further alleged that Lloyd's failed to make an effective compulsory audit of Mr H. Whilst Bailhache J was critical of some "misleading" promotions in the pamphlet, he did not regard it as an offer. The judge clarified that there had been no such reliance on the pamphlet: the assured previously insured its business in the company market until 1921, when it switched to Lloyd's merely because Mr H offered a cheaper premium. The judge held that Lloyd's did take reasonable precautions to ensure that underwriters should be solvent, as Mr H kept two sets of books: one set he showed to Lloyd's auditors and the other set he concealed from them. The former recorded that his underwriting account was in credit, but the latter contained his personal account which was heavily overdrawn. Bailhache J thus ruled that it was hardly possible for Lloyd's to detect such a fraud on the assumption that Mr H was an honest underwriter; since it was in this way deceived by Mr H, it was not liable to pay for his liability under the policy.

Despite the judgment in favour of Lloyd's, *Industrial Guarantee* led directly to a prohibition on the underwriting of credit risks at Lloyd's.[73] The Lloyd's Policy

72 It was reported that a further £100,000 was paid from the Corporation of Lloyd's resources and £88,468 from the Mutual Fund, a fund which the non-marine underwriters had voluntarily accumulated for some years and a precursor of the Central Fund established in 1927. See Julian Burling, *Lloyd's: Law and Practice* (1st edn, Routledge 2013) [2.33–4].

73 John Dunt, "When Marine Cargo Insurance Became Credit Risk Insurance" [2021] (3) LMCLQ 431, 431–2.

Signing Office (LPSO) was established to detect any such underwriting, and the following statement was required to be printed in every policy:[74]

> No policy or other contract dated on or after 1st January 1924 will be recognised by the committee of Lloyd's as entitling the holder to the benefits of the funds and/or guarantees lodged by the underwriters on the policy or contract as security for their liabilities unless it bears at the foot the seal of Lloyd's Policy Signing Office.

Today's ECI business at Lloyd's

It is suggested by the commentators that the Lloyd's regulations for specialist credit risk insurers have been much relaxed over the years, as ECI is now a "well-recognised class of business" underwritten at Lloyd's by specialist credit risk underwriters.[75] Nevertheless, the underwriting of ECI is still closely monitored and restricted. Lloyd's *Performance Management – Supplemental Requirements & Guidance* states that "Financial Guarantee risks have long been identified by Lloyd's as a class of business that can bring a high level of prudential risk to the Society if written without proper controls".[76] The document defines "Financial Guarantee insurance" as contracts of insurance against the risks of "the financial failure, default, insolvency, bankruptcy, liquidation or winding up of any person whether or not a party to the contract of insurance".[77] The document further stipulates the two largest classes of insurance within "Financial Guarantee insurance", namely "Credit Risk" (Risk Code "CR") and "Contract Frustration" (Risk Code "CF"). Both indemnify the assured for the non-performance of a valid contractual obligation, whereas the obligor under the former is a commercial entity, and the obligor under the latter is a government entity or a commercial entity controlled/owned by a government entity.[78] In arranging ECI, underwriters must apply the appropriate CR and CF risks codes[79] and comply with the special requirements for the writing on "Financial Guarantee" risks regarding premium income limits, appropriate capability and resource, assignment of the policy, insolvency of the

74 Burling (n 72) [2.35]. The functions of the LPSO are now performed by a separate company named "Xchanging Ins-sure Services". See < https://www.lloyds.com/market-directory/committees-and-associations/xchanging-ins-sure-services-xis-and-xchanging-claims-services-xcs> accessed 1 February 2022.

75 Dunt (n 73) 432.

76 See Lloyd's of London, *Performance Management - Supplemental Requirements & Guidance* (last updated in July 2020), 41 < https://www.lloyds.com/conducting-business/requirements-and-standards/supplemental-requirements-and-guidance/ > accessed 1 February 2022.

77 Ibid, 42.

78 Ibid, 43.

79 Lloyd's of London, "Market Bulletin Y47455 Financial Guarantee Insurance – Amendments to Requirements", 8 < https://www.lloyds.com/~/media/Files/The%20Market/Communications/Market%20Bulletins/2013/12/Y4755.pdf> accessed 1 February 2022.

insured, delegated writing, accelerated payment and fraudulent misrepresentations and claims.[80]

The website of Lloyd's provides detailed guidelines to policyholders on how to purchase political and credit risks insurance.[81] There are currently 44 managing agents at Lloyd's that can underwrite such risks.[82] Exporters and banks who wish to obtain ECI can contact those managing agents.

There have been several reported English cases which well explained how political and credit risks are underwritten in today's Lloyd's market. One typical example is *International Management Group (UK) Ltd v Simmonds*,[83] where the assured was a company responsible for the televising and distribution of the "Sahara Cup", an annual cricket tournament between India and Pakistan which was scheduled to take place in 1996–2000. The assured entered into an agreement between the cricket boards of those two countries. Under that agreement, the assured guaranteed an annual fee of US$ 0.5 m to the boards, and in return, it was granted exclusive rights to televise the events and to exploit other related commercial profits. The Sahara Cup duly took place in 1996–8, but in 1999, due to the increasing political tension between India and Pakistan, the Indian government refused to allow its team to participate. The Sahara Cup, however, was replaced by a trilateral match known as the "Toronto Cup", where the team of West Indies was invited to play against India and Pakistan separately. The Indian team was allowed to participate in the Toronto Cup in 1999. Given those situations, for the incoming Sahara Cup in 2000, the assured sought insurance against war and political risks, especially the risk of the cancellation of the tournament due to the political tension at that time. The assured initially tried to place an ordinary contingency risk cover through its broker, A. However, A did not have much experience in broking political risks, so it worked with a sub-broker, B, who was a specialist in this field. With the help of those brokers, the assured obtained a contingency risk cover subscribed by two leading underwriters and some following underwriters. The standard Lloyd's Contingency Policy at that time excluded losses arising from political risks. The assured, therefore, had to renegotiate with the underwriters who agreed to extend the coverage to certain political risks including losses arising from "the refusal of necessary permits, licenses or visas, or the withdrawal of any previously issued necessary permits, licenses or visas".[84] In this way, although such a risk "was hard to place" in the first place,[85] the assured eventually obtained the exact ECI cover it looked for.

80 Lloyd's of London (n 76) 41–5.

81 ECI products can be found in the "Market Directory" section on Lloyd's website, which includes "Political Risks, Credit & Financial Guarantee" as one type of "Specialty" risks. See <https://www.lloyds.com/> accessed 1 February 2022.

82 See <https://ldc.lloyds.com/market-directory/results?cobc=16&cob=126&name=> accessed 1 February 2022.

83 [2003] EWHC 177 (Comm), [2004] Llyod's Rep IR 247. The issue of this case concerned the assured's duty of fair presentation, which will be discussed in Chapter 4 of this book.

84 Ibid, [9-10].

85 Ibid, [146] (Cooke J).

The leading underwriters' role under ECI

ECI business at Lloyd's shall be placed by licensed and authorised specialist underwriters only.[86] Lloyd's *Performance Management – Supplemental Requirements & Guidance* states that:[87]

> The writing of Financial Guarantee classes requires a high level of technical expertise in the underlying risks. Where it is proposed that a syndicate will write any of the Financial Guarantee classes then Lloyd's will expect the managing agent to be able to demonstrate that it has suitable underwriting resources in place. In particular, Lloyd's will expect managing agents to have a suitably robust analytical resource to support the underwriting of any business. Managing agents should also have appropriate models in place, suitable to the types of risk being underwritten.
>
> …
>
> Other than where delegation is to a service company coverholder, Lloyd's is unlikely to agree plans for the writing of Financial Guarantee business in any of the classes listed where the risks are bound by way of delegated underwriting. This includes, in particular, binding authorities and line slips.

It is therefore important for underwriters to carefully check if they are capable of underwriting political and credit risks. However, that is sometimes a complicated task. In *ABN Amro Bank NV v Royal and Sun Alliance Insurance Plc*,[88] a recent case which involved a lengthy and complex piece of litigation, the broker sought to add a credit risk clause called the "Transaction Premium Clause" (TPC) in renewing a typical marine cargo insurance policy which was built around the Institute Cargo Clauses (ICC) (but also contained a number of tailored clauses). The TPC, which was intended to protect the assured bank against the risk of the non-payment by the buyers of the cargos, is indeed an unusual insuring clause in the marine cargo market where policies primarily cover the risks of physical loss of or damage to the insured cargos (PLOD risks) only. However, when the broker sent a slip containing the TPC clause to the leading underwriter for renewal, the latter merely skim-read it and then signed and stamped it without raising any specific questions on the TPC. Only after the buyers defaulted in payment did the leading underwriter realise that the TPC might render it liable to pay for the huge losses the assured suffered. In rejecting the claim, the underwriters raised a number of arguments regarding the construction of the TPC, non-disclosure, misrepresentation and the assured's duty to conduct quality checks of the goods. In particular, the leading underwriter contended that they were not licensed or authorised to write credit risks, and thus the coverage of the policy in question should not be extended to non-PLOD risks. Whilst all those issues will be dis-

86 Ibid, [202].
87 Lloyd's of London (n 76) 43–4.
88 [2021] EWHC 442 (Comm).

cussed in the following chapters of this book, it is sufficient here to note that the trial court rejected all of those arguments and held that the slip containing the TPC is a legally binding document. Clearly, Jacobs J did not treat the internal delegation requirements by Lloyd's as affecting the validity of the TPC.

The underwriters in *ABN Amro* appealed against the trial decision. Council for underwriters told the Court of Appeal that the TPC was "quietly inserted" into the renewed policy by the broker, and "it is like someone going to a car dealership and asking for a yacht". Council for the assured, on the other hand, argued that English law does not rewrite contracts even if there are "bad bargains".[89] In the appeal, the underwriters were only given permission to pursue one ground of appeal concerning the proper interpretation of the TPC. The Court of Appeal, in its concise judgment,[90] upheld Jacobs J's decision and held that the underwriters were liable to indemnify the assured for the losses under the TPC, which amounted to some £31m.

Despite all those controversies, what remains clear is that the leading underwriter in *ABN Amro* did not exercise sufficient caution in checking whether he was capable of underwriting political and credit risks. An example of good practice in similar situations can be found in *Harding Maughan Hambly Ltd v Compagnie Europeenne de Courtage d'Assurances et de Reassurances SA*,[91] where a peculiar political risk was presented to the leading underwriter who exercised sufficient caution. The assured in that case was a French trade company who wished to cover the risk that Sonangol, the Angolan state oil company, would fail to fulfil its obligation to supply it with 5,000–6,000 barrels of crude oil per day for a two-year period under an off-take agreement.[92] The off-take agreement, financed by a Swiss bank, provided that the assured was the operator of Block 3, an offshore oil block of Angola and that the physical movement of oil from that block was within the assured's control. The assured's attempt to insure the risk at Lloyd's as a "contract frustration" risk failed because the contract frustration market at that time was full up with Angolan debt and thus had no wish to further tranches of such risks.

The assured's brokers then presented the risk to a leading underwriter in the expropriation market, who indicated his willingness to underwrite the risk subject

89 Lexis, "Insurers appeal cocoa fraud decision (*ABN Amro v RSA*)" <https://www.lexisnexis.co.uk/legal/news/insurers-appeal-cocoa-fraud-decision-abn-amro-v-rsa > accessed 1 February 2022.

90 [2021] EWCA Civ 1789, [60]–[71]. It should be noted that the underwriters' appeal had been compromised between the hearing and the giving of the judgment, but the Court of Appeal, considering a number of factors, decided to give concise judgment on the underwriters' appeal. For details see Chapter 3 of this work.

91 [2000] 1 All ER (Comm) 225. See also Cheng Lin, "Understanding the Legal Nature of Export Credit Insurance: Lessons from *ABN Amro v RSA*" [2022] (3) JBL 225, 235.

92 An off-take agreement is an arrangement between a producer and a buyer to purchase or sell portions of the producer's upcoming goods, making it easier for producers to obtain financing. It is normally negotiated far in advance, often prior to the construction of manufacturing facilities and before actual production has begun. An off-take agreement can help the buyer lock in a price and guarantee the supply of a product in anticipation of future demand. See <https://www.investopedia.com/terms/o/offtake-agreement.asp> accessed 1 February 2022.

to a number of subjectivities regarding the underlying transaction.[93] In particular, he requested (a) a copy of the off-take agreement, (b) satisfactory evidence of the title of the oil and a letter of comfort signed by Sonangol, and (c) a legal opinion confirming the legality under Swiss law (which was the applicable law in that case) of documents (a) and (b) as well as the associated loan transaction. After these documents were provided by the brokers, the leading underwriter rightly noted a significant inconsistency between document (a) and (b): the former was worded as a straightforward Free on Board (FOB) sale and purchase agreement[94] which provided that the assured, as the buyer, would only become the owner of the oil after the product had passed through the loading pipeline onto the vessel; the latter, however, stipulated that the assured owned the oil from the signature of the off-take agreement. The leading underwriter thus requested further clarification on whether the assured was the owner of the crude oil "in the ground". The brokers sought to revise the off-take agreement and stipulate that the assured had an irrecoverable "right to receive" the oil from the signature of the agreement. Nevertheless, the Swiss law opinion indicated that such revision was still not specific and precise enough to constitute adequate evidence of the assured's ownership over the oil in the ground because the contractual oil had not been sufficiently identified (by being separated from a mass).[95] This rendered the leading underwriter critical of the placement of the risk. The brokers accordingly proposed a revised policy which more properly identified the subject matter insured. Whilst the details of the policy will be discussed in Chapter 3 of this work, it is sufficient here to note that the revised policy eventually convinced the leading underwriter that the risk could properly be written and the transaction proceeded smoothly.[96] *Harding* therefore provides a good example of how a leading underwriter could assess and underwrite political and credit risks in a diligent way so as to avoid potential disputes.

The relationship between leading and following underwriters under ECI

As with other types of insurance, ECI at Lloyd's is placed on a subscription basis.[97] The relationship between leading and following underwriters under ECI was explored in *ABN Amro*. The policy in that case was placed by one leading underwriter and thirteen following underwriters.[98] The written lines totalled more

93 For details see Chapter 4 of this work.

94 "FOB", the abbreviation of "Free on Board", is one of the International Commercial Terms ("Incoterms") published by the International Chamber of Commerce (ICC). The latest version of Incoterms rules, Incoterms 2020, is available on ICC's website. See < https://iccwbo.org/resources-for-business/incoterms-rules/incoterms-2020/> accessed 1 February 2022.

95 *Harding* [2000] 1 All ER (Comm) 225.

96 The issue of *Harding* was about the allocation of commission between brokers and sub-brokers, which will be analysed below.

97 Syndicates at Lloyd's may also delegate their authorities to other companies to underwrite ECI on their behalf. See, e.g., *Mann v Coutts & Co* [2003] EWHC 2138 (Comm), [2004] 1 All ER (Comm) 1.

98 *ABN Amro* [2021] EWHC 442 (Comm), [47].

than 135%, with the consequence that the written lines of the following market "signed down" to a lower percentage of the risk than they had wished to write, except that two underwriters had written on the basis that their percentage shares were "to stand" (i.e., not to be reduced).[99] The slip stated that the basis of the subscription agreement was the London Market Group's General Underwriters Agreement (GUA) (1.0 version, October 2001) with Marine Cargo Schedule 2003.[100]

The introduction section of the GUA (1.0 version) explains how it works in the following paragraphs, which were fully cited by the trial court in *ABN Amro*:[101]

> The GUA is an agreement between the subscribing underwriters on a particular contract relating to the level of delegated authority in respect of post placement alterations.
>
> The GUA structure provides a standard agreement that is referenced from the slip … The GUA is intended to be used with the new LMP Slip, but can be incorporated into any other form of slip. The slip should make clear reference to the GUA within the Subscription Agreement section under "Basis of Agreement to Contract Changes". For example, "*GUA October 2001 with Marine Hull Schedule May 2002*".
>
> The structure of the GUA enables its use for any class of business with each defining its particular requirements in the Class of Business Schedules. Class of Business Schedules have been defined for Non-Marine, Marine Cargo, Marine Hull, Marine Liability, Marine Energy, Excess of Loss & Treaty Reinsurance, Political Risks, Professional Indemnity and Terrorism.
>
> Each Schedule is split into three Parts, defining the Underwriters whose agreement is required for each type of alteration:
>
> Part 1 – Slip Leader only
> Part 2 – Slip Leader plus Agreement Parties
> Part 3 – All Underwriters
>
> ……

Clause 3 of the main text of the GUA (1.0 version) further states that:[102]

> 3.1 Only Alterations set out in the applicable Schedule Part 1 may be agreed by the Slip Leader alone on behalf of the Agreement Parties and Other

99 Ibid, [147].

100 See the GUA (1.0 version, October 2001) <https://lmg.london/wp-content/uploads/2019/07/GUA-and-Schedules-2012.pdf> accessed 1 February 2022. It should be noted that the London Market Group issued its latest (2.0) version of the GUA in February 2014, which did not change the substantive contents of the GUA (1.0 version). See <https://lmg.london/wp-content/uploads/2019/07/General-Underwriters-Agreement-version-2.0-February-2014.pdf> accessed 1 February 2022.

101 Ibid. See also *ABN Amro* [2021] EWHC 442 (Comm), [173]–[174].

102 See n 100 above.

Underwriters, each for its own individual signed proportion severally and not jointly.

3.2 Only Alterations set out in the applicable Schedule Part 2 may be agreed by the Slip Leader and Agreement Parties acting together on behalf of Other Underwriters, each for its own individual signed proportion severally and not jointly.

……

3.4 The Alterations set out in the applicable Schedule Part 3, and any Alteration that the Slip Leader and any Agreement Party so require, may be agreed only by all Underwriters, each for its own individual signed proportion severally and not jointly.

Part 3 of the GUA Marine Cargo Schedule 2003 stipulates that "any Alteration which increases the monetary exposure of the Underwriters (or of any of them) … shall be agreed only by all Underwriters each for its own proportion severally and not jointly".[103]

How the GUA and its Marine Cargo Schedule operate was elaborated by the trial court in *ABN Amro*. The policy in that case was annually renewed for many years, usually in February each year. In July 2015, the assured wished to insert the TPC and a non-avoidance clause (NAC) in the policy, and the broker sent the proposed endorsement (hereinafter referred to as the "July 2015 endorsement") to the leading underwriter. The endorsement was in the standard format subject to the GUA (1.0 version) with Marine Cargo Schedule 2003 and was scratched by the leading underwriter using the GUA Stamp B.[104] In the GUA Stamp B, the leading underwriter initialled the part of the box saying "Slip Leader Only", "thereby intimating that he did not consider that any of the following market needed to sign, or even see, the endorsement".[105] The TPC in the July 2015 endorsement was stipulated in Section 2, Clause 1.5, as a standalone provision "with no relevant link to any particular section of the policy or any part of the coverage elsewhere".[106]

In late January 2016, the leading underwriter and ten following underwriters (who were the 2nd–12th defendants in that case) scratched the slip for renewal (hereinafter referred to as the "unamended 2016 policy") which incorporated the July 2015 endorsement. However, in early February 2016, the broker further proposed an amended policy (hereinafter referred to as the "amended 2016 policy"), under which the location of the TPC had changed: it appeared twice, once in Section 1.5 where it already appeared, and again in Section 4, which "immediately followed" a non-PLOD extension in Section 3. The leading underwriter scratched this amended policy without informing those ten followers. Also, at this

103 Ibid. It should be noted that whilst the Marine Cargo Schedule 2003 was part of the GUA (1.0 version) document, Schedules under the GUA (2.0 version) are published separately.

104 Both the 1.0 and 2.0 version of the GUA include the GUA Stamp A and B in Clause 4. See n 100 above.

105 *ABN Amro* [2021] EWHC 442 (Comm), [52] (Jacobs J).

106 Ibid, [299].

time, another two underwriters (who were the 13th–14th defendants) subscribed to the amended 2016 policy as the new following underwriters.[107]

Whether the 2nd–12th defendants were bound by the July 2015 endorsement was not a central issue in *ABN Amro*, as all of the claims were made during the 2016 policy period.[108] However, they questioned whether they should be bound by the unamended 2016 policy only or by the amended 2016 policy as well. This, as they submitted, was relevant to the construction of the TPC: the fact that the TPC appeared as a standalone provision under the unamended 2016 policy would indicate that it covered PLOD risks only; however, under the amended 2016 policy, the fact that the TPC immediately followed a non-PLOD extension would mean that it could cover non-PLOD risks, too.

The key issue here, therefore, was whether the inclusion of the TPC constituted as an alteration which "increases the monetary exposure" of the underwriters under Part 3 of the GUA Marine Cargo Schedule 2003. If so, then the ten following underwriters were not bound by the amended 2016 policy. The trial court did not regard the TPC as "increasing the monetary exposure" of the underwriters. Jacobs J reasoned that prior to the TPC, the underwriters were already exposed to the potential for loss in relation to "every ton of" the assured's cargo subject to the maximum liability limits of the policy; the TPC did not constitute an increase in those limits, it only increased the "potential for loss" within the existing policy limits.[109]

ABN Amro illustrates the significance for following underwriters to carefully review every alteration under a renewed or endorsed policy. If the ten followers in that case had read the TPC when subscribing to the unamended 2016 policy, they could have questioned the purpose and effect of it and refused to sign. On the contrary, "none of them noticed the clause let alone read it carefully or asked questions about it".[110]

Notably, the policy in *ABN Amro*, as explained above, was placed in the marine cargo market, and thus the underwriters referred to the GUA Marine Cargo Schedule 2003. The (more) applicable schedule should be the GUA Political Risks Schedule 2006.[111]

ECI business in the company market

Apart from Lloyd's of London, exporters and banks can also obtain ECI coverage from private credit insurers in the London company market.[112] It should be noted

107 Ibid, [146].
108 Ibid, [92].
109 Ibid, [312–3].
110 Ibid, [293] (Jacobs J).
111 The full text of it is also included in the GUA (1.0 version). It should be noted that the latest (2.0) version of the GUA does not include the full text of GUA Schedules, but since it contains "minor editing changes" and "no changes in substantive content, i.e. to core GUA clauses or Schedules", the GUA Political Risk Schedule 2006 remains perfectly applicable. See n 100 above.
112 For the details of private credit insurers in the company market, see Gallagher, "Structured Credit and Political Risk Insurance Report and Market Update", 16 <https://www.ajg.com/uk/-/media

that the short-term limb of the ECGD had been privatised in December 1991, when it sold this part of the business to a Dutch private credit insurer, Nederlandse Credietverzekering Maatschappij NV (NCM) which was later renamed Atradius which, together with Euler Hermes, Coface and other private credit insurers, are providing various types of ECI products in the UK.[113]

The broker's role under ECI

Market protocols

London Market Group's "Contract Certainty Code of Practice" (CCCP) required that:[114]

> Contract Certainty Principles
> A. When entering into the contract
> The insurer and broker (where applicable) must ensure that all terms are clear and unambiguous by the time the offer is made to enter into the contract or the offer is accepted. All terms must be clearly expressed, including any conditions or subjectivities.
> ...
> A4. Broker actions
> The broker should provide the necessary risk and contractual information that represents the insured's demands and needs, in order to enable the agreement of all terms.

Although the CCCP is not a legal binding document, it reflects the "best practice" in the industry.[115] Brokers are therefore expected to comply with this guidance in placing political and credit risks.

Legal principles

The trial court in *ABN Amro* confirmed that, as with under other types of insurance, the broker under ECI owes duties of reasonable skill and care to the assured: (a) to procure the insurance cover which clearly and indisputably meets the assured's requirements; and (b) so did not expose it to an unnecessary risk of litigation.[116] Jacobs J further noted that concerning duty (b), it is well established by English

/files/gallagher/uk/news-insights/gallagher-scpr-market-update-jan-2021.pdf> accessed 1 February 2022.

113 See Andrews & Millett (n 21), [15-007]; Lomnicka (n 35), [25-017].

114 London Market Group, "Contract Certainty Code of Practice – September 2018", 3 < https://lmg.london/wp-content/uploads/2019/07/CC-COP-Sept-2018.pdf > accessed 1 February 2022.

115 *ABN Amro* [2021] EWHC 442 (Comm), [321] (Jacobs J).

116 Ibid, [864] (Jacobs J).

case authorities that the broker is liable for any costs which are irrecoverable from the underwriters.[117]

Broking political and credit risks in the marine cargo market?

To what extent does the broker bear such duties was examined in *ABN Amro*. As is explained above, the assured in that case sought insurance coverage for credit risks regarding its cargo and, with the help of its external lawyers, it prepared the TPC and required the broker to include that clause in amending and renewing the policy. The assured asked the broker whether the TPC was appropriately drafted to cover the credit risks it wished to insure. The broker gave a positive response, indicating that he had seen the leading underwriter and confirmed that the latter understood the TPC in the same way as the assured did: "anyway nothing much to worry about".[118] However, in fact the broker did not draw the TPC to the leading underwriter's attention, nor did he properly discuss that clause with the latter. The underwriters nevertheless skim-read and signed the amended policy, but they opted to reject the claim when the loss occurred under the TPC.

In addition to suing the underwriters, the assured also sued the broker (who was listed as the 15th defendant in that case), contending that (a) if the TPC was held ineffective and could not cover the claim, then the broker was in breach of its duties to procure the insurance cover that clearly and indisputably met its requirements; and (b) even if the TPC did respond to the claim, the broker was nevertheless liable for any irrecoverable costs it incurred in pursuing the underwriters.

Whilst the details of the judgement regarding the TPC will be discussed in the following chapters, it is sufficient here to note that the trial court held that the claim against the majority of the underwriters had succeeded, except that the claim against two underwriters (who were the 8th and 10th defendants in that case) failed because of an estoppel arising from a false statement made by the broker to them in relation to the TPC. It therefore became the trial court's task to decide whether the broker was liable for (i) any irrecoverable costs in circumstances where the cover was effective and (ii) the very substantial damages where the cover had been ineffective.[119]

The assured submitted that had the broker performed his duties, it would have sought and purchased alternative insurance coverage from specialist credit underwriters, which could have provided substantial protection against credit risks; alternatively, had such cover been not available, it would have wound up its transactions with the buyers so that it would have been no longer exposed to the credit

117 Ibid, [871] (Jacobs J). See also *FNCB Ltd v Barnet Devanney (Harrow) Ltd* [1999] Lloyd's Rep IR 459; *Talbot Underwriting Ltd v Nausch Hogan & Murray Inc* [2005] EWHC 2359 (Comm), [2005] 2 CLC 868; *Standard Life Assurance Ltd v Oak Dedicated Ltd* [2008] EWHC 222 (Comm), [2008] 2 All ER (Comm) 916.

118 *ABN Amro* [2021] EWHC 442 (Comm), [142].

119 Ibid, [875].

risks regarding the cargo.[120] In supporting its submission, the assured asserted that the broker did not provide advice that standalone ECI covers were available in the credit risk market, neither did he take adequate steps to ensure that the TPC was clear and undisputable: any reasonably competent broker would have explained the purpose of the TPC to underwriters, but what the broker actually did was merely handing the TPC over to the underwriters. Such a broking approach, in the view of the assured, was "perfunctory and superficial".[121]

The broker, relying on *Standard Life Assurance v Oak Dedicated*,[122] argued that he should not be held responsible for the consequences of underwriters "advancing spurious arguments" in relation to the construction of the TPC. The broker also submitted that the assured was relying on its external lawyers' advice in drafting the TPC, and thus any problems with the effect of the TPC shall be the responsibility of the external lawyers. Furthermore, the broker contended that his duty of care should be distinguished from a "duty to nanny": the underwriters were presumed to know their own business and to be able to form their own judgment of the risk to be placed. The broker thus believed that it was not his responsibility to ensure that the underwriters had read and understood the proposed slip that they were presented for agreement; if there was something they did not understand, they may either refuse to agree on it or ask the broker questions.

The trial court essentially rejected the broker's submissions. First of all, Jacobs J held that the assured was looking principally, but not exclusively, to its external lawyers for advice in preparing the TPC: it was also looking to the broker for its professional expertise. Therefore, the judge ruled that the broker's duty did not reduce, "still less disappear", because the TPC was drafted by the assured's external lawyers.

Jacobs J then referred to *Standard Life*,[123] where Tomlinson J ruled that "the coverage is clear in so far as it leaves no room for significant debate" but also admitted that "the risk of litigation can never be wholly avoided": the question was therefore whether a reasonably competent broker would have concluded that the policy wording was sufficiently clear to meet the assured's requirements. Accordingly, Jacobs J consulted with the expert witness about whether the broker should have (a) given the assured the proper advice at the outset that it should approach the political and credit risks market or, alternatively, (b) explained the TPC to the existing marine cargo risks underwriters. Based on the expert evidence, the judge held that the broker fell below the standard to be expected of a reasonably competent broker. Jacobs J held that the assured was never insistent on the marine cargo risk market being approached. It was merely proceeding on the assumption that the TPC was a possible change to which the existing underwriters might be willing to agree. Therefore, the starting point for the broker was to

120 Ibid, [874].
121 Ibid, [884].
122 [2008] EWHC 222 (Comm), [102] (Tomlinson J).
123 Ibid, [101–4] (Tomlinson J).

identify to its client the suitable specialist underwriters. The broker should have approached the existing underwriters to place political and credit risks only after the client had taken an informed decision to pursue this course, but no sensible client would have done so. Jacobs J reasoned that even if the broker opted to approach the marine cargo market, "going to see the wrong market made it all the more important" for him to explain to the existing underwriters what the TPC was intended to address so as to avoid the potential for future disputes. The TPC was "long and tightly drafted", and its full import would not necessarily be grasped by an underwriter on a first reading. The judge believed that the broker should ensure beyond any reasonable doubt that the cover was in place: "why take the chance, why not just do it?"[124] Therefore, in the judge's opinion, the careful drafting of a clause, in circumstances where that clause is unusual and unprecedented in the market in which the cover was being placed, could not reasonably be relied upon by the broker as providing protection against the unnecessary risk of litigation; any reasonably competent broker would be expected to specifically discuss the wording and consequences of any unusual clause with underwriters because that was "part and parcel of a broker's daily work".[125]

Jacobs J further commented that the underwriters' arguments concerning the construction of the TPC were not spurious because, as will be demonstrated in Chapter 3 of this work, those arguments paid little regard to the actual wording of the TPC. The underwriters focused on the factual matrix regarding the formation of the cover and the commercial consequences of rival interpretations, both of which should not be regarded as spurious. The judge also distinguished the unprincipled "duty to nanny" from the broker's general duties of care: the broker did not generally owe duties to his client to explain particular clauses, including unusual clauses, to the underwriters, but he should, in the interest of his clients, check whether the underwriters had the same understanding as the client in relation to the effect of such an unusual clause as the TPC. That was not about the duty to protect the underwriters; that was about the duty to protect his client.[126]

For the reasons above, the judge held that the broker failed his duties to the assured even on the premise that the TPC did provide the cover that was sought. The trial judgement of *ABN Amro* demonstrated the importance for the broker to place political and credit risks in the correct market and to ensure that the underwriters understand the insuring clauses (as well as any other significant clauses indeed) in the same way as the assured. It should be noted that the broker appealed against the trial court's decision on the estoppel issue only;[127] it no longer disputed its duties to the assured, thereby indicating that it has accepted the trial court's view that its broking approach in that case was far from professional. The trial judgment of *ABN Amro* on the broker's duties to the assured therefore remains

124 *ABN Amro* [2021] EWHC 442 (Comm), [921] (Jacobs J).
125 Ibid, [931] (Jacobs J).
126 Ibid, [938] (Jacobs J).
127 See *ABN Amro* [2021] EWCA Civ 1789.

good law. As is well summarised by the commentator, in preparing the policy wording, the broker bears the duty to the assured:[128]

> Not only to secure the required coverage but also to use wording that puts the coverage beyond reasonable doubt. If the wording is opaque and the outcome is litigation between the assured and the insurers as to its meaning, then the brokers are in breach of duty even though the outcome is ultimately favourable to the assured.

Notably, different from *ABN Amro*, the abovementioned *Harding* case[129] provides a very good example of how brokers could place political and credit risks diligently: when the brokers in this case sought to present the risk in the expropriation market, the leading underwriters requested further documentation and clarification for several times before finally agreeing to underwrite the risk. The brokers, however, were not "daunted":[130] they worked closely with the assured to obtain the requested documentation and clarification and kept in touch with the leading underwriters, explaining to them the nature of the risk[131] and proposing the revised insuring clause. It was the joint effort of the leading underwriter and the brokers that enabled the assured to eventually obtain the suitable ECI coverage for its off-take transaction.

The causal connection between the broker's breach and the assured's losses

In *ABN Amro*, concerning the causation issue, the assured contended that but for the broker's breach, it would either (i) have insured the transactions under an alternative credit risks cover; or (ii) if or to the extent that cover was unavailable, unwound existing transactions and not proceed with any new ones. As explained by Jacobs J, course (i) would have avoided 90% of the loss, with the remainder self-insured and involved paying a premium; course (ii) would have avoided 100% of the loss as the transactions would have been unwound. For the convenience of the trial, the assured was willing on both bases to give credit for the retention and premium under alternative credit risk cover, which meant that the court did not need to assess the relative chances of courses (i) and (ii) occurring.[132]

128 Robert Merkin, *Colinvaux's Law of Insurance* (2nd Supplement, 12th edn, Sweet & Maxwell 2021) [16-096].

129 [2000] 1 All ER (Comm) 225.

130 Ibid, 236.

131 The broker explained to the leading underwriters that the risk to be insured was not one of non-delivery of oil but expropriation: "we are not attempting to insure a non-delivery of oil … the oil being made available to the assured which amortizes the loan is granted … under the existing production sharing agreement. For as long as the assured is not affected by an expropriatory act in Block 3 there can be no loss". See ibid, 246.

132 See *ABN Amro* [2021] EWHC 442 (Comm), [943].

The broker argued that, but for any alleged breach, the assured would not have been able to obtain the cover it had under the TPC. Firstly, he contended that the price of a standalone ECI cover, rather than the existing cover under the TPC which was provided as a free add-on by underwriters in the context of a "large, valuable and popular risk", would be very high. The broker estimated that the premium rate would be about 2% of the value of the insured transactions, at least 1.85–1.90%. The assured would have considered that the high cost of such insurance far outweighed the benefit given the "apparent reliability" of the buyers. Secondly, even if the assured were interested in paying for such coverage, credit risk underwriters would not have agreed to place a policy covering the default of the buyers alone because the assured was engaging in adverse selection (i.e., picking the least attractive and riskiest part of its portfolio to insure). Thirdly, even if credit risk underwriters agreed to insure the risk of default of the buyers, they would exclude transactions that were concluded prior to the inception of the policy because ECI covers would have been a "risk-attaching" basis. Lastly, there would also be some contractual limitations. For instance, the maximum policy period would be five months (rather than the 12-month period under the existing policy), and the retention would be at least 50% (rather than the insured percentage of 90% under the existing policy); the assured would also be required to conduct quality checks of the goods under its transactions with the buyers.

The trial court referred to *Allied Maples Group Ltd v Simmons & Simmons*,[133] where Stuart-Smith LJ established that, where the defendant's negligence consists of an omission, in examining the causal link between the defendant's breach of contract and the claimant's losses, the court must consider both the acts of the claimant and any relevant third parties. On the one hand, the claimant must prove on the balance of probability that he would have taken action to obtain the benefit or avoid the risk. On the other hand, where the actions of third parties are in issue, the claimant does not have to prove on the balance of probabilities but needs to demonstrate a real or substantial chance that the third party would have acted so as to confer the relevant benefit or avoid the risk, the evaluation of the substantial chance being a question of quantification of damages.[134]

With regard to the claimant's conduct, the trial court was satisfied with the expert evidence which revealed that: the assured was making a margin of 3.25% on its transactions with the buyers, and thus the cost of ECI would still leave a decent and healthy margin; the assured would be willing to comply with any contractual limitations or requirements that the credit risk underwriters would have imposed because "there is no point paying a premium for cover and then declining to abide by the terms of the contract";[135] an ECI cover would be significant

133 [1995] 1 WLR 1602.

134 Ibid, 1610–1 (Stuart-Smith LJ), referred to by Jacobs J in *ABN Amro* [2021] EWHC 442 (Comm), [951-52].

135 For instance, the assured could carry out quality checks of the goods and pass the costs on to the buyers as part of the cost of financing. See *ABN Amro* [2021] EWHC 442 (Comm), [963], [1013] (Jacobs J).

for the assured's risk management.[136] Based on the abovementioned factors, Jacobs J held that ECI was a "necessary" rather than simply a "nice to have" for the assured:[137] if a standalone ECI cover were unavailable, the assured would have unwound the existing transactions with the buyer. The judge therefore ruled that on the balance of probabilities, the assured would have acted so as to obtain the relevant benefit or avoid the relevant risk in relation to its transactions with the buyers.

The trial court then identified two groups of potential third parties whose acts might confer the relevant benefit or avoid the risk. In relation to course (i), the question would be whether there was a real and substantial chance that credit insurers would have agreed to write insurance which would have provided protection against the assured's losses in that case. In relation to course (ii), the question would be whether there was a real and substantial chance that the buyers, if the transactions had been unwound, have made repayments to the assured.

In respect of course (i), Jacobs J ruled that there was a real and substantial chance that a standalone ECI cover would have been obtained. He noted that in 2015–16 there was a group of around 60 specialist credit risk insurers who could have been approached for cover. The market at that time was generally "soft" with sufficient capacity, and underwriters were actively looking for good business to write.[138] The judge rejected the broker's submission that the assured was engaging in adverse selection: the risk to be insured fell squarely within the bounds of standard trade credit insurance, and it was entirely normal for an assured to select a certain risk or group of risks from its portfolio to insure due to its credit profile or other concerns;[139] even if credit insurers had concerns on this regard, the assured would have either provided an acceptable explanation for seeking coverage on its transactions with the particular buyers or insured more of its clients within its portfolio "if that is what the insurers wanted".[140]

In respect of course (ii), Jacobs J held that there was clearly a real and substantial chance that the assured would have received significant repayments if course (ii) had been followed, because expert and documentary evidence showed that when the ECI cover was first sought in July 2015, the buyers had liquidity and were making substantial payments to the assured.

136 The expert witness in *ABN Amro* explained that ECI not only provided a second line of defence or an additional layer of protection but also lowered the assured's assessment of the probability of default. The assured could, therefore, for capital allocation purposes, allocate the exposure to insurers rather than the buyer, as the former had a better credit rating than the latter. That would reduce the assured's capital requirements for that part of the portfolio, and therefore the return on capital would be better. See ibid., [966].

137 Ibid, [969].

138 Ibid, [996].

139 Jacobs J noted that ECI sometimes operates as a "singleton" policy, where the assured can select an exposure to a particular counterparty to insure. See ibid., [992]. ECI can also operate on a "whole turnover" basis, where the assured can insure its transactions with multiple buyers as a whole.

140 Ibid, [994].

The trial court therefore concluded that the chain of causation between the broker's breach and the assured's losses had been established. It should be noted that the "but for" test in deciding the causation issue in insurance disputes has recently been reconsidered by the UK Supreme Court in *Financial Conduct Authority v Arch Insurance (UK) Ltd*,[141] where Lord Hamblen and Lord Leggatt criticised that the "but for" test is not applicable where there are multiple concurrent causes that lead to the loss. The Supreme Court replaced the "but for" test with an innovative "originating cause" approach in analysing the causal link between Covid-19 and pandemic-related losses. Nevertheless, the Supreme Court noted that the "but for" test remains to work in the vast majority of any area of law or ordinary life,[142] and thus the "but for" test was still followed by Jacobs J in the trial judgement of *ABN Amro*, which was delivered one month later than that of *FCA v Arch*.

It should also be noted that the Court of Appeal overruled the trial court's decision in *ABN Amro* regarding the estoppel defence raised by the 8th and 10th defendants. Whilst the details of the appeal judgment will be discussed in the following chapters of this book, it is worthwhile here to note that the 8th and 10th defendants were held by the Court of Appeal liable to indemnify the assured, which means that the assured now suffers no losses and accordingly the broker is no longer liable to the assured in respect of the 8th and 10th defendants' shares of indemnity, which amounted to some £3.3m. That was a narrow escape for the broker, but the trial court's reasoning on the causal link between the broker's breach and the assured's losses remains good law: "the [trial] judgment should give insurance brokers pause for thought, as they should possibly reconsider and review the rigour of their processes for communication between the assured and underwriters".[143]

The quantum issue regarding the broker's liability

The trial court in *ABN Amro* clarified that the quantum of recovery against the broker's liability in respect of 8th and 10th defendants should be based on the full amount of the cover that was provided by those two underwriters without a discount because the slip in that case was "substantially oversubscribed". Even if the two underwriters had declined to write the 7.5% share each of them wrote, the assured would still have had subscriptions to the cover which exceeded 100%.[144]

Jacobs J then accepted the assured's submission that the broker was liable for at least 90% indemnity that would have been payable under alternative cover. The judge was not persuaded by the broker's contention that the retention would be 50%, as it was based on the "adverse selection" argument which was held

141 [2021] UKSC 1.

142 Ibid, [183] (Lord Hamblen and Lord Leggatt).

143 Baris Soyer, "English Marine Insurance and General Average Law" [2021] *International Maritime and Commercial Law Yearbook* 84, 86.

144 *ABN Amro* [2021] EWHC 442 (Comm), [862].

incorrect. The judge was instead satisfied with the expert evidence demonstrating that "75–80% of all policies issued in the credit and political risks market are at 90% indemnity".[145]

The trial court also noted that credit would need to be given for the premium payable, but this would have been at the lower end of the range given by the experts. Expert evidence indicated that the overall premium for ECI depends upon the volume of business being transacted, and there would be a discount for volume. For instance, if the assured was required by credit risk insurers to insure its whole portfolio, it would then have to insure another four existing customers in addition to the buyers who defaulted in payment; however, the premium would not increase proportionately: it may be three times as much.[146] The possible premium rate range given by the expert witness was 1.35–2%. Taking all those factors into consideration, the judge ruled that the appropriate premium range should be 1.6%.

Jacobs J therefore concluded that, based on his decision that the 8th and 10th defendants were not liable to pay the claim, the broker's liability for its breach should be assessed on the basis of (2x7.5% of) 90% of the assured's losses less the premium of 1.6% of the amount of its transactions with the buyers. He clarified that the formula above would remain perfectly applicable in the event of a successful appeal by underwriters apart from those two defendants against the trial decision.[147] As explained above, whilst the underwriters' appeal had been compromised, and the 8th and 10th defendants were held by the Court of Appeal liable to pay the claim, the trial court's formula above remains valuable guidelines for future cases concerning the determination of the brokers' liability to the assured.

The broker's duty of care to the intended assignee of ECI

The broker bears the duty of care not only to the assured but also to the intended assignee under an ECI policy. In *Punjab National Bank v De Boinville and Others*,[148] a bank agreed to finance an exporter who sold goods to Sudan. The finance agreement between them provided that the bank undertook to negotiate the documents under the letter of credit issued by the buyer subject to the exporter procuring at its own cost and expense a political and exchange control risk insurance policy to cover the bank in respect of non-payment of the letter of credit and interest due or to become due.

The exporter and the bank placed insurance through brokers at Lloyd's and obtained four policies for the exporter's several shipments. The process of placing the ECI cover was entrusted to two individual brokers, Mr B and D, who were employees of W, a Lloyd's broking company, when placing the first and second

145 Ibid, [1012].
146 Ibid, [979].
147 Ibid, [1020].
148 [1992] 1 WLR 1138.

policies. Then Mr B and D moved to F, another brokerage firm at Lloyd's in May 1983 and placed the third and fourth policies thereafter. In the first and second policies, the definition of "assured" was "the bank a/c the exporter" (i.e., "the bank on account of the exporter"), but by amendments in both policies that definition was deleted and replaced by reference to "the exporter". In the third and fourth policies, the definition of the "assured" was "the exporter", and the exporter expressly assigned its rights to the bank. Subsequently, the buyer defaulted in payment, and the bank made claims under all four policies. The insurers did not dispute the title of the bank as an assured under the first and second policies. However, they rejected the claims under all four policies on the grounds of non-disclosure and misrepresentation. In case the insurers' allegations succeeded, the bank sought to exercise an alternative remedy against all those brokers (i.e., the individual broker Mr B, D and company W, F) for their failure to correct or make good any misrepresentation or non-disclosure. The brokers, however, argued that the bank was not the assured under any of those four policies, and thus they did not owe any duties of reasonable skill and care to it.

Neither the trial court nor the Court of Appeal was asked by the parties to consider issues regarding misrepresentation or non-disclosure. Instead, their task was to determine the following preliminary issues:

(a) Who was the assured under each of the policies?
(b) Was there a contractual relationship between the bank and any of the brokers?
(c) In the absence of a contractual relationship, did any of the brokers owe a duty of care to the bank?

The full text of the trial judgment was not reported, but it is sufficient here to note that the trial decision was fully upheld in the appeal. Regarding issue (a), the Court of Appeal held that on the true construction of the term "the bank a/c the exporter", the "assured" under the first and second policies referred to, or at least included the bank;[149] the assured under the third and fourth policies, on the other hand, was the exporter, who then assigned its rights to the bank.

With respect to issue (b), the Court of Appeal clarified that whether there was a contract for broking services depended on the instructions that the bank gave to the brokers, the response of the brokers to those instructions, and whether such instructions led to the inference that the brokers were contracting with the bank as a client. In relation to the first and second policies, Staughton LJ held that there was a contract for broking service between the bank and company W because both the exporter and the bank were giving instructions to W from time to time, and W did not positively decline to accept the bank's instruction or repudiate the inference that they were acting for the bank as a client. In relation to the third and fourth policies, the situation is more complex. The bank was not aware of the fact

149 The construction of the definition of "assured" in this case will be further discussed in the sections below.

that Mr B and D moved to company F until July 1983, when F dispatched the cover note and the bank responded by payment of premiums for those two policies. The judge accordingly held that there was a contractual relationship between the bank and F from July 1983. Staughton LJ further commented that the content of the broking contracts was not material for the court in making its judgement, as long as there was evidence as to the brokers' lack of reasonable skill and care.

The Court of Appeal then turned to address issue (c). Staughton LJ recognised that the bank did not have a contractual relationship with some of the brokers: on the one hand, between May 1983 and July 1983, the bank was not to its knowledge giving instructions to company F, and it was not to be an assured under the third and fourth policies, hence it had no contract with F; on the other hand, Mr B and D, throughout the broking history, did not have a contractual relationship with the bank as employees of W or F.

The brokers submitted that whether they owed a non-contractual duty of care to the bank depended on whether the relationship between them (1) falls within a recognised category in respect of which "it has been held that a duty exists", or (2) should fall within a recognised category by a justifiable increment to an existing category.

In respect of question (1), Staughton LJ identified three categories where a duty of care to avoid economic loss had been recognised: (i) the case where a professional man provides services to a client, (ii) agency, whether contractual or gratuitous, and (iii) negligent misstatement within the *Hedley Byrne* principle. His lordship ruled that the relationship between an insurance broker and his client fell within category (i). The judge referred to Lord Bridge of Harwich's statement in *Caparo Industries Plc v Dickman*:[150]

> In advising the client who employs him the professional man owes a duty to exercise that standard of skill and care appropriate to his professional status and will be liable both in contract and in tort for all losses which his client may suffer by reason of any breach of that duty.

Staughton LJ held that the principle above "applies as much to insurance brokers as to those who exercise any other professional calling, and to other professional activities which they carry on, besides giving advice".[151]

In respect of question (2), Staughton LJ found that the bank had financial interest in the transaction to be insured: ECI was a significant instrument to secure the repayment of its loan to the exporter; all relevant parties knew of the intended assignment to the bank of the third and fourth policies. Accordingly, his lordship held that it was a justifiable increment to rule that an insurance broker owes a duty of care to the specific person, not being a client, who he knows is to become an assignee of the policy, at least where that person actively participates in giving

150 [1990] 2 AC 605, 619.
151 *Punjab* [1992] 1 WLR 1138, 1152.

instructions for the insurance to the broker's knowledge. Company F, therefore, was held to owe a non-contractual duty of care to the bank.

The judge further dealt with the relationship between Mr B and D and the bank. Staughton LJ held that although it is not every employee of a firm or company providing professional services that owes a personal duty of care to the client, it depends what he is employed to do: in this case Mr B and D were evidently entrusted with the whole or nearly the whole of the task which their employers undertook; hence they both owed a personal duty of care to the bank, too.

In sum, *Punjab* illustrates the different circumstances where the brokers owed a duty of care to the intended assignee of an ECI policy: (a) companies W and F owed such a duty in tort concurrently with their contractual duty during their contractual relationship with the bank; (b) between May 1983 and July 1983, company F owed a duty of care to the bank by virtue of a justifiable increment to an existing category; and (c) individual brokers, Mr B and D, also owed a personal duty of care to the bank during their employment with companies W and F, respectively.

The role of sub-brokers under ECI

As a complex type of insurance, ECI transactions sometimes involve brokers as well as specialist sub-brokers who, due to unique expertise and experience, are in a better position to place the risks. The chain of brokers and sub-brokers under ECI and their respective roles were comprehensively examined in the abovementioned *Harding* case,[152] where the assured was a French trading company who wished to place the risk in the London market. There was a chain of five brokerage firms that contributed to the final placement of the complex expropriation risk:

- The first and second brokers were based in Paris. The first broker, as the producing broker of the assured, instructed the second broker to try to place the risk in the contract frustration market. That attempt failed due to the Angolan debt crisis discussed above.
- The third and fourth brokers were based in London. To find a solution, the second broker approached the third broker, who then introduced Mr B, an employee of the fourth broker, to the project. At this stage, the four brokers reached an agreement "in principle" that (i) the anticipated brokerage was 20% of the premium, (ii) the commission would be split 50/50 between Paris and London, and again evenly between the two Paris brokers and the two London brokers, respectively, and (iii) each broker would thus receive 5% of the premium.
- Mr B succeeded in a short while in placing the risk in the expropriation market, subject to certain subjectivities that were difficult to persuade the leading underwriter to remove. Whilst Mr B was working closely with the assured to provide requested clarification and documentation, the fourth broker decided to close down its political risks department and made Mr B redundant.

152 [2000] 1 All ER (Comm) 225.

- Mr B immediately obtained new employment with the fifth broker who was also based in London. Accordingly, the first broker decided to transfer the file (regarding the transaction to be insured) from the fourth broker to the fifth broker. The first broker then informed the third broker that its services were no longer required. At this stage, the first, second and fifth brokers agreed to share the whole commission between themselves, one-third each.
- The third broker sought agreement from the first broker about its share of the commission but was told to await the outcome. Mr B continued to seek a solution to the problem of overcoming the leading underwriter's subjectivities and, together with Mr P, his senior colleague at the fifth broker, he developed several changes to the slip and insurance wording. Mr P then met the leading underwriter, presented to him the revised slip and obtained his agreement in principle to the final placement of the risk. Mr B followed up this meeting by taking the leading underwriter through the whole documentation. Eventually, the risk was successfully placed, but the first broker declined to share any commission with the third broker.

The third broker then sued the first broker, claiming commission of 25% of the brokerage in accordance with the agreement, or alternatively quantum meruit, on the basis that it did what it was engaged to do and that its introduction of Mr B was the effective cause, or at least an effective cause, of the ultimate placing. The first broker argued that Mr B, so far from the solution to the assured's problem with the placement of the risk, was "an obstruction" to it, and thus the third broker was entitled to nothing.

The court identified three issues to be addressed. Firstly, was the agreement between the first to fourth brokers regarding the share of commission legally binding? Secondly, had the third broker been the, or at least an, effective cause of the final placing? Thirdly, if there was no binding agreement on commission but that the third broker was nevertheless entitled to a reasonable commission, then how much should it earn?

With respect to the first issue, Rix J found that the agreement between the first to fourth brokers was merely one in principle and thus was not intended to be legally binding.

With respect to the second issue, Rix J held that where the court faced two rival claimants for the same commission, it might have to determine which of the agents was the effective cause of the transaction because to hold that both were might lead to the client having to pay both agents a full commission. However, he noted that:[153]

> Where, however, as frequently occurs in insurance broking, numerous brokers are involved in chain, it seems to me that the test cannot be simply that of the effective cause. That is so even if the acts of all sub-brokers are attributed

153 Ibid, 251.

> to any broker higher in the chain: in such a case it would only be where the last sub-broker was the effective cause that all of the other brokers higher in chain could earn their commission. But such a rule would not seem to me to do adequate justice to the complexities of the situation. Thus, some of the brokers may be producing brokers and some placing brokers, and their roles, responsibilities and functions may be very different.

The learned judge then ruled that the third broker was an effective cause of the final placing of the risk as it had introduced Mr B, who had been the *sine qua non* of the placing of the risk; it was thus entitled to be paid in large part for that introduction. The judge further clarified that even if the appropriate test were to ask whether the third broker was the effective cause of the transaction, the result would be the same.

With respect to the third issue, Rix J found that after the services of the third broker were dispensed with, "there was still some not insubstantial further work to be done before the placement was finalised". Therefore, the judge found that the third broker was entitled to a reasonable remuneration of 20% of the brokerage.[154]

The *Harding* case demonstrates that where an ECI cover was placed by a chain of brokers and sub-brokers, the contribution of any of them to the placement of such a large and complex risk should not be neglected. As the third broker rightly submitted, it should not be so "badly treated by being left out in the cold". Moreover, the individual broker's effort should not be undervalued, too. Rix J rejected all criticism of Mr B by treating him as the "brains" behind the final successful placing of the risk which was completed with "the critical aid" of his "continuing involvement and … input into the overall strategy and development of documentation".[155] The judge, in the postscript of the judgment, commented that:[156]

> I cannot leave this case without expressing a substantial measure of concern about the need for a five-day trial in this matter. It is true that … it was only in the course of the litigation that the documentation was sufficiently pulled together to bring the whole history of this placing into order so as to permit a proper analysis and understanding of events. That is one of the things that litigation can achieve. Nevertheless, I regret that an unpleaded case of professional incompetence has been raised against Mr B … Underneath all this confusion was a real but limited point about the validity of a broker's claim for commission when its sub-broker has disbanded but the critical personnel have remained in place, albeit wearing a new broker's hat. That issue, if it had to be, could have been fought out at a fraction of the time and cost of this trial.

154 Ibid, 255.
155 Ibid, 253.
156 Ibid, 255–6.

Summary: is the formation process of ECI similar to that of general insurance contracts?

This research submits that the formation of ECI contracts is similar to the formation of general insurance contracts. The general view held that to conclude an insurance contract, the assured makes an offer by submitting a proposal form and that the insurer makes the acceptance by issuing a policy.[157] It is also widely accepted that the assured is deemed to know the usual terms and conditions of the policy he is applying for.[158] These rules on offer and acceptance remain perfectly applicable in the formation of ECI. The manner of dealing in ECI is similar to general insurance contracts. The ECA, as the insurer, is approached by the exporter or the bank who makes an offer. The only difference is that under ECI, they do not have to approach the UKEF via a broker, but the UKEF allows brokers to help them get the cover if necessary.[159] Furthermore, political and credit risks can, with the help of specialist brokers, be placed at Lloyd's of London through the subscription of leading and following underwriters, as is demonstrated in *International Management Groups*, *Harding*, *Punjab*, *ABN Amro*, *Mann v Coutts & Co* and *Banque Keyser Ullmann SA v Skandia (UK) Insurance Co Ltd and Others*.[160] The roles of underwriters and brokers under ECI were explored in detail by the courts in those cases, who all treated political and credit risks as no more than one category of specialty risks that can be insured at Lloyd's in the same way other types of risks are insured. All those factors indicate the legal nature of ECI as insurance.

The formation process of ECGs

How to conclude an ECG contract with the ECA?

Different from ECI, ECG products are provided by ECAs only. Lloyd's in the "additional requirements for the writing of Financial Guarantee risks" section of its *Performance Management – Supplemental Requirements & Guidance* states that:[161]

> Contracts of surety
>
> Underwriters are reminded that Lloyd's does not permit the writing of contracts of surety. Additionally, licensing restrictions apply to this class in most jurisdictions.

157 John Birds, *Modern Insurance Law* (10th edn, Sweet & Maxwell 2016) 89–90.

158 Merkin (n 8), [1-066].

159 For the list of the brokers approved by the UKEF, see < https://www.gov.uk/government/publications/uk-export-finance-insurance-list-of-approved-brokers/export-insurance-approved-brokers> accessed 1 February 2022.

160 [1987] 2 WLR 1300, 1302.

161 Lloyd's of London (n 76) 45.

Therefore, the UKEF appears to be the primary provider of ECGs in the UK. As explained above, ECG products are either buyer or supplier credit guarantees, which means that an ECG contract is always concluded between the ECA and the bank. However, the bank normally works closely together with the exporter in arranging an ECG transaction. For instance, to acquire the finance from a bank that is to be guaranteed by the UKEF's supplier credit guarantee scheme, the exporter needs to approach the UKEF via an approved bank which is a partner of the UKEF under the MGA.[162] Taking the UKEF's "Supplier Credit Financing Facility" as an example, to obtain that guarantee, the exporter and the bank should submit a proposal form together, in which they should disclose three parts of information: Parts A and B concern the background of the exporter and the bank, whereas Part C is about the details of the loan contract between the exporter and the bank.[163] The UKEF will, based on the contents of the proposal form, decide whether or not to issue a guarantee to the bank.

It should be noted that whether under a supplier or buyer credit guarantee, the guarantee contract is always a bilateral contract between the ECA and the bank. The ECA, in the meantime, tends to conclude a separate contract with the exporter so that the latter can be kept under certain contractual obligations.[164] The main contents of the ECG contract and the ECA-exporter contract will be discussed in Chapter 3 of this work.

Is the formation process of ECGs similar to that of general guarantee contracts?

The abovementioned formation process of ECGs is similar to that of general contracts of guarantee. Ordinary guarantees are bilateral contracts concluded between the surety and the creditor.[165] That is perfectly the case in the context of ECGs, under which the ECA acts as the surety and the bank as the creditor. The only difference between the formation of ECGs and general guarantees is that, in most contracts of guarantee, the offer is usually made by the surety to the creditor.[166] It was suggested by commentators that that is also the case in ECGs, namely that the ECA makes the offer to the bank, and the bank accepts the offer by granting finance to the exporter.[167] This research respectfully disagrees with that view: as explained above, under ECG transactions it is the bank that makes an offer to the ECA. Of course, that difference does not affect the legal nature of an ECG as a

162 See n 52 above.

163 See <https://assets.publishing.service.gov.uk/government/uploads/system/uploads/attachment_data/file/659457/supplier-credit-financing-facility-proposal-ukef-nov-2017.pdf> accessed 30 November 2020.

164 See n 52 above.

165 Andrews & Millett (n 21), [2-002].

166 James O'Donovan & John Phillips, *The Modern Contract of Guarantee* (English edn, Sweet & Maxwell 2003) 49.

167 Andrews & Millett (n 21), [15-009].

contract of guarantee. The ECA, as the surety, still undertakes to guarantee the bank in respect of the finance it provides to the exporter.

Are there any potential problems within the formation of ECI and ECGs?

The potential issue within the formation of supplier credit insurance

As explained above, the formation process of the basic ECI cover or buyer credit insurance is very straightforward. What seems problematic are supplier credit insurance transactions, where the ECA does not insure the bank directly but tends to issue an ECI policy to the exporter in the first place. After obtaining a cover, the exporter may include the bank as the co-assured or transfer its right under the policy to the bank. However, such arrangements must be clear and unambiguous; otherwise, the bank's eligibility to make a claim might be challenged.

In the abovementioned *Punjab* case,[168] the definition of "assured" under the first and second policies was "the bank a/c the exporter" (i.e., "the bank on account of the exporter") and the address of the "assured" was that of the bank, but by amendments in both policies that definition was deleted and replaced by reference to "the exporter". The brokers argued that the phrase "the bank a/c the exporter" should mean that the bank only acted as the agent of the exporter. The trial judge believed that it was the parties' intention that the bank was the assured despite the "ambiguous nature" of those two policies. The definition of "assured" was further examined in the appeal. The brokers referred to *Gadd v Houghton*,[169] a 19th-century case where a fruit broker had given a merchant a sold note reading "we sold to you on account of" the supplier. The court in that case held that the term "on account of" meant that the broker had contracted as an agent only. Staughton LJ, however, held that the decision on similar but different words used by a fruit broker in 1874 was "scarcely any authority for the meaning of words used in an insurance contract in 1983".[170] His lordship believed that the term "a/c", which meant simply "re", were merely a reference to remind the bank which of the bank's customers was concerned with the transaction to be insured; otherwise, there would have been no point in inserting the bank's name.

Staughton LJ then noted the fact that in subsequent amendments the phrase "the bank a/c the exporter" was deleted and replaced by reference to "the exporter", "with effect from inception". Nevertheless, his lordship remained very cautious in deciding whether it was permitted to have regard to deletions. Referring to a number of case authorities,[171] the learned judge ruled that: on the one hand, if

168 [1992] 1 WLR 1138.

169 (1876) LR 1 ExD 357.

170 *Punjab* [1992] 1 WLR 1138, 1146 (Staughton LJ).

171 *Louis Dreyfus & Cie v Parnaso Cia Naviera SA* [1959] 1 QB 498, 513 (Diplock J); *A & J Inglis v John Buttery & Co* (1878) 3 App Cas 552, 569 (Hatherley LJ); *M A Sassoon and Sons Ltd v International Banking Corporation* [1927] AC 711, 721 (Viscount Sumner); *London & Overseas*

the words were first inserted by the draftsman of the agreement and then deleted before signature, they must not be considered in construing the agreement;[172] on the other hand, if the words were deleted from a printed and signed form, then (a) such words can be looked at as a guide to the meaning of similar words in a neighbouring paragraph[173] or (b) the fact of deletion can serve as an aid to construction because if reflected what the parties did not want in their agreement.[174] Staughton LJ concluded that, if the parties to a concluded agreement subsequently agree in express terms that some words in it are to be replaced by others, one can have regard to all aspects of the subsequent agreement in construing the contract including the deletions. Therefore, the deletions of the term "the bank a/c" indicated the parties' intention to distinguish "the bank a/c the exporter" between "the exporter", thereby explaining that the initial description of the "assured" referred to, or at least included, the bank. His lordship further stated that in case he was wrong about deletions, he would still hold that, on the construction of the first and second policies, the bank was an assured because there was "plainly a distinction drawn by the draftsman" between the "assured" and "the exporter".[175]

Dillon LJ, in his concurring opinion, agreed that *Punjab National Bank* should be distinguished from *Gadd v Houghton*: whilst in *Gadd v Houghton* the term "a/c" was to indicate that the fruit broker was not to be personally liable under the sales contract, in this case the bank was to receive an indemnity rather than undertaking any liability. His lordship stated that whether looking merely at the definition of "assured" or reading the policy as a whole, he would "without hesitation" reach the conclusion that the bank was an assured, whether or not the only assured under the first and second policies.[176] Regarding the deletions, Dillon LJ further commented that he would "regard it as bizarre" if the law forbids looking behind the deletions and amendments in the present case, where such alterations had been effected by annexing a signed endorsement to the policy which itself stated to be part of the policy with effect from inception.[177]

Although the trial and appeal judgments of *Punjab* were both in favour of the bank, it does not mean that the wording of the "assured" (i.e., "the bank a/c the exporter") under the first and second policies was perfect. Indeed, such wordings might not eventually affect the bank's substantial right to the insurance money,

Freighters Ltd v Timber Shipping Co SA [1972] AC 1, 15-16 (Reid LJ); *Mottram Consultants Ltd v Bernard Sunley & Sons Ltd* [1975] 2 LIR 197, 209 (Cross of Chelsea LJ).

172 *London & Overseas Freighters* [1972] AC 1, 15–6 (Reid LJ).

173 This, as was explained by Diplock J, falls within the scope of the principle of *noscitur a sociis*. See *Louis Dreyfus & Cie* [1959] 1 QB 498, 513–5 (Diplock J) ("I must look first at the clause in its actual form without the deleted words, if I find the clause ambiguous, I think that I am entitled to look at the deleted words to see if any assistance can be derived from them in solving the ambiguity").

174 *London & Overseas Freighters* [1972] AC 1, 15–6 (Reid LJ); *Mottram Consultants Ltd* [1975] 2 LIR 197, 209 (Cross of Chelsea LJ).

175 *Punjab* [1992] 1 WLR 1138, 1149 (Staughton LJ).

176 Ibid, 1155 (Dillon LJ).

177 Ibid.

but certainly, they had caused extra delay and litigation costs to the bank in making a claim. The ECI industry has clearly realised this problem. As Staughton LJ noted in *Punjab*, by the time of the appeal:[178]

> There had been a directive from the Chairman of Lloyd's as to who should be the assured in this class of business, which may explain the change between the First and Second Policies, where the Bank were an assured, to the Third and Fourth where they were merely an assignee.

This requirement is now reflected in Lloyd's *Performance Management – Supplemental Requirements & Guidance* which states that:[179]

> All Financial Guarantee policies … must contain a condition that only allows assignment of the policy with the prior written agreement of underwriters. Where assignment of a policy does take place, the obligations placed upon the original insured by the terms of the policy must be transferred so that they become obligations of the assignee … It is acceptable to allow for the proceeds of a policy to be paid to a third party provided that the obligations on the insured under the terms of the policy remain with the insured.

Nevertheless, making the bank an assignee of ECI might not be the best solution, either. As is well elaborated by the commentator, from the bank's point of view, the assignment of an ECI policy has "a significant disadvantage":[180]

> The insurer, as debtor, can plead against the bank, the assignee, any defences or "equities" that it has against the seller, the assignor. Apart from being well established by authority, this right is usually expressly reserved by the insurer when it acknowledges the assignment. Thus, where the policy has been obtained by the seller by means of a fraud or of a misrepresentation in the proposal form, the insurer can avoid the policy and, in this way, defeat any claims raised by the bank under the assignment. Moreover, the bank can make a claim only in so far as it arises from a loss that is covered under the policy and only to the extent of the cover given to the seller.

Furthermore, an assignment of a policy may require registration. It was held by the court in *Paul and Frank Ltd v Discount Bank (Overseas) Ltd*[181] that an assignment of an ECI policy did not constitute a charge on "book debts" and therefore did not require registration. However, this decision was the subject of criticism in the light of well-established case law (in the context of domestic credit

178 Ibid, 1153 (Staughton LJ).
179 Lloyd's of London (n 76) 44.
180 Lomnicka (n 35), [25-028].
181 [1967] Ch 348.

insurance).[182] Notably, under s 859A of the Companies Act 2006 (Amendment of Part 25) Regulations 2013 (SI 2013/600), an assignment of a policy by a company, if effected by way of charge, will now require registration.

This research therefore submits that the ECA should directly issue the ECI policy to the bank in supplier credit insurance transactions. The root cause of all problems in *Punjab* was that, in arranging a supplier credit insurance transaction, the ECA does not directly insure the bank in the first place. That, in the author's opinion, is relatively problematic: since the exporter has gained the finance from the bank, it is the bank that bears the political and credit risks under a supplier credit insurance transaction. One might question the rationale behind such a problematic approach. This research suggests that there might be some historical reasons. Supplier credit insurance is a "top-up" product which was designed based on the basic ECI cover. In the early days when it was designed, ECAs were only familiar with exporters, as they were at that time the primary and main client of ECI. It then became natural for ECAs to issue a supplier credit insurance policy to exporters (as they did under a basic ECI cover) and then allow exporters to assign their rights under the policy to banks. Then such an approach became standard practice in the industry. However, what ECAs did not anticipate was that exporters might not always make a perfect (or, in other words, "standard") assignment arrangement. Another possible explanation is that ECAs might wish to keep the exporter at all times subject to the terms and conditions under the ECI policy, since the latter plays the primary role in the export transaction.

The reasons above, however, are not sound and persuasive. On the one hand, ECAs are now much more familiar with their bank clients than before. For instance, the UKEF has been working closely with the major commercial banks in the UK. On the other hand, the ECA can conclude a separate agreement with the exporter stipulating the latter's obligations. Therefore, there should be no reason why ECAs cannot directly insure the banks as it directly guarantees them under ECGs. This research submits that the formation process of supplier credit insurance transactions should be more straightforward: the insurance policy should be directly issued to the bank. Banks should seek to adopt such an approach in participating in supplier credit insurance transactions.

Is the formation process of ECGs as problematic as that of ECI?

Different from supplier credit insurance, the formation process of supplier and buyer credit guarantees is very straightforward: the guarantee contract is always concluded between the ECA and the bank; the bank can always make a direct claim when the buyer defaults in payment, and the ECA should always pay on demand as the surety. Therefore, the formation process of ECGs seems flawless to banks, as there has been no reported ECG case that indicates any relevant problem.

182 *Independent Automatic Sales Ltd v Knowles & Foster* [1962] 1 WLR 974. See also Lomnicka (n 35), [25-029].

In sum, from the perspective of the formation process, it appears that ECGs are friendlier than ECI to banks. That is perhaps why the UKEF now only provides supplier and buyer credit guarantees rather than supplier/buyer credit insurance. One might question if, in supplier credit insurance transactions, the ECA directly insures the bank as it does in supplier credit guarantees, will ECI be as friendly as ECGs? The following chapters aim to prove that even if that can be achieved, an ECI policy is still less pro-banks than an ECG contract, which is determined by their different legal characteristics.

References

Andrews, G & Millett, R, *Law of Guarantees* (7th edn, Sweet & Maxwell 2015)
Birds, J, *Modern Insurance Law* (10th edn, Sweet & Maxwell 2016)
Birds, J, Lynch, B & Paul, S, *MacGillivray on Insurance Law* (14th edn, Sweet & Maxwell 2018)
Burling, J, *Lloyd's: Law and Practice* (1st edn, Routledge 2013)
Clarke, M, *The Law of Insurance Contracts* (3rd edn, LLP Limited 1997)
Dunt, J, "When Marine Cargo Insurance Became Credit Risk Insurance" (2021) 3 LMCLQ 431
Gianturco, D, *Export Credit Agencies: The Unsung Giants of International Trade and Finance* (Quorum 2001)
Gürses, Ö, *Marine Insurance Law* (2nd edn, Routledge 2017)
ICISA, *A Guide to Trade Credit Insurance* (Anthem Press 2015)
Lewis, C, *Judicial Remedies in Public Law* (10th edn, Sweet & Maxwell 2014)
Lin, C, "Understanding The Legal Nature of Export Credit Insurance: Lessons from *ABN Amro v RSA*" (2022) 3 JBL 225
Lomnicka, E, "Export Credit Guarantees" in M Bridge (ed) *Benjamin's Sales of Goods* (11th edn, Sweet & Maxwell 2020)
Merkin, R, *Colinvaux's Law of Insurance* (12th edn, Sweet & Maxwell 2019)
O'Donovan, J & Phillips, J, *The Modern Contract of Guarantee* (English edn, Sweet & Maxwell 2003)
Padfield, A, *Insurance Claims* (2nd edn, Tottel Publishing 2007)
Salcic, Z, *Export Credit Insurance & Guarantees: A Practitioner's Guide* (Palgrave Macmillan 2014)
Soyer, B, "Risk Control Clauses in Insurance Law: Law Reform and the Future" (2016) 75 CLJ 109

3 Terms and conditions of ECI and ECGs

There is scant academic research on the legal nature of export credit insurance (ECI) and export credit guarantees (ECGs) from a contractual perspective. This chapter aims to fill this gap by scrutinising their terms and conditions which reflect the legal nature of ECI and ECGs as contracts of insurance and guarantee, respectively.

This chapter divides into three parts. The first part discusses the terms and conditions of ECI. It starts with the peculiar terms in ECI policies, such as the insuring and indemnity clause, the credit limit clause and the exclusions. In particular, it analyses the recent case of *ABN Amro Bank NV v Royal and Sun Alliance Insurance Plc*,[1] where a credit risk clause was inserted in a marine cargo insurance market. It then explores how ECI conditions precedent and warranties, the two most controversial types of insurance terms, operated and will operate before and after the IA 2015. As the UKEF indicates that its policies "take account of the Insurance Act 2015"[2] and that its "Export Insurance Policy" was updated in January 2017, this chapter's analysis will be given in light of the new provisions of the IA 2015. Before the IA 2015, the classification of insurance terms in common law included (1) warranties; (2) conditions precedent to the policy or the attachment of the risk; (3) conditions precedent to liability; (4) mere conditions and (5) terms descriptive of the risk which operate to suspend the risk during any period of the breach.[3] The IA 2015 reduced the significance of that classification to a minimum and moved from form to functionality.[4] What matters under the new regime is the substantial effects of the term, namely whether the term defines the risk as a whole or does it tend to reduce the risk of the loss of a particular kind, location or time. This chapter thus intends to explore whether the "Export

1 [2021] EWCA Civ 1789.

2 See UKEF, "Proposal Form: Export Insurance Policy (EXIP)" < https://assets.publishing.service.gov.uk/government/uploads/system/uploads/attachment_data/file/898048/10489_UKEF_Export_Insurance_Proposal_Form_20200331-fillable.pdf> accessed 1 February 2022.

3 Robert Merkin & Özlem Gürses, "Insurance Contracts after the Insurance Act 2015" [2016] 132 (3) LQR 445, 445–6.

4 Özlem Gürses, "Section 11 of the Insurance Act 2015: When Does a Term Define the Risk as a Whole in an Insurance Contract?" [2020] (3) JBL 184, 191–201.

DOI: 10.4324/b22864-3

Insurance Policy" is fully enforceable under the IA 2015 and, if not, what can be improved.

The second part analyses terms and conditions in ECGs. It takes supplier credit guarantees as an example and demonstrates that an ECG transaction often involves two separate contracts: the ECG contract between the export credit agency (ECA) and the bank, and the ECA-exporter contract between the ECA and the exporter. Furthermore, it shows that the ECG contract is a contract of guarantee where the bank is under no substantial obligations, whilst the primary obligations under ECGs are imposed on the exporter by the ECA-exporter contract. The third part demonstrates how this chapter contributes to the general theme of this book.

It should be noted that this chapter is not intended to cover all aspects of the terms and conditions in ECI and ECG contracts. The enactment of the IA 2015 does not affect the operation of terms which do not relate to the risk, such as the claim cooperation clause, notification and mitigation clause and subrogation protection clause.[5] Therefore, terms and conditions related to claim settlement and subrogation will be discussed in Chapters 5 and 6 of this work. Moreover, terms and conditions related to the duty of fair presentation will be analysed separately in Chapter 4.

The peculiar terms of ECI

The insuring and indemnity clause

ECAs normally use standard terms and conditions. Although ECI policies can be written and structured in various ways, their terms and conditions are more or less similar.[6] First of all, it can be said that every ECI policy includes an insuring and indemnity clause. An ECI policy can cover either a comprehensive bulk of commercial and political risks or certain tailored risks only.[7] Whatever the policy does, it always includes an insuring and indemnity clause which stipulates how the ECA or private credit insurer will pay the exporter for the loss.

The UKEF's insuring and indemnity clause

Clause 2.1 of the UK Export Finance's (UKEF) "Export Insurance Policy" specifies the commercial and political risks that the UKEF will insure:[8]

5 Merkin & Gürses (n 3) 451.

6 Zlatko Salcic, *Export Credit Insurance & Guarantees: A Practitioner's Guide* (Palgrave Macmillan 2014) 212.

7 Joe Blenkinsopp, "Political risk and trade credit policy wordings, and harmonisation in the context of the Insurance Act 2015", in *Berne Union Yearbook 2016*, 78–9 <https://www.berneunion.org/Search/keyword/2016%20yearbook>> accessed 30 November 2020.

8 Full text available at <https://assets.publishing.service.gov.uk/government/uploads/system/uploads/attachment_data/file/1041653/Docs_Policy_EXIP_SingleContract_All_Risks.pdf> accessed 1 February 2022.

(a) the failure of the Buyer to pay any Sum Due for a period of [six] months after the Due Date; or
(b) any act or omission of the Buyer in breach of any other obligation under the Contract which terminates, or results in the termination of, the Insured's obligation to supply any Goods and/or Services; or
(c) any: (i) act, decision or legislative or administrative measure of the government or courts of any country … or (ii) war, civil war, revolution or insurrection which, in either case, renders illegal or impossible the performance of any obligation under the Contract.

Clause 3 "Amount of Indemnified Loss" further provides that:[9]

> 3.1 In respect of any loss sustained by the Insured as a direct result of any failure referred to in Clause 2.1(a) UKEF will … pay the Insured Percentage of the amount of any Sum Due remaining unpaid by the Buyer, a Surety or any third person.
> 3.2 In respect of any loss sustained by the Insured as a direct result of any act or omission referred to in Clause 2.1(b) or any event or other matter referred to in Clause 2.1(c), UKEF will … pay the Insured Percentage of: (a) any costs which the Insured has incurred wholly and necessarily for the purpose of supplying any Goods and/or Services which, in consequence, it has not supplied, such amount not to be in excess of the amount which would have been payable by the Buyer under the Contract in respect of those Goods and/or Services, less: (b) any advance payment paid or accrued payable which is attributable to such Goods and/or Services … and (c) the value of any Goods and/or Services available for resale and any other benefit which the Insured may have received by not supplying such Goods and/or Services.

These clauses strongly indicate that ECI is a contract of indemnity insurance. As defined in the English law, insurance is an agreement under which, when a loss is suffered by the happening of an event insured against, the insurer will put the assured into the same position where he would have been had the event not occurred, but in no better position;[10] the essence of insurance is that the insurer pays to the assured what he has lost, no more than indemnity.[11] Clause 2 of the UKEF's policy reflects such a legal nature. The obligation of the UKEF under ECI is to compensate the exporter against loss arising from certain commercial and political events. Clause 3 further demonstrates how the UKEF will indemnify the exporter against his loss. Under Clause 3.1 the UKEF will pay the exporter the amount of the loss should it have delivered the goods, and under Clause 3.2 the

9 Ibid.
10 *Callaghan v Dominion Insurance Co* [1997] 2 Lloyd's Rep 541.
11 Robert Merkin, *Colinvaux's Law of Insurance* (12th edn, Sweet & Maxwell 2019) [4-007].

UKEF will pay the exporter the amount of the loss suffered in the pre-shipment stage. Those are strong indications suggesting that ECI is a contract of indemnity.[12]

Lloyd's definition of "Credit Risk" and "Contract Frustration"

Whilst the standard insuring clause of ECI policies issued by Lloyd's is not available online, Lloyd's in its *Performance Management – Supplemental Requirements & Guidance* provides a detailed definition of "Credit Risk" and "Contract Frustration" under the "Financial Guarantee Insurance" section, which also demonstrates that ECI is a contract of indemnity insurance:[13]

> Financial Guarantee insurance is defined as contracts of insurance (which includes any indemnity, guarantee, bond, contract of surety or other similar instrument, and references to "insurance" include reinsurance) where the insurer agrees to indemnify the insured against loss, or pay or otherwise benefit the insured in the event of any of the following:
>
> (1) the financial failure, default, insolvency, bankruptcy, liquidation or winding up of any person whether or not a party to the contract of insurance
> (2) the financial failure of any venture
> (3) the lack of or insufficient receipts, sales or profits of any venture
> (4) the lack of or inadequate response or support by sponsors or financial supporters
> (5) a change in levels of interest rates
> (6) a change of rates of exchange of currency
> (7) a change in the value or price of land, buildings, securities or commodities
> (8) a change in levels of financial or commodity indices
> (9) any liability or obligation under an accommodation bill or similar instrument.
>
> Within Financial Guarantee, the two largest classes written at Lloyd's are Credit Risk and Contract Frustration. These codes cover insurance that indemnify an insured, in relation to the provision of assets, goods, services and/or financing, either (1) for the non-performance of a valid contractual obligation or (2) in relation to the calling of a valid contractual bond.
>
> In Contract Frustration, the obligor is a government entity or a commercial entity controlled and/or majority owned by a government entity(ies). In Credit Risk the obligor is a commercial entity with a majority private ownership.

12 Ibid, [24-062].

13 Lloyd's of London, *Performance Management - Supplemental Requirements & Guidance* (last updated in July 2020), 42–3 < https://www.lloyds.com/conducting-business/requirements-and-standards/supplemental-requirements-and-guidance/ > accessed 1 February 2022.

Treating protracted payment default and insolvency of the buyer as separate risks insured

As demonstrated above, an insuring clause under ECI could cover many commercial and political risks. Among them, the buyer's protracted payment default and the buyer's insolvency, two commercial risks, are the most typical risks insured under ECI. It should be noted that they must be treated as separate, distinct and independent risks. In *Merrill Lynch International Bank Ltd (formerly Merrill Lynch Capital Markets Bank Ltd) v Winterthur Swiss Insurance Co*,[14] the assured bank provided a loan to EFL, a member company of Eurotunnel group who owns and operates the Channel Tunnel. Under the loan agreement, EFL must pay any amounts falling due on periodic (six-monthly) payment dates. This obligation was guaranteed by three other Eurotunnel group companies who, together with EFL, were defined by the policy as the "Eurotunnel Entities". The policy covered the assured's credit risk exposure in the following way: Clause 1(i)(a) concerned the risk of protracted payment default, namely the occurrence of a "Pre-Close Out Failure to Pay Event", which would materialise after the expiry of a 90-day period following the occurrence of a "Counterparty Failure to Pay"; Clause 1(i)(c) related to the insolvency of the buyer, namely the occurrence of a "Bankruptcy Trigger Event" where the assured would be entitled to terminate the loan agreement in advance. Clause 14 provided that:[15]

> "Bankruptcy Trigger Event" means the occurrence of a Counterparty Bankruptcy which occurs prior to the termination of the [loan agreement] following the occurrence of a Counterparty Failure to Pay.
>
> "Counterparty Bankruptcy" means any of the Eurotunnel Entities … institutes or has instituted against it a proceeding seeking a judgment of insolvency or bankruptcy or any other relief under any bankruptcy or insolvency law or other similar law affecting creditors' rights …
>
> "Counterparty Failure to Pay" means, after the expiration of any applicable (or deemed) grace period, a failure by any of the Eurotunnel Entities to make, when and where due, any payments to [the Bank] in accordance with the terms of the [loan agreement].

In July 2006, various Eurotunnel group companies, including the Eurotunnel Entities, instituted so-called "safeguard proceedings" in France which applied various prohibitions, stays and restrictions to their creditors. EFL, at this stage, had not defaulted in any periodic payment. The assured terminated the loan agreement and sought indemnity under Clause 1(i)(c). The insurer disputed that a "Bankruptcy Trigger Event" had occurred because, as a matter of construction, this term should only refer to bankruptcy which occurs after a "Counterparty Failure to Pay". Gloster J rejected the insurer's argument. The learned judge

14 [2007] EWHC 893 (Comm), [2007] 2 All ER (Comm) 846.
15 Ibid, [24]–[26].

clarified that under the loan agreement, the assured was exposed to two distinct and independent credit risks, namely the risk of the protracted payment default by the EFL and the risk of the insolvency of the Eurotunnel group. He thought it reasonable to suppose that the policy was intended to protect against each of the risks separately: before the actual termination of the agreement, bankruptcy posed an independent risk, which in some circumstances was "more of a credit risk than the failure of payment". He further held that, from a commercial point of view, it was unrealistic for the policy to exclude pre-termination bankruptcy, where there had been no prior failure to pay, as "an independent route to indemnification" and thereby to ignore the effect of a bankruptcy event on the credit risk faced by the assured and contemplated by the loan agreement itself. The judge thus held that the cover under Clause 1(i)(c) had been triggered notwithstanding that there had been no prior "Counterparty Failure to Pay".

Inserting a credit risk clause into a marine cargo policy?

The wording of the "transaction premium clause"

Where the assured seeks to insert a credit risk clause into other types of insurance policies than ECI, whether such a credit risk clause can operate as a full insuring clause as the abovementioned typical insuring clause under ECI could be a controversial issue. In *ABN Amro*,[16] the assured was a bank who had advanced working capital by way of structured commodities financing to the buyers to finance their trade in cocoa products under so-called "repo" transactions, where the buyers sold the cocoa products to the assured and then had an obligation to repurchase the goods from the assured at a specified time and (higher) price. The policy was placed with underwriters who were specialists in insuring cargo in warehouses and in transit, particularly the risk of physical loss of or damage to the cargo ("PLOD risks"). However, the policy contained an unusual clause, known as the "transaction premium clause" (TPC) which read as follows:[17]

> Underwriters note and agree that, in respect of any Transaction, it is hereby confirmed that the Insured is covered under this contract for the Transaction Premium that the Insured would otherwise have received and/or earned in the absence of a Default on the part of the Insured's client.
>
> "Actual Sale Price" means the sum received by the Insured upon the sale of the Subject Matter Insured to the applicable Exchange or to a third party on the open market.
>
> "Default" means a failure, refusal or non-exercise of an option, on the part of the Insured's client (for whatever reason) to purchase (or repurchase) the Subject Matter Insured from the Insured at the Pre-agreed Price.

16 [2021] EWCA Civ 1789.
17 Ibid, [3].

> "Pre-agreed Price" mean the amount for which the Insured's client had agreed to purchase (or repurchase) the Subject Matter Insured from the Insured as specified on the relevant invoice or in the relevant transaction documents, comprising the principal together with any premium or profit element payable to the Insured.
>
> "Transaction" means any transaction where, following a Default on the part of the Insured's client, the Insured sells the Subject Matter Insured to the applicable Exchange or to a third party on the open market.
>
> "Transaction Premium" means an amount that is equal to the difference in value between the Pre-Agreed Price and the Actual Sale Price.

The term "Subject Matter Insured" was defined as follows:[18]

> Interest
>
> All goods and or merchandise appertaining to the Insured's business for which the insured is the legal owner or for which the insured is at risk or responsible, contractually or otherwise …

The buyers defaulted in repurchasing the goods in 2016. The goods were of poor quality and the assured, after sustaining consequent financial losses when the goods were sold, sought indemnity against those losses under the TPC. The underwriters contended that, on its true interpretation and in the light of the admissible factual matrix and commercial consequences, the TPC did not cover non-PLOD risks such as the financial losses the assured suffered.

The construction of the TPC: textualism, contextualism, factual matrix and commercial consequences

In exploring the true interpretation of the TPC, the trial court in *ABN Amro* set out the established principles of contractual interpretation in English law in meticulous detail:[19] first, contractual construction is a "unitary exercise" where the court must consider the language used and ascertained what a reasonable person would have understood the parties to mean;[20] second, textualism and contextualism are not "conflicting paradigms" but are both tools to ascertain the objective meaning of the language;[21] third, the reliance on commercial common sense and surrounding circumstances should not be invoked to undervalue the importance of the

18 *ABN Amro* [2021] EWHC 442 (Comm), [168].

19 Ibid, [175]–[188]. Jacobs J clarified that "the principles which govern the construction of policies of marine insurance are those applicable to commercial instruments and indeed to contracts generally".

20 *Financial Conduct Authority v Arch Insurance (UK) Ltd* [2021] UKSC 1, [2021] 2 WLR 123, [48] (Lord Hamblen and Lord Leggatt); *Rainy Sky SA v Kookmin Bank* [2011] UKSC 50, [2011] 1 WLR 2900, [23]-[25] (Lord Clarke).

21 *Wood v Capita* [2017] UKSC 24, [2017] AC 1173, [13] (Lord Hodge).

wording;[22] fourth, the court should avoid re-writing the contract in an attempt to assist an unwise party or to penalise an astute party.[23] Jacobs J also referred to *Engelhart CIP (US) LLC v Lloyd's Syndicate 1221*[24] and clarified that since a marine cargo insurance policy primarily covers PLOD risks, clear words are needed if the parties wish to extend the coverage to non-PLOD risks.

Following the rules above, the judge analysed the parties' arguments in detail. The underwriters placed much emphasis on the factual matrix by arguing that they were not licensed or authorised to provide ECI which is "a separate line of cover", and that they only knew ECI business at a very general level. They also pointed to the "commercially absurd results" of providing ECI for free, which would mean an additional risk exposure totalling USD 2.5 billion.[25]

The assured accepted that ECI was a different class of business but argued that: it had paid high premiums under the policy; non-PLOD add-ons were common in the marine cargo market and, in this case, there were three such add-ons[26] in addition to the TPC under the policy; the market was generally "soft and difficult", and there was "overcapacity with underwriters straining to attract and retain business".[27]

In these circumstances, Jacobs J held that the factual matrix and commercial consequences served to underline the need for clear words for the cover to extend beyond normal PLOD coverage.

In dealing with the policy context, he noted that whilst paragraph (b) of the "General Conditions" stated that the policy was to cover PLOD risks, it was immediately followed by paragraph (c) stipulating that "all other conditions are more fully detailed in each respective section". He thus thought it necessary to consider all contractual terms in ascertaining the scope of the cover: since the policy contained three non-PLOD add-ons, the "General Conditions" could not be construed as a limitation denying non-PLOD coverage.[28]

In dealing with the words of the TPC itself, he found that (i) it was clear from the language that the TPC went beyond PLOD coverage, (ii) there was nothing in the wording of the TPC that provided a link to PLOD risks and (iii) the TPC contained several key expressions (e.g., "Transaction Premium" and "Default") which were not used elsewhere in the policy, each defined in a way unrelated to PLOD coverage.

The judge therefore concluded that the TPC was sufficiently clear to extend beyond PLOD coverage. He criticised the underwriters' argument as "not

22 *Arnold v Britton* [2015] UKSC 36, [2015] AC 1619, [18]–[19] (Lord Neuberger).

23 Ibid, [20] (Lord Neuberger). See also Cheng Lin, "Understanding the Legal Nature of Export Credit Insurance: Lessons from *ABN Amro v RSA*" [2022] (3) JBL 225, 227-9.

24 [2018] EWHC 900 (Comm), [2019] 1 All ER (Comm) 583, [39]–[41].

25 *ABN Amro* [2021] EWHC 442 (Comm), [198]–[205].

26 These add-ons were titled "Business Contingency Cover", "Fraudulent Documentation Cover" and "Additional Cover Confiscation and Expropriation". See ibid., [42]–[45].

27 Ibid, [213].

28 Ibid, [238].

appropriate", for it was primarily based not on the language but upon the policy context, factual matrix and commercial consequences in an attempt to circumscribe the ordinary and natural meaning of TPC.[29]

Both the underwriters and the brokers appealed. The underwriters were given permission to appeal against the trial court's decision on the interpretation of the TPC. However, the underwriters' appeal had been compromised between the hearing and the giving of appeal judgment. The underwriters and the assured prepared a draft order dismissing the appeal, and the underwriters asked for the judgment not to be delivered. The Court of Appeal, whilst approving the disposal of the underwriters' appeal, still decided to deliver judgment on both appeals because (a) the appeals were intimately connected, which means that it would have taken significant time to disentangle the points, (b) the parties were not unanimous in asking for the judgment not to be delivered[30] and (c) there was interest in the case in the insurance press.[31] The Court of Appeal in its concise judgment entirely upheld the trial court's decision on the interpretation of the TPC, confirming that the wordings of the TPC were clear and unambiguous.[32]

Rectification and an estoppel by convention?

As explained in Chapter 2 of this book, when the broker in *ABN Amro* presented the TPC to the leading underwriter in July 2015, neither the former explained its purpose nor the latter read it through carefully before signing the policy. The July 2015 endorsement then became the renewed policy scratched by all underwriters in 2016, the policy year when losses occurred.

In case their argument on construction failed, the underwriters advanced an alternative case based upon the communication between the broker and the leading underwriter, which would prevent, via rectification or an estoppel by convention, the assured from relying on the true construction of the TPC: the rectification argument was that both parties subjectively intended that the TPC did not provide standalone ECI cover; the estoppel argument was that the broker lacked protest in response to the leading underwriter's declaration as to his understanding of the TPC as providing PLOD coverage only, and thus the broker acquiesced in that assumption and it would be unjust to allow the assured to resile from it.

With respect to rectification, Jacobs J referred to *FSHC Holdings v GLAS Trust*[33] and clarified that an "outward expression of accord" is required to show that the parties shared a common intention that the document did not accurately record. He then cited *MacGillivray on Insurance Law* for the proposition that

29 Ibid, [260].
30 The assured and the broker were neutral but pointed out the benefits to the market of delivering the judgement. See *ABN Amro* [2021] EWCA Civ 1789, [9].
31 Ibid.
32 Ibid, [60]–[70].
33 [2019] EWCA Civ 1361, [2020] Ch 365 at [176].

"there is a presumption that a policy which is issued by the insurer and accepted by the insured contains the complete and final contract between the parties".[34]

With respect to estoppel, Jacobs J confirmed that an estoppel by convention arises if (i) there is a relevant assumption of fact or law, either shared by both parties or made by party B and acquiesced in by party A, and (ii) it would be unjust to allow party A to go back on that assumption.[35] He referred to *HM Revenue v Benchdollar*[36] (in the context of non-contractual dealings) and *Mitchell v Watkinson*[37] (in the context of contractual cases) and clarified that an assumption, whether shared by the parties or acquiesced in by one party, should be shown in an express way.

The judge then said that "ultimately, the present case turns upon the facts … rather than upon fine differences in the precise formulation of the principle".[38] After a lengthy treatment of the evidence, he concluded that the evidential foundation for rectification and estoppel did not exist.

In terms of rectification, he found no convincing proof to displace the natural presumption that the written contract is an accurate record of what the parties agreed. He noted that the presumption is reinforced in the context of the London insurance market by the Contract Certainty Code of Practice (CCCP), which is not a legally binding document but reflects the best practice of the industry by requiring that "the insurer should check that the proposed contract clearly identifies all of the terms by the time it formally commits to the contract".[39] Taking this into consideration, he commented that it would not have been difficult for the leading underwriter to add words at the start of the TPC saying "This clause applies in case of physical loss and damage to the cargo".[40] The judge was critical of the leading underwriter who "just did not take sufficient time to consider it when he first agreed it in July 2015, and did not do so thereafter".[41]

In terms of estoppel, he held that on the balance of probabilities, there was no alleged side-discussion or assumption capable of negating the clear policy wording the parties signed; furthermore, since the leading underwriter took no steps to clarify the true effect and scope of the TPC, there was "no injustice in saying that contractual terms should apply".[42]

34 John Birds, Ben Lynch and Simon Paul, *MacGillivray on Insurance Law* (14th edn, London: Sweet & Maxwell, 2018), [12-002].

35 *Blindley Heath Investments Ltd v Bass* [2015] EWCA Civ 1023, [2017] Ch 389 and *Aras and others v National Bank of Greece SA* [2018] EWHC 1389 (Comm), [2018] 6 WLUK 127 were cited by Jacob J in setting out the formulation for an estoppel by convention. See *ABN Amro* [2021] EWHC 442 (Comm), [325–6].

36 [2009] EWHC 1310 (Ch), [2010] 1 All ER 174.

37 [2014] EWCA Civ 1472, [2014] 11 WLUK 555, [52].

38 *ABN Amro* [2021] EWHC 442 (Comm), [331].

39 London Market Group, "Contract Certainty Code of Practice - September 2018", at <https://lmg.london/wp-content/uploads/2019/07/CC-COP-Sept-2018.pdf> accessed 1 February 2022.

40 *ABN Amro* [2021] EWHC 442 (Comm), [413].

41 Ibid, [428].

42 Ibid, [435–6].

Identifying the subject matter insured and drafting an appropriate insuring clause

ABN Amro demonstrates the English courts' insistence on contract certainty even if a signed contract might lead to a commercially unwise result for one party. Both the trial and appeal courts in *ABN Amro* were critical of the underwriters: Jacobs J held that the TPC was apparently very carefully drafted, but the leading underwriter read it through only once "in a meeting which lasted around 15 minutes" before signing the slip; as far as the following underwriters were concerned, "none of them noticed the clause let alone read it carefully or asked questions about it".[43] Sir Geoffrey Vos further commented that "underwriters are bound by the terms of the slip to which they subscribe, whether they read it or not".[44] Underwriters of all types of insurance business, therefore, should learn from this case and always read the policy carefully before agreeing to its terms.

Indeed, both the underwriters and the brokers in *ABN Amro* were confused by the complexity of the "repo" transaction. The Court of Appeal rightly noted that (by citing *MacGillivray on Insurance Law*):[45]

> The genius of the London market is to set out the elements of a complex transaction involving large sums of money in one short document - the slip. Usually the slip is worded with care by persons experienced in the terms used by the market. Sometimes, however, it is difficult to ascertain the parties' intention from the wording of the slip. Difficulties are caused by the use of abbreviations and delay in producing the detailed wording to set out their meaning in full, by the use of standard wordings of acknowledged pedigree but not always appropriate to the particular transaction and creating either repugnancy or surplusage, and by the practice of incorporation by reference.

ABN Amo reveals that underwriters and brokers in the London market, except for those who specialise in credit risk, only knew at a very general level the legal nature of ECI, which was the root cause of all controversies in this case. Otherwise, the underwriters would have rejected the risk at the outset and the broker, alternatively, would have placed the risk with the UKEF or specialist private credit risk insurers. It is therefore vital for parties who wish to arrange ECI to identify the subject matter insured under ECI and draft an appropriate insuring clause.

The underwriters in *ABN Amro* believed that the TPC covers no more than PLOD risks largely because the "Subject Matter Insured" under the policy is the cargo itself. But they failed to recognise that the real subject matter insured under the TPC is the "Transaction Premium" (i.e., financial losses) the assured would suffer following the buyer's default in repurchasing the cargo. In other words, the subject matter insured here has shifted from "cargo" to "Transaction Premium".

43 Ibid, [291–3]
44 *ABN Amro* [2021] EWCA Civ 1789, [98].
45 *ABN Amro* [2021] EWHC 442 (Comm), [168].

This is why both the trial and appeal judges treated the TPC as a standalone coverage clause.[46]

The wisdom of identifying the subject matter insured under ECI was better illustrated in *Harding Maughan Hambly Ltd v Compagnie Europeenne de Courtage d'Assurances et de Reassurances SA*,[47] where the risk was successfully placed in the suitable sub-market within the broad political risk market, which enabled the parties to avoid potential disputes. The background of *Harding Maughan Hambly* has been discussed in Chapter 2: the assured was the operator of Block 3 (an offshore oil block of Angola) who wished to cover the risk that the Angolan state oil company (of which the operating name is "Sonangol") would fail to fulfil its obligation to supply it with the specified amount of crude oil that was to be sourced from Block 3 under an off-take agreement. As was commented by Rix J, the placing of such risks "lay awkwardly between the two markets of contract frustration and expropriation".[48] The assured's attempt to place the risk in the contract frustration market failed because of the Angolan debt crisis, and thus it had to try the expropriation market which did not have the indigestion problem with the Angolan debt crisis. The learned judge explained that "the essence of the expropriation market is that it is necessary to find an asset which is subject to the risk, and not merely a contractual arrangement which is imperilled by embargo or frustration": the expropriation market is asset-based, whereas the contract frustration market is trade-based.[49]

To obtain an expropriation risk cover, the assured's brokers presented to the leading underwriter in July 1994 an initial draft of a slip which read as follows:[50]

> TYPE: Political Risks
>
> INTEREST: Crude oil owned by the Assured in/off-shore Angola to a value of up to US$58,500,000
>
> CONDITIONS: This insurance is to indemnify the Assured for their ascertained net loss arising from the occurrence, during this period of insurance of any event covered by the wording attached hereto …
>
> Expropriation
>
> 1. EXPROPRIATION Means an act occurring within the Policy period not limited to expropriation but including also confiscation, nationalisation, requisition and sequestration by law, order or administrative action of the Foreign Government which:
>
>   (a) Expressly and permanently deprives the Assured of all or part of their share holding/equity in Block 3 Offshore Angola … or

46 Ibid. See also *ABN Amro* [2021] EWCA Civ 1789 at [70].
47 [2000] 1 All ER (Comm) 225.
48 Ibid, 246 (Rix J).
49 Ibid, 231 (Rix J).
50 Ibid, 230–1.

(b) Expressly and permanently deprives the Assured of all or part of its current assets those being (in relation to this insurance) crude oil as identified herein and the related pledge and confirmation of ownership given to the Assured by Sonangol as attached hereto. or

(c) Expressly and selectively prevents or restricts the production of oil from Block 3 … so as to cause the temporary cessation (beyond the end of the waiting period herein) or the permanent and total cessation of the production of oil from Block …

The leading underwriter questioned whether the risk was suitable for an expropriation cover. The brokers explained that the intention of the policy was (a) that the assured owned an asset in the form of crude oil production from Block 3 to be delivered and exported from Angola through time in repayment of the loan and (b) that the insurance policy will therefore respond to a claim arising as a result of the assured's inability to export the asset from Block 3 as a result of an action of the Angolan Authorities. Nevertheless, the leading underwriter remained doubtful whether the assured owned the crude oil in the ground or merely had the right to receive it after being sourced from Block 3, as inconsistencies existed between the document of title to the oil and the off-take agreement.[51] The brokers, after consulting with the assured and its external lawyers, presented to the leading underwriters in March 1995 a revised policy which included the following changes:[52]

(1) The "TYPE" heading was changed from "Political Risks" to "Expropriation";
(2) The bank who financed the off-take transaction was added as a co-assured;
(3) The "INTEREST" section was amended so as to delete reference to "Crude oil owned by the Assured" and to read instead-

> The Assured's existing interest in Block 3 Offshore Angola and additional collateral given by Sonangol in relation to a loan provided to Sonangol by the Assureds.

(4) The previous wording under Clause 1 (b) was replaced with the new wording which read as follows-

> Expressly and/or effectively deprives the Assured of all or part of their fixed and/or current assets located in/offshore Angola and/or collateral given by Sonangol in relation to production from Block 3 Offshore Angola.

Rix J commented that the revised policy more properly identified the subject matter insured as the assured's interest in Block 3 and, "very importantly", the collateral relating to the loan, the performance of which reflected an asset that could be insured under an ECI (expropriation) cover.[53] Such revisions shifted attention

51 For details, see Chapter 2 of this work.
52 *Harding* [2000] 1 All ER (Comm) 225, 243.
53 Ibid, 245.

from the assured's title of the oil (i.e., PLOD coverage) to its interest in the underlying transaction as a whole (i.e., non-PLOD coverage), which convinced the leading underwriter that the risk could properly be written. Eventually, the insured transaction "passed off without any difficulty".[54]

The measure of indemnity under ECI

The maximum liability clause

In terms of the measure of indemnity in indemnity insurance, there is a difference between a valued and an unvalued policy. Under the Marine Insurance Act 1906 (MIA 1906), a valued policy specifies the agreed value of the subject matter insured,[55] whereas an unvalued policy does not specify the value insured of the subject matter insured but, subject to the limit of the sum insured, leaves the insurable value to be subsequently ascertained.[56] ECI is normally an unvalued policy, which can be inferred from the term "maximum liability" and "insured percentage". The term "Maximum Liability" is printed on the front page of the UKEF's "Export Insurance Policy", indicating the maximum amount of loss for which the UKEF will indemnify the exporter. The term "Insured Percentage" is also stipulated on the front page, where the UKEF undertakes to pay up to 95% of the "Maximum Liability".[57]

The credit limit clause

In addition, ECI normally also include a peculiar clause called "credit limit". The credit limit is the highest amount of cover that an ECA grants to the assured regarding its transaction(s).[58] The purpose of the credit limit is to determine the limit of indemnity.[59] The credit limit can be either comprehensive or individual but is in most cases individual: the former covers the whole turnover of the assured's business with various buyers, whereas the latter concerns the assured's transac-

54 Ibid, 246 (Rix J).

55 In valued policies, the insurer usually makes express provisions on the measure of indemnity. See Merkin (n 11), [11-017-027].

56 The MIA 1906, ss 27–8.

57 See n 8 above.

58 Salcic (n 6) 36–7. The amount of the credit limit will depend to a large extent on the ECA's perception of the risk as well as on the volume of previous dealings between the exporter and the buyer(s). However, once a credit limit has been fixed, it remains in force unless it is varied or withdrawn by the ECA. See Eva Lomnicka, "Export Credit Guarantees", in Michael Bridge (ed.), *Benjamin's Sales of Goods* (11th edn, Sweet & Maxwell 2020), [25-019]. Notably, an ECAs might give a "nil" credit limit endorsement in regards to a certain buyer, which means that the assured's transaction with that buyer is not included in the ECI cover. See, e.g., in *Close Invoice Finance Ltd v Watts* [2009] EWCA Civ 1182, [22].

59 Merkin (n 11), [24-068]; Birds and others (n 34), [33-021]. The credit limit is of a revolving nature; as payments are made that reduce the buyer's outstanding amounts, further transactions with them up to the agreed limit may be covered by the policy. See Lomnicka, ibid.

tion with a specific buyer.[60] Where the credit limit is of a comprehensive nature, it equals to the maximum liability of the policy; where it is granted to cover the assured's transaction with a specific buyer, the total amount of all such credit limits equals to the maximum liability. For instance, if the maximum liability of an ECI policy is £1m, then the assured may be granted a credit limit of £0.5m for its transaction with buyer A and another credit limit of £0.5m for buyer B. The insurer's liability is capped by the credit limit multiplied by the insured percentage.

How the credit limit clause determines the limit of indemnity was considered in *Hill and Lichtenstein Ltd v Export Guarantee General Manager*,[61] where the credit limit for the assured exporter's transaction with a specific buyer was NZ$90,000. The ECI policy stipulated that the insured percentage was 85% and provided that the credit limit was to determine the maximum amount recoverable. However, the debt of that buyer amounted to NZ$116,250. The assured argued that it was entitled to be paid either 85% of the total loss or at least 85% of the total loss capped by the credit limit of NZ$90,000. Rejecting the assured's submission and clarifying that the assured could only recover 85% of the credit limit of NZ$90,000, the court explained that the credit limit was designed to define the maximum sum recoverable in respect of any one debtor, and the 85% cap was to be applied to each claim in regard of that debtor.

How the credit limit clause "cuts down" the ECA's liability was further elaborated in *Kent Engineering & Foundry Ltd v Export Credits Guarantee Department*.[62] The insured percentage in that case was 90%. The credit limit was £62,500 for each particular buyer, and therefore the maximum amount the ECA was liable to pay under each credit limit was £62,500 × 90% = £56,250. The assured exporter suffered losses in respect of two consignments of goods to the same buyer. The amounts of the first and second losses were £49,895 and £52,524. The assured contended that the credit limit should apply to each loss. Parker J, however, held that it was clear and unambiguous from the wording of the policy that the credit limit applied to the totality of claims arising in relation to a specific buyer rather than each loss. Therefore, the ECA should pay £49,895 × 90% = £44,906 under the first claim. In respect of the second claim, although the assured sought to be paid a sum of £52,524 × 90% = £47,271, the ECA's liability was capped by the credit limit, and it should only pay £56,250 – £44,906 = £11,344.

A credit limit can fluctuate during the currency of a policy, a decision made by the court in *Moore Large & Co Ltd v Hermes Credit & Guarantee Plc*.[63] The dispute in that case was whether the aggregate loss had exceeded the credit limit. The assured was covered under an ECI policy against the risk of "Qualifying Debts" due to the buyer's insolvency. The amount of the loss, namely the "Qualifying Debts", was

60 *Moore Large & Co Ltd v Hermes Credit & Guarantee Plc (sued as Credit & Guarantee Insurance Co Plc)* [2003] EWHC 26 (Comm), [2003] 1 Lloyd's Rep 163, [3] (Colman J); See also *Simon Container Machinery Ltd v Emba Machinery AB* [1998] 2 Lloyd's Rep 429, 435 (Jack J).

61 [1972] NZLR 802.

62 [1983] 2 Lloyd's Rep 556.

63 [2003] EWHC 26 (Comm), [3] (Colman J).

ascertained by "Qualifying Invoices" made upon the delivery of respective goods. The assured was granted an initial credit limit of £0.6m. Due to the Christmas peak orders, the parties adjusted the credit limit, which was £0.6m from 1 March 2000 to 30 September 2000 ("Period 1"), and £2.5m from 1 October 2000 to 31 October 2000 ("Period 2"). The buyer went insolvent during Period 2, but the delivery of goods took place in Period 1. The loss amounted to £1.5m. The insurer rejected the claim, arguing that the credit limit of £0.6m in Period 1 should apply because the date of the Qualifying Invoices fell within Period 1. The assured submitted that the credit limit of £2.5m in Period 2 should apply because the insolvency occurred within Period 2. The determination of the applicable credit limit was therefore the key issue in this case: if the credit limit of Period 1 should apply, then the loss had exceeded the £0.6m credit limit; otherwise, the loss had not exceeded the £2.5m credit limit of Period 2. The relevant clauses of the policy read as follows:

> This Insurance Cover
> Subject to the terms and conditions of this policy the Insurer will indemnify the Insured in respect of Insured Loss arising in respect of the … Qualifying Debt, directly and naturally suffered by the Insured as a result of Insolvency of the Customer occurring within the period of Insurance.
>
> Insured Loss:
> Such amount of … Qualifying Debt as shall not exceed Credit Limit as shall have arisen as a result of Insolvency of the Customer occurring within the Period of Insurance.
>
> Credit Limit:
> The limit in respect of credit, as approved by the Insurer for the purposes of this policy, to be extended by the Insured to the Customer as specified in the Schedule.
>
> Qualifying Debt:
> Such amount of Qualifying Invoice … as shall remain unpaid after Due Date.
>
> Qualifying Invoice:
> Invoice delivered to the Customer and being in respect of goods sold and services provided by the Insured to the Customer during the Period of Insurance pursuant to the terms of the Contract.

The judgment was for the assured for the following reasons. Firstly, Colman J observed that there was no express provision that the accumulation of pre-existing debts as reflected on Qualifying Invoices should not exceed the credit limit at any time.[64] Secondly, the definition of "Insured Loss" clearly indicated that it

64 See ibid, [21–2], where Colman J stated that:

> Had it been the purpose of the policy to limit the indemnity by reference to the relationship to Credit Limit of each separate invoice at the date of its issue one would have expected as

was quantifiable only following insolvency. Thirdly, the constituent outstanding debts under ECI were a running aggregate, which can be higher than the credit limit for some time but fall below the limit later following the payment of some pre-existing invoices. The historical credit limit can be reduced by the time of insolvency. Fourthly, it would be more consonant with the commercial purpose of a credit limit clause with reference to the financial liability of the customer that the limit should be applied upon insolvency and not at the date of each invoice.[65]

Hill and Lichtenstein, *Kent Engineering & Foundry* and *Moore Large* showed that the credit limit clause operates closely with the insuring and indemnity clause. It determines the limit of indemnity under ECI. All those cases indicate that by including the credit limit clause, ECI is a contract of indemnity insurance.

Distinguishing an insuring clause from a measure of indemnity clause

It is important to distinguish an insuring clause from a measure of indemnity clause: the former defines the scope of coverage, whereas the latter merely provides the measure of indemnity under the coverage. This distinction can sometimes be controversial. The policy in *ABN Amro* contained a "Basis of Valuation" (BOV) clause, which was clearly a measure of indemnity clause in relation to PLOD risks:[66]

> Market Value at date of claim provided that the market value shall be no less than the Market Value as used at the date of purchase. For the purposes of this clause the term "Market Value" shall mean the relevant published Exchange future price or any other price stated in the Insured's underlying purchase contract, call option contract or any other document relevant to the purchase …

In supporting the argument on the construction of the TPC, the underwriters contended that the BOV clause would not cover the entire field of potential loss and that the TPC, after being inserted into the policy in July 2015, should be read as an expansion of the measure of indemnity. The essence of the underwriters' submission was that: the BOV clause was focused on the market value at the date of purchase of the goods by the assured, and thus its purpose was to ensure that the assured recovered no less than the price relating to its purchase of the cocoa

---

a matter of ordinary drafting technique to find that the definition of Qualifying Invoice or possibly Qualifying Debt alluded expressly to this limit on the scope of the indemnity … Nowhere in the policy wording is it expressed by reference to the amount of an individual invoice or to the date when such invoice was issued.

65 Ibid.
66 *ABN Amro* [2021] EWHC 442 (Comm), [267].

products from the buyers; on the other hand, the measure of recovery under the TPC was focused on the "Pre-Agreed Price" which related to the repurchase of the goods by the buyers. There was therefore a difference in approach taken by the BOV clause and by the TPC. Whilst the TPC had no application if the cargo was a total loss, it would have potential value in a situation where there was, for example, damage to the cargo. In that situation, the assured would have the option of valuing the loss under either the BOV clause or the TPC. The underwriters thus submitted that the TPC should be interpreted as applying only to calculate the measure of indemnity in relation to PLOD risks.

Jacobs J did not consider this argument to be sound or persuasive or to provide a reasonable alternative interpretation of the TPC for a number of reasons:[67]

First, if the parties were concerned that the BOV clause was inadequate to cover the full field of market-related loss as a result of PLOD perils, then "one would not expect the BOV clause to be expanded upon by a wholly separate clause, which makes no reference to the BOV clause itself, and uses very different terminology".[68]

Second, there was nothing in the wording of the TPC itself which suggests that the parties were addressing any inadequacy in the BOV clause. The TPC was simply a formula for calculating the loss the assured would suffer due to the default of payment by the buyer.

Third, if the TPC was intended to be an enhanced BOV clause, then it would make no sense for it to have no application in circumstances where the goods were destroyed or damaged so as to be incapable of re-sale.

Fourth, the underwriters' argument gave an unnecessarily restrictive meaning to the wide words of the BOV clause. It was relevant to consider the nature of the "repo" transactions: such transactions were a very usual way in which a bank would advance funds to its customers, with the result that it would acquire the ownership of goods for a temporary period and the customer would repurchase them later. The need for the assured bank to insure the goods here arose from its ownership of goods acquired in this way via transactions involving the purchase of goods and agreements relating to their repurchase. The BOV clause expressly referred to the "Insured's call option contract", and there is no reason to confine these words to call option contracts in favour of the assured, i.e., where the assured could call for goods. In fact, there was no evidence that the assured entered into such contracts. On the contrary, under "repo" transactions, one would more naturally expect that the "call options" would give the buyers the right to call for goods. This was consistent with the reference in the definition of "Default" under the TPC: the buyers would be calling for goods from the assured, not the other way round. In these circumstances, the BOV clause was sufficient to enable the assured to assess Market Value by reference to prices payable by the

67 Ibid, [269]–[279].
68 Ibid, [270].

buyers under the obligation to repurchase or the price payable upon exercise of the call option by the buyers.

Fifth, the interpretation of the TPC as an expansion of the BOV clause would render the TPC without any practical effect: the TPC, as "a lengthy and carefully drafted bespoke additional clause, introduced by way of amendment to a policy which already had a BOV clause" should not be devoid of any practical meaning to become "linguistic overkill".[69]

Jacobs J thus regarded the TPC as a "self-contained coverage clause",[70] a decision that was upheld in the appeal where Sir Geoffrey Vos confirmed that the TPC was sufficiently clear: "these are words of coverage, not simply of a basis of valuation or measure of indemnity".[71]

The exclusion clause

Exclusion clause: general

Whilst an ECI policy covers certain types of commercial and political risks, as expected, it may also exclude some perils. An exclusion clause in the ECI policy may pose some general limitations on the insured perils. For instance, loss resulting from failure by the exporter to perform the sales contract or comply with any relevant law is not covered.[72] Besides, there may be a limitation on the geographical scope of the export business. In *G&GB Hewitt Ltd v SA Namur-Assurances du Credit*,[73] the assured, a meat wholesaler and processor, was insured under an ECI policy that covered commercial risks but excluded political risks. The exclusion clause read as follows:

> This policy shall not cover
>
> 15.7.1 losses due to a delay in transfer to the United Kingdom of payments made by a customer to the insured, or
> 15.7.2 losses resulting from fluctuations in rates of exchange, or
> 15.7.3 losses arising from the delivery of goods or the rendering of services in respect of which the export from the insured's country of residence and/or business or the import into the same of such goods or services is or may become prohibited or for which HM Customs or similar export, import or exchange licences, or other prescribed consents are lacking.

During the currency of the policy, the assured supplied meat to its customer, C, who was based in England and had a substantial export trade business. Subsequently, due to the EU ban on the export of beef from the UK, C's business

69 Ibid, [273].
70 Ibid, [255].
71 [2021] EWCA Civ 1789, [70].
72 Lomnicka (n 58), [25-023].
73 [1999] 1 All ER (Comm) 851.

was heavily hit, and C went insolvent. The assured claimed against the insurer, but the insurer rejected the claim relying on Clause 15.7.3. The assured argued that Clause 15.7.3 only applied to trans-border transactions, but the insurer contended that it could rely on Clause 15.7.3 so long as the goods supplied by the assured to C were coincidentally the subject matter of the export ban and the reason why the customer failed to pay was attributable to the export ban. The court rejected the insurer's submission, holding that Clause 15.7.3 only applied to goods which were to "cross an international frontier" and that the insurer was liable to pay. The court read Clause 15.7 as a "coherent whole" and held that since Clause 15.7.1 and 15.7.2 applied only if the assured was the exporter, so did Clause 15.7.3. The court further rejected the insurer's request to investigate whether the goods supplied by the assured to the customer had been identified or appropriated[74] as goods for the customer's export business, as that was an irrelevant point.[75]

Moreover, the limitation regarding the timing of the transaction was considered in *British Credit Trust Holdings v UK Insurance Ltd*,[76] a domestic credit insurance case where the assured was a finance company running a motor car hire–purchase business. The credit risk policy provided an "umbrella cover" which insured each hire-purchase agreement ("Agreement") the assured concluded with customers. Clause 5(n) provides that:

> No legal action may be brought under this insurance in respect of any Agreement unless the Insured has complied with all the provisions of the insurance in relation to such Agreement and any such legal action must be commenced within one year after any loss occurs in respect of such Agreement.

Although Clause 5(n) itself was not an exclusion clause, it created a cut-off date which limited some potential legal actions brought by the assured. However, the parties disputed the true construction of Clause 5(n). The insurer submitted that any legal action must be brought within one year after the first loss under the umbrella cover occurred. The insurer alleged that once there was a loss in any Agreement, the one-year period started and applied to any future losses. The assured argued that the one-year period applied on a contract-by-contract basis and the time bar must be calculated separately in each individual Agreement. The court accepted the assured's submission. Morison J held that although Clause 5(n)

74 The insurer in that case was relying on the concept of "appropriation/identification" in international sales. Art 67(2) of the United Nations Convention on Contracts for the International Sale of Goods (CISG) provides that "the risk does not pass to the buyer until the goods are clearly identified to the contract, whether by markings on the goods, by shipping documents, by notice given to the buyer or otherwise". However, the concept of "appropriation/identification" only concerns the transfer of risk from the seller to the buyer in international sales. The court therefore treated the insurer's argument as irrelevant.

75 Ibid.

76 [2003] EWHC 2404 (Comm), [2004] 1 All ER (Comm) 444.

was "curiously worded", it had to be read "against the commercial background of the policy". He further pointed out that in each Agreement, a separate loss would be ascertained, and that Clause 5(n) cannot be construed to establish a one-year window to preclude any future claims in respect of losses occur one year after the occurrence of the first loss, as such interpretation would not be within the contemplation of the parties.[77]

Exclusion of documentation risk

In addition to general exclusions on some perils, under supplier/buyer credit insurance, most ECAs around the world, if not all of them, would include a particular exclusion clause on the documentation risk. The term "documentation risk" refers to the risk that the bank cannot receive payment because of the invalidity, illegality or unenforceability of the loan agreement with the buyer.[78] Banks sometimes make errors in the loan agreement: for instance, they may simply omit to obtain the required signature of the buyer or to include a clear schedule for the repayment of the loan. ECAs normally exclude documentation risk in ECI policies because it is difficult for them to scrutinise "a huge number of different international contracts that are governed by various national laws".[79] Some typical wording of the exclusion clause on documentation risk from the Berne Union members are cited below:

> **Sample wording A:**[80]
> The consequences of negligence, errors and inaccuracies in the description of documents linked with the Export Contract and the Loan Agreement covered by this insurance are borne only by the Insured.
>
> **Sample wording B:**[81]
> [The Insurer] shall take no responsibility as regards the contractual documentation relating, in particular, to the Contract and to collaterals. The Insured shall be held solely liable for the validity and the description of the Contract by the latter, and potentially the interpretation it gives of it, even if [the Insurer] has been sent the contractual documents or has made some observations about them.
>
> **Sample wording C:**[82]
> The Insured person is responsible for the validity of the Buyer credit and contracted security, compliance with the Export Contract with the Buyer credit and checking whether the documentary conditions of the loan have been met.

77 Ibid, [18]–[20].
78 Salcic (n 6) 28.
79 Ibid, 29.
80 See Clause 10.1(e) of KUKE's policy.
81 See Clause 16.1 of Credendo's policy.
82 See Clause 6.2 of HBOR's policy. For similar wordings, see Clause 5(3) of Euler Hermes Germany Government's policy and Clause 4.2 of Finnvera's policy.

It is also, at its own expense, required to prove the validity of these documents, as well as demonstrate the occurrence of the Insured event and the amount of Damage.

The documentation risk exclusion clause may not provide a direct indication of the legal nature of ECI, but it helps to reveal a significant difference between ECI and ECGs: whilst such exclusion is usually included in ECI policies, it is rarely seen in ECG contracts, which will be further discussed in the following sections of this chapter. Under ECGs, ECAs tend to bear the documentation risk, which indicates that an ECG is client-friendlier to banks than ECI.

Specific exclusions under Lloyd's ECI policies

ECI covers placed at Lloyd's are subject to the following specific exclusions:

- **The insolvency of the assured.** This should be distinguished from the insolvency of the buyer, a commercial risk that is normally insured under ECI. Lloyd's *Performance Management – Supplemental Requirements & Guidance* provides that "all policies must contain an exclusion in respect of any loss arising from the insolvency of the insured". Nevertheless, Lloyd's recognises that due to market practice, such a full exclusion may not be achievable (e.g., where the ECI cover is reinsured by ECAs), and thus, on a request received from the managing agent, Lloyd's may agree not to use this full exclusion.[83]
- **Price fluctuation.** Lloyd's *Performance Management - Supplemental Requirements & Guidance* indicates that Lloyd's is unlikely to agree plans that involve the writing of political risks where the primary risk is the price risk such as (a) currency fluctuation risk, (b) commodity price fluctuation risk, (c) financial market fluctuation risk or (d) property/land price fluctuation risk.[84]
- **Nuclear, chemical, biological or radioactive material used as a weapon (NCBR risk).** Lloyd's *Performance Management-Supplemental Requirements & Guidance* requires the inclusion of NCBR exclusions in all classes of policies issued at Lloyd's. In the case of Credit Risk and Contract Frustration, however, Lloyd's recognises that where the assured is a bank or other financial institution then it may seek to have any NCBR exclusion removed to allow it to take credit for the insurance for the purposes of setting regulatory capital. Lloyd's may therefore agree to the removal of NCBR exclusions in such policies as part of the business planning agreement process.[85]

83 Lloyd's of London (n 13) 44.

84 Ibid, 45.

85 Nevertheless, managing agents must ensure that they comply with the requirements for reporting NCBR exposures; syndicates must also have the matching back-to-back reinsurance or the exposure must be within their net risk appetite. See ibid., 43.

In addition, Lloyd's Market Association developed a series of model clauses for specific exclusions under political risk policies:[86]

- **Cyber risk**. Lloyd's Market Association's "Political Risk Cyber Endorsement" (document references: LMA5408, LMA 5427[87] and LMA 5427B[88]) affirm cyber coverage under ECI (i.e., losses arising from the normal operation of computer system) but exclude losses as a result of harmful cyber actions.
- **Communicable disease/pandemic risk**. Following the outbreak of the COVID-19 pandemic, Lloyd's Market Association published its "Political Risk Communicable Disease Exclusion" (document reference: LMA5501[89]) which bars coverage for losses arising from any governmental measures to curb the spread of any communicable disease.

The specific exclusions above show that syndicates at Lloyd's, as private credit insurers, are very cautious in underwriting political risks due to limited capacity and risk appetite. On the contrary, such exclusions are not seen in ECI policies issued by ECAs. In particular, whilst private credit insurers tend to exclude pandemic risks, ECAs have shown strong support for exporters and banks to deal with difficulties caused by the COVID-19 pandemic.[90] In particular, the UKEF has launched the "General Export Facility", a new scheme to give exporting small and medium-sized enterprises (SMEs) access to the working capital they need to recover from COVID-19.[91] As the Berne Union stated in its recent report, "the role of an ECA is typically to fill market gaps and to provide capacity for higher-risk transactions".[92] That is consistent with the mission of the UKEF, which is to

86 It should be noted that all model clauses drafted by Lloyd's Market Association are purely illustrative and distributed for the guidance of LMA members, who are free to agree to different conditions or amend as they see fit. LMA model clauses are available on the Lloyd's Wordings Repository (LWR) at <www.lloydswordings.com> and/or on the LMA website at < https://www.lmalloyds.com/LMA/Underwriting/Wordings/LMA/lma_wordings.aspx?hkey=d2594463-c8f3-4dcc-8907-0791904224c0>.

87 Full text available at < https://www.lmalloyds.com/LMA/News/LMA_bulletins/LMA_Bulletins/LMA20-026-PD.aspx > accessed 1 February 2022.

88 Full text available at < https://www.lmalloyds.com/LMA/Underwriting/Wordings/LMA/lma_wordings.aspx?hkey=d2594463-c8f3-4dcc-8907-0791904224c0 > accessed 1 February 2022.

89 Full text available at <https://www.lmalloyds.com/LMA/Underwriting/Non-Marine/Political_Risks/LMA/Underwriting/Non-Marine/Political_Risks.aspx?hkey=ef5f8580-99aa-49cd-9d84-b0297f822008> accessed 1 February 2022.

90 ICISA, "Overview of Covid19 policy developments December 2020" <https://www.icisa.org/documents/overview-of-covid19-policy-developments-december-2020/> accessed 1 February 2022.

91 UKEF, "Radical shake up to government export finance support for small businesses" <https://www.gov.uk/government/news/radical-shake-up-to-government-export-finance-support-for-small-businesses> accessed 1 February 2022.

92 Berne Union, "Export Credit Insurance Industry Response to COVID-19", 3 <https://www.berneunion.org/Articles/Details/506/Robust-response-to-the-COVID-19-pandemic-from-the-export-credit-insurance-industr> accessed 1 February 2022.

ensure that no viable UK export should fail for lack of finance from the private market.[93]

Conditions and warranties under ECI before and after the IA 2015

ECI conditions before the IA 2015: the effects of the breach of conditions precedent to liability

In common law, insurance conditions can be classified as conditions precedent to the validity of the policy, conditions precedent to the inception of the risk, conditions precedent to liability and bare conditions.[94] Firstly, conditions precedent to the policy must be satisfied before the parties can be treated as having contracted at all, and conditions precedent to the risk means that the risk is not attached if such conditions are not complied with.[95] Secondly, conditions precedent to liability entitles the insurer to reject a claim in respect of a loss should there be a breach.[96] Thirdly, the breach of bare conditions will entitle the insurer either to terminate the entire policy if the condition goes to the root of the policy or to claim damages if the condition is minor.[97] Whether a term can be classified as "condition precedent" is a matter of construction.[98] Conditions precedent can be created either by using the word "condition precedent"[99] or by an express statement of the remedy for the breach.[100]

It has been well established that a general clause in an insurance policy purporting to make compliance with obligations in the policy a condition precedent to the insurer's liability could indeed have that effect.[101] Like other types of insurance policies, ECI policies usually include such a general clause.[102] However, one might question whether the breach of such a clause would relieve the insurer of all its liabilities under the policy or only the liability to pay a particular tainted claim if the policy wording is very widely drafted. This was explored in the context of ECI in *Kazakstan Wool Processors (Europe) Ltd v Nederlandsche Credietverzekering Maatschappij NV*,[103] where the conditions precedent in question were stipulated

93 See n 91 above.
94 Merkin (n 11), [8-005].
95 Ibid, [8-006].
96 Ibid, [8-007].
97 Ibid, [8-008].
98 Özlem Gürses, *Marine Insurance Law* (2nd edn, Routledge 2017) 343.
99 *Royal & Sun Alliance Insurance Plc v Dornoch Ltd* [2005] EWCA Civ 238, [2005] Lloyd's Rep IR 544, [19].
100 *Eagle Star Insurance Co Ltd v Cresswell* [2004] EWCA Civ 602, [2004] Lloyd's Rep IR 537. See also the abovementioned *British Credit* case, where Clause 5 (n) was not stated to be a condition precedent but Morison J held that the compliance with it would constitute a condition precedent to the insurer's liability. See *British Credit* [2003] EWHC 2404 (Comm), [23].
101 *London Guarantie Co v Fearnley* (1880) 5 App Cas 911.
102 See, e.g., Clause 11(viii) of the policy in *Merrill Lynch* [2007] EWHC 893 (Comm), [62].
103 [2000] 1 All ER (Comm) 708.

together with a termination clause. The policy provided that the assured should make monthly declarations of goods despatched and, if there were no goods to be despatched in a certain month, a nil declaration had to be submitted. Clause 13 of the policy provided that:

> Observance of stipulations
>
> (1) Due payment of all premiums (and other charges) specified in Schedule 1, and the due performance and observation of every stipulation in the policy or the proposal, shall be conditions precedent to any liability on our part.
> (2) In the event of any breach of any condition precedent we also have the right to retain any premium paid and give written notice terminating the policy and all liability under it.

The policy covered 14 months ending in August 1998. During the currency of the policy, the ECA had paid the assured the first claim. In May 1998, the assured failed to make a nil declaration and did not pay the respective monthly premium. In the meantime, some buyers defaulted, and the assured made the second claim concerning goods despatched between the first claim and May 1998. Clause 3 of the policy provided that the amount of loss should be ascertained after a waiting period of six months after the original due date of payments. The ECA purported to terminate the policy, contending that it was not liable for all its liability and was entitled to recover the payment of the first claim.

The trial court first confirmed that the conditions in dispute were conditions precedent to liability. The court then divided the ECA's liabilities in the present case into three categories: (a) previous liability, which was the ECA's payment for the first claim; (b) contingent liability, which referred to the second claim which was "still to crystallise" because the waiting period after non-payment had not expired as at the date of termination; and (c) future liability, namely the ECA's further liability to the loss occurring after the assured's breach. Toulson J read Clause 13 separately. He held that Clause 13(1), which relates to conditions precedent, only had the effect of suspending the ECA's liability in respect of those claims in relation to which the assured had breached the conditions precedent. Therefore, he rejected the ECA's submission that its payment in relation to its previous liability should be recovered. However, he held that Clause 13(2), which related to termination, entitled the ECA to be discharged of its contingent and future liabilities.[104]

The reasoning in the trial judgment was upheld by the Court of Appeal, who confirmed that under Clause 13(1), due payment of premium and performance were conditions precedent to liability only in respect of the risk for which the premium was payable or to which the stipulations referred, and that under Clause

104 *Kazakstan Wool* [1999] 2 All ER (Comm) 445.

13(2), the right to terminate the policy did not include claims which had been paid but did include contingent and future liabilities.[105]

It should be noted that although the assured lost the case, it did not lose because it breached conditions precedent under Clause 13(1). It failed on the further ground of termination under Clause 13(2),[106] in the absence of which the insurer would still be liable to the assured's second claim. The court in *Kazakstan Wool* construed conditions precedent to liability in a narrow way, insisting that the insurer should only be allowed to reject a claim tainted by the assured's breach of the condition precedent related to that particular claim. In the court's opinion, the assured's failure to make a nil declaration of goods despatched and the monthly payment of premium in May 1998 was irrelevant to its second claim regarding the loss occurring before May 1998. Therefore, the ECA should not be discharged of the liability to pay the second claim merely because of the assured's breach of that condition precedent. As is well elaborated by the commentator, *Kazakstan Wool* is an informative case authority which indicates that:[107]

> Where the insurer is given a contractual right to terminate (e.g., upon any breach by the insured), the effect of termination will depend upon the contract terms. One would generally expect that termination would prevent liability arising for losses occurring after the date of termination, and that it would not affect liabilities which had already been settled. The position with regard to contingent losses (e.g., where a waiting period after non-payment of a debt has not expired as at the date of termination) is more difficult. Appropriately drafted terms can relieve the insurer of liability for such losses upon termination.

The court's interpretation of conditions precedent in *Kazakstan Wool* was confirmed later in *Aspen Insurance UK Ltd v Pectel Ltd*,[108] a liability insurance case where Clause 4(a) of the policy provided that the assured should give the insurer an immediate written notice of probable loss and Clause 13 provided that the cover was conditional on "the assured paying premiums and observing the terms and conditions of this insurance". The assured breached Clause 4(a). The court held that whilst the breach of payment of premiums may discharge any of the insurer's liabilities, failure to observe other terms and conditions can only enable the insurer to reject the tainted claim. Teare J reiterated that there had to be a

105 Waller LJ delivered dissenting opinions, arguing that the right to terminate only affected future liabilities, which would arise if the policy was continued and not contingent liabilities, which was already in existence under the policy. Waller LJ further pointed out that if a breach of any stipulation would entitle the ECA to be released from every liability past, present and future, the condition precedent would "seem to have a limited role to play". See *Kazakstan Wool* [2000] 1 All ER (Comm) 708.

106 Merkin (n 11), [8-019].

107 Birds and others (n 34), [33-025].

108 [2008] EWHC 2804 (Comm), [2009] Lloyd's Rep IR 440.

"conditional link" between the assured's obligation to give notice and the underwriters' obligation to pay the claim, a decision consistent with that in *Kazakstan Wool*.

It should be noted that the result of *Kazakstan Wool* would remain intact should it be judged under the new regime of the IA 2015, because the new law only regulates terms which are not risk-defining and which would tend to reduce the risk of losses of a particular kind, location and time. The condition precedent in question in *Kazakstan Wool*, namely the declaration requirement, did not relate to the risks at all, so it would stay entirely unaffected. The influence of the IA 2015 on ECI policies will be further discussed in the next sections below.

ECI conditions after the IA 2015: risk-defining or risk-mitigating?

In a questionnaire survey distributed by the Berne Union to its members in 2016, a question was asked about the potential influences of the IA 2015 on the members' policy wording.[109] The respondents to that survey, whose ECI policies are governed by English law (including the UKEF), all believed that their policies should be subject to the IA 2015 if the policy was issued after 12 August 2016, the date when the IA 2015 came into force. They further indicated that they either had amended their wording according to the changes in the IA 2015 or were in the process of doing so.[110] However, their focus was heavily on the duty of fair presentation. The changes, reflected in ss 10 and 11 of the Act, were seldom mentioned in their responses. Although at the very least the abovementioned survey showed that the Berne Union members regarded their ECI policies as insurance contracts, whether their amended wording can operate well under the new law is still to be tested. The paragraphs below will take the UKEF's "Export Insurance Policy" as an example to scrutinise that issue.

Clause 6 of the "Export Insurance Policy": is it a condition precedent to liability?

Clause 6 "Conditions of Cover" of the "Export Insurance Policy" provides that:[111]

> 6.1 Unless and to the extent that UKEF otherwise expressly agrees in writing, if, at any stage, the Insured:
>
> (a) departs from the terms of the Contract or agrees to or acquiesces in any variation of them or any departure from them by the Buyer in relation to (i) the identity of the buyer, (ii) the Buyer's country, (iii) the

109 Cheng Lin, "Berne Union Academic Survey: The Legal Nature of Buyer Credit Insurance and Buyer Credit Guarantee", *The BUlletin (The Official Newsletter of the Berne Union)*, January 2020, 26 <https://www.berneunion.org/Articles/Details/489/January-BUlletin-Mega-Trends-and-Trade> accessed 1 February 2022.

110 Ibid.

111 See n 8 above.

destination of the goods, (iv) the Terms of Payment, (v) the Purchase Price, (vi) a reduction in the proportion of UK content to below 20%, or (vii) the identity of any agent, unless that variation or departure would be a Permitted Variation;

(b) materially departs from the terms of the Contract or agrees to or acquiesces in any variation of them or any departure from them by the Buyer in relation to the nature of the Goods and/or Services;

(c) assigns, mortgages, charges, pledges or otherwise disposes of this Policy or any rights arising under it or the benefit of it;

(d) uses the name of Her Majesty's Government or UKEF or the insurance provided under this Policy directly in connection with the raising of funds from the capital markets …; or

(e) fails promptly to provide UKEF with any information, in writing, that UKEF may request from time to time regarding the progress and performance of the Contract, then UKEF shall have no liability under this Policy.

6.2 If, at any stage, without UKEF's express approval in writing, the Insured:

(a) materially departs from the terms of the Contract or agrees to or acquiesces in any material variation of them or any material departure from them by the Buyer in a way that falls outside Clause 6.1(a) or 6.1(b) above, unless that variation or departure would be a Permitted Variation;

(b) materially fails to comply with the terms of any component of the Contract Suite[112] …;

(c) waives or releases, or fails to take all necessary actions to preserve the legal enforceability of, its rights under any component of the Contract Suite;

(d) fails to take all necessary actions to preserve the legal enforceability of any security for the performance of the Buyer's obligations, or does something which prejudices its rights against any surety for payment; or

(e) assigns, mortgages, charges or pledges or otherwise disposes of all or part of the Contract Suite or any of its rights or interests thereunder, including its right to recover in respect of loss,

then UKEF shall not be liable under this Policy in respect of a loss unless the Insured can show that the act or omission in question could not have increased the risk of that loss taking place.

It is submitted that the conditions stated in Clause 6 above should be classified as conditions precedent to the UKEF's liabilities. Although express wording such as

112 Under Clause 1.1 of the "Export Insurance Policy", "Contract Suite" means the Contract itself and all agreements, financial instruments (including, without limitation, any letter of credit or bill of exchange), undertakings, consents, authorisations or other documents relating to the Contract or issued in connection with any payments made or to be made under it. See ibid.

"conditions precedent" and "the insurer will not be liable to pay any claim" are not used in Clause 6, the phrase "the UKEF shall have no liability/shall not be liable under this Policy" can achieve the same effect. The remedies for the assured's breach of the obligations under Clause 6 are that the UKEF can reject potential claims under the policy. Clause 6 is neither a condition precedent to the validity of the policy nor a condition precedent to the attachment of the risk because the UKEF here clearly treats the contract as having been concluded and the risk as having been attached. It is not a bare condition, either, since the remedy of non-liability is attached to the clause. Therefore, the wording of Clause 6 indicates that they are conditions precedent to the UKEF's liabilities.

How to determine whether a term is risk-defining or risk-mitigating?

Even if the provisions of Clause 6 are not conditions precedent to liability, that no longer matters under the IA 2015 which reclassified insurance policy terms by moving from form to functionality.[113] Before the IA 2015, the common law laid great emphasis on the legal classification of insurance terms. Where a term was drafted as a "condition precedent" to the insurer's liability (and the court confirmed the insurer's terminology), then if that term was breached by the assured and loss occurred, the insurer was not liable even if the breach is trivial and irrelevant to the loss in question.[114] That was, obviously, disproportionately severe to the assured. The IA 2015 discards the technical categorisation and changes the rule. Section 11 of the IA 2015 stipulates that if a term does not define the risk as a whole and if compliance with that term would tend to reduce the risk of the loss of a particular kind, location or time, then where the assured breaches that term, the insurer would be still liable if the assured can prove that the non-compliance of the term could not have increased the risk of loss which actually occurred in the circumstances in which it occurred.

Therefore, what now matters under the new regime is whether a term defines the risk as a whole (risk-defining) or whether it tends to reduce the risk of a particular loss (risk-mitigating). If a term defines the risk as a whole, then s 11 is not applicable at all. The function of such a term is to "assist risk assessment" generally from the outset of the contract.[115] Therefore, if such a term is broken, the insurer will not be liable regardless of the relationship between the breach and the loss. The IA 2015 does not define the meaning of a term that defines the risk as a whole. However, the Law Commissions has provided some guidance, indicating that such term will "have a general limiting effect … not linked to a specific risk sector".[116] The Law Commissions added that such term would tend to "affect

113 Merkin & Gürses (n 3) 449.

114 Baris Soyer, "Risk Control Clauses in Insurance Law: Law Reform and the Future" [2016] 75 CLJ 109, 110.

115 Ibid, 117.

116 Law Com. No. 353, *Insurance Contract Law: Business Disclosure; Warranties; Insurers' Remedies for Fraudulent Claims; and Late Payment*, [18.35].

either the whole risk or a significant part of the risk", thereby being of a general as opposed to specific importance.[117] It is widely acknowledged that whether a term is risk-defining should be determined on a case-by-case basis, and there is no obvious solution other than "judicial good sense".[118]

It is further suggested by the commentators that some criteria can help determine whether a term defines the risk as a whole.[119] Firstly, risk definition terms express the object of the policy. If it is "absolutely clear" that the insurer would not have agreed to underwrite any other circumstances than those outlined by the clause, then that clause is risk-defining. If a clause relates to some evident aspect of the risk, without which the risk could potentially increase, then that clause is a risk-mitigating term which is subject to s 11(3) of the IA 2015. The difference between those two types of terms is that "whilst the former is concerned with the performance of the contract, the latter deals with one of the characteristics that are collateral to the object of the contract".[120] Secondly, risk definition terms are the main terms rather than ancillary terms, as they qualify the subject matter insured and constitute an essential part of the risk identified. A helpful analogy can be found in the Court of Justice of EU's interpretation of s 64 of the Consumer Right Act 2015 of the UK, which provides that a term of a consumer contract may not be assessed for fairness if it specifies the main subject matter of the contract, subject to the transparency and prominence requirement. The EU court held that "a term that defines the very essence of the contractual relationship, which sets out the essential obligations of the contract characterising it, falls within the notion of the 'main subject matter of the contract'".[121] Thirdly, risk definition terms are restrictions or limitations inherent in the risk. The insurer might sidestep s 11 by artificially drafting a clause as "risk definition" rather than "exclusion",[122] but cases from Australia and New Zealand have shown that for a term to be risk-defining, it should contain inherent restrictions on the nature of risks that are intended to be accepted, paid for and covered, rather than mere exclusions.[123]

Is Clause 6 subject to s 11 of the IA 2015?

Whilst the judicial determination of risk definition terms in English law remains to be observed, the abovementioned guidance is helpful for this chapter's discussion of Clause 6 of the "Export Insurance Policy". The UKEF has drafted Clause 6 in two parts. Clause 6.1 relates to the assured exporter's obligations under the "Contract", i.e., the underlying export contract; and Clause 6.2 relates

117 Stakeholder Note: Terms Not Relevant to the Actual Loss reproduced in H.L. Paper 81, 47.

118 Merkin & Gürses (n 3) 455.

119 Gürses (n 4), 191–201.

120 Ibid.

121 *Kasler v OTP Jelzalogbank Zrt* (C-26/13) [2014] 2 All ER (Comm) 443.

122 Rob Merkin & Özlem Gürses, "The Insurance Act 2015: Rebalancing the Interests of Insurer and Assured" [2015] 78 (6) MLR 1004, 1014.

123 Merkin & Gürses (n 3) 456.

to its obligations under the "Contract Suite", i.e., the surrounding documents of the export contract such as financial instruments (e.g., letter of credit or bill of exchange). Clearly, the UKEF regards Clause 6.1 as entirely risk-defining and Clause 6.2 as entirely risk-mitigating, because it stipulates that under Clause 6.1 it will not be liable whether the assured's breach is relevant to the loss or not, whilst under Clause 6.2 it will not be liable unless the assured can show that his breach could not have increased the risk of the loss in question. Clause 6 shows that the UKEF has taken account of s 11 of the IA 2015, but does it reflect a thorough understanding of s 11? Is the entire term in Clause 6.1 risk-defining, and does Clause 6.2 relate to risks of particular loss? Can Clause 6 fully operate under s 11? Is the UKEF entitled to deny liabilities by relying on Clause 6 under the new law? A closer investigation into Clause 6 is needed before answering these questions.

Clause 6.1 imposes several obligations on the assured. It can be said that Clause 6.1(a) and (b) are indeed terms that define the risk as a whole, as they describe every essential item of information about the underlying transaction. These terms, clearly, have a general limiting effect on the risk the UKEF insures as a whole rather than a specific risk sector. Breach of these terms will render the UKEF's general risk assessment in tatters.[124] Therefore, Clause 6.1(a) and (b) fall outside the scope of s 11, and the UKEF can reject the claims should the exporter breach them. However, Clause 6.1(c)–(e) can hardly be said to be risk-defining. All requirements under Clause 6.1(c) concern the specific risk that the exporter's rights under the policy might be affected by the exporter's certain legal behaviour to dispose of the rights. Therefore, Clause 6.1(c) relates to the risk of the loss of a particular kind, that is, the loss as a result of the exporter's arbitrary disposal of its legal rights under the export contract. Clause 6.1(d) relates to the export's undertaking not to engage in the capital market, and this would also tend to reduce the risk of the loss of a particular kind. Clause 6.1(e) relates to the exporter's obligation to provide information, which is not related to risk at all, and the IA 2015 does not touch upon non-risk clauses. Therefore, Clause 6.1(c) and (d) should at least arguably be subject to s 11, and the exporter's breach cannot entitle the UKEF to deny liability without questioning the relation between the breach and the loss under s 11(3). It is thus very doubtable whether Clause 6.1(c) and (d) are in compliance with s 11 of the IA 2015.

Clause 6.2 also includes different types of terms. It is submitted that Clause 6.2(a) and (b) are also risk-defining. These two provisions prevent the assured from "materially departing" from them, which indicates that they describe an essential part of the risk that the UKEF has agreed to cover. However, Clause 6.2(c)–(e) are terms related to the risk of loss of particular kinds. Where the exporter breaches the obligations under Clause 6.2(c)–(e), as stipulated in Clause 6.2, the examination under s 11(3) of the IA 2015 should be carried out. Since the IA 2015 does not prevent the insurer from including a more favourable clause for the assured,

124 Soyer (n 114) 119.

breach of the obligations under Clause 6.2(a) and (b) can also be subject to such examination. Therefore, Clause 6.2 is entirely in compliance with s 11.

However, an insured-friendlier clause as seen in Clause 6.2(a) and (b) might not be the real purpose of the draftsman of the "Export Insurance Policy". It is submitted that Clause 6 can be drafted in a better way that can clearly reflect the objectives of the UKEF: The first part of Clause 6 should include terms that are now stipulated in Clause 6.1(a) and (b) as well as Clause 6.2(a) and (b). As they are risk-defining terms, it is perfectly fine for the UKEF to stipulate that it will be not liable without any test on the relationship between the breach and the loss. The second part, on the other hand, should include the rest of the terms in Clause 6.1 and 6.2, which related to the risk of particular times. If the assured breaches those terms, whether the UKEF is liable or not will depend on the examination of the relationship between the breach and the loss. Besides, the UKEF can use specific statements in the policy wordings to indicate how key terms should all fall to be treated under the IA 2015. For instance, they can expressly state which terms are to be considered as s 11 terms of the Act. Such expression is not conclusive because whether a term is risk-defining should be determined by the court, but it will be helpful to the court in doing so. Some private credit insurers in the ECI industry have already drafted such wordings in order to provide greater clarity to the parties and the court.[125] Moreover, the UKEF can contract out of s 11 by meeting the transparency requirement under the Act, which will be discussed in the following sections of this chapter.

The paragraphs above show that although Clause 6 is not very well-drafted, and there is no doubt that the drafting of Clause 6 is clearly influenced by the changes brought about by s 11 of the IA 2015. When drafting the "Export Insurance Policy", the UKEF regarded it as a contract of insurance and tried to make its stipulations compliant with the new law, despite some infelicities in drafting.

ECI warranties after the IA 2015

Clause 11 of the "Export Insurance Policy"

In the context of insurance law, a warranty means a promise by which "the assured undertakes that some particular thing shall or shall not be done, or that some condition shall be fulfilled, or whereby he affirms or negatives the existence of a particular state of facts".[126] Warranties used to be "the most draconian class of term"[127] in insurance law before the IA 2015 because under common law (and as codified by the MIA 1906) breach of warranty would enable the insurer to be discharged from its liability automatically, even if the breach is remedied before any loss arises and even if the breach has no casual connection

125 Blenkinsopp (n 7) 78–9.
126 The MIA 1906, s 33(1).
127 Merkin & Gürses (n 122) 1011.

with the loss.[128] The IA 2015 removed these harsh features to a very great extent. Section 10(2) of the IA 2015 provides that the risk is only suspended (instead of being automatically terminated) until the breach is remedied. Section 11(3) provides that there should be a link between the breach and the loss if the warranty tends to reduce the risk of the loss of a particular kind, location and time.[129] There were very few disputes on warranties in English ECI cases before the IA 2015,[130] and at the time of this work being written, warranties under the IA 2015 have not been tested by the court yet. Therefore, the following paragraphs will focus on the warranty stipulated in the UKEF's "Export Insurance Policy", which should be read subject to the IA 2015.

In non-marine insurance, warranties can be express only.[131] A warranty can be created by the use of the word "warranty" or "it is warranted that" in connection with a particular term.[132] The "Export Insurance Policy" follows this wording and stipulates a warranty related to the exporter's anti-corruption undertaking in Clause 11.2:[133]

> The Insured represents and warrants that it has not:
>
> a) engaged in, authorised or consented to any Corrupt Activity in relation to the Contract or any Related Agreement;
> b) failed to report to the relevant authorities any Corrupt Activity in relation to the Contract or any Related Agreement of which it has become aware.

The UKEF then stipulates the consequences of the exporter's breach of the anti-corruption warranty in Clause 11.4:[134]

> Then UKEF shall be discharged from any liability under this Policy and may cancel this Policy with effect from its commencement and in either event (i) UKEF shall be entitled to retain all premium which it may have received and

128 The MIA 1906, ss 33–4.

129 S 11(4) of the IA 2015 provides that s 11 can be applied in addition to s 10, which means warranties should also be read subject to s 11.

130 The only relevant English ECI case in the pre-IA 2015 era is *International Management Group (UK) Ltd v Simmonds* [2003] EWHC 177 (Comm), [2004] Llyod's Rep IR 247, in which the policy contained a warranty that the assured "shall ensure that all necessary licences, visas and permits are obtained within sufficient time prior to the Insured Event". The assured failed to do so and subsequently suffered losses. The court simply held that a warranty had to be "strictly complied with" and the assured's breach entitled the ECA to be discharged from liability. It should be noted that the ECA in that case rejected the claim relying not only on the assured's breach of warranty but also on its breach of the condition precedent and duty of disclosure. All those submissions were accepted by the court. The details of *International Management Group* are discussed in Chapters 2 and 4 of this book.

131 *Euro-Diam Ltd v Bathurst* [1988] 2 All ER 23.

132 Merkin (n 11), [8-053].

133 See n 8 above.

134 Ibid.

(ii) the Insured shall on demand repay to UKEF all sums which UKEF may have paid to the Insured under this Policy.

It is clear that the UKEF in Clause 11 stipulates a more severe outcome of the assured's breach of its anti-corruption warranty, which is different to s 10 of the IA 2015. Instead of the suspension of cover, the UKEF provides that the assured's breach will result in full discharge of its liability under the policy and, furthermore, the cancellation of the entire policy at the UKEF's option. Whether Clause 11 can operate under the IA 2015 in this way should be examined step by step by answering the following questions: (1) Does it define the risk as a whole, does it tend to reduce the risk of any loss, or is it unrelated to risk at all? (2) Is the breach of the anti-corruption warranty remediable? (3) Has the UKEF fulfilled the transparency requirement under the IA 2015 when contracting out?

Does Clause 11 conflict with ss 10 and 11 of the IA 2015?

It is submitted that Clause 11 should be read subject to ss 10 and 11 as well as ss 16 and 17 of the IA 2015. To begin with, s 10 should apply to Clause 11. Section 10(2) provides that the insurer has no liability under a contract of insurance in respect of any loss occurring, or attributable to something happening, after the breach of warranty but before the breach has been remedied. However, this suspensory rule is not reflected in Clause 11 at all. Perhaps one justification is that the UKEF believes that once the assured breaches the anti-corruption warranty, the breach is not remediable. It is true that some warranties, due to their nature, cannot be remedied because the breach may continue to have an adverse impact on the risk even though the breach is remedied. In other words, it is sometimes impossible to bring the risk back to the level with which the insurer was content.[135] The UKEF further stipulate the optional right of cancellation as the consequence of the assured's breach of the anti-corruption warranty. Therefore, the wording of Clause 11 *prima facie* does not conflict with s 10 of the Act.

Meanwhile, Clause 11 is not compliant with s 11 of the IA 2015. It seems that Clause 11 does not define the risk as a whole but does tend to reduce the risk of the loss of a particular kind, which is loss caused by corruption activities. Clause 11 does not describe or limit the overarching object of the policy; neither does it constitute an essential part of the scope of the risk. The risks insured by the "Export Insurance Policy" are certain commercial risks (i.e., the non-payment by or insolvency of the buyer) and political risks (e.g., war, civil disturbance, expropriation and nationalisation). Clause 11 does not define the essential scope of any commercial or political risks at all. On the contrary, Clause 11 tends to reduce the risk of loss of a particular kind, i.e., the loss caused by the assured's corruption activities. Indeed, corruption is very harmful to export transactions because it "distorts the normal trade patterns" and gives the exporter unfair advantages

135 Soyer (n 114) 113.

in doing business.[136] International regulations such as art 12 of the OECD Convention on Combating Bribery of Foreign Public Officials in International Business Transactions require ECAs to comply with relevant procedures to combat bribery and corruption.[137] In particular, the UKEF bears the obligation to (a) conduct anti-bribery due diligence procedures in arranging ECI and (b) report all suspicious bribery circumstances to the Serious Fraud Office (SFO) of the UK.[138] Therefore, if the assured is found to be engaged in corruption activities, the export contract might be rendered illegal and unenforceable, thereby causing loss to the assured. However, Clause 11 tends to reduce the risk of such loss only: it should be read subject to s 11(3) of the IA 2015, but it does not include any stipulation on the test of the link between the breach and the loss. Therefore, it is submitted that the wording of Clause 11 conflicts with s 11(3).

Did the UKEF intend to contract out of ss 10 and 11 of the IA 2015?

It thus can be seen that the UKEF's stipulations on the consequences of the assured's breach of Clause 11 seem to conflict with the outcomes set by ss 10 and 11 of the IA 2015. Did the UKEF wish to contract out of ss 10 and 11, and can Clause 11 have that effect? Under the IA 2015, if an insurer wishes to contract out of the new law,[139] transparency requirements must be met. Section 16(2) provides that any term of a non-consumer insurance contract which would put the insured in a worse position than he would be in under the provisions of the IA 2015 is of no effect unless the transparency requirements have been satisfied.[140] According to s 17, the transparency requirements include two limbs: (1) the insurer must take sufficient steps to draw the disadvantageous term to the insured's attention before the contract is concluded; (2) the disadvantageous term must be clear and unambiguous as to its effect.[141] Section 17(4) further provides that in determining whether the transparency requirements are met or not, the characteristics of insured persons of the kind in question and the circumstances of the transaction should be considered. It should therefore be questioned whether the UKEF has satisfied the transparency requirements when contracting out.

136 Anders Grath, *The Handbook of International Trade and Finance* (Kogan Page 2008) 21.

137 See also arts V and IX of the OECD Recommendation of the Council on Bribery and Officially Supported Export Credits.

138 For instance, in *Director of the Serious Fraud Office v Airbus SE* [2020] 1 WLUK 435, when arranging an ECI cover for Airbus, the UKEF detected bribes paid by third parties hired by Airbus in order to secure aircraft orders. The UKEF duly reported that to the SFO and accordingly, Airbus had fully cooperated with the criminal investigation, completely changed its management and compliance structures and agreed to pay a disgorgement of profits, a financial penalty, and the SFO's costs. The court thus approved a deferred prosecution agreement entered into between the Serious Fraud Office and Airbus.

139 The IA 2015 does not permit contracting out of s 9 which abolishes the basis of the contract clauses in business insurance.

140 The IA 2015, s 16(2).

141 Ibid, s 17(2)–(3).

On the one hand, Clause 11.4 is clearly a "disadvantageous term" as it would put the insured in a worse position according to the definition of "disadvantageous term" in s 17(1) of the IA 2015. It can be said that Clause 11.4 itself is clear and unambiguous; on the other hand, has the UKEF taken sufficient steps to draw Clause 11.4 to the assured's intention before concluding the contract? It is suggested by both the Law Commissions and the commentators that whether the assured is a big corporate entity assisted by in-house lawyers and brokers or a small-sized business with limited experience, it would normally be necessary for the insurer to stipulate (a) that certain sections of the Act are not applicable; and (b) the legal effects and consequences for displacing these sections.[142] The UKEF in Clause 11.4 does not stipulate that ss 10 and 11 of the IA 2015 are discarded. There is no evidence that the assured's attention has been drawn to them before the policy is concluded. Therefore, it is submitted that when drafting Clause 11.4, the UKEF does not meet the transparency requirements the IA 2015 provided on contracting out.

The paragraphs above demonstrate that although the UKEF seems to have taken into account s 11 of the IA 2015 in drafting Clause 6, it has failed to draft Clause 11 as required by the new law. One sentence would have sufficed to achieve contracting out of the IA 2015 – if that was what the UKEF desired to do: "Sections 10 and 11 of the IA 2015 do not apply to this policy".

An example of an anonymous Berne Union member's policy that is compliant with the IA 2015

The discussion above focuses on the UKEF's ECI policy wording before and after the IA 2015. It seems that the UKEF has not made sufficiently thorough revisions according to the changes in the new law. In the meantime, this research has discovered that in the international industry, there has been an anonymous Berne Union member's ECI policy which is highly compliant with the IA 2015. The applicable law of that policy is English law, and the policy wording has been thoroughly amended to comply with the changes in the IA 2015. It is therefore worthwhile to analyse that policy in the following paragraphs.

The policy includes three parts where the IA 2015 is expressly mentioned to be applied or to be contracted out of. Firstly, Clause 20 "Duty of Fair Presentation" provides that the assured should comply with s 3 of the IA 2015, while the parties agree that s 4 of the IA 2015 shall not apply. Clause 20 also states that s 8 and Sch 1 of the IA 2015 shall apply. Secondly, Clause 21 "Observance of Stipulations" provides that s 11 of the IA 2015 shall not apply. Thirdly, Clause 22 "Fraud" provides that s 12 of the IA 2015 shall not apply. Clause 20 and 22 will be further discussed in Chapters 4 and 5 of this research, respectively, whereas the focus here is Clause 21.

142 See n 116 above, [29.50]. See also Soyer (n 114) 119.

Clause 21 provides that:

(1) Payment of all premiums in full at the time We require and the due performance and observance of every stipulation that is within Your direct control in the Policy shall be a condition precedent to any liability on our part.
(2) If You fail to comply with any of the conditions of this Policy, such failure will not be deemed to have been excused or accepted by Us unless We say so in writing.
(3) Section 11 of the Insurance Act 2015 shall not apply to Clause 21(1). If You do not undertake the due performance and observance of every stipulation in the Policy, We may rely on such non-compliance to exclude, limit or discharge Our liability, in accordance with the wording of Clause 21(1), even if Your non-compliance could not have increased the risk of the loss which actually occurred in the circumstances in which it occurred.

It is submitted that Clause 21 (3) is an excellent example of "contracting out" which satisfies the transparency requirement under s 17 of the IA 2015. It first expressly provides that s 11 of the IA 2015 shall not apply. Then, it further indicates that the insurer may rely on the assured's non-compliance to exclude, limit or discharge its liability. Moreover, it stipulates that the insurer is entitled to do so even if the non-compliance could not have increased the risk of the loss in question. Therefore, Clause 21 (3) is sufficiently clear and unambiguous. It is of course a disadvantageous term under s 17 of the Act, but as long as the insurer takes sufficient steps to draw such a clause into the assured's attention, the transparency requirement under s 17 will be perfectly satisfied.

The discussion of the abovementioned policy wordings that are compliant with the IA 2015 supports the argument of this chapter that ECAs, inclusive but not limited to the UKEF, regard ECI as contracts of insurance and accept that principles of insurance law should apply to ECI policies. The anonymous Berne Union member's policy is a very typical example. Choosing English law as the applicable law, that member regarded its ECI policy as insurance and made thorough amendments of its wordings to comply with the changes of the IA 2015.

Alteration of the ECI policy

Where the ECI policy is issued on a subscription basis at Lloyd's, any alteration should be made subject to London Market Group's General Underwriters Agreement (GUA) Political Risk Schedule 2006.[143]

Summary: the legal nature of ECI reflected by its terms and conditions

This research submits that the terms and conditions in ECI reflect its legal nature as insurance. The reasons are given below.

143 For details, see Chapter 2 of this work.

Firstly, under the insuring clause, the ECA is undertaking an "insurance obligation" as defined by case law and the English regulatory guidance. The English court in *Prudential v Commissioners of Inland Revenue*[144] described insurance as a contract whereby one party (the insurer) promises in return for a money consideration (the premium) to pay to the other party (the assured) a sum of money or to provide him with a corresponding benefit upon the occurrence of one or more specified events.[145] Detailed guidance on the definition of insurance is provided by the Financial Conduct Authority (FCA)'s *Perimeter Guidance*, which follows the descriptions of insurance in *Prudential*. In the view of the FCA, insurance is a contract under which the "provider" undertakes (1) in consideration of one or more payments; (2) to pay money or provide a corresponding benefit (including in some cases services to be paid for by the provider) to a "recipient"; (3) in response to a defined event the occurrence of which is uncertain (either as to when it will occur or as to whether it will occur at all) and adverse to the interests of the recipient.[146] Those three elements constitute an "insurance obligation", and the FCA is likely to treat a contract as insurance if that contract contains "an identifiable and distinct obligation that is, in substance, an 'insurance obligation'".[147] The insuring clause in the ECI policy exactly imposes such an "insurance obligation" on the ECA: it will, in return for the premium, pay the money to the exporter should it suffer from a loss as a result of an uncertain commercial or political event. By doing so, the ECA fulfils its "insurance obligation".

Secondly, the indemnity clause, together with the maximum liability clause, the insured percentage clause and the credit limit clause, further indicate that ECI is a contract of indemnity and, particularly, a contract of indemnity insurance. As a legal dictum says, "indemnity is the controlling principle in insurance law".[148] Apart from contingency insurance such as life and accident insurance, most types of insurance are indemnity insurance.[149] The court in *Gould v Curtis*[150] drew a distinction between contingency insurance and indemnity insurance: in the former class, a loss is not required, and the insurer will pay a fixed sum of money on the happening of a particular event, whether or not that event is adverse to the assured; in the latter class, the loss is an essential element, and the assured's recovery is quantified by reference to the amount of his loss.[151] That said, a contract of indemnity insurance is a contract whereby the insurer undertakes to indemnify the

144 [1904] 2 KB 658.

145 Birds and others (n 34), [1-001].

146 FCA, *The Perimeter Guidance Manual, Chapter 6: Guidance on the Identification of Contracts of Insurance*, [6.3.4] <https://www.handbook.fca.org.uk/handbook/PERG/6/?view=chapter> accessed 1 February 2022.

147 Ibid, [6.6.7(1)].

148 *Castellain v Preston* (1883) 11 QBD 380, 386 (Brett LJ).

149 Robert Merkin, *Colinvaux and Merkin's Insurance Contract Law* (Sweet & Maxwell 2021) [A-0004].

150 [1913] 3 KB 84, 95.

151 Merkin (n 11), [1-040].

assured, in the manner and to the extent thereby agreed, against losses.[152] The principle of indemnity always operates with a maximum liability clause and an insured percentage clause which limit the insurer's liability to the loss.[153] In the context of ECI, the credit limit clause helps the operation of the indemnity clause by stipulating the comprehensive limit of indemnity or the limit of indemnity to the loss caused by a specified buyer. Those clauses together show that under ECI, the ECA will indemnify the exporter for the loss by paying an agreed amount of money.

Thirdly, ECI shares many common terms with other types of insurance. As the FCA suggests, a contract is more likely to be regarded as a contract of insurance "if the contract is described as insurance and contains terms that are consistent with its classification as a contract of insurance".[154] ECI satisfies that criterion. An ECI policy is normally described as "insurance" and, in addition to the insuring clause and indemnity clause discussed above, it always includes some exclusions and conditions precedent and warranties. All those terms are common in other types of insurance, which indicates that ECI is one among the various types of insurance contracts.

Lastly, from a practical view, ECAs and private credit insurers regard their ECI policies as contracts of insurance and assume that their policies are subject to the principles of insurance law. In England, the UKEF clearly states that its "Export Insurance Policy" is to be read subject to the IA 2015, and Clause 6 of the "Export Insurance Policy" reflects the UKEF's effort in amending its policy wording in compliance with the new provisions in s 11 of the Act. Although there is much to be improved in the drafting of the UKEF's policy, it is doubtless that the UKEF regarded its policy as insurance. A more straightforward example can be found in the anonymous Berne Union member's policy, of which the wordings have been amended to comply with the IA 2015. That policy provides the perfect wordings to "contract out" under the transparency requirement of the Act, which, again, supports the argument of this research that ECAs regard ECI as contracts of insurance to which insurance law should apply.

Terms and conditions of ECGs

Whilst an ECI policy is a bilateral contract between the ECA and the assured, an ECG normally involves a tripartite transaction between the ECA, the bank and the exporter. In addition to the ECG contract concluded by the ECA and the bank (hereinafter referred to as "the ECG contract"), there is always a separate contract, which often takes the form of a list of general terms and conditions between the ECA and the exporter (hereinafter referred to as "the ECA-exporter contract"). Therefore, an ECG arrangement normally consists of two parts: the ECG contract and the ECA-exporter contract. The following paragraphs aim to show that (1) the

152 The MIA 1906, s 1. See also Merkin (n 149), [A-0003].

153 Ibid, [A-0009].

154 FCA (n 146), [6.6.8.(3)].

ECG contract is a contract of guarantee, whilst the ECA-exporter contract is not a contract of guarantee but one to which general rules of contract law should apply; and (2) the bank is under no substantial obligations under an ECG, whereas the main obligations under an ECG are imposed on the exporter.

For most types of the UKEF's ECG products, samples of the ECG contract and the ECA-exporter contract are not available online. The only product that contains sufficient information and materials for this research is the "Supplier Credit Finance Facility", a supplier credit guarantee product explained in Chapter 2. It can be learned from the UKEF's website[155] that under the "Supplier Credit Finance Facility" scheme, the UKEF grants the bank a "Certificate of Approval" as a document setting out the basic terms of the UKEF's support to the bank. A sample of the "Certificate of Approval" is not available online. It is not clear whether the UKEF signs an ECG contract with the bank. In the meantime, the UKEF prepares a detailed ECA-exporter contract named "Supplier Credit Finance Facility – Standard Terms and Conditions" for the exporter (hereinafter referred to as "the SCFF contract"), which is available online[156] and will be the focus of the following discussion.

It should also be noted that there are only three reported English ECG cases, namely *Credit Lyonnais Bank Nederland NV (now Generale Bank Nederland NV) v Export Credits Guarantee Department*,[157] *Crown Aluminium Ltd v Northern and Western Insurance Co Ltd*[158] and *Export Credits Guarantee Department v Universal Oil Products Co*.[159] Despite these difficulties, this research tries to extract as much useful information as it can from the very limited materials about ECGs in the context of English law. It will also take account of relevant information collected from the Berne Union Academic Survey.

The ECG Contract

The guarantee clause: general

"A guarantee is a binding promise of one person to be answerable for a debt of another if that other defaults".[160] An ECG contract is one type of contract of guarantee. Under an ECG contract, the ECA does not indemnify the bank against its loss as a result of a series of commercial and political events as it does under ECI. Instead, the ECA simply guarantees the bank against the failure of the buyer to pay his debt. This fundamental difference is well demonstrated by a sample guarantee clause provided by an anonymous Berne Union member:

155 See <https://www.gov.uk/guidance/supplier-credit-financing-facility> accessed 1 February 2022.

156 See <https://assets.publishing.service.gov.uk/government/uploads/system/uploads/attachment_data/file/889491/supplier-credit-terms-and-conditions.odt> accessed 1 February 2022.

157 [1999] CLC 823.

158 [2011] EWHC 1352 (TCC).

159 [1983] 1 WLR 399.

160 *Yeoman Credit Ltd v Latter* [1961] 1 WLR 828.

> [The ECA] hereby guarantees to Lender, as surety and not as primary obligor, the payment of the Guaranteed Amount of the obligations of each Debtor to Lender, as and when the same shall become due under each Financing, up to the Guaranteed Amount applicable thereto, provided that such Financing satisfies the terms and conditions provided herein. In no event shall the liability of [the ECA] hereunder with respect to any Financing exceed the Guaranteed Amount of such Financing.

It can be seen from the guarantee clause above that the ECG contract is a contract of guarantee, where the ECA will pay the bank the loss up to a certain percentage of the value of the export contract. An ECG contract is different from other types of contracts of indemnity including an ECI contract: a guarantee is different from a contract of indemnity because the latter is "a contract by one party to keep the other harmless against loss"[161] where a primary liability is assumed by the indemnifier whether or not a third party makes default;[162] by contrast, in guarantees, the guarantor assumes a secondary liability to the creditor for the default of the principal debtor who remains primarily liable.[163] In other words, a contract of guarantee is different from a contract of insurance because in insurance the insurer agrees to pay upon the happening of a specified event, whilst in guarantees the guarantor promises to pay if the principal debtor defaults.[164] The difference of ECGs and ECI are consistent with the distinctions drawn as above: whilst an ECI policy protects the assured exporter against the loss as a result of certain commercial and political risks, an ECG contract simply protects the bank against the default of payment by the buyer, no matter what kind of events cause the buyer's default in payment. Therefore, it seems straightforward that an ECG contract is a contract of guarantee, where the ECA is the guarantor, the bank is the creditor and the buyer is the principal debtor.

The guarantee clause must mirror the terms of the underlying contract of sale

Discrepancies between the ECG and the terms of the underlying contract of sale might result in potential disputes. For instance, in *Crown Aluminium*,[165] the guarantee clause under the ECG provided that:

> We … (hereinafter known as Guarantor) … declare that in consideration of the advancement of credit referred to in the agreement forming part of and attached to this Guarantee and in consideration of the payment by the

161 Ibid, 831.
162 *Guild & Co v Conrad* [1894] 2 QB 885.
163 See n 161 above.
164 *Dane v Mortgage Insurance Corp* [1894] 1 QB 54, 61 (Lord Esher M.R); *Prudential* [1904] 2 KB 658, 664 (Channel J).
165 [2011] EWHC 1352 (TCC).

> Trade Debtor of the guarantee fee, we hereby guarantee unconditionally and irrevocably to the Trade Creditor, in respect of all sums due at 16 April 2009 as defined within Bill of Exchange (No. CA1) from the Trade Debtor, under the terms of the Contract of Sale subject to the limit of this Guarantee of £96,266.72 …
>
> "Default" is defined as the failure of the Trade Debtor to honour the contractual obligations as set forth in the Contract of Sale.
>
> Should the Trade Debtor default against payments to the Trade Creditor, the Trade Creditor must for the Guarantee to be effective, give notice within thirty (30) days to the guarantor in writing to cure the Trade Debtor's default. With the said notice the following documents must be included: copies of the Contract of Sale, the Guarantee, and an authorised statement detailing the non-payment by the Trade Debtor.

The bills of exchange CA1 covered several invoices issued by the exporter (i.e., the Trade Creditor) to the buyer (i.e., the Trade Debtor). However, the due dates of these invoices were either the end of February or the end of March 2009, well before the due date of payment stated in CA1 and the guarantee clause (i.e., 16 April 2009). Therefore, the ECG clearly did not mirror the terms of the contract of sale, as it reflected "the more generous terms of credit" instead of "being tied to the terms of payment as defined in the underlying contract of sale and as stated in the relevant invoices".[166]

The buyer failed to pay under the bill of exchange and the exporter, on 17 April 2009, sent a notice to the guarantor indicating that it intended to make a call under the ECG. Copies of the ECG, the invoices as well as an authorised statement detailing the non-payment were attached to the notice. The guarantor rejected the claim on the ground that the form and content of the notice did not comply with the terms of the ECG: first, the exporter failed to give notice within 30 days after the due date of the earliest invoice; second, the exporter failed to attach a copy of the contract of sale (i.e., the purchase orders).

Both submissions were rejected by Edward-Stuart J. With respect to the first submission, he accepted the witness evidence which indicated that the underlying contract of sale was superseded by the incorporation into the guarantee of CA1, in that the payment obligations stated in the invoices were replaced by a single obligation to make payment of the sums shown in the invoices by 16 April 2009 as stated in CA1. Accordingly, the judge held that on the true construction of the guarantee clause, the guarantor's obligation to pay under the ECG arose only if the payment was not made on 16 April 2009, irrespective of any prior failure by the buyer to make payment by reference to the dates on which the invoices were issued. The judge thus held that the exporter submitted the notice promptly.

With respect to the second submission, Edward-Stuart J noted that the only obligation relating to payment was that the buyer had to make payment of the

166 Ibid, [33] (Edward-Stuart J).

sums stated in the invoices by the date stated in CA1: since the "sums due at 16 April 2009" were the amounts making up the total sum of £96,266.72, which was stated in CA1, the terms of the original contracts under which those sums were originally payable were no longer relevant to the operation of the ECG. Accordingly, the judge considered that the only document that determined the buyer's, and hence the guarantor's, liability under the ECG was CA1. He thus ruled that the expression "Contract of Sale" in the guarantee clause must be construed as referring to CA1, because there was no other document that was relevant to the Trade Debtor's obligation to pay the exporter. Edward-Stuart J admitted that this was "a rather forced construction" of the language of the guarantee, but he believed that any other reading would result in absurdity or incoherence.[167]

Although the judgment of *Crown Aluminium* favoured the exporter, this case shows the importance for the parties under ECGs to draft a guarantee clause that mirrors the underlying contract of sale in order to avoid potential disputes. In fact, prior to the ECG cover in question, the guarantor in *Crown Aluminium* had issued some earlier ECGs that operated smoothly. The guarantee clause in those ECGs read as follows:

> We hereby guarantee unconditionally and irrevocably to [the exporter] … in respect of all sums due as listed in Schedule A to this document from [the buyer] … under the terms of the Contract of Sale subject to the limit of this guarantee of £95,903.50 …

Schedule A was in these terms:

> Invoices summary [the exporter] – [the buyer]
> Note that this [ECG] covers the invoices listed below.
> [Four invoices were then listed, giving for each invoice: the invoice number, date, project name and amount.]

Edward-Stuart J commented that the due dates for payment could only be derived from the invoices or contracts of sale themselves: it was therefore "reasonably clear" that the liability under those ECGs would arise at the moment that the buyer failed to make payment of the amount shown on any of the invoices by the date required by that particular contract.[168]

The guarantee clause covers genuine underlying transactions only

It should also be noted that whilst the guarantee clause under ECGs is straightforward, the guaranteed underlying transaction must always be a genuine one. In *Credit Lyonnais*,[169] the ECA issued an ECG to a bank that financed the exporter

167 Ibid, [70]–[71].
168 Ibid, [64].
169 [1999] CLC 823.

by purchasing the bills of exchange and also issued an ECI policy to protect the exporter against the risk of the non-payment by the buyer.[170] The guarantee clause (Clause 2) under the ECG provided that:

> [The ECA] hereby guarantees payment to the Bank of the face value of any Guaranteed Instrument which has been duly presented for payment or presentation of which for payment has been prevented by circumstances beyond the control of the Bank or its correspondents and which remains unpaid six months after the due date of payment thereof against surrender to the insurer, if so required, of the relevant Guaranteed Instrument duly endorsed.
>
> "Guaranteed Instrument" means … any sterling bill of exchange drawn by the exporter and accepted by a buyer …

The bills of exchange had never been honoured, and the bank found that they were forged by the exporter. The bank made a claim to the ECA under the ECG. Hobhouse LJ clarified that what the ECG guaranteed was the "acceptance" of the bills of exchange by the buyer:[171]

> The drawing of a bill of exchange imposes no obligation upon the drawee to accept or pay the bill … Once a bill has been accepted the acceptor comes under an obligation to pay the bill at its maturity and if he fails to do so the bill has been dishonoured by non-payment. The subject matter of the guarantee is the acceptance and the guaranteed obligation is the acceptor's obligation to pay the bill at maturity. It is not a guarantee of any obligation of the exporter. This is further confirmed by the requirement that the bank (the beneficiary of the [ECG]) shall have purchased the accepted bill without recourse. The liability that is guaranteed is the liability of the buyer created by his acceptance of the bill. This is the meaning … which is consistent with the scheme of the [ECG] and of the [ECI] policy to which it refers and is ancillary.

The learned judge then held that the forged bills of exchange in this case were never "accepted" because the relevant drawees were fictitious and the signatures were all forged. Relying on s 24 of the Bills of Exchange Act 1882 which provided that forged signatures were "wholly inoperative" and no right to enforce payment could be acquired through or under such signatures, the judge ruled that "no obligation of any acceptor to pay the bills of exchange ever arose": there was accordingly "no liability which was guaranteed by [the ECG], no primary liability to which the liability of [the ECA] was secondary".[172]

170 How an ECG is used with ECI to support supplier credit transactions will be analysed in Chapter 7.

171 *Credit Lyonnais* [1999] CLC 823, 846.

172 Ibid, 846–7.

The exclusion on the documentation risk?

As demonstrated above, ECAs normally exclude the documentation risks under ECI. Meanwhile, this research observes that ECAs may be willing to bear the documentation risks under ECGs. For instance, a standard term buyer credit guarantee contract collected through the Berne Union Academic Survey provides that:[173]

> The liability of [the ECA] shall not be impaired or discharged by reason of … the loan agreement being or becoming … invalid, illegal, unenforceable or void, in whole or in part, for any reason whatsoever.

The fact that the documentation risk is borne by the ECA indicates that the bank will be protected more broadly under ECGs than ECI.

The bank's rights and obligations under ECGs

Under an ECG contract, once the bank, as the creditor, has provided finance to the buyer and paid the guarantee fee, there are generally no other substantial obligations on the bank. That is because a guarantee, in its legal nature, is unconditional and on-demand. As a unilateral instrument, a guarantee normally includes no promissory obligations on the creditor.[174] The creditor's rights to enforce the guarantee arises automatically upon the default of the principal debtor.[175] In other words, a guarantor becomes liable as soon as the payment is not made or the default occurs under the principal contract.[176] Therefore, under an ECG contract, once the buyer defaults in payment and the bank makes a claim, the ECA becomes liable to pay. It should be noted that under English law of guarantee, there is no general obligation on the creditor to notify the guarantor of the principal debtor's default in advance before the creditor can enforce the guarantee,[177] unless otherwise expressly provided.[178]

Of course, under guarantee, the parties are free to stipulate some conditions precedent to the operation of the guarantee or to the guarantor's liability. The rules of conditions precedent in the law of guarantee are similar to their counterpart rules in insurance law before the IA 2015. Breach of a condition precedent to the operation of the guarantee means that the guarantee never becomes operative,[179] and breach of a condition precedent to the guarantor's liability will

173 Cheng Lin, "Why Export Credit Agencies Provide Guarantees in addition to Insurance: A Contractual Perspective" [2021] (1) LMCLQ 149, 153.

174 *Ankar Pty Ltd v National Westminster Finance (Aust) Ltd* (1987) 162 CLR 549, 556.

175 *Keene v Devine* [1986] WAR 217 at 223; *Rickaby v Lewis* (1905) 22 TLR 130.

176 James O'Donovan & John Phillips, *The Modern Contract of Guarantee* (English edn, Sweet & Maxwell 2003), [10-116].

177 *Moschi v Lep Air Services Ltd* [1973] AC 331, 356 (Lord Simon of Glaisdale).

178 *Eshelby v Federated European Bank Ltd* [1932] 1 KB 423; *Clydebank and District Water Trustees v Fidelity & Deposit Co of Maryland* (1915) SC 362.

179 *Molsons Bank v Cranston* (1918) 45 DLR 316.

automatically discharge the guarantor's liability.[180] A condition precedent to liability should be strictly complied with; otherwise, the guarantor will be entitled to be discharged for the most trivial departure from it.[181] Since a guarantee is not a contract of insurance, s 11 of the IA 2015 is not applicable, and the common law rules governing conditions precedent in guarantee remain intact.

However, even if conditions precedent in a guarantee can be harsh, there is in fact little room for the guarantor to use conditions precedent. This is because, as mentioned above, under a guarantee, the creditor generally does not bear many substantial obligations. The guarantor can only require the creditor to obey certain formalities before enforcing the guarantee.[182] The most common condition precedent is to require the creditor to serve notices of default of the principal debtor.[183]

The general rules above perfectly apply in the context of ECGs. In practice, most ECAs do not impose very heavy obligations on the bank under ECGs. The Berne Union Academic Survey found that its members tend to only include two conditions precedent under ECGs: (a) that the bank should duly provide the loan and (b) that the bank should pay the guarantee fee. Other obligations, such as notification of probable loss and mitigation of loss, are generally not drafted as conditions precedent.[184] Furthermore, for obligation (a) and (b) to be treated as a condition precedent, the English court required that they need to be stipulated in an express way.[185]

In sum, respondents to the Berne Union Academic Survey regarded ECGs as unconditional when asked about the advantages of a guarantee compared with insurance. They said that they rarely reject claims made by banks under an ECG contract. Some of the ECAs' opinions are cited below:[186]

- A guarantee cannot be disputed, and because of that, it is preferred by the bank, whilst an insurance policy has to be complied with so that the policy is more complicated or riskier to the bank;
- A guarantee is preferred by banks as it does not contain a number of clauses that restrict the conditions of compensation;
- A guarantee is binary[187] and comprehensive as opposed to insurance, which is subject to conditions, exclusions and procedural requirements;
- Guarantees are highly preferred by banks as they are "unconditional, irrevocable and payable on first demand". For the same reasons, however, the cost for the bank (i.e., the premium) is generally higher compared to the insurance policy.

180 O'Donovan & Phillips (n 176), [8-11].
181 *Tricontinental Corp Ltd v HDFI Ltd* (1990) 21 NSWLR 689.
182 O'Donovan & Phillips (n 176), [10-07].
183 Ibid., [10-95].
184 Lin (n 109) 26.
185 For instance, Edwards-Stuart J in *Crown Aluminium* rejected the guarantor's submission that the payment of the guarantee fee was a condition precedent of the ECG as there was no such express wording. See *Crown Aluminium* [2011] EWHC 1352 (TCC), [77].
186 Lin (n 109) 26–7.
187 Ibid. The word "binary" here probably means that a guarantee operates in a straightforward way where the guarantor either pays in full or refuses to pay at all.

The paragraphs above demonstrate that under an ECG contract, the bank, as the creditor, does not bear many substantial obligations. Once the foreign buyer defaults in payment, the bank is entitled to claim against the ECA, because an ECG is unconditional and on-demand as a contract of guarantee.

The ECA-exporter contract

While under an ECG contract, the bank is not under any substantial obligations, the main obligations under ECG transactions are imposed on the exporter in a separate ECA-exporter contract. The exporter is not a party under the ECG contract. In the general law of guarantee, a guarantee is a contract between the guarantor and the creditor,[188] but in the context of an ECG arrangement, the ECA usually concludes a separate contract with the exporter. As mentioned above, the ECA-exporter contract under the "Supplier Credit Finance Facility" scheme is the SCFF contract, which stipulates the exporter's rights and obligations.[189]

On the front page of the SCFF contract is a general provision in bold:

> Important
>
> The UKEF will only make support available to a Bank, in respect of the Export Contract detailed in a Supplier Credit Finance Facility Proposal to enable that Bank to provide finance for a maximum of 85% of the value of that Export Contract on the understanding that you will at all times observe and be bound by the conditions detailed below, together with such other conditions in the relevant Certificate of Approval as are expressed to apply specifically to you.

This general provision demonstrates that the SCFF contract is binding to the exporter. In this provision, the word "you" refers to the exporter, and the word "Bank" means the bank that finances the exporter. The UKEF will provide a guarantee to the bank only if the exporter complies with all conditions in the SCFF contract as well as in the "Certificate of Approval". Therefore, as will be seen in the following paragraphs, under an ECG the obligations are primarily imposed on the exporter.

Core clauses on the exporter's obligations

The core clauses under the SCFF contract are analysed below.

Clause 1 provides that once the bank has confirmed that it will finance the exporter by purchasing the negotiable instruments, the exporter must ensure that the negotiable instruments are all enforceable and intact in their legal effect.

Clause 2 provides that once the bank has allowed the exporter to draw money, the exporter must do so by obeying all procedural requirements such as providing evidence of export/performance of service.

188 *Duncan, Fox & Co v North and South Wales Bank* (1880) 6 App Cas 1, 11.

189 See n 156 above.

Clause 5 deals with the exporter's duty of disclosure to the UKEF, which will be discussed in Chapter 4 of this work.

Clause 7 is a warranty under which the exporter warrants and undertakes that it has not engaged, and will not engage, in any corrupt activities.

The SCFF contract only includes the abovementioned clauses as the exporter's obligations. The purpose of those clauses is to ensure that the exporter obtains finance in a business-like way. Once the procedural requirements are met, the UKEF will issue an ECG cover to the bank, and the bank will provide finance to the exporter.

The UKEF's remedies for the exporter's breach

The ECA-exporter contract is not a contract of guarantee. It is a separate and independent contract concluded between the ECA (as the guarantor) and the exporter (as the principal debtor). Therefore, general principles of contract law, rather than the principles of guarantee law, should apply. If the exporter breaches the ECA-exporter contract, the ECA is entitled to the remedies in accordance with general contract law, as well as the remedies stipulated in the ECA-exporter contract. However, it seems that the contractual remedies spelt out under the SCFF contract are somehow patchy:

Clause 7 provides that if the exporter breaches the anti-corruption warranty, it should, on demand, pay to the UKEF any amounts that the UKEF has paid to the bank in respect of any loss the bank has incurred in respect of the payments for the purchase of any negotiable instruments.

Clause 9 stipulates the UKEF's remedies for the exporter's breach of Clause 5, the duty of disclosure. Clause 9 provides that without prejudice to Clause 7, if any statement or warranty made by the exporter is incorrect or untrue, the exporter should, as the case may be, (a) repurchase for cash from the bank for the negotiable instruments; or (b) pay to the UKEF any amounts it has paid to the bank in respect of the loss that the bank has incurred.

What seems particularly surprising is that the UKEF has not expressly stipulated its contractual remedies for the exporter's breach of Clauses 1 and 2. What can be applied is only the general provision on the front page which stipulates that the UKEF will provide the ECG "on the understanding that" the exporter will obey "the conditions detailed below". But what are the legal effects of that general provision?

A relevant case law authority is *Universal Oil*,[190] a buyer credit guarantee case where in addition to the ECG contract between the UKEF and the bank, the UKEF concluded an ECA-exporter contract titled "premium agreement" with the exporter. Clause 7(1) of the "premium agreement" set out the remedies for the exporter's breach:

190 [1983] 1 WLR 399.

> The premiums hereby payable are not intended to and do not cover payments made by the UKEF to the Bank when … the Exporter is in default under the terms of the contract. In the above circumstances the Exporter will on demand pay to the UKEF a sum equal to that paid by the UKEF to the Bank as aforesaid.

By providing Clause 7(1), the ECA wished to be entitled to a right of recourse should the exporter default in the performance of obligations. The exporter failed to pay the £1m premiums for the guarantee, and the buyer defaulted in payment. The ECA paid the bank the loss at £39m and then relied on Clause 7(1) to claim reimbursement from the exporter. The exporter argued that Clause 7(1) was a penalty clause which should be null and void.[191] The Court of Appeal, relying on a number of case law authorities,[192] rejected the exporter's submission and held that once the party drafted a remedy provision based on a "genuine pre-estimate of the damages",[193] then the provision was not a penalty clause. That decision was upheld by the House of Lords, who confirmed that under Clause 7(1) the ECA was only seeking to recover no more than its actual loss.

Universal Oil indicated that the ECA's remedies for the exporter's breach under the ECA-exporter contract could be very harsh: the exporter had to pay to the UKEF £39m for its breach of paying the £1m premiums. The exporter in the appeal made a very persuasive submission, saying that such a clause was included in almost every ECA-exporter contract at that time in the UK, and exporters could not negotiate this clause at all. The exporter further pleaded that since there was no source to obtain finance from the bank other than via the ECG cover from the UKEF, the court's attitude towards such a clause would be important not only to the exporter itself, but also to every other exporter and the export industry in the UK. Despite all that pleading, the House of Lords held that such a clause was the only way for the UKEF to secure the finance from the bank; otherwise, the bank would not be willing to provide such a large sum of the loan. In particular, Lord Roskill stated that:[194]

> One purpose, perhaps the main purpose, of the law relating to penalty clauses is to prevent a plaintiff recovering a sum of money in respect of a breach of

191 In English contract law, where the parties to a contract agree that, in the event of a breach, the contract-breaker shall pay to the other a specified sum of money, the sum fixed may be classified by the courts either as a penalty (which is irrecoverable) or as liquidated damages (which are recoverable). The difference between them is that the latter do not extravagantly exceed a genuine attempt to estimate in advance the loss which the claimant would be likely to suffer from a breach of the obligation in question. Whether a clause is a penalty clause or a "genuine pre-estimate of the damages" is a matter of law and, in particular, a question of construction. See H.G. Beale, *Chitty on Contracts* (33rd edn, Sweet & Maxwell 2018), [26-190]–[26-197].

192 *Dunlop Pneumatic Power Co Ltd v New Garage Co Ltd* (1915) AC 79; *Bridge v Campbell Discount Co* (1962) AC 600; *Alder v Moore* (1961) 2 QB 57.

193 *Universal Oil* [1983] 1 Lloyd's Rep 448.

194 *Universal Oil* [1983] 1 WLR 399, 402-04 (Lord Roskill).

> contract committed by a defendant which bears little or no relationship to the loss actually suffered by the plaintiff as a result of the breach by the defendant. But it is not and never has been for the courts to relieve a party from the consequences of what may in the event prove to be an onerous or possibly even a commercially imprudent bargain.

It should be noted that the law of penalties has been largely rewritten by the UK's Supreme Court in *Cavendish Square Holding BV v Makdessi*.[195] The court in *Cavendish v Makdessi* clarified that whilst a clause may be enforceable if it meets the traditional "genuine pre-estimate of the damages" test, the true test is whether the party to whom the sum is payable had a legitimate interest in ensuring performance by the other party and the sum payable in the event of the breach is not extravagant or unconscionable in comparison to that interest.[196] It is submitted that even under the new test established in *Cavendish v Makdessi*, Clause 7 in *Universal Oil* would not be treated as a penalty clause, since it reflected the ECA's "legitimate interest" under that ECG cover without being extravagant or unconscionable. In particular, Lord Roskill's statement above was quoted by the Supreme Court in *Cavendish v Makdessi* as a guiding principle which "is worth restating at the outset of any analysis of the penalty rule, because it explains much about the way in which it has developed":[197]

> There is a fundamental difference between a jurisdiction to review the fairness of a contractual obligation and a jurisdiction to regulate the remedy for its breach. Leaving aside challenges going to the reality of consent, such as those based on fraud, duress or undue influence, the courts do not review the fairness of men's bargains either at law or in equity. The penalty rule regulates only the remedies available for breach of a party's primary obligations, not the primary obligations themselves. This was not a new concept in 1983, when [*Universal Oil*] was decided … And it provided the whole basis of the classic distinction made at law between a penalty and a genuine pre-estimate of loss, the former being essentially a way of punishing the contract-breaker rather than compensating the innocent party for his breach.

It therefore seems that under ECG transactions, the main obligations are imposed on the exporter, and the ECA's remedies for the exporter's breach under the ECA-exporter contract could be harsh. In the absence of contractually expressed remedies, the UKEF may claim damages according to general rules of contract law should the exporter breach Clauses 1–2 of the SCFF contract. Nevertheless, it

195 [2015] UKSC 67, [2016] AC 1172. See also William Day, "A Pyrrhic victory for the doctrine against penalties: *Makdessi v Cavendish Square Holding BV*" [2016] (2) JBL 115.

196 Beale (n 191), [26-190].

197 *Cavendish v Makdessi* [2015] UKSC 67, [12]–[13] (Lord Neuberger and Lord Sumption). Lord Roskill's principle above was also recently followed by the court in *Adare Finance DAC v Yellowstone Capital Management SA* [2020] EWHC 2760 (Comm), [2020] 10 WLUK 285, [98].

is submitted that the UKEF should revise its ECA-exporter contract and make express provisions on its remedies for the exporter's breach of Clauses 1–2, but avoiding the application of the law against penalties. As long as the UKEF stipulates the contractual remedies which (a) are based on the genuine pre-estimate of the likely loss, (b) reflect the ECA's legitimate interest in the guarantees and (c) are not extravagant or unconscionable in comparison to that interest, they will not conflict with the law of penalties.

Summary: the legal nature of ECGs reflected by its terms and conditions

The discussion above reveals that the ECG transaction is a tripartite arrangement between the ECA, the bank and the exporter. It includes two contracts: the ECG contract between the ECA and the bank, and the ECA-exporter contract between the ECA and the exporter.

On the one hand, the terms and conditions of the ECG contract indicate that the legal nature of an ECG contract is a contract of guarantee. It is different from a contract of insurance: under an ECG, the ECA undertakes to pay the bank the loss straight away if the buyer defaults in payment. An ECG contract is unconditional to the bank, as the ECA is liable to pay the bank on demand. The bank is normally under no substantial obligations under an ECG.

On the other hand, the ECA-exporter contract is not a contract of guarantee. It is a separate contract concluded between the ECA and the exporter to ensure that the exporter complies with all the requirements concerning its obtaining finance from the bank. Without such a contract, the bank may not be willing to provide finance. The main obligations of the ECG transaction are imposed on the exporter. Therefore, whilst an ECG transaction is bank-friendly, it is not always exporter-friendly. The ECA's remedies for the exporter's breach can be very harsh.

Conclusion

This chapter has explored the legal nature of ECI and ECGs from the perspective of their contractual terms and conditions. It contributes to the overarching theme of this book in the following aspects.

Firstly, are ECI and ECG contracts of insurance or guarantee in their legal nature? This question is explored by the detailed analysis in this chapter. The terms and conditions of ECI and ECGs indicate that they are contracts of insurance and guarantee, respectively.

Secondly, can principles of insurance law and guarantee law apply to the contracts of ECI and ECGs, respectively? As far as this chapter is concerned, the English courts construed ECI contracts in the same way as they construe other types of insurance contracts. The peculiarities of ECI are scarcely mentioned by the courts. The UKEF, as well as the anonymous Berne Union member, also treated their policies as being subject to the IA 2015. It can therefore be said that from the perspective of contractual terms and conditions, principles of insurance law fully apply to ECI contracts. Likewise, principles of guarantee law apply to ECG contracts, as analysed in the paragraphs above.

Thirdly, what are the differences between ECI and ECGs? This chapter submits that from a contractual perspective, ECGs are significantly different from ECI because:

(1) An ECG transaction is usually a tripartite arrangement which includes the ECA, the exporter and the bank. It normally includes two contracts, the ECG contract and the ECA-exporter contract. An ECI policy is usually a bilateral contract between the ECA and the exporter/bank;
(2) An ECG contract covers the bank's loss should the buyer default in payment no matter what event has caused the loss, whilst the risks covered by an ECI policy are limited to certain commercial and political events. Therefore, ECI provides a smaller scale of protection to the bank than ECGs. In particular, whereas the documentation risk is generally excluded by the ECA under ECI, it may be borne by the ECA under ECGs;
(3) The terms and conditions in ECG transactions are very precise and straightforward. The ECG contract and the ECA-exporter contract are both less lengthy than an ECI policy which generally includes more complicated terms and conditions provisions. As pointed out by the commentator, the ECA under ECI is "very often dealing with complex underlying activity and contractual documentation".[198]

References

Beale, H, *Chitty on Contracts* (33rd edn, Sweet & Maxwell 2018)

Birds, J, Lynch, B & Paul, S, *MacGillivray on Insurance Law* (14th edn, Sweet & Maxwell 2018)

Cheng Lin, "Understanding the Legal Nature of Export Credit Insurance: Lessons from *ABN Amro v RSA*" (2022) 3 JBL 225

Day, W, "A Pyrrhic Victory for the Doctrine against Penalties: Makdessi v Cavendish Square Holding BV" (2016) 2 JBL 115

Grath, A, *The Handbook of International Trade and Finance* (Kogan Page 2008)

Gürses, Ö, "Section 11 of the Insurance Act 2015: When Does a Term Define the Risk as a Whole in An Insurance Contract?" (2020) 3 JBL 184

Lin, C, "Why Export Credit Agencies Provides Guarantees in addition to Insurance: A Contractual Perspective" (2021) 1 LMCLQ 149

Lomnicka, E, "Export Credit Guarantees" in M Bridge (ed) *Benjamin's Sales of Goods* (11th edn, Sweet & Maxwell 2020)

Merkin, R, *Colinvaux and Merkin's Insurance Contract Law* (Sweet & Maxwell 2021)

Merkin, R, *Colinvaux's Law of Insurance* (12th edn, Sweet & Maxwell 2019)

Merkin, R & Gürses, Ö, "Insurance Contracts after the Insurance Act 2015" (2016) 132 (3) LQR 445

198 Blenkinsopp (n 7) 78–9.

Merkin, R & Gürses, Ö, "The Insurance Act 2015: Rebalancing the Interests of Insurer and Assured" (2015) 78 (6) MLR 1004

O'Donovan, J & Phillips, J, *The Modern Contract of Guarantee* (English edn, Sweet & Maxwell 2003)

Salcic, Z, *Export Credit Insurance & Guarantees: A Practitioner's Guide* (Palgrave Macmillan 2014)

Soyer, B, "Risk Control Clauses in Insurance Law: Law Reform and the Future" (2016) 75 CLJ 109

4 The duty of fair presentation under ECI and ECGs?

This chapter consists of four parts. The first part examines how the duty of fair presentation in English insurance law applies to export credit insurance (ECI) contracts. Until now, the IA 2015 has not been the subject of litigation before the English courts in the context of ECI. Hence the analysis will focus on the ECI cases decided under the MIA 1906 of which the principles applied to all types of insurance. This part aims to show that the general rules in relation to the duty of fair presentation in insurance law applied to the English ECI cases, and those cases, in turn, contributed to the development of these general rules. The second part explores the misrepresentation and non-disclosure in export credit guarantee (ECG) contracts. A guarantee is not a contract *uberrimae fidei*, but misrepresentations and non-disclosure could vitiate the contract, and there is a tendency that the UK Export Finance (UKEF) is importing the duty of fair presentation into its ECG business. The third part then proposes a unified approach in English law regarding the duty of fair presentation in ECI and ECGs, and the fourth part addresses the issues that do not fall within the scope of the duty of fair presentation but are closely related to the theme of this chapter: the assured's post-contractual duty of disclosure under ECI, the insurer's duty of utmost good faith under ECI, the ECA's vicarious liability for its employees' fraud and the bank's duty to investigate the genuineness of the underlying transaction.

The duty of fair presentation under ECI

The materiality test

Material facts: general

In English ECI cases, the courts followed the materiality test under s 18(2) of the MIA 1906 which provided that "every circumstance is material, which would influence the judgment of a prudent insurer in fixing the premium or determining whether he will take the risk". The materiality test in English law is an objective test[1] and

1 *Brit Uw Limited v F & B Trenchless Solutions Limited* [2015] EWHC 2237 (Comm), [2016] Lloyd's Rep IR 69.

DOI: 10.4324/b22864-4

mere influence test[2], which were fully applied by the English courts in deciding whether the misrepresented or undisclosed facts were material in ECI cases. The courts had identified five categories of material facts in the context of ECI. All those facts fall within the scope of "physical hazard"[3] in insurance law and will still be applicable under s 7(3) of the IA 2015 which provides that "a circumstance or representation is material if it would influence the judgement of a prudent insurer in determining whether to take the risk and, if so, on what terms".

First, information about the foreign buyer's financial standing was deemed material.[4] In *Morgan Grenfell & Co Limited v SACE Istituto Per I Servizi Assicurativi Del Commercio*,[5] SACE, the Italian ECA, issued a buyer credit insurance cover to an English bank against the risks of the non-payment by the buyer. The buyer was a state-owned entity of Equatorial Guinea.[6] The loan agreement was guaranteed by the local government, so the bank believed that this sort of governmental guarantees was sufficient and did not investigate the financial standing of the buyer or the viability of the project. Unfortunately, the buyer refused to pay, and no recovery was received from the government. SACE argued that the bank failed to disclose the buyer's financial standing and the viability of the project. The court held that had those facts been disclosed, the likelihood of the occurrence of the insured event would be "clearly less" and such matter would influence a prudent insurer in deciding whether to take the risk. The applicable law in that case was Italian law, but Clarke LJ deemed the foreign law as "a question of fact to the satisfaction of the judge"[7] and substantially followed the materiality test in English law. His lordship confirmed that to constitute a material fact, it "must be so important that, had it been known by the insurer, the insurance contract would either not have been concluded at all or would only have been concluded on different terms and conditions".[8]

Second, the assured's failure to conduct due diligence on the foreign buyer's financial standing was also held material. In *Morgan Grenfell*, SACE further submitted that the bank's failure to investigate the foreign buyer's financial standing increased the probability of the insured event occurring and thus was material for disclosure. Clarke LJ accepted this submission because the

2 *Pan Atlantic Ins Co Ltd v Pine Top Ins Co Ltd* [1995] 1 AC 501.
3 Özlem Gürses, *The Insurance of Commercial Risks: Law and Practice* (5th edn, Sweet & Maxwell 2017), [3-027].
4 For an early case authority treating the buyer's financial standing as a material fact under credit insurance, see *Anglo-Californian Bank Ltd v London and Provincial Marine and General Insurance Co Ltd* (1904) 20 TLR 665.
5 [2001] EWCA Civ 1932, [2002] CLY 2729.
6 ECAs normally insure exporters or banks in their home countries only. See Zlatko Salcic, *Export Credit Insurance & Guarantees: A Practitioner's Guide* (Palgrave Macmillan 2014) 135. However, in *Morgan Grenfell*, although the assured bank was based in the UK, it financed two Italian exporters who were conducting overseas construction business. That was why SACE, as the ECA of Italy, was willing to provide ECI to the assured.
7 *Morgan Grenfell* [2001] EWCA Civ 1932, [45] (Clarke LJ).
8 Ibid, [134]–[135].

disclosure of that information would certainly influence a prudent insurer in determining whether to take the risk or not. However, it should be noted that in *Credit Lyonnais Bank Nederland NV (now Generale Bank Nederland NV) v Export Credits Guarantee Department*,[9] which is an ECG case, a similar defence was advanced before the court, but Longmore J held that the bank was under no duty to investigate the genuineness of the underlying transaction and that the bank's failure to do so was not a material fact and need not be disclosed. Hence, the English court's view on this matter is not consistent, which reflects their different approaches towards the materiality test in ECI and ECGs: in ECI cases, the court tends to adopt a more stringent approach on the assured's duty of disclosure and is likely to confirm a wider range of material facts.[10] The details of *Credit Lyonnais* will be further discussed in the following sections of this chapter.

Third, in terms of commercial risks, the levels of previous trade and any excess of the credit limit granted by the ECA are also material facts. As explained in Chapter 3, the credit limit means the highest amount of cover which an ECA provides to the assured for a specific buyer during a certain period.[11] If, during that period, the total sales amount exceeds the credit limit due to the seasonal peak orders or market need fluctuations, the exporter will need to seek to vary the ECI contract and change the credit limit.[12] In *Moore Large & Co Ltd v Hermes Credit & Guarantee Plc*,[13] Hermes, a major private credit insurer in the UK, required the exporter to make quarterly declarations on the level of trades in the previous quarter and on whether the trade amount had exceeded the respective credit limit. Those facts were regarded as material by the court because the disclosure of these facts would raise questions for a prudent insurer as to the financial strength of the buyer.

Fourth, in terms of political risks, the local government's previous refusal to grant permits to the insured transaction is a material fact that the assured must disclose. In *International Management Group (UK) Ltd v Simmonds*,[14] to which the background has been explained in Chapter 2, the assured, prior to concluding the ECI contract, merely disclosed that the bilateral Sahara Cup was replaced by the tripartite Toronto Cup due to "the political situations" in 1999. However, the assured did not disclose the facts that (1) regarding the Sahara Cup 1999, the Ministry of Sports of India had written a letter to BCCI, the cricket board of India, advising the latter not to participate in that tournament; (2) regarding

9 [1996] CLC 11.

10 John Birds, Ben Lynch and Simon Paul, *MacGillivray on Insurance Law* (14th edn, Sweet & Maxwell 2018) [33-020].

11 Lord Mance, Iain Goldrein, Robert Merkin, *Insurance Disputes* (3rd edn, Informa 2011) 633.

12 It is well established that the duty of disclosure applies to a variation of the policy involving an extension of cover, even for a limited period. See *Manifest Shipping v Uni-Polaris Ins Co* [1997] 1 Lloyd's Rep 360, 370.

13 [2003] EWHC 26 (Comm), [2003] 1 Lloyd's Rep 163.

14 [2003] EWHC 177 (Comm), [2004] Llyod's Rep IR 247.

the Sahara Cup 2000, there had been articles written by "prominent journalists and well-connected people with BCCI" who predicted that the Indian government would by no means allow its team to play against Pakistan in any bilateral games. It turned out that the Indian government forbade its team to play not only in the Sahara Cup 2000 but also in any trilateral/multilateral events. The assured thus suffered great losses. The insurer alleged that the assured had breached the duty of utmost good faith because of the failure to disclose the fact (1) and (2). The court first clarified that "there was little dispute about the applicable law", stating that the ECI policy in that case was a contract of insurance which was subject to the principle of utmost good faith.[15] Then, citing s 18(2) of the MIA 1906, Cooke J applied the prudent insurer test in determining the materiality of the fact (1) and (2). The judge regarded the fact (1) as "highly material to the underwriter's assessment of the risk" because it indicated that the Indian government might not allow its team to participate in 2020, whether the tournament would be of a bilateral or trilateral/multilateral nature. As for the fact (2), Cooke J distinguished immaterial, loose rumours from hard intelligence, believing that the fact (2) belonged to the latter. Both facts were held material for the assured to disclose.

Fifth, any peculiarities of the underlying transaction are likely to be treated as material facts by the insurer. In *Harding Maughan Hambly Ltd v Cie Européenne de Courtage d'Assurances et de Réassurances SA and another*,[16] the assured (the operator of Block 3 Offshore Angola) wished to cover the risk that Sonangol (the Angolan state oil company) would fail to fulfil its obligation to supply it with the specified amount of crude oil that was to be sourced from Block 3 under an off-take agreement financed by a Swiss bank. When the risk was presented to the leading underwriter, he indicated his interest to insure subject to a number of subjectivities regarding the assured's off-take transaction:[17] (a) confirmation that the physical movement of oil was within assured's control and out of Sonangol's control; (b) satisfactory explanation of the "route structure" for oil funds and how the proceeds from the oil liftings were allocated and paid to the lending bank(s); (c) satisfactory evidence of title to oil and/or funds from the oil and legal opinion as to the priority of this title over other creditors; (d) review of the off-take agreement; (e) basis of valuation; and (f) confirmation that the assured had had no problems (and were unaware of others having problems) that could give rise to a loss – especially had there been any temporary cessation. The leading underwriter also required certain documentation to be submitted.[18]The assured and its brokers duly provided the clarification and documentation and, during the placement of the risk, the first payment on the loan under the off-take transaction had also been made. Rix J commented that all those factors

15 Ibid, [135].
16 [2000] 1 All ER (Comm) 225.
17 Ibid, 232.
18 Ibid, 233. For details, see Chapters 2 and 3 of this work.

indicated that the agreement between the assured and the Angolan Government was working and eventually influenced the leading underwriter's decision to insure this risk.[19]

Facts that make the risk attractive to the insurer

There are some facts that might make the risk attractive to insurers under ECI. For instance, as Jacobs J noted in *ABN AMRO Bank NV v Royal and Sun Alliance Insurance Plc*,[20] the underwriters would welcome the bank (who financed the buyers under "repo" transactions discussed in Chapters 2 and 3) as an assured for the following reasons:[21]

> [The Bank] was an internationally well-regarded corporation whose business underwriters would have sought to secure. There were also other features of the risk that made it attractive. It had a short duration: each repo transaction was three months, at the end of which the Bank could decide whether or not to roll over. The security structure was good, because the Bank had legal title to the goods, not merely a security interest. The countries where the risks were situated were attractive. The most recent financial statements of [the buyer] showed a picture of increased income and profit.

A "new raft" of disclosure where ECI is provided as an add-on cover?

The paragraphs above focus on the material facts that the assured needs to disclose when it places a standalone ECI policy. One might question what (else) the assured needs to disclose if it inserts a credit risk clause as an add-on to an insurance policy of other types. This was exactly the case in *ABN Amro*, where the underwriters advanced an argument, though not a central one, that including ECI in a marine cargo policy would open up "a whole raft of underwriting considerations" and "a new raft of areas for disclosure",[22] and that they would not know the rating approach, the typical terms or the material facts to be considered in deciding whether a particular risk was acceptable. Neither the trial nor appeal judgement directly addressed this issue because it was elaborated as part of the abovementioned "factual matrix" submission. Nevertheless, inference can be made from Jacobs J's following statement:[23]

> Information about the trade credit market, including matters relating to the underwriting approach, could no doubt have been obtained by underwriters

19 Ibid, 245.
20 [2021] EWHC 442 (Comm).
21 Ibid, [990].
22 Ibid, [202].
23 Ibid, [217].

> … via contacts or colleagues, if they were interested in finding anything out. To that extent, such information was reasonably available to the parties and could be said to form part of the factual matrix.

This should be read together with his clarification on whether the "Transaction Premium Clause" (TPC) itself was an unusual circumstance the assured should disclose:[24]

> An insurer who writes an open cover in favour of a commodity trader must be taken to be aware of the whole range of circumstances that may arise in the course of carrying on a business of that kind. In the present case there was nothing unusual in the nature of the business carried on by the Bank. On the contrary, the financing of stock by way of repo transactions was entirely normal.

Whilst the policy in *ABN Amro* was governed by the MIA 1906, Jacobs J's analysis above remains perfectly applicable in the light of ss 3(5)(c), 5(2)(b) and 7(4)(a) of the Insurance Act 2015: if the underwriter, when insuring the main risk (e.g., the PLOD risks in *ABN Amro*), has known all material facts about the underlying transaction, then the assured bears no additional duty of disclosure when obtaining ECI as an add-on. Otherwise, it must disclose all material facts about the underlying transaction it knows or ought to know.

The inducement test

Section 8(1) of the IA 2015 codified the inducement test that did not appear in the MIA 1906 but was established in *Pan Atlantic Ins Co Ltd v Pine Top Ins Co Ltd*.[25] In addition to satisfying the materiality test, the insurer must also prove that, but for the assured's breach, he would not have taken the risk or would have taken it on different terms. The test of inducement is a subjective test, which means the actual insurer must prove on the balance of probabilities of the inducement[26] and that the evidence from the insurer is of great importance.[27] The Law Commissions suggested that the evidence to establish inducement could include "pricing manuals and models, contemporaneous policies and oral evidence from the individual underwriter or expert witnesses".[28] The English courts followed that guidance in deciding relevant ECI cases.

24 Ibid, [631].

25 [1995] 1 AC 501.

26 Robert Merkin, *Colinvaux's Law of Insurance* (12th edn, Sweet & Maxwell 2019) [7-165].

27 *Laker Vent Engineering Ltd v Templeton Insurance Ltd* [2009] EWCA Civ 62, [2009] Lloyd's Rep IR 704; *Lewis v Norwich Union Healthcare Ltd* [2010] Lloyd's Rep IR 198; *Persimmon Homes Ltd v Great Lakes Reinsurance (UK) Plc* [2010] EWHC 1705 (Comm), [2011] Lloyd's Rep IR 101.

28 Law Com. No. 353, *Insurance Contract Law: Business Disclosure; Warranties; Insurers' Remedies for Fraudulent Claims; and Late Payment*, [11.76].

Firstly, the ECA's questionnaires in its standard application form were accepted by the court to prove inducement by the insurers. In *Morgan Grenfell*, the court noted that on the placement of the risks, no queries were raised by SACE about information about the buyer's financial standing. Clarke LJ was critical of SACE for its failure to make relevant enquiries and thought that in making enquiries SACE "had operated bureaucratically and its underwriting technique was certainly formulaic". His lordship therefore held that SACE failed to satisfy the court that had the disclosure been made, it would have "elicited any unfavourable response or reaction to the application".[29]

Secondly, the internal correspondence within the ECA was accepted as evidence for the inducement test. In *Moore Large*, there had been rumours that the assured's parent company had defaulted on agreements with banks prior to the variation of the policy. The underwriter of Euler Hermes asked for a meeting with that parent company and obtained a financial briefing on its current financial position and its future financial viability. After that, the underwriter reported this to the central credit committee of Euler Hermes, and the committee agreed to vary the policy relying on this report. The correspondence between the underwriter and the central committee convinced the court that Hermes was concerned about the assured's financial standing.[30]

Thirdly, the witness evidence by the ECA's employees, especially its underwriter who dealt with the assured in dispute, could also serve as evidence. In *Moore Large*, Hermes's underwriter stated that:[31]

> If I had known at that time that the claimant was already trading at a level in excess of the then agreed Credit Limit … I think that I would for all the reasons set out above, have insisted on a meeting … as a pre-condition to approval being given.

Colman J accepted the witness statement and held that it was the underwriter's honest belief that he would indeed have called for a further meeting before agreeing to vary the policy if the disclosure was made.

Lastly, if ECI is placed on a subscription basis, then the following underwriters are likely to be treated as having been induced if the inducement test is established in favour of the leading underwriters. In *International Management Group*,[32] the risks were underwritten by two leading underwriters and several followers. Cook J held that had the leading underwriters known the fact (1) and (2), they would have either expressly excluded liability in the event of lack of the Indian government's permission to the insured transaction or declined to underwrite it at all. The inducement test was therefore clearly established in favour of the leading underwriters. As

29 *Morgan Grenfell* [2001] EWCA Civ 1932, [138]–[141].
30 *Moore Large* [2003] EWHC 26 (Comm), [60].
31 Ibid, [65].
32 [2003] EWHC 177 (Comm).

for the following underwriters, Cook J pointed out that the risk insured in that case was of a specialised nature and, to underwrite such a risk, the following underwriters relied heavily on the leading underwriters. Therefore, the assured was deemed as having induced the following syndicates to take the risk, too.

Non-disclosure of the existence and purpose of specific policy clauses?

The non-disclosure of the Transaction Premium Clause and the Non-avoidance Clause

It might seem strange if an insurer seeks to avoid the policy due to the non-disclosure of certain policy clauses it did not carefully read. Nevertheless, this unusual situation was illustrated in *ABN Amro*, where the assured sought to insert the Transaction Premium Clause (TPC) as well as a Non-avoidance Clause (NAC) in renewing a marine cargo policy. The underwriters signed the slip without carefully reading through the wording of those two clauses. In case the argument on the construction of the TPC failed, the underwriters made an alternative submission that the policy should be avoided because the broker did not disclose the existence and purpose of those two clauses. The wording of the TPC has been cited in Chapter 3, and the NAC read as follows:[33]

> The Underwriters will not:
>
> (a) Seek to avoid or repudiate this contract for non-disclosure or misrepresentation other than fraudulent non-disclosure or fraudulent misrepresentation; or
>
> (b) Rely on, or assert any breach of warranty as grounds for the Underwriters to be discharged from any liability other than where the warranty was given fraudulently; or
>
> (c) Seek damages for or seek to reject a claim for loss on the grounds of: (i) Non-disclosure or misrepresentation other than fraudulent non-disclosure or fraudulent misrepresentation; or (ii) Any breach of warranty other than where the warranty was given fraudulently.

The underwriters argued that the assured should have disclosed the existence and purpose of the TPC and NAC. The policy was governed by the Marine Insurance Act 1906 and Jacobs J, referring to s 18(3)(b) of the Act, held that the assured need not disclose the existence of them because "the terms of the policy that the underwriter subscribes … are clearly either known or presumed to be known to the insurer".[34]

The judge then relied on *Iron Trades Mutual Insurance v Companhia De Seguros Imperio*[35] and ruled that the assured need not disclose the purpose of the

33 *ABN Amro* [2021] EWHC 442 (Comm), [464].

34 Ibid, [597].

35 (1992) Lloyd's Rep IR 213, 224.

two clauses, either, since "the insurer is presumed to know his own business and to be able to form his own judgment of the risk; the proposer is under no duty to offer the insurer advice; the duty relates to facts not opinions".[36]

Nor did he accept that the existence and purpose of the TPC constituted an unusual circumstance. He said that the TPC did not "involve a minor tweak to standard wording which might perhaps go unnoticed",[37] and thus a reasonably careful underwriter presented with such "a lengthy and unfamiliar clause" would be prompted to make further enquiries if interested in its true effect and purpose.

The "comprehensive" effect of the NAC

The assured in *ABN Amro* argued that the NAC would preclude any avoidance for non-fraudulent non-disclosure, such as the alleged non-disclosure of the TPC and NAC. The underwriters, however, contended that the non-disclosure of the presence of the NAC had two consequences: (a) it would prevent reliance on the NAC itself, and (b) it would render the entire contract void. The underwriters invited the trial court to decide this issue, which they believed "would be a matter of interest for any prudent underwriter" because "the clause would be material to the risk being written, since it restricted the nature and extent of the insured's disclosure about the risk".[38]

This was indeed a tricky issue. To deal with it, Jacobs J started with the following statement:[39]

> The starting point is the principle that a person who signs a document knowing that it is intended to have legal effect is generally bound by its terms, whether he has actually read them or not … this is an important principle of English law which underpins the whole of commercial life: any erosion of it would have serious repercussions far beyond the business community.

Then, referring to a number of case authorities where the NAC had been given effect,[40] Jacobs J clarified that the true effect and scope of the NAC should depend on its language. Given that the NAC had been agreed by underwriters in a signed document, the only relevant question was whether the NAC extended, as a matter of construction, to all non-fraudulent non-disclosure. He clarified that there was no "residual category" of non-fraudulent disclosure (i.e., the alleged non-fraud-

36 Ibid.
37 *ABN Amro* [2021] EWHC 442 (Comm), [599].
38 Ibid, [456]–[457].
39 Ibid, [472].
40 *ABN Amro* [2021] EWHC 442 (Comm), [466], [473]-[484]. The relevant case authorities include: *Toomey v Eagle Star (No. 2)* [1995] 2 Lloyd's Rep 88; *HIH Casualty and General Insurance Ltd v New Hampshire Insurance Co and others* [2001] EWCA Civ 735; *HIH Casualty and General Insurance Ltd v Chase Manhattan Bank* [2003] UKHL 6; *Mutual Energy Ltd v Starr Underwriting Agents Ltd* [2016] EWHC 590 (TCC).

ulent disclosure of the NAC itself) that the underwriters could rely on to avoid the contract as a whole. The learned judge further commented that the NAC was not collateral or separable or akin to an arbitration or jurisdiction clause,[41] and thus it was impermissible to isolate innocent non-disclosure affecting the NAC itself. Since the underwriters did not allege any fraudulent non-disclosure, Jacobs J held that the policy (including the NAC itself) survived and the underwriters' non-disclosure defences failed.[42] In sum, *ABN Amro* shows that the NAC is a "comprehensive"[43] clause: it "stands or falls with the policy as a whole".[44]

The non-disclosure of the TPC and NAC in light of the IA 2015?

This research submits that Jacobs J's analysis of the non-disclosure of the TPC and NAC in *ABN Amro* remains perfectly applicable in light of the IA 2015. Should the policy be governed by the new law, the assured can, relying on ss 3(5)(c) and 5(2)(b) of the IA 2015, establish that such a circumstance constitutes a piece of "relevant information" held by the insurer and "readily available" to the individual leading underwriter, a fact which the insurer ought to know. Of course, as is suggested by the commentator, if the amendments of a policy for renewal are in some way buried or hidden, then the assured or its broker must make a fair representation of those terms. Otherwise, the insurer could justifiably argue that the presentation was not reasonably clear and accessible to a prudent insurer as required by s 3(3)(b) of the IA 2015.[45]

Misrepresentation as the foundation for an estoppel to circumvent the application of the NAC?

Two following underwriters in *ABN Amro*, who are the 8th and 10th defendants of the case, advanced a separate argument on misrepresentation. As explained in Chapter 2, the TPC and NAC were first introduced in July 2015. The leading underwriter scratched the July 2015 endorsement but did not instruct the broker to circulate it to the following market, which included the 8th and 10th defendants.

41 See *HIH Casualty and General Insurance Ltd v New Hampshire Insurance Co and others* [2001] EWCA Civ 735, [2001] 2 All ER (Comm) 39, [182] (Rix LJ); *HIH Casualty and General Insurance Ltd v Chase Manhattan Bank* [2003] UKHL 6, [2003] 1 All ER (Comm) 349, [98] (Lord Hobhouse); *Enka Insaat Ve Sanayi AS v OOO Insurance Company Chubb* [2020] UKSC 38, [2020] 1 WLR 4117, [41], [61]–[63], [232].

42 *ABN Amro* [2021] EWHC 442 (Comm), [477], [484].

43 Ibid, [476].

44 Robert Merkin, *Colinvaux's Law of Insurance* (2nd Supplement, 12th edn, Sweet & Maxwell 2021) [7-374].

45 Ibid, [7-302]. It should be noted that in *ABN Amro* Jacobs J rejected the allegation that there was any "moral fault" on the part of the broker by making a subtle revision of the wording in a disguised way. He noted that the TPC was a prominent clause originally presented to the leading underwriter as part of a three-page document, which should be read by a professional underwriter before he signs. See *ABN Amro* [2021] EWHC 442 (Comm), [621].

Accordingly, those two following underwriters were not aware of the TPC and NAC. The broker honestly believed that the leading underwriter had agreed on the TPC on behalf of the entire following market. However, it was clarified by Jacobs that only the leading underwriter, and not the following market, was bound by the TPC and the NAC contained in the July 2015 endorsement.[46]

When the prior year's policy was renewed to become the 2016 policy, each of the underwriters, including the 8th and 10th defendants, scratched or signed, and was given a copy of the 2016 policy wording including the TPC and the NAC, but none of them carefully read it through. When the broker presented the renewal to those two underwriters, they were told that the renewal policy was "as expiry".

The two underwriters thus alleged that the broker made a misrepresentation which would establish an estoppel by convention which prevented the assured from relying on the TPC and NAC. Jacobs J accepted that there had been a non-fraudulent misrepresentation and clarified that different from other underwriters, these two underwriters made the assumption that the terms which they were considering were "as expiry", which was the result of the positive statement made by the broker during the renewal broke. The judge did not criticise them for not reading through the 2016 policy as following underwriters, and thus he thought it unjust to allow the assured "whose broker acquiesced in the assumption" to go back on it.[47] He further stated that the NAC did not apply to the "as expiry" misrepresentation as the foundation for an estoppel by convention:[48] The potential advantage of the argument from the perspective of these underwriters is that it potentially circumvents the difficulties in their avoidance case, and in particular the effect of the NAC and affirmation.

Therefore, these two underwriters were held not liable to indemnify the assured, and accordingly, the broker became liable to the assured in respect of the two underwriters' share of the indemnity. Both the underwriters and the broker appealed, but the underwriters chose to compromise their appeal. The broker's appeal thus became the focus. They did not dispute their duties to the assured but questioned Jacobs J's decision on the "as expiry" misrepresentation case. The broker contended that the parties were at cross purposes about the meaning of "as expiry": the broker understood "as expiry" to include the TPC and NAC, whereas the 8th and 10th defendants understood "as expiry" as not including them. Referring to *Jones v Lydon*,[49] the broker argued that an estoppel by convention by acquiescence could not succeed if the party making the representation did not know that the other party had a different understanding.

Sir Geoffrey Vos held that the subjective nature of a conventional understanding and acquiescence requires the meaning of a representation to be determined by how a reasonable representee would understand it. He ruled that a reasonable

46 For details, see Chapter 2.
47 Ibid, [698].
48 Ibid, [695].
49 [2021] EWHC 2321 (Ch), [2021] 8 WLUK 149, [58] (Mann J).

representee in the position of the two underwriters would plainly understand "as expiry" as not including those two clauses. Nevertheless, he held that it would not be unjust for the assured to resile from the assumption that the policy did not include the TPC and NAC because "the clear law" is "that underwriters are bound by the terms of the slip to which they subscribe, whether they read it or not".[50]

Sir Geoffrey Vos also overruled the trial decision that the "as expiry" misrepresentation argument could circumvent the application of the NAC. Referring to *HIH Casualty v Chase Manhattan Bank*,[51] the judge reiterated that exclusion clauses were to be construed strictly against those they protected, and the clearest language was required to exclude or waive legal rights. He found that the NAC does not expressly preclude reliance on an estoppel, and therefore "it bites on the estoppel whether it is an estoppel by convention or representation – both being based on the 'as expiry' misrepresentation". He further commented that:[52]

> For completeness, I should say that … the [trial] judge was wrong to say … that "the potential advantage of the estoppel argument … is that it potentially circumvents the difficulties in their avoidance case, and in particular the effect of the NAC and affirmation". The [trial] judge assumed that the NAC only prohibited **avoidance** for non-fraudulent misrepresentation and overlooked the fact that it also prohibits **rejection of a claim** for non-fraudulent misrepresentation.
>
> (Emphasis added by Sir Geoffrey Vos)

Therefore, the 8th and 10th defendants were held liable to the assured, and the broker was released of their liability.

Waiver

In English ECI cases concerning misrepresentation and non-disclosure, the courts not only applied the rules in general insurance law but also contributed to the development of the general rules, particularly to the rules concerning the insurer's waiver of the right to disclosure and the insurer's waiver of the right to avoidance.

Waiver of the assured's duty to disclosure: the "frame of reference" formulation

According to s 3(5) of the IA 2015, in the absence of enquiry, the assured need not disclose a circumstance if "it is something as to which the insurer waives information". The waiver can be either express or implied, but most disputes arose on the

50 *ABN Amro* [2021] EWCA Civ 1789, [98].
51 [2003] 2 Lloyd's Rep 61, [11] (Lord Bingham).
52 *ABN Amro* [2021] EWCA Civ 1789, [96].

implied waiver.[53] The general principle of implied waiver is that the absence of enquiries by the insurer on certain facts does not necessarily mean that the facts are immaterial, and whether there is a waiver should be decided on a case-by-case basis.[54] English insurance cases have not been consistent in this area; hence, it is not easy to formulate clear guidance from them.[55] Nevertheless, in *Morgan Grenfell*, the court developed the "frame of reference" formulation, which is helpful to decide whether the insurer has impliedly waived its right of disclosure.

In *Morgan Grenfell*, before taking the risk, SACE failed to ask questions about the foreign buyer's financial standing and the project's viability, and the assured bank asserted that this constituted an implied waiver of the disclosure of these facts. Under the "frame of reference" formulation established by the court, a fact is immaterial unless it "(a) falls within the scope of a question specifically asked in the proposal or (b) falls, for reasons of consistency, within the frame of reference set by the proposal".[56]

Applying that test to the case, Clarke LJ scrutinised the questionnaire in SACE's standard proposal form and found that no questions were specifically raised about the buyer's financial standing and the viability of the project. Therefore, these facts did not fall within category (a) of the test.

His lordship then turned to determine whether these facts fell within the frame of reference set by the proposal. First, he found that prior to the present application, the assured had made many applications for SACE's buyer credit insurance covers over the past decade, but none of these application forms included questions on the buyer's financial standing and the project's viability. Second, he noted that in the promotion manuals published in previous years, SACE stated that for the evaluation of political risks, the central aspect was the evaluation of country risk ("whether the foreign state or public entity will be good for the money"). The factors of the buyer's financial standing and the project's viability were not mentioned at all. Third, he reviewed the basis on which SACE calculated premiums and found that for political risks it fixed the premiums exclusively by reference to the specific country risk regardless of the buyer's financial standing and the project's viability. Taking all the evidence into consideration, Clarke LJ ruled that those facts did not fall within category (b) of the test. Therefore, the court held that SACE had waived its right to disclosure of those facts.

Morgan Grenfell demonstrated clearly how the court dealt with the issue of waiver of the duty of disclosure in the context of ECI. Clarke LJ, approving the trial judge, developed the "frame of reference" test to determine whether the implied waiver can be established. Under that formulation, if a certain fact is not specifically asked, it is deemed to have been waived by the insurer unless it falls

53 Merkin (n 26), [7-274-298].

54 *Schoolman v Hall* [1951] 1 Lloyd's Rep 139; *Arterial Caravans v Yorkshire Insurance* [1973] 1 Lloyd's Rep 169; *Doheny & ors v New India Assurance Company Ltd & ors* [2004] EWCA Civ 1705, [2005] 1 All ER (Comm) 382.

55 Merkin (n 26), [7-278-298].

56 *Morgan Grenfell* [2001] EWCA Civ 1932, [80].

within the frame of reference set by the insurer's questionnaires. His lordship further pointed out that the proper interpretation of the "frame of reference" test is "ultimately evidential", and the court must "ultimately depend on the nature and particular circumstances of each case".[57] Clarke LJ gave good examples of the evidential factors a court can take into consideration in insurance cases: the history of the transaction between the assured and the insurer, the manuals, prospectus or booklets published by the insurer and the way the insurer calculated premiums. Those factors are not only common in ECI cases but also can be found in other types of insurance cases. Therefore, the "frame of reference" test contributed to the development of the rules on the insurer's waiver of the assured's duty of disclosure.

Waiver of the right to avoid the contract: the "legal advice" presumption

Even if the materiality and inducement tests both have been satisfied, the insurer will still need to take positive action to inform the assured of avoiding the contract (or other proportionate remedies under the IA 2015), as failure to do so may result in a finding of waiver. To establish a waiver by affirmation, the assured must prove that the insurer has made an unequivocal statement that it would be bound by the contract and that it knows that it has the right to avoid the contract.[58] These principles were confirmed in the context of ECI in *ABN Amro* by Jacobs J, who noted that affirmation provided "a second complete answer" (apart from the application of the NAC) to the suggested avoidance.[59] However, it is sometimes difficult for the assured to prove the insurer's knowledge of the right of avoidance. In *Moore Large*, the court introduced the "legal advice" presumption to address the problem.

In *Moore Large*, Euler Hermes focused on the issue of an aggregation clause. However, neither in its original defence nor in its solicitor letter to the assured did Euler Hermes raise the issue of non-disclosure. In the amended defence, it raised the argument of non-disclosure for the first time, but it still made no express reference to the right of avoidance. The assured therefore claimed that Euler Hermes had waived its right to avoid the contract for non-disclosure. Euler Hermes, on the other hand, argued that by the time of the amended defence, it knew nothing about its right of avoidance.

The court accepted that Euler Hermes had made an unequivocal statement that it would be bound by the policy. Colman J pointed out that under the principle of avoidance in insurance law, for the court to establish an affective affirmation, the insurer must have knowledge of all the facts related to the right of avoidance.[60] However, the judge found it difficult for the assured to prove that

57 Ibid, [95]–[98].
58 Özlem Gürses, *Marine Insurance Law* (2nd edn, Routledge 2017) 92–5.
59 *ABN Amro* [2021] EWHC 442 (Comm), [448], [529], [541].
60 *The Kanchenjunga* [1990] 1 Lloyd's Rep 391.

because the legal documents between Euler Hermes and its solicitor were privileged and inaccessible. To solve this "evidential problem", the learned judge referred to relevant case authorities. He held that the insurer's knowledge of the legal rights should be inferred from the fact that the insurer received legal advice[61] unless the insurer could prove that it was never told by its legal advisers of a certain legal tactic or choice.[62] Colman J added that even without the legal advice, as a professional credit insurer, Euler Hermes was generally acquainted with the rules of avoidance for non-disclosure. He therefore held that Euler Hermes had elected to affirm the policy and was disentitled to avoid the ECI contract.

Moore Large solved the evidential difficulties in the waiver of avoidance by introducing the "legal advice" presumption.[63] The court exempted the assured from proving that the insurer knew about the right of avoidance. Instead, Colman J established the assumption that the insurer knows such consequences unless he proves he did not know. *Moore Large* also showed the importance for an ECA to make the correct "tactical decisions" in legal proceedings of a dispute concerning the insured's breach of the duty of fair presentation.[64] In the amended defence, Euler Hermes tried very hard to persuade the court on the issue of materiality and inducement but eventually lost the issue of the waiver and therefore was not entitled to avoid the policy. If it insisted on the assertion of non-disclosure and expressly claimed avoidance before the trial, it would have been entitled to avoid the policy. Unfortunately, Euler Hermes debated fiercely on the issue of aggregation instead, which made the court hold that it had regarded the policy as binding.

The UKEF's questionnaire in the ECI cover proposal form

It is evident that the UKEF has gained experiences from *Morgan Grenfell* which led it to develop a very detailed questionnaire in the ECI application form. The form is designed in a way providing clear guidance to determine the issue of materiality and inducement in future ECI disputes.

Taking the UKEF's "Export Insurance Policy" as an example, to obtain the cover, the exporter should submit an "Export Insurance Policy Proposal Form",[65] in which he must provide information on his corporate details, nature of business, turnover, credit control and collections, buyer details, trading information,

61 *Peyman v Lanjani* [1985] 1 Ch 457.

62 *Evans v Bartlam* [1937] AC 473, 479.

63 Mance and others (n 11) 155; Alison Padfield, *Insurance Claims* (2nd edn, Tottel Publishing 2007) 207.

64 John Lowry, Philip Rawlings, Robert Merkin, *Insurane Law: Doctrines and Principles* (3rd edn, Hart 2011) 135.

65 See <https://assets.publishing.service.gov.uk/government/uploads/system/uploads/attachment_data/file/898048/10489_UKEF_Export_Insurance_Proposal_Form_20200331-fillable.pdf> accessed 1 February 2022.

other insurance arrangements, export contract and broker (see Appendix 4.1 of this book).

Section 15 of the "Export Insurance Policy Proposal Form" also requires the exporter to make the following confirmations and acknowledgements:[66]

By signing and submitting this Proposal:

> (1) you confirm that the information contained in this Proposal and any related discussions or correspondence constitutes a fair presentation of the risk to include all material facts and circumstances; and
> (2) you acknowledge that: (a) you should contact us or your broker (if applicable) if you are in any doubt as to what constitutes a material fact; (b) we will rely on the information, statements and declarations in this Proposal when deciding whether, and on what terms, to issue any policy; and (c) you must continue to disclose material facts to us and any changes to material facts after the date of signature of this Proposal until the date cover commences under any policy unless this would, or might reasonably be considered to, constitute the offence of "tipping off" under s 333A of the Proceeds of Crime Act 2002.

Therefore, the UKEF now raise very detailed questions concerning the exporter, the buyer, the underlying transaction and the viability of the project. It also requires the exporter to make specific confirmations and acknowledgements. All of these can help protect the UKEF on the issue of materiality and inducement in future ECI disputes.

It should be noted that the "Export Insurance Policy" is a basic ECI cover where the assured is the exporter. Where the ECA issues a supplier/buyer credit insurance policy, the assured who is under the duty of fair presentation will be the bank. Nevertheless, ECAs might also contain a separate clause requiring the exporter (who is financed by the bank) to disclose any material facts about the transaction. For instance, the annex section of SERV's buyer credit insurance policy requires the exporter to declare:[67]

> Duty of disclosure
>
> We are aware that we shall provide full and accurate information about any circumstances of the export transaction that are materially relevant to the granting of the export credit insurance during the application procedure and after the insurance applied for has been granted. This also includes answering [the ECA]'s questions regarding the identity of persons who are or were involved on their behalf in arranging the export contract (Agents), and the reason for and amount of any payments to those persons.

66 Ibid, 10.
67 See SERV's policy, 7.

Contractual clauses in relation to the duty of fair presentation

Stipulating the duty of fair presentation as a condition precedent to liability?

In addition to the detailed questionnaires contained in the proposal form for the assured to complete, ECAs or private credit insurers may also include express contractual provisions in their ECI policies stipulating that the assured was subject to the duty of fair presentation. Such provisions can be stipulated as conditions precedent to the insurer's liability. For instance, the ECI policy in *International Management Group* included a clause stating:

> It is a condition precedent to this insurance that Assured has:
>
> (i) Diligently made all necessary enquiries and truthfully declared all material facts likely to influence a prudent underwriter in determining: (a) Whether or not to accept the risk; (b) The premium; and (c) The conditions, exclusions and limitations;
>
> (ii) No knowledge at the inception of any matter, fact or circumstance, actual or threatened that increases or could increase the possibility of a loss under this insurance.

In this case, the insurer relied on the assured's breach of both the duty of utmost good faith and that condition precedent. Having established the non-disclosure case, Cooke J nevertheless thought it was necessary to analyse the issue of the breach of conditions precedent. The learned judge held that the effect of the latter was basically the same as avoidance by underwriters for non-disclosure, except that the insurer had an option whether or not to "take advantage of the provision" and keep the premiums (in the absence of fraud). It is also suggested by the commentator that such a condition precedent might be useful for the insurer in that it (a) "removed the need for proof of inducement" and (b) required the assured to investigate the existence of possible material facts, "a duty which the common law does now recognise".[68]

Notably, *International Management Group* was decided in the regime of the MIA 1906. It is necessary to examine whether the analysis above remains applicable under the IA 2015. On the one hand, the IA 2015 provides proportionate remedies for the breach of the duty of fair presentation. The insurer is entitled to keep the premiums if the assured's breach is deliberate or reckless[69] or, of course, fraudulent,[70] but it should return the premiums in all other circumstances. Therefore, where the assured breaches a condition precedent, and that breach is neither fraudulent nor deliberate or reckless, then the insurer can still have

68 See "Coverage, Warranties and Utmost Good Faith: Sports Events and Cancellation Cover" [2003] (15) *Insurance Law Monthly*.

69 The IA 2015, Pt 1, Sch 1.

70 Ibid, s 12(2).

an option whether or not to keep the premiums. On the other hand, although s 11 of the IA 2015 reduced the harshness of insurance contractual terms, such as warranties and conditions precedent, that does not affect the effect of conditions precedent regarding the duty of fair presentation. What constitutes a risk-defining term has been discussed in detail in Chapter 3 of this research. However, it is worthwhile here to briefly analyse the conditions precedent in the context of the duty of fair presentation: such clauses clearly "have a general limiting effect" rather than being "linked to a specific risk sector".[71] The insurer's decision on whether to underwrite/refuse to underwrite the risks as a whole or to exclude some of the risks depends on the assured's strict compliance with such clauses. Therefore, conditions precedent in relation to the duty of fair presentation fall outside the scope of s 11. It thus can be seen that stipulating the assured's duty of fair presentation as a condition precedent to liability may still bring some advantages to the insurer under the IA 2015.

Non-avoidance clause

Turning the coin, an ECI policy can also include certain clauses that protect the assured under the duty of fair presentation. One typical example is the NAC discussed above. As was confirmed by both the trial court and the Court of Appeal in *ABN Amro*, the NAC "is a common exclusion clause in the marine market, intended to apply to a non-disclosure or misrepresentation made on behalf of the insured in breach of the duty to disclose under sections 18 and 20 of the MIA 1906".[72] It is perfectly fine for the assured to include an NAC in ECI under the IA 2015, provided that it contracts out of relevant provisions under the new law in compliance with the transparency requirements.[73]

Is the creditor under ECG subject to the duty of fair presentation?

The creditor is under no duty of disclosure: Credit Lyonnais

Whilst there are a few English ECI cases concerning the duty of fair presentation, there is so far only one ECG case in which the English courts dealt with the issues of misrepresentation and non-disclosure: in *Credit Lyonnais*,[74] an exporter concocted wholly fictitious sales contracts supported by fraudulent bills of exchange with forged acceptance in the name of imaginary foreign buyers. A bank was persuaded by the exporter to purchase the bills of exchange and apply for Export Credits Guarantee Department (ECGD)'s ECG cover. The transaction was facilitated by Mr P, an employee of the ECGD, who was bribed by the exporter and had

71 Stakeholder Note: Terms Not Relevant to the Actual Loss reproduced in H.L. Paper 81, 47.
72 *ABN Amro* [2021] EWCA Civ 1789, [94].
73 See Merkin (n 26), [7-372].
74 [1996] CLC 11.

knowledge of the scheme to defraud the bank. In concluding the ECG, the ECGD asked the bank the details of the exporter and the buyer and was told that the management of the exporter was "respectable, trustworthy, highly able and efficient" and that no difficulties occurred in the exporter's business. However, the bank in fact did not check the factual accuracy of its answers. The fraudster exporter disappeared after receiving £10m from the bank, who then claimed against the ECGD in contract and in tort (which will be discussed at the end of this chapter).

With respect to the claim in contract, the ECGD defended on the grounds of misrepresentation and non-disclosure. Confirming that the applicable law in the present case was the law of guarantee rather than insurance law, Longmore J (the trial judge) confirmed the alleged misrepresentation but rejected the non-disclosure argument:

On the issue of misrepresentation, Longmore J held that the bank was making a representation that it had a genuine factual basis for its answers as to the exporter's business. However, as it in fact had no factual basis for its answers, the judge held that the bank was making a material misrepresentation.

On the issue of non-disclosure, however, Longmore J held that the bank was under no general duty to investigate the genuineness of the underlying transaction and to disclose any unusual matters to the ECGD; to do so would be applying the duties of an insured to an insurer and there was no authority for that. He confirmed that a bank is under an obligation to reveal to a surety anything in its transaction with its customer which revealed the position of the customer as different from that which the surety would normally expect, particularly if it affected the nature or degree of the surety's responsibility, but he pointed out that in the present case the non-disclosure was about the purported export contracts and their financing and did not relate to the transaction between the banker and its customer. Besides, suspicions as to the genuineness of the export contracts did relate to such a transaction, but since the bank was required to disclose knowledge rather than mere suspicions, it did not have to disclose the suspicions to the ECGD.[75]

Thus, misrepresentation was found in *Credit Lyonnais*, but non-disclosure was not. Longmore J thus held that the ECGD was entitled to rescind the ECG contract because it relied on the misrepresented information as mentioned above.[76] It should be noted that the trial court did not address the inducement issue, whereas the Court of Appeal clarified that the bank's misrepresentation did not induce the ECG, since Mr P, when authorising the issuance of the ECG, was aware of the fraud. The ECGD was thus held not entitled to rescind the ECG. However, Stuart-Smith LJ ruled that the bank's claim in contract still failed because (a) (as discussed in Chapter 3 of this book) an ECG only covers genuine transactions and (b) the bank's losses were caused by its own recklessness in checking the genuineness of the transaction.

75 Ibid, 12–3.
76 See *Credit Lyonnais* [1999] CLC 823, 830–5.

General rules on misrepresentation and non-disclosure in the law of guarantee

Credit Lyonnais reflected the general rules the English court adopted when deciding issues of misrepresentation and non-disclosure in contracts of guarantee. Unlike insurance law, there is no statutory law imposing on the creditor a duty of fair presentation to the surety, but case law has provided much guidance in this area. The basic point is that since a contract of guarantee is not a contract *uberrimae fidei*,[77] the creditor is under no duty of fair presentation as the insured would be under a contract of insurance. However, misrepresentation and certain non-disclosure could vitiate a contract of guarantee in some situations.

Misrepresentation of material facts by the creditor could entitle a surety to rescind the contract.[78] Sureties are entitled to true, honest and accurate answers to their questions about any matters germane to the guarantee.[79] Although an early case suggests that the surety was entitled to rescind the contract even for minor misrepresentations,[80] the currently accepted rule is that to rescind a contract of guarantee, the surety must prove that a misrepresentation is material in accordance with the general principles of contract law.[81]

Therefore, the scope of misrepresentation in contracts of guarantee looks substantially the same as that in contracts of insurance. To establish a creditor's misrepresentation there is also a requirement on materiality although it is not codified as is the materiality test in an insured's misrepresentation under s 7 of the IA 2015. The creditor's misrepresentation could be made on a broad scope of matters including "the financial position or state of accounts of the principal debtor, the creditor's policy and intentions as to terms of the principal contracts, the need and purpose of the guarantee and the extent of the surety's liability under the guarantee".[82]

However, there is no general duty of full disclosure under the contract of guarantee, except that the creditor must disclose "any unusual feature" of the contract between itself and the debtor.[83] There is a later authority which extended the duty of disclosure as to unusual features of the "contractual relationship" between the creditor and the principal debtor which "makes it materially different in a potentially disadvantageous respect from what the guarantor might naturally expect",[84]

77 *Seaton v Heath* [1899] 1 QB 782, 792 (Romer LJ).

78 *Mackenzie v Royal Bank of Canada* [1934] AC 468.

79 *Westminster Bank Ltd v Cond* (1940) 46 Com Cas 60.

80 *Davies v London and Provincial Marine Insurance Co* (1878) 8 Ch D 469.

81 *North Shore Ventures Ltd v Anstead Holdings Inc* [2011] EWCA Civ 230, [2011] 2 Lloyd's Rep 45; *Bank of India v Riat* [2014] EWHC 1775 (Ch). See also the Hon Mrs Justice Geraldine Andrews & Richard Millett QC, *Law of Guarantees* (7th edn, Sweet & Maxwell 2015), [5-006].

82 James O'Donovan & John Phillips, *The Modern Contract of Guarantee* (English edn, Sweet & Maxwell 2003), [4-36].

83 *North British Insurance Co v Lloyd* (1854) 10 Ex 523; *Railton v Matthews* (1844) 10 Cl & F 934; *London General Omnibus Co v Holloway* [1912] 2 KB 72.

84 This means that even an informal arrangement between the creditor and the debtor should be disclosed if it has any unusual feature. See *Royal Bank of Scotland v Etridge* [2001] UKHL 44, [2002] Lloyd's Rep 343.

but still, the duty of disclosure in the context of guarantees was limited to the scope of "any unusual feature".

It thus seems that the scope of non-disclosure in contracts of guarantee is much narrower than that in insurance contracts. English guarantee cases indicated that the creditor must only disclose "unusual features" related to its contract with the debtor, and anything beyond that need not be disclosed. In insurance contracts, on the other hand, an insured should disclose every material circumstance related to the risks. The scope of "material facts" is much broader than the scope of "unusual features". This is perhaps why the English courts reached different conclusions in *Credit Lyonnais* and *Morgan Grenfell*: in *Credit Lyonnais*, an ECG case, the bank was held under no duty to investigate the underlying transaction and failure to do so need not be disclosed, whereas in *Morgan Grenfell*, an ECI case, the bank was held under such duty and the failure to do so was held a material fact that needed to be disclosed. Those cases show the courts' different attitudes towards the duty of disclosure in ECI and ECG contracts.

Such divergence could pose significant difficulties for the UKEF. Although the UKEF is entitled to full disclosure under ECI, it has a very limited right of disclosure under ECGs. As is illustrated in Chapter 2, the transaction structures of supplier/buyer credit insurance and supplier/buyer credit guarantees could be very similar, and the only difference is whether the UKEF acts as an insurer or a surety. Taking *Credit Lyonnais* as an example, under a supplier credit guarantee, to assess the risks the UKEF needs sufficient information about the bank (the creditor), the exporter and the foreign buyer (the principal debtor). Under the general rules in the law of guarantee, the bank only needs to disclose any unusual features related to its contract with the foreign buyer, but, as Longmore J pointed out in *Credit Lyonnais*, it had in fact no contractual relationship with the foreign buyer, so it needed to disclose almost nothing. However, what if the UKEF issues a supplier credit insurance cover to the bank? The bank will then be obliged to make full disclosure about the exporter and the foreign buyer, as seen in *Morgan Grenfell*. That seems unfair to the UKEF, especially as it now only offers guarantee products for supplier/buyer credit transactions.

That issue was further examined by the Berne Union Academic Survey, in response to which the Berne Union members thought that whether under ECI or ECGs, the following facts are always material for them to assess the risks:[85]

- The financial standing of the buyer/borrower;
- The genuineness of the underlying export contract;
- The country risks;
- The financial standing of the exporter and other skills of the exporter;

85 Cheng Lin, "Berne Union Academic Survey: The Legal Nature of Buyer Credit Insurance and Buyer Credit Guarantee", *The BUlletin (The Official Newsletter of the Berne Union)*, January 2020, 27 <https://www.berneunion.org/Articles/Details/489/January-BUlletin-Mega-Trends-and-Trade> accessed 1 February 2022.

- The bank's and exporter's compliance with the Corporate Social Responsibility (CSR), Anti-Money Laundering (AML) and Know Your Customer (KYC) requirements.

Therefore, ECAs believe they should be entitled to equal access to the abovementioned information under ECI and ECGs, but clearly, the current English guarantee law does not establish such a rule. Is that a shortcoming of the law which needs to be reformed? To examine that question, it is necessary to explore the rationale for the general rule of the creditor's limited duty of disclosure.

The rationale for the creditor's limited duty of disclosure: does it apply to ECGs?

The distinction between credit insurance and credit guarantees in terms of the duty of disclosure is well elaborated in *MacGillivray on Insurance Law*:[86]

> This distinction is not an easy one to apply in practice, since both types of contracts involve an undertaking to pay upon the event of a default by another, and it turns on the construction of the agreement in issue. Where the guarantor (whether described as "surety" or "insurer") is engaged by the debtor and is also a party to a transaction with the creditor whereby he guarantees its performance by the debtor or agrees to answer in some other manner for the debt, default or miscarriage of another, then the agreement is a contract of surety, because it creates the tripartite contractual relationship of creditor, debtor and surety. If, however, the guarantor is engaged by the creditor and charges a realistic premium in consideration for paying a set sum in the contingency of the creditor suffering a default by the debtor, but his obligation is not mentioned in or required by the original contract between the creditor and debtor, then the guarantee given is in substance made in the form of an insurance. It is quite logical that there should be a duty of disclosure owed to the insurer by the creditor, since there is no reason why the insurer should be conversant with the situation of the debtor. In a contract of surety, however, the surety is engaged by the debtor, and has as good a chance of knowing or discovering facts relevant to the debtor's capacity to perform as the creditor.

It thus seems that, among the varied reasons to justify the general rule of the creditor's limited duty of disclosure under a contract of guarantee, the most crucial one is that the surety is assumed to be acquainted with the principal debtor's position and will have ready access to its financial statements. He is presumed to know that the guarantee is intended to secure repayment of the debt and that dissatisfaction with the principal debtor's account is the probable reason for the creditor to

86 Birds and others (n 10), [17-101].

insist on such a guarantee.[87] This is because, in general, the surety provides the guarantee out of mere motives of friendship with the debtor or due to some business association, but not as a result of any direct bargaining between the creditor and the surety. Suretyship can arise between husband and wife, company and directors, mortgagor and mortgagee, landlord and tenant, vendor and purchasers, contractor and subcontractor.[88] In all those relationships, it is reasonable to assume that the surety knows the risks.

Other reasons why the creditor is under a limited duty of disclosure include practicalities, business efficacy and confidentiality requirements. In *Hamilton v Waston*,[89] Lord Campbell suggested that no bankers would "rest satisfied" if full disclosure of all material facts were required as it is "quite unnecessary" to do so. In *London General Omnibus Co Ltd v Holloway*,[90] Farwell LJ stressed that full disclosure might result in the bank's breach of its duty of confidence to its clients, namely the principal debtors.

However, this research argues that the abovementioned rationales do not fit easily into the context of ECGs. To conclude an ECG contract, it is the creditor, i.e., the bank, who bargains with the surety, i.e., the UKEF. The UKEF has no means of knowledge about the principal debtor. The principal debtor can be either the exporter (under supplier credit guarantees) or the foreign buyer (under buyer credit guarantees). In particular, if the debtor is a foreign buyer, it would be extremely difficult for the UKEF to conduct overseas investigations. Even if the debtor is an exporter who is based within the UK, it will also be a huge cost for the UKEF to investigate every exporter in every single transaction before granting an ECG cover. The only evidence that the UKEF can rely on is the export contract and the relevant underlying documents, but even an export contract could be forged, as seen in *Credit Lyonnais*. Moreover, by issuing ECG covers, the UKEF is using the state fund of the UK, which comes from every taxpayer. The UKEF should make good use of the fund and try to avoid any unnecessary loss. The value of business efficacy and the duty of confidence in certain contracts of guarantee should not outweigh the very value of business safety in the context of ECGs.

Therefore, it is submitted that there should be a wider duty of disclosure in ECG contracts. An ECG is a special contract of guarantee, and it operates in much a similar way as an ECI. In ECI contracts the UKEF relies on the bank's disclosure of every material circumstance concerning the underlying export contract and the buyer's financial standing, which is also the case in ECGs. Since it is entitled to the full disclosure in ECI contracts under the IA 2015, why should it be deprived of such a right in ECG contracts? The court in *Credit Lyonnais* simply followed the general rules in guarantee law, which seems overly conservative and unsatisfactory. It would be more appropriate if the courts impose on the bank

87 *Fitzgerald v Jacomb* (1873) 4 AJR 189, 190.
88 O'Donovan & Phillips (n 82), [1-40], [1-113-114].
89 (1845) 12 Cl & F 109.
90 [1912] 2 KB 72.

a duty of disclosure of every material circumstance to the UKEF in future ECG cases. The proposal on what the law should be is provided below.

A tendency that the ECA is importing the duty of fair presentation into ECG business?

Express contractual provisions on the duty of full disclosure?

Although *Credit Lyonnais* reflected the English court's conservative attitude towards the non-disclosure issues in ECG contracts, the case law leaves it open for the parties themselves to provide that the creditor must disclose certain specific matters to the surety.[91] The UKEF seems to take such a strategy. There is said to be "an increasing tendency"[92] that the UKEF is trying to import the duty of fair presentation, especially the duty of disclosure, into its ECG contracts with the banks. Whilst this research has not found direct evidence that the UKEF imports the duty of disclosure into its ECG contracts with the bank, it is reasonable to conclude that the UKEF gives the exporter a critical role in the conclusion of its ECG contracts with the bank.

As explained in Chapters 2 and 3, in the UKEF's ECG business, it is the exporter who acts as the co-applicant together with the bank for the guarantee, although it is not a party to the ECG contract between the UKEF and the bank. Whilst the bank, as the creditor, is under a very limited duty of disclosure and may also know little about the foreign buyer, the exporter is usually acquainted with the export business with the foreign buyer. The UKEF, therefore, tends to impose a contractual obligation on the exporter to make full disclosure. For example, in the "SCFF Contract", the UKEF provides a wide scope of the exporter's duty of disclosure:[93]

> 5.1 You must promptly inform the UKEF on becoming aware of -
>
> 5.1.1 any circumstances that might materially affect the support to be, or being provided by the UKEF for the financing of the Export Contract; and
>
> 5.1.2 any changes in the Export Contract or any events that affect or may affect its performance".

The UKEF further provides in Clause 9 that:[94]

> If any statement made by you in the Proposal or in any Warranty is incorrect or untrue in any respect which is considered by the UKEF to be material, the UKEF may send to you a notice withdrawing its support for the purchase of

91 *Lee v Jones* (1864) 17 CB (NS) 482.

92 See Andrews & Millett (n 81), [15-009] and fn 29 of that paragraph.

93 See <https://assets.publishing.service.gov.uk/government/uploads/system/uploads/attachment_data/file/889491/supplier-credit-terms-and-conditions.odt> accessed 1 February 2022.

94 Ibid.

> any Negotiable Instruments … and, without prejudice to any rights and remedies at law to which the UKEF may be entitled as a result of such untruth or incorrectness, you will, if so required by the UKEF, immediately … repurchase for cash from the Bank of the Negotiable Instruments purchased by the Bank.

By including these provisions, the UKEF requires the exporter, rather than the bank, to undertake the duty of disclosure. If the exporter breaches the duty, the UKEF is entitled to withdraw the ECG, and the bank is entitled to repurchase or repayment of the facilities. Without a doubt, that approach can keep the UKEF better informed of the underlying export transaction and assess the risks, but a problem may arise when the exporter concocts a wholly fictitious transaction as seen in *Credit Lyonnais*. If the exporter is fraudulent and disappears, it cannot be forced to repay the money to the bank, but the bank would still ask the UKEF to perform the ECG contract to pay for the loss. However, the "SCFF Contract" is concluded between the UKEF and the exporter, and thus it has no legal effect on the bank due to the doctrine of privity of contract. Should the UKEF's right to "withdraw the support" under the "SCFF Contract" mean that it can avoid its ECG contract with the bank? Should the bank bear the loss if the exporter is fraudulent, given that *Credit Lyonnais* does not oblige a bank to investigate the genuineness of the underlying transaction? If such a situation happens in an ECI case, the UKEF can cite *Morgan Grenfell* to argue that the bank should bear the loss because it should have conducted the investigation; but in ECG contracts, the UKEF lacks such case law authority. Will the "SCFF Contract" be sufficient to protect the UKEF's rights? This is still to be tested by the court, but it seems that the UKEF is unlikely to be fully protected by such standard terms and conditions, simply because the bank is not a party to them and should not be bound by them.

Detailed questionnaires for the exporter and the bank to complete

In addition to making express provisions on the exporter's duty of disclosure in the ECA-exporter contract, the UKEF now also designs questionnaires in its standard application forms for the exporter and the bank to complete.

Taking the "Export Working Capital Facility" (a supplier credit guarantee product analysed in Chapter 2) as an example, the UKEF requires two forms to be submitted before it assesses the exporter's application. The first is the "Exporter Questionnaire",[95] which needs to be completed by the exporter only. In that questionnaire, the UKEF makes detailed enquiries on the exporter's corporate details, customer base, exporting experience, capital structure, internal management

95 See < https://assets.publishing.service.gov.uk/government/uploads/system/uploads/attachment_data/file/578136/ukef-bss-ewcs-export-questionnaire.pdf>, accessed 1 February 2022.

and financial facilities (see Appendix 4.2 of this book). Besides, the exporter is required to make the following certification that it:[96]

(a) acknowledges that UKEF will rely on the information in this form (when completed) for the purpose of deciding whether to issue any guarantee at the request of the exporter;
(b) certifies that the facts stated by the exporter in this form are true and that the exporter has neither misrepresented nor omitted any material fact which might have a bearing on UKEF's decision to issue any guarantee on the application of the guarantee requested above;
(c) agrees that for the purposes of this form it shall be deemed to have knowledge of any fact or circumstance, if that knowledge is possessed by one or more of its directors or by the person signing this form on the exporter's behalf;
(d) shall advise UKEF promptly of any changes that may occur to the details shown in this form.

The second form that the UKEF requires is the "Standalone Guarantee Application Form",[97] which should be completed by the exporter and the bank together. The exporter should provide information on its corporate details, export contract details, ancillary details, working capital facility to be guaranteed and its trade agents (if applicable). The bank, on the other hand, should also disclose its corporate details, relationship with the exporter, working capital facility to be guaranteed and security for the guarantee (see Appendix 4.3 of this book).

The "Standalone Guarantee Application Form" requires the exporter and the bank to make certain certifications. The exporter's relevant certifications read as below:[98]

Section 11

(e) The exporter certifies, for the benefit of UKEF and the bank, that the representations and declarations made, and facts stated, by the exporter in this form ... are true and that the exporter has neither misrepresented nor omitted any material fact which might have a bearing on the guarantee requested above.
(f) The exporter agrees that for the purposes of this form, the exporter shall be deemed to have knowledge of any fact or circumstance, if that knowledge is possessed by one or more of its directors or by the person signing this form on its behalf.
(g) The exporter undertakes to UKEF and the bank promptly of any changes that may occur in the details shown in this form.

96 Ibid.
97 See <https://assets.publishing.service.gov.uk/government/uploads/system/uploads/attachment_data/file/618142/EWCS-BSS-stand-alone-application-20170609.pdf> accessed 1 February 2022.
98 Ibid.

(h) The exporter authorises the bank to provide to UKEF such information as UKEF may from time to time require in connection with the export contract or the export contract's performance.

The bank's certifications in Section 17 of the "Standalone Guarantee Application Form" are:[99]

> In each case, the bank (1) represents that the statements made and information provided in this form are true and correct; (but makes no representation as to the truth or correctness of any statement made by the exporter in the other sections of this form); and (2) acknowledges that UKEF will rely on the statements and information in this form when deciding whether or not to enter into the contract.

To instruct the exporter and the bank to complete the two forms above, the UKEF provides a "Guidance on Applying for Export Capital Facility Scheme", in which it explains why it raises the questions in the two forms and expressly reminds the parties that it will place "considerable reliance" on the information in the questionnaire and application form.[100]

It can be seen from the paragraphs above that the UKEF now has very detailed questionnaires for both the exporter and the bank. In addition to answering the questions in the abovementioned two forms, the exporter and the bank are also required in the proposal forms to make the respective certification that they have neither misrepresented nor omitted any material facts and acknowledge that the UKEF will rely on the statements and information in the forms when considering whether to issue the guarantee or not.

By requiring the exporter and the bank to complete the questionnaire and make the certification, the UKEF imports the duty of fair presentation into its ECG business. It clearly raises questions on the material facts that it will rely on when considering the application for the guarantee, which in fact poses a duty of disclosure to both the exporter and the bank. The certification made by the exporter and the bank also makes the duty of fair presentation binding in a clear way. All of that enables the UKEF to know the underlying transaction and foreign buyer in ECG business.

However, there may still be similar problems in the extreme situation mentioned before: what if the export transaction is fraudulent? The bank does answer certain questions in the "Standalone Guarantee Application Form", but those questions are not related to the export transaction and the foreign buyer. Moreover, Section 11(e) and (g) and Section 17 of the "Standalone Guarantee Application Form" all imply that the UKEF understands that the bank knows little about the

99 Ibid.

100 See <https://assets.publishing.service.gov.uk/government/uploads/system/uploads/attachment_data/file/421225/Exporter_Questionnaire_and_Application_Form_-_Guidance_Notes.pdf> accessed 1 February 2022.

buyer. It is the exporter who should, "for the benefit of the UKEF and the bank", make a fair presentation of the risks, and the bank makes no representation as to the truth or correctness of any presentation made by the exporter. Therefore, it can be said that the questionnaire can help the UKEF reduce the risks of fraud but cannot protect it completely. The following section will also offer solutions to this problem.

Proposal: a unification of English law on the duty of fair presentation in ECI and ECGs

What is the current law?

Insurance law and ECI contracts: before and after the IA 2015

The English cases demonstrate a significant divergence in the duty of fair presentation under ECI and ECGs.

The duty of fair presentation in insurance law thoroughly applies to ECI contracts. The English ECI cases present a clear picture of how the duty of fair presentation operates in ECI contracts: *Morgan Grenfell* illustrates the importance of making sufficient enquiries and the risks the ECA might otherwise be taking: a waiver of the right to disclosure. *Morgan Grenfell*, *Moore Large*, *International Management Group* and *ABN Amro* all indicate that in order to avoid the insurance contract, the ECA must prove that the fact undisclosed or misrepresented is material, and that the non-disclosure or misrepresentation has induced it to take the risk or to conclude the ECI contract on different terms; *Moore Large* also show that even if the ECA has met the materiality and inducement tests, should it waive the right of avoidance, it is no longer entitled to avoid the ECI policy.

Moreover, ECI cases have contributed to the development of relevant rules in general insurance law on the duty of fair presentation and post-contractual duty of disclosure. *Morgan Grenfell* established a "frame of reference" formulation to determine whether the ECA's failure to ask specific questions amounts to an implied waiver of the duty of disclosure. *Moore Large* confirmed the "legal advice" assumption that where the insurer made no express reference to the right to avoidance in the proceeding, if it cannot prove that it was not told by its legal advisers of this right, it would be assumed to have known of and waived the right. The decisions in *Morgan Grenfell* and *Moore Large* are both applicable to other types of insurance cases and will be the authorities for the courts to decide on similar matters.

Although the ECAs lost in both *Morgan Grenfell* and *Moore Large*, that does not mean that English law is hostile to the ECAs in relation to the duty of fair presentation in ECI contracts. On the contrary, those cases show that the courts are very likely to favour the ECA when it comes to the materiality and inducement tests. If certain facts are not disclosed or are misrepresented by the insured, the court tends to decide that those facts are material and have induced the ECA to take the risk or conclude the contracts on different terms as long as the ECA can provide sufficing and convincing evidence. Therefore, it can be said that the ECA is entitled to a full scope of the duty of fair presentation in ECI contracts in English law. Besides, English courts have been very cautious when deciding a plea of waiver of disclosure. Whether there is a waiver of disclosure will depend on the true construction of the terms of the questions actually asked,[101] and it has long been established that the essence of the duty requires the assured not only to correctly answer the questions raised by the insurer but also to spontaneously disclose any other material facts.[102] Therefore, an assured's allegation of waiver "cannot easily be reconciled with" the principle that he bears the duty of spontaneous disclosure.[103] As the Law Commission pointed out, a limited disclosure provision is not to be used as an instrument of deception.[104]

It should be noted that ECI policies are now to be read entirely under the IA 2015.[105] Although there has not yet been a decided ECI case under the new regime, it can be said that the IA 2015 rebalanced the interests of the ECAs and the assured on the duty of fair presentation.

On the one hand, there are provisions that would at least *prima facie* be in favour of the ECAs.

Section 4(6) of the IA 2015 provides that whether an individual or not, the assured ought to know "what should reasonably have been revealed by a reasonable search of information" available to himself, "whether the search is conducted by making enquiries or by any other means". This provision extends the principle under s 18(2)(b) of the MIA 1906 that the assured should disclose facts that he ought to know in the ordinary course of business, thereby imposing on him a "positive duty" to "uncover material circumstances".[106] The imputation of "blind eye knowledge" is also stipulated under s 6(1) of the IA 2015. Applying those changes to ECI contracts (especially supplier credit insurance and buyer credit insurance), the ECA could insist that the assured bank is under the duty to do a reasonable search and disclose the details about the exporter, the foreign buyer and the underlying transaction. If, particularly, the bank suspects that the underlying transaction is fraudulent, then it should conduct due diligence and disclose relevant facts to the ECA. Although the term "reasonable search" is entirely new and its definition is yet to be tested by the courts, the ECA can at least argue that all the information above can be revealed by the bank's reasonable search. In this way, the ECAs can be entitled to an even broader scope of the right to disclosure.

101 *Doheny v New India Assurance Co Ltd* [2004] EWCA Civ 1705.

102 *Huguenin v Rayley* (1815) 6 Taunt 186; *Wheelton v Hardisty* (1857) 8 E&B 232; *Glicksman v Lancashire & General* [1927] AC 139; *Bond v Commercial Assurance* (1930) 35 Com Cas.171; *Misirlakis v The New Zealand Insurance Co Ltd* (1985) 3 ANZ Insurance Cases 60–633;*Wayne Wilkinson Insurance Ltd v Kaiaua Downs Ltd* (1995) 8 ANZ Insurance Cases 75–782.

103 Merkin (n 26), [7-279].

104 See n 28 above, [7.40].

105 The UKEF's "Export Insurance Policy" expressly stipulates that IA 2015 applies to the ECI contracts.

106 Merkin (n 26), [7-104].

The IA 2015 also makes detailed provisions on the knowledge of the assured when the assured is not an individual but a legal person or organisation. Section 4(3) provides that an insured who is not an individual knows what is known to the individual(s) who are "part of the insured's senior management or responsible for the insured's insurance". Section 4(8) defines the terms "senior management" and "responsible for the insured's insurance". In the context of ECI, the exporter would seem inevitable to be a company, so the exporter needs to disclose what is known or ought to be known to its senior managers and the individuals who are responsible for the placement of insurance; failure to do so will give the ECA the remedy of breach of the duty of fair presentation.

On the other hand, there are some changes which might benefit the assured.

The IA 2015 provides a "lesser form" of performance of the duty of disclosure.[107] Section 3(4)(b) stipulates that, if the disclosure "gives the insurer sufficient information to put a prudent insurer on notice that it needs to make further enquiries" on the material facts, the assured would comply with the duty of fair presentation. In the context of ECI, whilst this new law is in favour of the assured, it also reminds the ECA to always ask the right questions and "probably adds nothing" to the principle of waiver of disclosure.[108] As long as the ECA prepares detailed questionnaires, there would be little possibility for the assured to argue that it complies with the duty of disclosure under s 3(4)(b) of the Act, should it fail to answer the questions correctly.

The insurer's knowledge is re-enacted in s 5 of the Act, which not only concerns the knowledge of individuals within the insurer's organisation but also defines information held within it. Section 5(2)(b) particularly assumes that information "readily available" to the underwriting team would be imputed to the insurer's knowledge. That is a significant change that pre-existing law is inconsistent with.[109] In the context of ECI, if some information regarding previous refusals, loss and claims is not passed by the individuals within the ECA to the underwriting team, then the assured might not need to disclose, as such information could be "readily available" to the underwriter and the ECA ought to know it. Although the term "readily available" still awaits judicial determination, it will benefit the assured to some degree.

The assured's agent's duty of disclosure under s 19 of MIA 1906 is removed by IA 2015, which stipulates what knowledge of the assured's agent can be imputed to the assured in ss 4(4), 4(5) and 4(8)(b). It remains to be observed what effect such a change will bring in the context of ECI.

Moreover, the IA 2015 replaces the sole remedy under the MIA 1906 with a proportionate remedies scheme.

Under the MIA 1906, the only remedy for the breach of duty of utmost good faith would be the avoidance of the contract, subject to repayment of premiums

107 Rob Merkin & Özlem Gürses, "The Insurance Act 2015: Rebalancing the Interests of Insurer and Assured" [2015] 78 (6) MLR 1004, 1009.

108 Ibid.

109 Merkin (n 26), [7-267].

in the absence of fraud, but this "all or nothing" approach was replaced with proportionate remedies which are stipulated in Sch 1 of the IA 2015. The remedies for breach of the duty of fair presentation under the new regime are less draconian to the assured. ECA can also benefit from the new remedies, especially in cases such as *Moore Large* where a plead of waiver of the right to avoid is raised by the assured: under the old law, the right to avoid is a purely self-help remedy,[110] thus if the insurer fails to exercise the right, a waiver might be found. However, under the IA 2015, the proportionate remedies (including avoidance) become "a statutory code" of remedies which can only be exercised with the assistance of the court.[111] Whilst it is still possible that waiver of the right to proportionate remedies may be found in ECI cases under the new regime, the IA 2015 provides a clear guideline for the ECA, indicating which remedy can they assert according to different situations provided in Pt 1 and 2 of the Sch 1 of the Act. These detailed provisions will help reduce the possibility of waiver, as the ECA will be very informed of their rights under the new law.

Based on the analysis above, this research submits that ECAs were well protected by the common law and the MIA 1906 and will be even better protected by the IA 2015 on the duty of fair presentation to some degree. Nevertheless, they should make good use of their rights and avoid vital mistakes such as the waiver of the duty of disclosure and the waiver of the right to avoid the contract, as seen in *Morgan Grenfell* and *Moore Large*, respectively.

Law of guarantees and ECG contracts

Turning the coin, the English guarantee law is far less developed than English insurance law on the duty of fair presentation. English guarantee cases lack a precise formulation of the creditor's duty of disclosure,[112] but all of them indicated that the creditor only needs to disclose "any unusual feature" in the contractual relationship between itself and the debtor. Case law has also established that the following facts need not be disclosed:[113]

(a) The principal debtor's existing indebtedness to the creditor[114], previous defaults[115] or credit rating;[116]
(b) The fact that the principal debtor whose account is guaranteed had overdrawn his account or consistently exceeded the overdraft limit;[117]

110 *Brotherton v Aseguradora Colseguros SA* (No.2) [2003] EWHC 1741 (Comm), [2003] Lloyd's Rep IR 746.
111 Merkin (n 26), [7-363].
112 Donovan & Phillips (n 82), [4-06].
113 Ibid, [4-20].
114 *National Provincial Bank of England Ltd v Glanusk* [1913] 3 KB 335.
115 *Roper v Cox* (1882) LR Ir 200.
116 *Hamilton v Waston* (1845) 12 Cl & Fin 109.
117 *Commercial Bank of Australia Ltd v Amadio* (1983) 151 CLR 447.

(c) The likely future indebtedness or liability of the principal debtor to the creditor;[118]
(d) The principal debtor's conduct and behaviour, including the principal's irresponsibility in operating the business;[119]
(e) The object or expected use of the advance secured by the guarantee or the purpose of the guarantee itself;[120]
(f) Any anticipated logistical or technical difficulties which the principal debtor may have in discharging the principal obligations;[121]
(g) The fact that the purchase price payable under the contract guaranteed greatly exceeds the true value of the property purchased.[122]

Accordingly, the English court had a conservative approach towards the issue of misrepresentation and non-disclosure in ECG contracts. Although *Credit Lyonnais* is the only ECG case in English law, it means much: it shows that the court would allow the ECA to avoid the ECG contract if there is a misrepresentation but would be reluctant to impose a duty of disclosure on the insured. Although in *Credit Lyonnais* the ECA was entitled to avoid the guarantee, this case shows that in English law the ECA is entitled to a very limited scope of disclosure under ECG contracts. The bank only needs to disclose the "unusual features" related to the contractual relationship between itself and the debtor.

Despite the limitations seen above, the UKEF is importing the duty of fair presentation into its ECG business by (a) making express contractual terms under the ECA-exporter contract to require the exporter to make full disclosure and (b) developing detailed questionnaires for the exporter and bank to complete. In this way, the UKEF circumvents the case law and requires the exporter and the bank to disclose material facts that it wishes to know. However, one problem remains unsolved. That is, as has been mentioned before, what if the export transaction is fraudulent? Should the bank or the UKEF bear the loss?

What should the law be?

This research submits that the law concerning the duty of fair presentation should be unified in the ECI and ECG contracts.

On the one hand, current insurance law works well in ECI contracts, and thus there is not much to interfere or add to. The courts strictly applied the general rules on the duty of fair presentation in insurance law, which entitles the ECA to the full right of a fair presentation by the insured. The full application of the relevant principles of insurance law to ECI contracts also provides certainty for both the UKEF and the insured in the ECI disputes. Moreover, as is analysed

118 *Goodwin v National Bank of Australia Ltd* (1968) 117 CLR 173.
119 *Bank of Scotland v Henry Butcher & Co* [2001] 2 All ER (Comm) 691.
120 *Westminster Bank Ltd v Cond* (1940) 46 Com Cas 60.
121 *Trade Indemnity Co Ltd v Workington Harbour & Dock Board* [1937] AC 1.
122 *Pooraka Holdings Pty Ltd v Participation Nominees Pty Ltd* (1991) 58 SASR 184.

above, the new law, namely the IA 2015, can also well protect the ECA. When the court determines the definitions and scope of the new terms such as "reasonable search", "readily available" and "further enquiries" in the IA 2015 in the future, there will be more certainty in ECI cases.

On the other hand, one might question what can be altered in the law in ECG contracts to amend the current law of guarantee which does not fit well to the unique characteristics of ECGs. This research submits that although the ECG contract is not a contract *uberrimae fidei*, the scope of the duty of disclosure should be broadened. The rationale for the limited duty of disclosure in general guarantee contracts is not necessarily relevant in ECGs. An ECG is a special type of guarantee, and it operates differently from other kinds of guarantee: although an ECG contract is concluded between the ECA and the bank, it is always the exporter who applies for the cover. As the surety, the ECA has no means of knowledge about the principal debtor, whether the debtor is the exporter or the foreign buyer. The reasons for a limited duty of disclosure in general guarantee contracts, such as practicalities and business efficacy, do not well apply to the context of ECGs. Besides, there is no concern of the bank's breach of confidence so long as there is written consent by the exporter which authorises the bank to reveal relevant information in connection with the export contract.[123] Therefore, it would be unfair for the ECA to have such a very limited scope of the right of disclosure under ECGs, compared with the right of disclosure it would be entitled to in ECI contracts. The English law of guarantee should never stop developing in such a rapidly changing commercial world.

First, the creditor should disclose not only "any unusual feature" in its contractual relationship with the principal debtor, but also "every material fact" which would significantly affect the surety's risks and influence the surety in deciding whether to offer the guarantee and if so, on any terms. There has been one Commonwealth case authority indicating that the duty of disclosure should be extended to material facts as well as unusual facts. In *Westpac Securities v Dickie*,[124] Hardie Boys J suggested that a creditor's failure to disclose a material fact will vitiate the guarantee if that fact is inconsistent with the presumed basis of the contract. Case law also allows the parties to extend the scope of the duty by express contractual provisions.[125] The UKEF should impose a contractual duty on the bank to disclose every material fact concerning the ECG contract and the underlying transaction. The court should recognise the legal effect of such a clause in future ECG disputes and further establish a materiality test formulation on the creditor's duty of disclosure.

Second, the creditor should disclose not only material facts which he knows but also material facts that he ought to know. That might seem radical in the context

123 See, e.g., Section 11(h) of the "Standalone Guarantee Application Form".

124 [1991] 1 NZLR 657, 662–3.

125 See *Formica Ltd v Secretary of State acting by the Export Credits Guarantee Department* [1995] Lloyd's Rep 692.

of English law, but an Australian case took this view. In *Pooraka Holdings Pty Ltd v Participation Nominees Pty Ltd*,[126] the Supreme Court of South Australia suggested that the creditor must disclose circumstances that (a) the creditor knows or ought to know, (b) the surety is unaware of, and (c) the creditor appreciates, or ought to appreciate, might affect the surety's decision to offer the guarantee. This formulation would be beneficial for English courts to decide future ECG cases.

Third, fraud should be disclosed in any case, even if the creditor has a mere suspicion of fraud and even if the fraud does not arise in the contractual relationship between the creditor and the principal debtor. The English courts in *Credit Lyonnais* and *National Provincial Bank of England Ltd v Glanusk*[127] both held that the creditor bank's suspicions of fraud of the principal debtor need not be disclosed. This conservative view has received scholarly criticism: it would be "somewhat odd" if the creditor is obliged to disclose an unusual contractual term of the principal agreement, but not the knowledge or suspicion of fraudulent practices of the principal.[128] Australian cases, again, can provide some valuable guidelines: The court in *Fitzgerald v Jacomb*[129] held that the belief that the principal debtor was defrauding the creditor by forgery must be disclosed. *Westpac Banking Corp v Robinson*[130] further required that a "virtual certainty of fraud" in respect of the principal debtor's own internal operations should be disclosed and that the duty to disclose the fraud should prevail over the duty of confidentiality in a banker–customer relationship. English courts should take those approaches when deciding ECG cases and require the creditor bank to disclose to the ECA the following circumstances: (a) any fraudulent behaviour of the exporter, even if such behaviour does not arise from the bank–exporter contractual relationship where the ECG takes the form of a supplier credit guarantee; (b) any fraudulent behaviour of the foreign buyer, even if such behaviour does not arise from the bank-buyer contractual relationship where the ECG takes the form of a buyer credit guarantee; and (c) any suspicion of (a) and (b). The creditor's duty to disclose any fraud situations should be as broad as possible.

Fourth, the mere imposition of a broader duty of disclosure on the bank in the questionnaires in the proposal form is not a sufficient response to the UKEF' tendency to import the duty of fair presentation into ECGs. The law should also scrutinise the legal effect of ECA-exporter contracts such as the "SCFF Contract" and clarify whether it should bind the bank and whether the UKEF's right of withdrawal means it can avoid the ECG contract. This research submits that the doctrine of privity of contract should always be followed. The exporter's breach under the ECA-exporter contract should by no means affect the validity of the ECG contract.

The proposal discussed above will help develop a unified legal system governing ECI and ECGs: The bank's duty to disclose "material facts" under ECG

126 [1991] 58 SASR 184.
127 [1913] 3 KB 335.
128 Donovan & Phillips (n 82), [4-13].
129 (1873) 4 AJR 189.
130 (1990) ASC [56-002].

contracts as a creditor will substantially equal to its duty of disclosure under ECI contracts as an assured in accordance with insurance law. The bank needs to disclose not only what it knows but also what it ought to know under ECGs, which can be mirrored in ECI contracts where insurance law principles on the assured's knowledge are applicable. The requirement on the bank to disclose fraud or suspicion of fraud in ECGs will also resemble the "blind eye knowledge" provision in ECI. Thus, a unified approach by the courts would not only provide consistency in the materiality test in ECI and ECG contracts, but also avoid making different decisions on similar matters as shown in *Morgan Grenfell* and *Credit Lyonnais*, and reduce the possibilities of a totally fraudulent transaction.

To summarise, it is submitted that the law should apply unified standards towards the duty of fair presentation in ECI and ECG contexts and provide more certainty for the parties. The main source of the law of guarantee is the case law; hence the courts play a fundamental role in reforming the law in this area. It remains to be seen how the English court will deal with the duty of fair presentation in ECG cases in the future.

What steps can the UKEF take?

In ECI contracts, the UKEF is entitled to the full right of fair presentation of the risk by the insured, but it should make good use of such right. It should make as detailed enquiries before the conclusion of the ECI contracts as it can, and once it finds out that the insured has breached the duty, it should avoid the contract in time by giving express and unequivocal notice to the insured. Failure to do so may render every effort it makes to establish the materiality and inducement fruitless, and result in a finding of the waiver of the duty of disclosure and the loss of the right to avoid the contract.

The UKEF should also respond to the changes and potential challenges that the IA 2015 brings to ECI contracts.

Firstly, it should in its policies define "reasonable search" under s 4(6) as there is no judicial definition yet. The Law Commission has suggested that whether a search is reasonable "will depend on the size, nature and complexity of the business".[131] It is also proposed by the Law Commission that the parties could "discuss and reach agreement on the nature of the search to be undertaken", and that the process will be easier "by the development of industry-produced protocols on the types of search which are expected".[132] These suggestions would benefit the UKEF, whose proposal forms now available to the exporters are uniform, regardless of the size and nature of the exporter's business. The UKEF should develop different proposal forms for exporters with small business, medium and large business and multinational business. The more complex the business is, the more detailed the questionnaire should be. It should also reach an agreement

131 See n 28 above, [8.83].
132 See n 28 above, [8.85].

with the assured on the scope, method and extent of the "reasonable search" that the assured needs to undertake. For instance, under supplier credit insurance and buyer credit insurance where the assured is the bank in both cases, the UKEF could produce standard terms and conditions stipulating that the bank should search the genuineness of the underlying transaction, the financial standing of the buyer as well as the viability of the project to be insured.

Secondly, as a result of s 5(2)(b), the UKEF should make sure that information "readily held" within its internal departments can always be passed to its underwriting committee. The information on previous application refusals, claim history and credit assessment records of UK exporters should all be stored in a unified database which can be searched by the underwriting team with a simple click. This is because the UKEF will be assumed to know all the information held within itself, even if the assured does not make such disclosure.

Thirdly, although its questionnaires are already very detailed, the UKEF's proposal forms do not leave room for the assured to write about anything other than answers to the questionnaires. That is particularly significant where the application is made online nowadays and electronic forms without a blank section for the assured to disclose "any other material facts" may result in a finding of waiver of further information under s 3(4)(b) of the IA 2015.[133]

In ECG contracts, on the other hand, the bank is currently under no duty of fair presentation to the UKEF, which requires the UKEF to protect itself by importing the duty of fair presentation into its ECG business. The UKEF responds to the court's conservative decision in *Credit Lyonnais* by including express contractual provisions in the ECA-exporter contract requiring the exporter to make full disclosure. That is helpful for the UKEF to know and assess the risks, but it would be better if the UKEF could make similar provisions in its ECG contract requiring the bank to disclose every material fact it knows or ought to know. More importantly, the UKEF should make as detailed and pertinent questionnaires as possible at the conclusion stage of ECG contracts. The current ECG application forms look fine, but whether the questionnaires and the certification in those forms can effectively protect the UKEF is still to be tested by the court. Before that, the UKEF should always raise as detailed enquiries to the bank as it can to detect any potential fraud. If the UKEF has made enquiries as to certain facts and the exporter or bank fails to provide a correct answer, the court will be likely to treat it as material misrepresentation, which gives the UKEF a better chance to vitiate the contract than under the rule of limited disclosure in guarantee law. As the legal saying goes, "the insurer's clamour at loss time must meet a traditionally high judicial decibel standard if it is to drown out its silence at premium taking time".[134] Asking more detailed questions, therefore, is always the better and safer choice.

133 Merkin (n 26), [7-289].

134 See B. Harnett, "The Doctrine of Concealment: A Remnant in the Law of Insurance" [1950] (15) Law and Contemporary Problems 391, 406.

Miscellaneous

Whilst the focus of this chapter is the assured's duty of fair presentation under ECI and ECGs at the conclusion stage of the contract, for the convenience of the reader, the following sections aim to address some critical and cautionary topics reflected by English case law that do not fall within the scope of the duty of fair presentation but remain highly relevant to the theme of this chapter.

The assured's post-contractual duty of disclosure under ECI: the "common interest" test and the legal professional privilege

The English case law on ECI contributes not only to the development of rules on the insured's duty of fair presentation before the conclusion of the insurance contract but also to the rules on the insured's post-contractual duty of disclosure. *Formica Ltd v Secretary of State acting by the Export Credits Guarantee Department*[135] offered a valuable insight into the duration of the insured's post-contractual duty of disclosure and the discovery of documents in insurance proceedings.

In this case, the insured exporter under the ECGD's basic ECI cover suffered from non-payment by the foreign buyer and was aware that the buyer had gone into liquidation. At that time there was a third-party company who was the assured's competitor seeking to purchase the buyer company. The insured commenced legal proceedings to stop the purchase and then made a claim to the ECGD. The ECGD argued that the assured was in breach of the duty of disclosure under Article 4(a) of the policy which provided that the assured should disclose promptly "at all times during the operation of the guarantee all facts in any way affecting the risks guaranteed". Colman J confirmed that the policy in question was a contract of insurance and, by seeking the true construction of the policy, the judge pointed out that the operation of the cover and the duty of disclosure under Article 4(a) ceased at such time, as there was no longer any risk of loss in relation to a given contract which could be affected by any information that might be provided. His lordship held that once there had been a default by a buyer and once all prospect of further recovery in respect of the sales contract had been lost, the assured was no longer under a duty of disclosure.

The ECGD made an alternative submission applying to discover the documents concerning the legal proceedings the insured took to stop the purchase. The assured claimed legal privilege[136] on the documents, but the ECGD argued that the documents came into existence in furtherance of their common interest of maximising the recovery of the foreign buyer's outstanding debts.

135 [1994] CLC 1078.

136 In common law, all things reasonably necessary in the shape of communication to the legal advisers are protected from production or disclosure in order that legal advice may be obtained safely and sufficiently. See *Wheeler v Le Marchant* (1881) LR 17 Ch D 675, 681.

Colman J first cited *CIA Barca de Panama SA v George Wimpey & Co Ltd*,[137] in which the court established the rule of common interest privilege: if A and B have a common interest in litigation against C and there is no dispute between A and B at that point, then in the litigation between A and B, neither A nor B can claim legal professional privilege for documents which came into existence in relation to the earlier litigation against C; his lordship then referred to *Buttes Gas & Oil Co v Hammer (No.3)*[138] where Lord Denning stated that the parties have common interest if they can be treated "as if they were partners in a single firm or departments in a single company", and *Bank of Nova Scotia v Hellenic Mutual War Risks Association (Bermuda) Ltd (The Good Luck)*[139] where Saville J required the interest must be so close "that the parties concerned could (had they chosen to do so) have used the same solicitor or other lawyer". Colman J then came up with a supplemental test: if the parties have a common interest, the party to whom the documents are passed is subject to a duty of confidence which the law will protect in the interests of justice.

Applying these approaches to the circumstances in the present case, Colman J recognised the following factors: (a) the ECGD insured 90% of the risks, and the assured bore the rest 10% of the risk; (b) the ECGD's policy provided that the assured should "take all practical measures" to minimise the loss at the request of the ECGD; and (c) under the principle of subrogation, it was commonplace for insurers to take over the recovery of claims against third parties by the insured. Taking all these factors into consideration, the judge held that the ECGD and the assured could be treated as if they were partners in a single firm or department and could have used the same solicitor. Further, the judge believed that had the documents been passed to the ECGD, it would bear the confidential duty on them. Therefore, there was a common interest between the ECGD and the assured, which could destroy the assured's legal privilege on the claimed documents.

Formica v ECGD contributes to developing the rules on the assured's post-contractual duty of disclosure in two aspects. First, it demonstrates how the insurer could make contractual provisions on the duration of the insured's duty of disclosure and in what way the court construed the provisions. In this case, the ECGD tried to provide a wide duration of the duty by using the words "at all times during the operation of the policy", but the court interpreted it as a rather limited duration which ended when the loss occurred. Moreover, this case is consistent with *Manifest Shipping Co Ltd v Uni-Polaris Insurance Co Ltd (The Star Sea)*,[140] in which the court held that once it comes to the proceeding stage, the duty of disclosure ceases to operate and the dispute is governed by civil procedure rules. As the IA 2015 does not touch upon the assured's post-contractual duty of disclosure, *Formica v ECGD* will be applicable under the new regime. Second and more

137 [1980] 1 Ll Rep 598, 615.
138 [1981] QB 223, 242–3.
139 [1982] 2 Ll Rep 540, 542.
140 [2001] 1 Lloyd's Rep 389.

importantly, it addresses the issue of the discovery of documents in the context of insurance proceedings. The discovery of documents, a very critical topic in civil procedure and evidence law,[141] had not been mentioned in insurance cases before. In this case, Colman J thoroughly reviewed relevant previous cases in civil procedure law and showed how the court reasoned on the discovery issue: to destroy the respondent's legal privilege on the documents, the applicant must share a common interest with the respondent. To further establish the common interest, the applicant must prove that they can be treated as if they were "partners in the same department" and "could share the same solicitor", and that had he been passed the documents, he would have been under the duty to keep them confidential. Moreover, Colman J took the particularities of insurance into consideration. The facts that the insured itself bore 10% of the risks, the risk control provisions in the policy, along with the principle of subrogation, were all regarded by his lordship as relevant factors to help the court establish the insurer's common interest in the assured's legal documents. This case links insurance law with relevant rules in civil procedure law, which would be meaningful for the court to decide similar matters in insurance cases.

The insurer's duty of utmost good faith under ECI

It has been well established that the obligation to disclose material facts is a mutual one imposing reciprocal duties on the insurer and the assured,[142] and s 17 of the MIA 1906 also confirms that the duty of utmost good faith is a mutual one. The occasions where disclosure by the insurer is required may, in practice, be rare since the circumstances material to the insurance will ordinarily be known only to the proposed insured. Nevertheless, such occasions may arise. In *Banque Keyser Ullmann SA v Skandia (UK) Insurance Co Ltd and Others*,[143] the banks provided loans to the buyer companies controlled by a Mr B. The securities offered were ECI policies and gemstones with certified valuations. The banks were named co-insured or assignees under the ECI policies relating to the loans to protect them against failure to repay. A firm of Lloyd's brokers, acting as the banks' agent, arranged ECI covers through their manager, Mr L, and each policy contained a fraud exclusion clause precluding liability in respect of "any claim or claims arising directly or indirectly out of or caused directly or indirectly by fraud, attempted fraud, misdescription or deception by any person, firm, organisation or company". Mr L arranged to place the insurance in layers and the insurance company through its senior underwriter, Mr D, issued "held covered" notes on a temporary basis. Although the insurance cover was not complete, L issued cover notes representing

141 See Charles Hollander, *Documentary Evidence* (12th edn, Sweet & Maxwell 2015), [19-06]; Paul Matthews & Hodge M Malek, QC, *Disclosure* (5th edn, Sweet & Maxwell 2016), [11-01]; Alison Padfield, *Insurance Claims* (2nd edn, Tottel Publishing 2007) 130.

142 *Carter v Boehm* (1766) 3 Burr 1162.

143 [1991] 2 AC 249.

that the cover was complete, and the lead bank advanced money under the first loan agreement. Mr D, although fully aware that L had deliberately concealed from the banks the gap in the insurance cover, continued to underwrite further loans provided by the banks, without reporting the matter either to the brokers or the insurance company, or informing the banks of Mr L's deceit. The buyer defaulted in payment, the gemstones proved of comparatively little value, and Mr B disappeared with the banks' money. The banks claimed reimbursement from the insurance companies under the insurance policies. In the course of the trial, the banks reached a settlement with the brokers and conceded that, by reason of the fraud exclusion clause, the insurers were not liable under the policies. However, the banks claimed damages from the insurers for their breach of the duty of utmost good faith, a "novel" and "bold" claim that had not been supported (and rejected) by any case authorities.[144]

The trial court (Steyn J) gave judgment for the banks, holding that the insurers had been in breach of their duty of the utmost good faith to the banks in failing to disclose Mr L's deception to them. The banks were thus held entitled to rescind the contract and demand the return of the premium, but that was not pursued by the banks. The court then turned to decide whether the banks were entitled to damages for the insurers' breach. Steyn J noted that in the ordinary course, the right to avoid the policy would be an adequate remedy for the aggrieved insurer if the assured breaches the duty of disclosure; and in the rare case where the insurer breaches the duty of disclosure, avoidance of the policy and the return of the premium may constitute sufficient relief for the assured if he became aware of the non-disclosure before the occurrence of the contingency against which he had intended to insure. If, however, he became aware of it only after the occurrence of the contingency, relief of this nature may be quite inadequate. He then said:[145]

> Once it is accepted that the principle of the utmost good faith imposes meaningful reciprocal duties, owed by the insured to the insurers and vice versa, it seems anomalous that there should be no claim for damages for breach of those duties in a case where that is the only effective remedy. The principle *ubi jus ibi remedium* succinctly expresses the policy of our law.

The learned judge pointed out that on the facts of the present case, an order for the return of the insurance premiums, even if still available, would be a "derisory" remedy in relation to the true loss if there had been a breach of duty by the insurers which caused the loss. Observing that "occasionally judges have to apply an existing remedy to a new situation when a right already recognised by the law is not adequately protected", he ruled that "justice and policy considerations combine in requiring me to rule that in principle an insured can claim damages from

144 *Banque Keyser* [1990] 1 QB 665, 774–5 (Slade LJ).
145 *Banque Keyser* [1987] 2 WLR 1300, 1132.

an insurer arising from loss suffered by the insured as a result of a breach of the obligation of the utmost good faith by the insurer".[146]

The Court of Appeal confirmed that the duty of utmost good faith is a mutual one and ruled that the insurer must disclose all facts known to him which are material either to (a) the nature of the risk sought to be covered or (b) the recoverability of a claim under the policy which a prudent insured would take into account in deciding whether or not to place the risk for which he seeks cover with that insurer. Slade LJ thus upheld the trial decision that the insurers' breach of the duty of utmost good faith had foreseeably caused the banks to suffer loss. However, his lordship rejected the banks' submission that a breach of the duty of utmost good faith would give rise to a remedy in damages. The judge noted that s 17 of the MIA 1906 did not appear to contemplate a remedy in damages for non-disclosure, being silent on the point, but making express provision for avoidance. His lordship further reasoned that the legal origin of the alleged right to damages was founded "neither on tort nor on contract nor on the existence of a fiduciary duty nor on statute". The judge also held that the insurers did not owe the banks a duty under the common law of negligence to prevent them suffering financial loss through the fraud of Mr L. His lordship concluded that:[147]

> Like the [trial] judge we deplore the fact that we live in a world in which commercial dishonesty, such as that of [Mr L], is rampant. Like him we wish it could be eliminated, particularly from the insurance markets of the world, and not least the London insurance market. But we cannot regard our decision in the present case an appropriate instrument for seeking to achieve that purpose.

The House of Lords confirmed that the duty of utmost good faith is a mutual one but clarified that the duty of the insurer, as of an assured, "goes no further than a disclosure of matters material to the risk".[148] Therefore, the facts the insurers concealed were held immaterial as such facts did not relate to the assessment of the risk to be insured but concerned "the recoverability of a claim under the policy". Turning to the common law duty of care, Lord Templeman pointed out that when two parties are negotiating a contract *uberrimae fidei*, neither party was under a duty to the other to disclose that the other's agent was dishonest or negligent or incompetent. His lordship thus held that Mr D's failure to disclose to the banks the dishonesty of Mr L was only blameable "as a matter of business ethics" and did not amount to a breach of "any legal duty". Furthermore, the House of Lords rejected the reasoning shared by the Court of Appeal and the trial court that the non-disclosure by Mr D of Mr L's dishonesty was an effective cause of the banks' loss of the further loans. Lord Templeman distinguished the cause of (a)

146 Ibid.
147 *Banque Keyser* [1990] 1 QB 665, 805.
148 *Banque Keyser* [1991] 2 AC 249, 262 (Lord Templeman).

the advance of the further loans from the cause of (b) the loss of the advance of the further loans: whilst the cause of (a) was Mr L's dishonesty, the cause of (b) was the buyer's fraud. In other words, but for the buyer's fraud, the banks would have suffered no loss even if being induced to advance further loans by Mr L's dishonesty. Accordingly, their lordships ruled that the insurers' failure to inform the banks of Mr L's dishonesty was not causative of the banks' loss.

The appeal and final decisions of *Banque Keyser* have widely attracted academic criticism as they "have certainly not helped to enforce commercial morality in the London insurance market".[149] *Banque Keyser* established "a rather narrow duty of disclosure on an insurer" and "a fairly ineffective remedy limited to avoidance and return of the premium".[150] Moreover, it seems difficult to accept the House of Lords' "somewhat narrow" analysis of causation. On the one hand, the distinction drawn by Lord Templeman arguably ignored the evidence advanced by the banks that if they had known of Mr L's misconduct they would have made no further loans to the buyer. On the other hand, the fact that Mr L's fraud was not connected with the buyer's fraud should not deny the banks the right to benefit from the fact that knowledge of Mr L's conduct would, by chance, have saved them from the consequences of the buyer's fraud.[151] *Banque Keyser* therefore demonstrated the "insuperable problems" in imposing damages as a sort of relief "purely as a matter of common law". The imbalance and unfairness showed in this case "indicates the desirability of a regime containing sufficient flexibility to take account of the circumstances of the particular case".[152]

It was thus suggested by the commentators that a statutory duty should be created requiring the payment of damages by the insurer or insured to compensate the other for losses resulting from a failure to disclose material facts known to him. In 2010, as part of their insurance law reform project, the Law Commissions published a working paper titled "Insurance Contract Law Issue Paper 6: Damages for late Payment and the Insurer's Duty of Good Faith" ("Issue Paper 6")[153] which suggested a reversal of the rule in *Banque Keyser*. In Issue Paper 6, the Law Commissions suggested that the statutory law should provide the parties with appropriate remedies if the duty of utmost good faith is breached: in particular, if an insurer acts in bad faith in a way that causes foreseeable loss to the policyholder, damages should be available. In the meantime, the Law Commissions did not treat the duty of utmost good faith as an implied term or one that gives rise

149 F.A. Trindade, "The Skandia Case in the House of Lords" [1991] (107) LQR 24, 28. See also John Birds, *Modern Insurance Law* (10th edn, Sweet & Maxwell 2016) 161–4; P Macdonald Eggers, "Remedies for the failure to observe the utmost good faith" [2003] (2) LMCLQ 249, 275.

150 Birds (n 149) 161.

151 David Allen, "Non-Disclosure: Hairshirt or Halo?" [1992] (55) MLR 96, 101.

152 Ibid., 100. See also A. H. Hudson, "Duty of Disclosure Again" [1991] (1) LMCLQ 18, 23; Letizia Chetcuti, "The Insurer's Post-Contractual Duty of Good Faith: Search for a Balanced Regime" [2010] (16) 6 Journal of International Maritime Law 446, 446–3.

153 Law Commissions, "Insurance Contract Law Issue Paper 6: Damages for Late Payment", 40–3 <https://www.lawcom.gov.uk/project/insurance-contract-law/> accessed 1 February 2022.

to an action in tort or delict. They proposed to treat this duty "as a separate, non-excludable duty, giving rise to specific remedies".[154] However, there was "wide opposition" to this proposal, and the Law Commissions did not proceed with it in their final report of the project.[155] Ultimately, they merely recommended that good faith was enshrined as a general interpretive principle in insurance law "as a shield not a sword", and that "judicial intervention may be appropriate in an extreme case".[156] The insurer's pre-contractual duty of fair presentation does not subsequently appear in the Insurance Act 2015.[157] Thus, as is observed by the commentator, "whilst *Banque Keyser* might have heralded an exciting judicial development of a broad duty of good faith in insurance law, sadly that seems unlikely now to happen".[158]

The ECA's vicarious liability for its employee's fraud?

In *Credit Lyonnais*, in addition to the abovementioned claim in contract, the exporter also made a claim against the ECGD in tort: to induce the bank to participate in the transaction, the exporter bribed Mr P, a senior officer of the ECGD, to "oil the wheels" and avoid asking any "awkward questions". To facilitate the transaction, Mr P signed an "acceptability letter" confirming that the forged bills of exchange were "valid and enforceable in the UK" and advised the bank to regard them "as acceptable for this transaction". Mr P then authorised the issuance of several ECGD's ECG covers.

Mr P had passed away when the bank detected the fraud and suffered the losses, so the bank sued the ECGD on the grounds that (a) Mr P knowingly acted fraudulently in that he was bribed by the exporter to issue the ECGs; (b) Mr P was personally liable in tort for its loss; (c) Mr P in making the underwriting decision, albeit for corrupt motives, was acting within the course of his employment; and (d) accordingly, the ECGD was vicariously liable for Mr P's corrupt underwriting.

The trial court held that the bank's claim in tort failed because Mr P did not have the requisite knowledge of the exporter's deceit to be a joint tortfeasor, but this finding was overruled by the Court of Appeal. Stuart-Smith LJ clarified that Mr P had sufficient knowledge of the exporter's fraud and had a common purpose with him, and thus Mr P was personally liable to the bank both in a conspiracy to deceive and as a joint tortfeasor in the tort of deceit. However, the judge held that the issuance of the ECG was not within Mr P's actual or ostensible authority, and thus the deceit did not occur in the course of his employment with the ECGD.

154 Ibid.
155 Law Commissions, "Insurance Contract Law: Business Disclosure; Warranties; Insurers' Remedies for Fraudulent Claims; and Late Payment", 327, at <https://www.lawcom.gov.uk/project/insurance-contract-law/> accessed 1 February 2022.
156 Ibid, 297, 327.
157 Özlem Gürses, "What Does Utmost Good Faith Mean" [2016] (27) Insurance Law Journal 124, 129–30.
158 Birds (n 149) 164.

The bank appealed again and this issue was further elaborated by the House of Lords. Lord Woolf MR, based on evidence, clarified that Mr P had sufficient authority to issue the ECG and said that:[159]

> This case therefore raises starkly the question of whether, in the case of a joint tort, it is sufficient to make the master liable if the acts of his servant for which he is responsible, do not in themselves amount to a tort but only amount to a tort when linked to other acts which were not performed in the course of the employee's employment.
>
> The other acts may or may not be in the course of the employee's employment whether the other acts are performed by the same person or a different person. In addition, if by a different person, that person may or may not be a fellow employee...
>
> The conduct for which the servant is responsible must constitute an actionable tort and to make the employer responsible for that tort the conduct necessary to establish the employee's liability must have occurred within the course of the employment. If the tort is committed jointly, then it is conduct which is within the course of the employment sufficient to constitute the tort, irrespective of which tortfeasor performed the acts, which is necessary ... For vicarious liability what is critical, as long as one of the joint tortfeasors is an employee, is that the combined conduct of both tortfeasors is sufficient to constitute a tort in the course of the employee's employment.

His lordship then identified three acts in this case: (a) Mr P's issuance of the ECG, which was in the course of his employment with the ECGD; (b) Mr P's issuance of the "acceptability letter", which was not within his employment;[160] and (c) the exporter's fraud, which of course fell outside the course of Mr P's employment, either. The learned judge held that "there was nothing unlawful" in act (a) because the ECG, as a genuine contract, did not deceive the bank; it was the combined conduct of act (b) and (c) which constituted a tort, but neither of them fell within the course of Mr P's employment. ECGD was thus held not vicariously liable to the bank.

The bank's duty to investigate the genuineness of the underlying transaction?

The law should reconsider the very extreme situation illustrated in *Banque Keyser* and *Credit Lyonnais*: where the export transaction is fraudulent, should

159 *Credit Lyonnais* [1999] CLC 823, 862.

160 This finding derived from the trial judgment where Longmore J "loosely compared" ECGD to a large insurance company where officials who are not particularly senior make underwriting decisions. He clarified that "unlike an underwriter's scratch on an underwriting slip prepared by an insurance broker", Mr P's signature of the "acceptability letter" was not "something that was itself communicated to the bank": it would thus be outside the usual authority of someone in Mr P's position to make a fundamental departure from the terms of the ECG. See *Credit Lyonnais* [1996] CLC 11, 40.

the ECA or the bank bear the ultimate loss? This research suggests that there should be a balance in the interest of both parties: it seems unfair if the law simply leaves all the loss to be borne by the ECA. On the other hand, if it is the bank who is to bear all the loss, it might discourage the banks from participating in ECG business and thereby undermine the ECG's purpose of promoting trade and economy. One possible solution for the English courts is to confirm that whether under ECI or ECGs, the bank bears the duty to conduct due diligence on the genuineness of the underlying transaction and the buyer's financial standing and to disclose such information to the ECA by checking the custom and logistical documents as well as underlying contracts and invoices. A prudent bank is expected to do so, which is not only in the ECA's interest but also in the bank's own interest. Although this issue has not been centrally disputed in reported English ECI or ECG cases, inference can be made from the existing case authorities:

In the context of ECI, as pointed out by Clarke LJ in *Morgan Grenfell*, the fact that a prudent banker would only enter into certain projects if it had ECA backing cannot of itself mean that it would be willing to enter into any and every transaction, however suspect, if it had ECA backing. A prudent bank would care for the success even of transactions covered by the ECA, since their success or failure can affect a bank's public reputation and future relationship with the ECA; a prudent bank would therefore at least get down to the key facts related to each transaction.[161] Also, in *Svenska Handelsbanken v Sun Alliance and London Insurance Plc*,[162] a domestic credit insurance case, Rix J confirmed that it was the bank who bore the responsibility of investigating the credit risk of the underlying transaction and to further represent that to the insurer: it was reasonable to assume that the bank's standard lending criteria would involve such credit analysis. The judge held that the bank's failure to conduct credit analysis constituted a breach of the policy, and the insurer was therefore released from liability.

In the context of ECGs, Stuart-Smith LJ in *Credit Lyonnais* did not address whether it was an (implied) condition precedent under ECGs that the bills of lading should be authenticated. However, his lordship was clearly critical of the bank who did not adopt "the usual practice whereby the exporter hands to his bankers the unaccepted bills of exchange, the original bills of lading, the invoice and any other requisite documents for presentation to the buyer through the banking system".[163] That was confirmed by the House of Lords, where Lord Woolf MR said that had the bank exercised sufficient caution in entering into the ECG transaction, the fraud in this case would have been avoided. It is therefore always crucial for the bank to detect frauds and avoid potential loss.

161 *Morgan Grenfell* [2001] EWCA Civ 1932, Annex B, [8].
162 [1996] CLC 833.
163 *Credit Lyonnais* [1999] CLC 823, 829.

It should be noted that the UKEF also acknowledges that it will conduct due diligence in relation to the underlying transactions, too. For example, its "Guidance on Applying for Export Capital Facility Scheme" states that:[164]

> UKEF is helping the bank provide support under the Bond Support and Export Working Capital Schemes. It may have no prior relationship with the exporter and therefore needs to undertake some due diligence, both to understand the company and the export contracts it is seeking to support.

In addition, Section 10.2 of the "Standalone Guarantee Application Form" imposes the exporter a duty to permit and help the UKEF to conduct due diligence.

This research therefore submits that once the bank has made the investigation with the care and skill that would ordinarily be expected of a prudent bank, the risk should be transferred to the ECA. This formula has been recently confirmed by the English court in *ABN Amro* in the context of the assured's duty to prevent and mitigate the loss. As explained above, the buyer defaulted in repurchasing the goods under the "repo" transactions, and the goods, when resold by the banks in the open market, were of poor quality. The bank thus suffered huge losses, and criminal proceedings had since been pursued against the leading executives of the buyer company, alleging various conspiracies to commit fraud. All executives were eventually pleaded guilty and were sentenced to terms of imprisonment. Jacobs J rejected the underwriters' submission that the bank failed to take reasonable precautions to prevent and mitigate the loss by verifying the quality of the goods or obtaining quality certificates. The judge held that the bank had complied with normal banking practice and procedures in relation to its approach to collateral: the buyer, a longstanding client of the bank for over ten years, was a reputable company who never defaulted in payment before, and the bank had conducted a very detailed level of due diligence on the buyer and obtained protection through the contractual terms agreed in the loan agreement. The judge thus accepted the expert evidence that it was not market practice for banks, when advancing funds under "repo" transactions, to "arrange inspections of commodities owned by large companies which have stocks all over the world, and who were financing those stocks on a constant basis".[165] Therefore, the bank in *ABN Amro* was held neither reckless nor negligent in taking reasonable precautions to prevent or mitigate the loss: as long as it had investigated the genuineness of the underlying transaction and the financial standing of the buyer, the risk was borne by the insurer.

References

Allen, D, "Non-Disclosure: Hairshirt or Halo?" (1992) 55 MLR 96
Andrews, G & Millett, R, *Law of Guarantees* (7th edn, Sweet & Maxwell 2015)

164 See n 100 above.
165 *ABN Amro* [2021] EWHC 442 (Comm), [751].

Birds, J, *Modern Insurance Law* (10th edn, Sweet & Maxwell 2016)

Birds, J, Lynch, B & Paul, S, *MacGillivray on Insurance Law* (14th edn, Sweet & Maxwell 2018)

Eggers, P, "Remedies for the Failure to Observe the Utmost Good Faith" (2003) 2 LMCLQ 249

Gürses, Ö, *Marine Insurance Law* (2nd edn, Routledge 2017)

Gürses, Ö, *The Insurance of Commercial Risks: Law and Practice* (5th edn, Sweet & Maxwell 2017)

Gürses, Ö, "What Does Utmost Good Faith Mean" (2016) 27 Insurance Law Journal 124

Harnett, B, "The Doctrine of Concealment: A Remnant in the Law of Insurance" (1950) 15 Law and Contemporary Problems 391

Hollander, C, *Documentary Evidence* (12th edn, Sweet & Maxwell 2015)

Lowry, J, Rawlings, P & Merkin, R, *Insurance Law: Doctrines and Principles* (3rd edn, Hart 2011)

Mance, L, Goldrein, I & Merkin, R, *Insurance Disputes* (3rd edn, Informa 2011)

Matthews, P & Malek, H, *Disclosure* (5th edn, Sweet & Maxwell 2016)

Merkin, R, *Colinvaux's Law of Insurance* (12th edn, Sweet & Maxwell 2019)

Merkin, R & Gürses, Ö, "The Insurance Act 2015: Rebalancing the Interests of Insurer and Assured" (2015) 78 (6) MLR 1004

O'Donovan, J & Phillips, J, *The Modern Contract of Guarantee* (English edn, Sweet & Maxwell 2003)

Padfield, A, *Insurance Claims* (2nd edn, Tottel Publishing 2007)

Salcic, Z, *Export Credit Insurance & Guarantees: A Practitioner's Guide* (Palgrave Macmillan 2014)

Trindade, F, "The Skandia Case in the House of Lords" (1991) 107 LQR 24

5 The claim handling process under ECI and ECGs

This chapter explores the claim handling process under export credit insurance (ECI) and export credit guarantees (ECGs) by scrutinising the preconditions to indemnification under each type of contract. The first part of this chapter analyses two peculiar and unique clauses in ECI, i.e., the "waiting period" clause and the "arbitration award/judgment" clause, both of which could potentially prolong the claim handling process under ECI. It argues that despite the controversies of these two clauses, they are essential for the export credit agency (ECA) to ascertain the loss and protect its subrogation right; hence they do not contradict the principles of insurance law. Nevertheless, these two clauses could be burdensome to the assured. This chapter proposes a fairer waiting period clause and "arbitration award/judgment" clause, respectively, in order to address their harshness.

The second part turns to explore the claim provisions under ECI which are also commonly seen in all types of insurance contracts, such as the general claim handling clause, the acceleration clause, the notification and mitigation clause and the fraudulent claim clause, in order to draw a full picture of how the claim handling process works under ECI. It demonstrates that ECAs take the IA 2015 into account in drafting these clauses, which further indicates that they regard their ECI policies as contracts of insurance.

The third part then analyses the claim handling process under ECGs. It explores whether the waiting period clause and the "arbitration award/judgment" clause exist in ECGs and whether the claim handling process in ECGs is straightforward and speedy. It also analyses the claim provisions in ECGs, such as the general claim handling clause, the refund of payment clause and the notification and mitigation clause, and examines whether and how these clauses indicate the unconditional and on-demand nature of ECGs. By comparing the preconditions to indemnification under ECI and ECGs, this chapter seeks to explore the legal nature of them, respectively.

The fourth part studies the Loan Market Association's "Single Currency Term Buyer Credit Agreement for Use in Export Credit Agency Supported Finance Transactions", a model loan agreement for ECA-supported buyer credit transactions. It aims to show the interrelationship between the ECI/ECG

DOI: 10.4324/b22864-5

contract and the underlying loan agreement in respect of claim handling and indemnification. The last part concludes how this chapter contributes to the theme of this book.

It is necessary to clarify the selection of topics covered in this chapter. First, whilst the waiting period clause and the "arbitration award/judgment" clause can be drafted in various ways, they always relate to the claim handling processes in ECI. Therefore, these two clauses are discussed in this chapter rather than Chapter 3 (terms and conditions of ECI and ECGs). For the convenience of discussion, the interrelationship of these two clauses and the ECA's subrogation right will also be included in this chapter, whereas all other issues regarding subrogation will be discussed in Chapter 6 (subrogation and recoveries under ECI and ECGs). Second, as the duty not to make a fraudulent claim and the duty of utmost good faith are divorced in English law, the fraudulent claim clause in ECI policies will be analysed in this chapter rather than Chapter 4 (the duty of fair presentation under ECI and ECGs). Third, whilst the ECA's obligation to indemnify the claim within a reasonable time will be discussed throughout this chapter, the remedies for the ECA's late payment will not be touched because there have yet been any relevant ECI cases in English law. Fourth, the assignment of the assured's right to the ECA and the assured's obligation to collect debts after being indemnified will be discussed in Chapter 6, too, whilst these obligations are generally embedded in the claim provisions under an ECI policy.

It is also worthwhile to explain the samples of standard form ECI policies and ECG contracts analysed in this chapter. In addition to the UK Export Finance's (UKEF) "Export Insurance Policy" which is available on its website, the Berne Union Academic Survey has collected standard term ECI policies governed by English law from two anonymous members. These three policies will be discussed in detail throughout this chapter. In the meantime, in order to better analyse the peculiarities of the waiting period clause and the "arbitration award/judgment" clause, this chapter will also extensively refer to relevant wordings in ECI policies from other jurisdictions that are available online. Moreover, the sample ECG contracts shared by anonymous Berne Union members will also be studied so as to explore the claim provisions in ECGs.

The peculiar preconditions which could prolong the claim handling process under ECI

The waiting period clause

Time of loss under ECI policies?

ECAs invariably stipulate a waiting period clause in their policies, which provides that the ECA will not indemnify the assured straight away on the due date of the buyers' payment but will apply a waiting period instead, only after which will the ECA make the indemnification. The waiting period usually lasts 180 days/6 months from the due date. A sample of the waiting period clause can be found in Clause 2.1 of the UKEF's policy:[1]

> If the Insured sustains a loss as a result of the failure of the Buyer to pay any Sum Due for a period of [six] months after the Due Date … UKEF will … pay to the Insured …

According to the waiting period clause, whilst the assured should notify the ECA of the buyer's non-payment on the due date, it is not entitled to make the formal claim until the waiting period expires, when the ECA begins to handle the claim and indemnify the assured. That is also the case in the private credit risk market. Lloyd's, in its *Political Risk & Credit Claims Statement of Best Practice*, also divides the political and credit risks claim settlement process into four stages: (a) the assured notifies of a possible claim or circumstance that may give rise to a claim; (b) the waiting period is triggered; (c) the underwriters determine recovery strategy at the time of reserving if possible; and (d) the waiting period expires, and the claim becomes validated.[2]

It thus seems that the waiting period clause is a peculiar ECI term that prolongs the indemnification process. One might question why ECAs do not indemnify the assured straight away on the due date of the buyer's payment but apply a waiting period instead. When is the loss deemed to occur under the ECI policy? Does the loss occur on the due date of the buyer's payment, or does the loss materialise on the expiry date of the waiting period?

The answer should be found in the ECI policy wording. The Berne Union Academic Survey revealed that although the waiting period clause is stipulated in various ways in different ECI policies, all of the policies collected provide that the loss should be deemed to occur on the expiry date of the waiting period. Some policies express the word "loss" or "date of loss" in the definitions part of the policy. For instance, a sample wording from an anonymous Berne Union member provides that the "date of loss" shall mean the date on which the "non-payment" occurs, whereas the "non-payment" occurs on the expiry date of the waiting period.[3] Some policies specify the date of loss in the insuring clause. For instance, Clause 2.1.2 of Credendo's policy provides that the policy covers "non-payment" which occurs "when the insured cannot recover the payment of a certain, liquid and due claim" that "remains unpaid at the end of the waiting period".[4]

1 Full text available at <https://assets.publishing.service.gov.uk/government/uploads/system/uploads/attachment_data/file/1041653/Docs_Policy_EXIP_SingleContract_All_Risks.pdf> accessed 1 February 2022.

2 See Lloyd's of London, *Performance Management - Supplemental Requirements & Guidance* (last updated in July 2020), 55 < https://www.lloyds.com/conducting-business/requirements-and-standards/supplemental-requirements-and-guidance/ > accessed 1 February 2022.

3 See also Clause 11.3 of EGAP Czech's policy, Clause 3.11 of NEXI's policy and Clause 4.1 of SERV's policy.

4 See also Clause 2.1 of the UKEF policy (as seen above), Clause 4(4) of EH Germany's policy and Clause 6 of OeKB's policy.

Some policies stipulate the waiting period clause as an individual provision. For instance, Clause 2.5 of EKN's policy provides that "loss on a claim will be considered to have occurred only after the lapse of the waiting period".[5]

Section 6(c) of the European Commission Directive 98/29/EC on Harmonisation of the Main Provisions concerning Export Credit Insurance for Transactions with Medium and Long-Term Cover ("Directive 98/29/EC")[6] also provides that the loss under an ECI policy materialises on the expiry date of the waiting period, which is consistent with the ECAs' policy wordings cited above.

It thus seems that no matter in what way the waiting period clause is stipulated, under ECI the loss is always regarded as occurring on the expiry date of the waiting period rather than the due date of the buyer's payment. This raise questions such as "Why do ECAs provide such an artificial date of the occurrence of the loss?" and "Does it indicate that ECI is not insurance?" In order to answer those questions, it is necessary to explore the rationale behind the waiting period clause.

The rationale behind the waiting period clause

The primary purpose of ECAs' waiting period clause is to enable the ECA to ascertain whether the buyer's payment is temporarily delayed, for instance, "due to minor difficulties that can be resolved shortly".[7] In international trade, it is not uncommon for buyers to delay payment for a couple of days after the debt becomes due. The waiting period can also allow the ECA to examine the case and assess whether the non-payment is caused by political events or commercial events, as the insured percentages are different for political risks and commercial risks. Besides, during the waiting period, the ECA and the assured can take actions to mitigate or avoid the loss.

To interpret the abovementioned rationale in the language of insurance law, the function of the waiting period is to facilitate the ECA to verify and ascertain the loss, as ECI only covers the buyer's "protracted delay" rather than its merely temporary delay in payment.[8] This was confirmed by the English court in *Kent Engineering & Foundry Ltd v Export Credits Guarantee Department*,[9] where Parker J recognised that it was common ground in the export credit industry that a loss under an ECI policy occurs at "the date of ascertainment of loss", i.e., the date

5 See also Clause 1.2.5 of ODL's policy.
6 EC *Official Journal* L148/22.
7 Zlatko Salcic, *Export Credit Insurance & Guarantees: A Practitioner's Guide* (Palgrave Macmillan 2014) 167. See also *Export Credits Guarantee Department v Davenport (Shoes) Limited* [1983] 2 WLUK 36, where Ackner LJ explained that when the buyer defaulted in payment on the due date, the loss "was a probable one" because, for instance, due to congestion at the port of destination, the buyer had only recently obtained delivery of the goods from the customs and had made an application to the central bank of its country for funds to be remitted, but that required permission and had been delayed due to the shortage of foreign exchange.
8 See *Euler Hermes UK Plc v Apple Computer* [2006] EWCA Civ 375, [22] (Moore-Bick LJ).
9 [1983] 2 Lloyd's Rep 556, 558 (Parker J). The main issue of that case was about subrogation and recoveries, which will be discussed in Chapter 6.

when the waiting period elapses rather than the due date of payment. The same conclusion has been shared by the English courts in many other ECI or domestic credit insurance cases.[10]

Therefore, where there is strong evidence that the buyer is unable to pay, then the waiting period is no longer necessary and should be shortened or cancelled. Section 24(b) of the Directive 98/29/EC provides that:

> No claim waiting period need apply:
>
> (1) when, in the case of a private debtor, the non-payment is due to the debtor's insolvency, either *de jure* or *de facto*,
> (2) in case of a bilateral intergovernmental debt restructuring agreement.

Section 24(b) is also widely adopted by ECAs in their policies.[11] Clause 2.2 of the UKEF's policy stipulates an even somehow narrower scope for the waiting period to apply, providing that the waiting period "shall be reduced as to expire" on the date of (1) any intervening court order which renders the assured's performance of any obligations under the sales contract illegal or impossible, or (2) the provision of evidence satisfactory to UKEF of the insolvency of the buyer, which prevents the buyer from making the payment. The fact that the waiting period can be reduced or cancelled again indicates that the purpose of such a clause is to enable the ECA to ascertain the loss.

For a very similar purpose, the waiting period clause is also included in certain insurance policies other than ECI. For instance, health insurance policies typically include a general waiting period of 30–90 days so that any disease contracted within this period will not be indemnified, except for accident cases.[12] There can be various specific waiting periods in a health insurance cover. For instance, a pre-existing conditions exclusion waiting period, which could last 12–48 months, excludes the indemnification of the assured for pre-existing conditions (e.g., cancer or cardiovascular) during that period. The assured, however, can be indemnified for non-pre-existing conditions such as the flu. A maternity waiting period, ranging from 10 to 12 months, also prevents the assured from claiming maternity costs within that period.[13] The purpose of the waiting period in health insurance

10 See *Kazakstan Wool Processors (Europe) Ltd v Nederlandsche Credietverzekering Maatschappij NV* [2000] CLC 822; *Merrill Lynch International Bank Ltd (formerly Merrill Lynch Capital Markets Bank Ltd) v Winterthur Swiss Insurance Co* [2007] EWHC 893 (Comm), [2007] 2 All ER (Comm) 846, [24]-[25], [51]; *ECGD v Davenport* [1983] 2 WLUK 36; *British Credit Trust Holdings v UK Insurance Ltd* [2003] EWHC 2404 (Comm), [2004] 1 All ER (Comm) 444; *ABN AMRO Bank NV v Royal and Sun Alliance Insurance Plc* [2021] EWHC 442 (Comm), [776], [795].

11 Similar provisions can also be found in Clause 12(a) of Atradius DSB's policy and Clause 2.5.1 of EKN's policy.

12 The waiting period is also referred to as the "elimination period" or the "qualifying period" in the health insurance industry. See <https://www.myinsuranceclub.com/guides/waiting-period-in-health-insurance> accessed 1 February 2022.

13 See <https://www.pacificprime.com/plans/information/waiting-period/> accessed 1 February 2022.

is to ensure that the insurer only indemnifies the loss which is covered by the policy. Likewise, the waiting period can also be found in dental, property, auto or business interruption insurance policies.[14] The waiting period clause in these policies can take different forms,[15] but the rationale behind it is always to enable the insurer to ascertain the loss.

Claiming the interest that accrues during the waiting period?

The waiting period clause could prolong the claim handling process under ECI. A follow-up question will thus be about the interest that accrues during the waiting period (hereinafter referred to as "the waiting period interest").[16] Should ECAs compensate for the delayed indemnification by paying the waiting period interest? This work found that although almost every ECA provides a waiting period clause in their policies, their attitudes towards the waiting period interest are totally different. Whilst some ECI policies remain silent on this issue, some expressly exclude the waiting period interest. For instance, a sample wording from an anonymous Berne Union member provides that "loss shall mean the amount of principal due but not paid as at the date of loss, excluding any interest, penalty interest, fees, charges or similar ..."[17] Conversely, other policies expressly cover the waiting period interest. For instance, Clause 2.1.2(b) of Credendo's policy covers "the late interest due and payable under the [underlying contract] during the waiting period".[18]

As can be seen above, different ECAs take different approaches to the coverage of the waiting period interest. The Berne Union Academic Survey interviewed some members who did not cover the waiting period interest and asked about the reasons behind their approach:

(1) Some members explained that the coverage of the waiting period interest is additional and optional in their ECI products and that the assured has to pay

14 For instance, in the United States, some property insurance policies provide that when a named storm is in the area, new policies will not go into effect until after the storm passes. Some auto insurance policies place a 60-day waiting period which gives the insurers a chance to decide if the driver fits within their risk profiles. See <https://www.investopedia.com/terms/w/waiting-period.asp> accessed 1 February 2022.

15 The waiting period in some policies can have the effect of deductibles, and in some policies the waiting period is placed before the cover comes into effect rather than before the indemnification process. See <https://www.irmi.com/term/insurance-definitions/waiting-period-deductible> accessed 1 February 2022.

16 The waiting period interest is also called "post-maturity interest" in ECI industry. See, e.g., s 7(b) of the Directive 98/29/EC.

17 Similar provisions can also be found in the definition part of the UKEF's policy, Clause 2(2) of EH Germany's policy, Clause 3.1.3 of EGAP Czech's policy, Clause 16.1 of HBOR's policy, Clause 2.5 of NEXI's policy, Clause 6(1) of KUKE's policy and Clause 2(2) of OeKB's policy.

18 See also Clause 2 of ASHRA's policy, Clause 10.2 of Finnveras' policy, Clause 14(a) of Atradius DSB's policy, Clause 3.1.2 of ODL's policy and Clause 1.3 of SERV's policy.

an additional premium if it wishes to extend the cover to the waiting period interest.[19] They observed that very few of their clients chose to purchase this additional coverage.

(2) Some members also indicated that under certain types of their ECI products, e.g., buyer credit insurance covers, the restructuring of the insured project[20] is very common if the buyer fails to pay on the due date. In such circumstances, the assured will sign a so-called "standstill agreement" with the buyer, and the buyer will not be deemed as defaulting in payment. Therefore, no default interest accrues, and if the ECA indemnifies the default interest, it could have no respective recovery claim against the buyer.

However, the rationale above might not seem very convincing. Regarding explanation (1), it could be argued that some ECAs expressly include the waiting period interest in their ECI cover without charging any additional premiums. Explanation (2), on the other hand, is more persuasive in certain ECI covers which insure the construction of a project but cannot apply in all other types of ECI products which insure the sales of goods. Therefore, the ECA can make an exceptional provision regarding the restructuring of a project under a buyer credit insurance cover, but it should not generally exclude the waiting period interest in the policies of all types of ECI products.

It is therefore necessary to explore whether the waiting period interest should be covered from a legal perspective and, particularly, to question whether the waiting period interest should be covered in English law. The analysis should start with exploring the English law's position on default interest itself. The common law did not recognise the interest for late payment of sums due in the absence of express contractual provisions,[21] but this position was gradually reversed by the statutory law. Section 35A of the Senior Courts Act 1981 entitles the court to exercise the discretion to award interest and to fix the period and rate of the interest. Section 49 of the Arbitration Act 1996 also allows the arbitration tribunal to award interest. Furthermore, under ss 1 and 4 of the Late Payment of Commercial Debts (Interest) Act 1998, it is an implied term in a contract for the supply of goods or services that the debt under such a contract carries a simple interest which runs from the day after the due date of payment. It thus seems that if the sales contract stipulates that it is governed by the English law and any dispute will

19 This has been codified by s 29(b) of OECD's Agreement on Officially Supported Export Credits. For details see Chapter 7 of this work.

20 Restructuring is an action taken by a company to significantly modify the financial and operational aspects of the company, usually when the business is facing financial pressures. Restructuring is a type of corporate action taken that involves significantly modifying the debt, operations or structure of a company as a way of limiting financial harm and improving the business. See <https://www.investopedia.com/terms/r/restructuring.asp> accessed 1 February 2022.

21 *London, Chatham and Dover Railway Co v South Eastern Railway Co* [1893] AC 429. See also Robert Merkin, *Colinvaux's Law of Insurance* (12th edn, Sweet & Maxwell 2019), [11-264]; H.G. Beale, *Chitty on Contracts* (33rd edn, Sweet & Maxwell 2018), Chapter 26, Section 12.

be heard by the English court, then the statutory interest shall apply. Meanwhile, where a contract is governed by foreign law, according to s 12(2) of the Late Payment of Commercial Debts (Interest) Act 1998, the statutory interest does not apply. It thus seems that an express default interest clause in the underlying sales/loan contract is always essential for the assured if it wishes to claim default interest against the buyer. Therefore, in ECI transactions, the assured does normally in the underlying contract provide that the buyer should pay the principal amount (plus contractual interest) as well as the default interest should it fail to make a payment on the due date. In other words, the assured is generally entitled to claim the default interest from the buyer. However, the question here is, can the assured claim the default interest, i.e., the waiting period interest, from the ECA under the ECI policy?

The English court in *AB Svensk ExportKredit v New Hampshire Insurance*[22] confirmed that in the context of ECI the assured should be compensated by the insurer the default interest "for being kept out of their money", whereas the court did not provide detailed case authorities and reasoning for reaching this conclusion. The core issue in that case was whether the insurer was entitled to control the assured's proceedings prior to indemnification; hence the issue regarding the waiting period interest was only addressed briefly.[23] Meanwhile, that issue was further addressed in the context of insurance contracts generally by Tomlinson J in *Hellenic Industrial Development Bank v Atkin (The Julia)*.[24] The learned judge suggested that the assured should be compensated for being kept out of its money by being awarded the interest:[25]

> In a commercial action … if the defendant has had the use of money to which the claimant was entitled, fairness requires that the claimant be compensated for the notional cost of borrowing the same amount over the same period.

Of course, the common law also allows the insurer to postpone the running of interest for not indemnifying the assured because of conducting a reasonable investigation into the claim,[26] but this applies only when (a) the claim was sufficiently unusual as to require special investigation[27] or (b) where there is evidence of a commercial practice of a later date of payment without an interest obligation.[28] However, it is submitted that this cannot be an excuse for the ECA to exclude the waiting period interest: the waiting period applies to every claim made by the assured, whether usual or unusual, and there is no evidence of a

22 [1988] 3 WLUK 387.
23 The details of this case will be discussed in Chapter 6 of this book.
24 [2002] EWHC 1405 (Comm), [2003] Lloyd's Rep IR 365 [16].
25 Ibid.
26 *Kuwait Airways Corp v Kuwait Insurance Co SAK (No 3)* [2000] 1 All ER (Comm) 972.
27 *Quorum AS V Schramm* [2002] 2 All ER (Comm) 179.
28 *The Julia* [2003] Lloyd's Rep IR 365, [12].

"commercial practice" for excluding the waiting period interest in ECI industry. Moreover, since almost every ECI policy regards the "loss" as occurring on the expiry date of the waiting period, such a "loss" should include both the principal amount (plus contractual interest) on the due date and the interest which accrues during the waiting period. This research argues that since the ECA takes an artificial date of loss which prolongs the indemnification, it should accordingly compensate the assured for doing so by covering the waiting period interest. This view is supported by the European Commission and stipulated in s 7(b) of the Directive 98/29/EC:

> Cover for credit risk shall include the amount (principal and interest) owed by the buyer under the commercial contract or by the borrower under the loan agreement, including interest accruing after the due date (post-maturity interest).

The proposal for a fairer waiting period clause for the assured

Based on the discussion above, this research calls for ECAs to include a fairer waiting period clause for the assured, under which the waiting period interest should be covered. In particular, ECAs should consider the following points in drafting their waiting period clause.

First, the waiting period clause should require that the assured includes a default interest clause in its sales contract with the buyer, which ensures that the ECA can exercise its subrogation right to the default interest against the buyer. A good example can be found in EKN's specimen policy.[29] Clause 2.1 of EKN's policy provides that the policy "can" cover the waiting period interest, and Clause 3.2 further provides that should the policy cover the waiting period interest, "it must be expressly stated in the contract that the debtor is obliged to pay default interest".[30]

Second, it is necessary to expressly stipulate how to fix the waiting period interest rate. Most ECI policies do not specify the waiting period interest rate, which may cause uncertainties to the parties. The ECI policy should provide that if the assured and the buyer have agreed on the default interest rate in the sales contract, then the waiting period interest should be fixed in accordance with such rate.[31] The policy can also cap the waiting period interest rate by the appropriate

29 As a document of general terms and conditions, EKN's policy does not include specific wordings but offer detailed guidance on the wordings.

30 Clause 14(a) of Atradius DSB buyer credit insurance policy also provides that the waiting period interest shall be reimbursed only if it is payable by the buyer under the loan agreement. See also Clause 10.2 of Finnvera's policy.

31 For instance, Clause 19.3 of CESCE's policy provides that the default interest rate should not be higher than the contractual interest rate. Clause 1 of EKN's policy provides that the default interest rate should be fixed on the basis of the market interest rate (which is the Stockholm Interbank Offered Rate) with the addition of a margin of 0.25%.

prevailing interbank rate, e.g., US Prime Rate for dollars and EURIBOR (Euro Interbank Offered Rate) for euros.[32] That is because ECI is a contract of indemnity insurance and the assured is not supposed to make a profit by providing a very high default interest rate. Such an interbank rate has been referred to by the English court in *AB Svensk ExportKredit*.[33] A buyer credit transaction was arranged in this case. The assured, a Swedish bank, in its loan agreement provided that the buyer shall pay the default interest should it fail to repay on the due date and the default interest rate should be 1.5% higher than the contractual interest rate. The ECI policy does not expressly provide whether and how the waiting period interest should be covered. The court decided that the waiting period interest should be covered by the insurer, and the rate should be fixed on the basis of the rate of interest "at which a borrower in Sweden of the credit standing of the assured could, at the time of … [the buyer transaction], have borrowed the sum of … [the buyer credit transaction]". The court decided that the appropriate reference was the Stockholm Interbank Offered Rate.[34]

By paying the principal amount (plus the contractual interest) and the capped waiting period interest, the ECA can ensure that the assured suffers no loss and makes no profit. Some sample wordings collected through the Berne Union Academic Survey read as follows:

> **Sample wording A:**[35]
> [The ECA] does not pay indemnification for default interest for a period longer than six (6) months. Default interest may be indemnified up to a maximum of 2% per annum above the annual contractual interest rate of the Credit.
>
> **Sample wording B:**[36]
> The waiting period interest … shall be reimbursed … on the basis of the rate stated in the Loan Agreement, but shall not exceed the prevailing interbank rate for the currency in which the Insured Receivable must be paid (EURIBOR for euros and LIBOR for other currencies) for a period equal to the Waiting Period …
>
> **Sample wording C:**[37]
> The unpaid amount of the Claim … which may be increased as applicable by late interest due under the Contract during the Waiting Period, it being

32 It should be noted that LIBOR (London Interbank Offered Rate) was abolished in 2021. For the transition from LIBOR to risk-free rates, See Bank of England, "Transition from LIBOR to risk-free rates", <https://www.bankofengland.co.uk/markets/transition-to-sterling-risk-free-rates-from-libor> accessed 1 February 2022.

33 [1988] 3 WLUK 387.

34 Ibid. A similar decision can be found in *The Julia* [2005] Lloyd's Rep IR 365, [19], a marine insurance case where Tomlinson J adopted the US Prime Rate in awarding the interest for the assured.

35 See Clause 10.2 of Finnvera's policy.

36 See Clause 14(a) of Atradius DSB's policy. For a similar provision see Clause 2 of ASHRA's policy.

37 See Clause 5.2.2(a) of Credendo's policy.

understood that the rate opposable to [the ECA] for the calculation of such late interest may not exceed:

(i) for any Claim in euros: the 6-month Euribor rate established on the contractual due date on which it is unpaid, or if no Euribor rate is available, the reference rate commonly used by major European banks to grant loans in euros; and
(ii) for any Claim in currencies other than the euro: the 6-month Libor rate of the currency in question established on the contractual due date on which it is unpaid or if no Libor rate is available, the reference rate commonly used by major international banks to grant loans in the currency concerned.

Should the Euribor, Libor or any other reference rate become negative, the late interest rate shall be equal to 0% per annum.

Third, the waiting period interest shall not include any penalties and damages against the buyer. The common law established that the purpose of interest is to ensure that the creditor does not suffer any loss, rather than punishing the debtor.[38] Damages for late payment, on the other hand, are available in common law only if the creditor can plead and prove that the loss is caused by the late payment of the debtor,[39] and it would be practically impossible in the indemnification process for the ECA to determine that in each claim. ECI only covers "the debtor's regular payment commitments",[40] so penalties and damages fall outside of the scope of an ECI cover. The exclusion of penalties and damages is widely found in ECI policies[41] and is included in s 7(b) of the Directive 98/29/EC.

Fourth, for the avoidance of doubt, it would be helpful to stipulate that the total amount of loss that the ECA is obliged to pay, including both the principal amount (plus contractual interest) and the waiting period interest, shall not exceed the maximum liability of the ECI policy.[42] Without such a provision, the assured may argue that the maximum liability only caps the principal amount (plus contractual interest).

Based on the analysis above, this research proposes a model waiting period clause as follows:

(1) [The ECA] is obliged to indemnify the assured after a waiting period of [six] months from the due date of the buyer's payment.
(2) The waiting period in Clause (1) shall not apply:

38 *BP Exploration Co (Libya) Ltd v Hunt (No.2)* [1979] 1 WLR 783. See also *The Julia* [2005] Lloyd's Rep IR 365.
39 *Sempra Metals Ltd v Inland Revenue Commissioners* [2007] UKHL 34, [2008] 1 AC 561.
40 See the commentary attached to Clause 2.2.2 of EKN's policy.
41 See, e.g., Clause 2.1.2(b) of Credendo's policy, Clause 2(2) of EH Germany's policy and Clause 1.5 of SERV's policy.
42 See, e.g., Clause 15.4 of ASHRA's policy.

(a) If the assured provides evidence satisfactory to [the ECA] of the buyer's insolvency; or
(b) If any intervening court order is made which renders the assured's performance of any obligations under the sales contract illegal or impossible; or
(c) In case of a bilateral intergovernmental debt rescheduling agreement.

(3) With regard to Clause (2), the loss shall be deemed to occur on the date when circumstances (a), (b) or (c) takes place. In all other circumstances, the loss shall be deemed to occur on the expiry date of the waiting period.
(4) The interest which accrues during the waiting period ("the waiting period interest") shall be covered by the policy, whereas the total amount of loss, which includes the principal amount, the contractual interest and the waiting period interest, shall not exceed the maximum liability of the policy.

The waiting period interest shall be fixed on the default interest rate agreed by the parties in the underlying export contract, but such rate shall not exceed the prevailing interbank rate for the currency in which the principal amount and contractual interest are paid.

Any further ancillary claims, e.g., penalties, damages or compound interest, shall not be covered under the policy.

The "arbitration award/judgment" clause

The controversies of the "arbitration award/judgment" clause

In addition to the waiting period clause, an ECI policy may include another clause which could prolong the indemnification process. The Berne Union Academic Survey found that over 70% of the respondents in their ECI policies include a term to the effect that should any dispute arise from the underlying contract between the assured and the buyer, the assured must obtain an arbitration award or a judgment which establishes its rights before it can be paid by the ECA (hereafter referred to as the "arbitration award/judgment" clause). As explained above, the Berne Union Academic Survey takes buyer credit transactions as the survey scenario, under which many members believe that the dispute between the assured (i.e., the bank) and the buyer is rather rare. However, there are still over 70% of respondents who include such a clause in their buyer credit insurance policies. It can be said that under a basic ECI or a supplier credit insurance policy that supports the business between the exporter and the buyer, a dispute will be more likely to arise, and therefore, there will be an even higher percentage of ECAs or private credit insurers stipulating an "arbitration award/judgment" clause.[43]

The "arbitration award/judgment" clause can be stipulated in various ways according to the different structures of the policies. For instance, it can be included

43 The author through the Berne Union Academic Survey interviewed a product manager from an anonymous Berne Union member who explained the application of the "arbitration award/judgment" clause to different types of ECI covers as follows:

under the "insured risks" clause or "insured amount" clause[44] or can be drafted as part of the exclusions.[45] It can also be stipulated as a condition precedent to liability under the claim handling/indemnification clause[46] or as one of the general principles of the policy.[47] No matter how the "arbitration award/judgment" clause is structured, it could restrict or, at least, prolong the indemnification under the ECI policy. A sample wording of the "arbitration award/judgment" clause in Clause 2.3 of the UKEF's policy reads as follows:

> Where a dispute exists between the Buyer and the Insured concerning or affecting the Buyer's obligation to pay the sum in question … UKEF shall (unless and to the extent that it may otherwise agree in writing) have no liability unless and in so far as the Insured has obtained (at its own expense and risk) an Arbitration Award or Judgment determining that the Buyer is obliged to pay the sum and is not justified in refusing or failing to do so.

The "arbitration award/judgment" clause is also stipulated under s 29 of the Directive 98/29/EC. Such a clause is questionable in at least three aspects: (1) What does the word "dispute" mean, and does the "arbitration award/judgment" clause have a large scope to apply? (2) Is such a clause unfair to the assured and is there any statutory or judicial control of it? (3) Does it contradict the principles of insurance law (e.g., the principle of subrogation) and thereby indicate that ECI is not a contract of insurance? The following paragraphs will analyse these questions by discussing *Euler Hermes UK Plc v Apple Computer*[48] and the Berne Union members' wordings.

Firstly, what does the word "dispute" mean? That is a frequent area of disagreement between the ECA and the assured. Is it a genuine reason or a mere

---

> The dispute is extremely seldom under buyer credit insurance which covers a loan agreement provided by a bank. Usually, the existence of the loan claim is not being disputed. Seldom cases might be that (a) the accrual of the loan interest is disputed; (b) the loan is in violation of local law (e.g., Sharia rules); and (c) the applicable law or place of jurisdiction is disputed. In such cases, we would indemnify straight away once a final judgement has been obtained. We will indemnify before this if it is evident that the legality/validity of the claim is being disputed without any good reason and is abusive. In practice, most of the disputes arise under supplier credit insurance covers, where the quality of the delivered merchandise or the works executed by the exporter are being claimed as insufficient/defective and the buyer refuses (full or partial) payment because of this. In such cases, the above said would apply *mutatis mutandis*.

44 See, e.g., Clause 2.3 of UKEF's policy, Clause 5(2) of EH Germany's policy and Clause 12.4.2 of EGAP Czech's policy.

45 For instance, a sample wording from an anonymous Berne Union member provides that "any loss which is the subject of dispute shall be excluded from cover until the dispute is finally resolved".

46 See, e.g., Clause 8.3 of Finnvera's policy, Clause 5.3 of SERV's policy and Clause 14.3 of KUKE's policy.

47 See, e.g., Clause 5.1.4 of Credendo's policy and Clause 13.2 of ODL's policy.

48 [2006] EWCA Civ 375, [2006] Lloyd's Rep IR 691.

excuse? Does it refer to a dispute related to the performance of the underlying contract only, or can it cover any dispute between the assured and the buyer? It might seem strange that most ECAs do not define the term "dispute" in their "arbitration award/judgment" clause. The Berne Union Academic Survey only collected two sample wordings in this respect:

> **Sample wording A (in the context of basic ECI) (from an anonymous Berne Union member):**
> A "dispute" is … in respect of the quality of the goods delivered, conditions of delivery, etc, between the exporter and the buyer relating to the execution of the export contract by the exporter, irrespective of whether such dispute relates to the shipment or any other transaction between the two.
>
> **Sample wording B (in the context of buyer credit insurance):**[49]
> The term "Dispute" means charges (in and out of court) filed by the Debtor in relation to the Receivables of the Policyholder where the Debtor fails to acknowledge the claims of the Policyholder for the payment of Receivables, particularly questioning the chargeability of the Receivables, the performance or proper performance of the duties and obligations by the Policyholder resulting from the Credit Agreement in principle or amount, or files mutual claims that have not been accepted by the Policyholder, or withholds its Receivables against the Receivables of the Policyholder that have not been accepted by the Policyholder.

It thus seems that ECAs are likely to draw a broad definition of "dispute". One might question how would the English court construe the term "dispute" and, in particular, would the court construe it in favour of the assured?

As discussed in Chapter 3, in English law, a contract of insurance is subject to the general rules of construction which apply to any type of contract:[50] where the clause is interpreted in two different ways by the parties, the court is entitled to prefer the interpretation which is consistent with business common sense;[51] if the policy is ambiguous, the court may construe a policy against the party who drafted it if the policy is ambiguous.[52] However, the English courts did not permit the artificial creation of ambiguity,[53] nor did they accept that a clause was ambiguous merely because it could "produce a both unexpected and irrational result".[54] It thus seems that the scope of the application of the principle of *contra proferentem* is relatively narrow.

That is also the case in the context of ECI. In *Euler Hermes*,[55] the ECI policy had excluded the ECA's liability for "any loss where there is a dispute" between

49 See Clause 1.19 of KUKE's policy.
50 Merkin (n 21), [3-001].
51 *Rainy Sky SA v Kookmin Bank* [2011] UKSC 50, [2012] 1 All ER 1137.
52 *Simmonds v Cockell* [1920] 1 KB 843, 845 (Cockburn CJ). See also Merkin (n 21), [3-026].
53 *Hare v Barstow* (1844) 8 Jur 928, 929 (Lord Denman CJ).
54 *Carlingford Australia General Insurance Ltd v EZ Industries Ltd* [1988] VR 349.
55 [2006] EWCA Civ 375.

the exporter and the buyer. However, it did not define the term "dispute". The assured exporter distributed goods to its buyer in Saudi Arabia until the summer of 2000, when it decided not to renew the distributorship. The buyer did not challenge the exporter's performance of the sales contract but claimed compensation for the termination of distributorship and withheld payments on goods previously supplied by the exporter. The exporter argued that the buyer's claim did not fall within the scope of "dispute" in the exclusion clause of the policy. Reading the policy as a whole, the court held that in the absence of any indication to the contrary, the term "dispute" could refer to any dispute between the exporter and the buyer which resulted in the protracted default in payment. *Euler Hermes* indicates that the principle of *contra proferentem* does not apply to the "arbitration award/judgment" clause. The scope of the term "dispute" could be very broad under this clause.

Secondly, is the "arbitration award/judgment" clause unfair to the assured, and is there any statutory or judicial control of it? Such a clause is apparently "burdensome" to the assured[56] because it has to at its own expense take legal proceedings of which the outcome is very uncertain. However, in English law, there seems to be little statutory or judicial control of ECI policy terms which are deemed "unfair" by the assured. In terms of statutory control, since the "arbitration award/judgment" clause does not tend to reduce the risk of the loss of a particular kind, location and time, it falls out of the scope of s 11 of the IA 2015. It is, in any case, ancillary to the scope of the cover.[57] This means that where the "arbitration award/judgment" clause is drafted as a condition precedent to liability, the assured cannot rely on s 11(3) of the IA 2015 to restrict the ECA's right to preclude its liability. Moreover, whilst the Financial Conduct Authority's *Insurance Conduct of Business Sourcebook* (ICOBS) provides general requirements that an insurer must "handle claims promptly and fairly" and must not "unreasonably reject a claim",[58] it does not address how to determine whether a term is unfair in the context of commercial insurance. Therefore, it seems that the assured cannot rely on any English legislation or regulation to challenge the validity of the "arbitration award/judgment" clause.

In terms of judicial control, in common law, the English court can prevent the insurer's reliance on "particularly onerous" terms unless they are expressly brought to the attention of the assured.[59] However, they have not developed a clear formulation to determine whether a term is "particularly onerous". Such an issue, therefore, has to be decided on a case-by-case basis. In *Euler Hermes*,[60] following the abovementioned non-payment by the buyer, the exporter claimed against the ECA and indicated that it would soon commence legal proceedings against the

56 Salcic (n 7) 95.
57 For detailed discussion on s 11 of the IA 2015, see Chapter 3 of this research.
58 The Financial Conduct Authority's Insurance Conduct of Business Sourcebook, Section 8.1.1.
59 *US Trading Ltd v AXA Insurance Co Ltd* [2010] Lloyd's Rep IR 505; *D&J Koskas v Standard Marine Insurance Co Ltd* (1927) 27 Ll L Rep 59.
60 [2006] EWCA Civ 375.

buyer. Relying on the assured's statement, the ECA concluded a claim settlement agreement which required the exporter to "take action" to establish that it was entitled to the buyer's payment. After the ECA paid the claim, the exporter subsequently decided not to begin such legal proceedings because doing so was not in its "commercial interest". The ECA then claimed to recover the insurance proceeds because the exporter breached the claim settlement agreement. The exporter argued such a clause was "absurd" and onerous because to obtain an arbitration award or judgment in favour of itself in a foreign jurisdiction was out of its control. The court pointed out that it would be irrelevant to enquire into the exporter's chances of establishing its rights because this was a contractual obligation under the claim settlement agreement. However, Moore-Bick LJ believed that it would be necessary to consider whether there was "any significant likelihood" that such an arbitration award or judgment would be unable to be enforced in Saudi Arabia, which should be proved by the expert witness evidence. The court then relied on the expert witness evidence to conclude that the "arbitration award/judgment" clause was not unfair. It thus seems that the English court is not likely to regard the "arbitration award/judgment" clause as "particularly onerous" or unfair.

Thirdly, does the "arbitration award/judgment clause" contradict the general principles of insurance law (e.g., the principle of subrogation), thereby indicating that ECI is not a contract of insurance? In *Euler Hermes*, the exporter submitted that the ECA could have exercised its rights of subrogation to take proceedings in its name to mitigate the loss and, having failed to do so, could not recover payment from the assured. The court rejected this argument. Moore-Bick LJ pointed out that neither the ECA nor the exporter would be keen to embark on litigation at their own expense. Relying on the claim settlement agreement which created a contractual obligation on the exporter to establish an undisputed right to the debt, his lordship explained that if the exporter failed to do so, it would mean that the ECA suffered damage as a result of having paid a loss which it was not bound to pay under the exclusion of the ECI policy. His lordship further assumed that if the ECA exercised its subrogation right to take proceedings against the buyer and those proceedings led to the recovery of the debt, it would have only recovered no more than it already stood to recover from the exporter by way of damages for breach of contract without incurring any expense. In such circumstances, there would be no ground for saying that the ECA ought reasonably to have embarked at its own expense on litigation which would have yielded it "no practical benefit".[61] *Euler Hermes* thus indicates that the "arbitration award/judgment" clause does not contradict the principle of subrogation.

However, it is submitted that *Euler Hermes* has its limitation as a case law authority: the "arbitration award/judgment" clause in that case was included in the claim settlement agreement on the understanding that the exporter intended to commence a legal proceeding against the buyer. The court's decisions regarding questions (1)–(3) were all heavily based on this background. Whilst the judgment

61 Ibid, [54].

is indeed helpful to answer questions (1) and (2), with respect, its approach to question (3) is far from convincing. His lordship's reasoning was that, since the claim settlement agreement obliged the exporter to commence legal proceedings, it did not contradict the principle of subrogation. However, it should be questioned what the solution would be if the "arbitration award/judgment" clause is embedded in the standard form ECI policy and the assured has no option but to accept it due to the imbalance of the bargaining power. The assured would wish that the insurer pay it first and then subrogate into its shoes to exercise its rights against the third party (i.e., the buyer) because it will never be eager to engage in burdensome legal proceedings against the third party by itself. Unfortunately, the judge did not scrutinise the details of the principle of subrogation. As the exporter in *Euler Hermes* argued, the ECA could first pay the exporter and then exercise its subrogation right against the buyer. One issue that must be specifically taken into account here is the reimbursement of legal costs. The Berne Union Academic Survey found that whilst most respondents expressly reimburse the "collection cost", over 50% of the respondents do not reimburse the legal costs the assured incurs under the "arbitration award/judgment" clause.[62] This means that if there is no dispute at all, the assured will be indemnified by the ECA and after that, where the assured is required by the ECA to collect recoveries against the buyer, the legal cost incurred will be reimbursed. But if there is a dispute between the assured and the buyer, the assured must at its own expense sue the buyer. The distinction between these two situations can be rather blurred. Where the assured suffers a loss as a result of political events or the insolvency of the buyer, there is little doubt that the ECA should pay and should reimburse the assured's legal cost in collecting debts. However, where non-payment occurs, the buyer is very likely to raise some reasons for withholding its payment, and the ECA could thus argue that since there is a "dispute", the assured must establish an undisputed right to the debt at its own expense. That would, as a result, be very harsh to the assured. It thus seems that *Euler Hermes* did not provide a thorough analysis of the "arbitration award/judgment" clause. To better examine the "arbitration award/judgment" clause, it is necessary to scrutinise the rationale behind this clause and explore its interrelationship with insurance law principles, such as the principle of indemnity and the principle of subrogation.

The rationale behind the "arbitration award/judgment" clause: a prerequisite of indemnification and subrogation

This research submits that despite the controversies of the "arbitration award/judgment" clause, it functions as a prerequisite of the assured's indemnification and the ECA's subrogation right.

62 Most ECI policies remain silent on this issue, whereas some expressly exclude the reimbursement of the legal cost under the "arbitration award/judgment" clause. For instance, a sample wording from an anonymous Berne Union member provides that "any costs by the incurred by the Insured in proving a claim under the policy shall be borne by the Insured".

In practice, ECAs have their reasons for stipulating the "arbitration award/judgment" clause. In international trade, it is possible that a buyer is not satisfied with the quality or quantity of the exporter's performance of the sales contract and withholds the payment. Equally, it is also possible that the exporter denies any breach of the sales contract. If the buyer mistakenly believes that the exporter has not performed its obligations, then the buyer's refusal is in practice called "unjustified repudiation". If, on the contrary, the buyer has pertinent groundings to refuse to pay, it is called "justified repudiation"[63] which will not be covered by ECAs.[64] However, ECAs normally do not assess whether the buyer's refusal is justified or not because it would be difficult for them to "assess all the facts and the contractual provisions" of the contract between the exporter and the buyer.[65] They believe that the only way for the assured to establish its rights is to obtain an arbitration award or a judgment.

To interpret the abovementioned rationale in the context of insurance law, the aim of the "arbitration award/judgment" clause is to require the assured to prove and establish the existence and amount of its loss so that it can be indemnified by the ECA. For instance, Clause 5.3 of SERV's policy provides that:

> If the claim for which indemnity is requested or any joint liability of third parties as documented in the insurance policy is disputed, [the ECA] may request that proof of the existence of the claim, maturity, and absence of defences and objections be established by a judgement of the court having competent jurisdiction.

Such key words as "prove", "ascertain", "establish", "confirm", "determine" and "settle" are widely seen in Berne Union members' ECI policies.[66]

That is consistent with the common law principle that in contracts of indemnity, no obligation arises on the part of the insurer to pay a claim until the insured has suffered a loss.[67] This principle is applicable in ECI, which is one type of indemnity insurance. ECI only covers the risk of the buyer's default in payment to which the assured is entitled. If the buyer's non-payment results from the assured's breach of the underlying contract, then it should not be the loss covered by the ECI policy. By obtaining an arbitration award or a judgment, the assured will be able to prove its right to the buyer's payment and thus establish and quantify the loss it suffered. That is a precondition for the assured to be indemnified under the ECI policy.

63 Salcic (n 7) 27. See also Eva Lomnicka, "Export Credit Guarantees", in Michael Bridge (ed.), *Benjamin's Sales of Goods* (11th edn, Sweet & Maxwell 2020), [25-022].

64 For instance, Clause 5.1.5 of Credendo's policy provides that "the indemnity paid by Credendo to the Insured may not become a source of enrichment for the latter beyond the benefit taken from the partial performance of the Contract".

65 Salcic (n 7) 95, 180.

66 See, e.g., Clause 2.3 of UKEF's policy, Clause 5.1.4 of Credendo's policy, Clause 5(3) of EH Germany's policy and Clause 8.3 of Finnvera's policy.

67 *West Wake Price & Co v Ching* [1957] 1 WLR 45, 49 (Devlin J).

Based on the very similar purpose, a similar provision can also be found in some liability insurance policies, in which the common law requires the assured to establish its liability by an arbitration award, a judgment or a settlement agreement.[68] By obtaining an arbitration award or a judgment, the assured will be able to ascertain its liability to the third party so that it can prove its loss under the policy and be indemnified by the insurer. The assured under liability insurance can also prove its loss by reaching a settlement agreement with the third party, which is not common in ECI policies, but the Berne Union Academic Survey found that some ECAs would also recognise the resolution of a dispute via negotiations and mediation. Liability insurance and ECI share some common characteristics: they are both contracts of indemnity, and they both cover the loss relating to the third party. Under liability insurance, the loss is ascertained by the assured's liability to the third party, and under ECI the loss is determined by the assured's right against the third party (i.e., the buyer). In both cases, the loss needs to be established and quantified by an arbitration award, a judgment or by other means, as a precondition for the assured to be indemnified.

Moreover, the "arbitration award/judgment" clause does not contradict the principle of subrogation. On the contrary, it is the prerequisite for the ECA to exercise its subrogation right. The common law has established that the insurer does not have a subrogation right if the insured has no right to action.[69] If there is a dispute between the assured and the buyer as a result of the assured's breach of the underlying sales contract, then the assured is not entitled to the buyer's payment, and thus the ECA cannot exercise its subrogation right against the buyer. The common law has also established that the right of subrogation arises only after the insured is indemnified by the insurer.[70] Where there is a dispute about the buyer's non-payment, the ECA will not pay to the assured until it has obtained an arbitration award or judgment establishing its right; hence it cannot exercise its subrogation right at this stage. Once the assured has obtained such an arbitration award or judgment, the ECA will then indemnify the loss ascertained by the arbitration award or judgment. After that, the ECA can exercise its subrogation right relying on the decisions that it followed. Therefore, the "arbitration award/judgment" clause is a prerequisite of the ECA's subrogation right.

Should the ECA make indemnification straight away after the assured has obtained an arbitration award or a judgment?

After the rationale behind the "arbitration award/judgment" clause is clarified, there remains a follow-up question about how it operates. That is, should the ECA indemnify the assured straight away after it has obtained an arbitration award or a judgment that establishes the buyer's obligation to pay? This seems to depend

68 *Post Office v Norwich Union Fire Insurance Society Ltd* [1967] 2 QB 363.
69 *Simpson v Thomson* (1877) 3 App Cas 279; *Buckland v Palmer* [1984] 1 WLR 1109.
70 *Page v Scottish Insurance Corp* (1929) 98 LJKB 308, 311 (Scrutton LJ).

on the policy wordings, and there could be three possible stipulations: (1) the ECA indemnifies the assured straight away after the assured has obtained such an arbitration award or a judgment. In other words, the indemnification begins on the date when such an award or a judgment is given by the arbitration tribunal or the court; (2) the ECA indemnifies the assured on the date when the buyer is obliged to pay under the arbitration award or the judgment, e.g., a month after the award or the judgment is made; (3) the ECA suspends the indemnification until the enforcement of such an arbitration award or a judgment in the buyer's country. This research found that most ECI policies do not include express provisions on this issue. No example of the category (1) or (2) above was found, and, in respect of category (3), there were only two policies which stipulate that if the arbitration award or the judgment is obtained by default, then indemnification may be held in abeyance pending its enforcement in the buyer's country.[71] To explore the rationale behind such a provision, the author, through the Berne Union Academic Survey, interviewed a legal counsel of a Berne Union member's claim department, whose explanation is cited below:

> Prior to compensation, we do require enforcement of a default judgment. Enforcement of normal judgments, however, is not required before compensation. The rationale is the following: default judgments are rendered by the court without having heard the arguments of the defendant. Indeed, for such a judgment to be rendered, the defendant cannot have appeared in court. Consequently, as default judgments are only based on the arguments presented by the plaintiff, a higher scrutiny standard is required and we compensate once the default judgment has been enforced in the country where enforcement is sought.

Therefore, except for default judgments, in practice, most ECAs will indemnify the assured straight away after it has obtained an arbitration award or a judgment, although they do not expressly provide so in their policies. This can also be implied from the "arbitration award/judgment" clause in their policies: such clause normally provides that the ECA will not indemnify the assured "unless" it has proved its loss by obtaining an arbitration award or a judgment, which means that once the assured has done so, there is no reason for the ECA to further postpone the indemnification.

Furthermore, it is equally necessary to explore how the waiting period clause operates together with the "arbitration award/judgment" clause. Should a waiting period run after the assured has obtained an arbitration award or a judgment? There could also be three possible approaches: (1) the waiting period does not run if the "arbitration award/judgment" clause applies,[72] which means that the ECA

71 See Clause 5.1.4 of Credendo's policy and Clause 13.2 of ODL Luxembourg's policy.

72 For instance, the policy in *Euler Hermes* provides that the waiting period "shall not run" if the "arbitration award/judgment" clause applies. See *Euler Hermes* [2006] EWCA Civ 375, [2].

will indemnify the assured straight away after it has obtained such an arbitration award or a judgment; (2) these two clauses operate together, but the waiting period is fixed from the due date of the buyer's payment. As it will always take longer than the waiting period to resolve the dispute, the waiting period will invariably elapse before the assured resolves the dispute, and the outcome would still be that the ECA indemnifies the assured when it has obtained such an arbitration award or a judgment; (3) these two clauses operate together, but the waiting period starts to run after the assured has obtained an arbitration award or a judgment. The indemnification process would be prolonged for the greatest length of time in this situation.

This research found no ECI policies that contain stipulations about this issue, but it might be said that approach (2) represents the current practice in the industry. The author, through the Berne Union Academic Survey, interviewed some experienced legal counsels from several Berne Union members and revealed that ECAs would generally insist that the "original" waiting period must always run from the due date of the buyer's payment whether there is a dispute between the assured and the buyer or not. In the meantime, they also admitted that the waiting period clause would have little effect in the case of such a dispute, as the waiting period is most likely to elapse before the dispute is resolved.[73] Approach (3), meanwhile, should by no means be the correct one. Since the waiting period clause and the "arbitration award/judgment" clause are both intended to facilitate the ECA to ascertain the existence and the amount of loss, after the assured has proved its right by fulfilling the obligations under the "arbitration award/judgment" clause, there is no need for a waiting period to run again. This research submits that approach (1) is the best for the ECA to avoid any doubt.

Mitigating the harsh consequences of the "arbitration award/judgment" clause

The paragraphs above explored the "arbitration award/judgment" clause in detail. Although justifiable with its commercial considerations, this clause may cause harsh consequences to the assured. For instance, the scope of the "dispute" can be very broad, and the assured may have to commence legal proceedings at its own cost. Moreover, the indemnification process could be further prolonged if the ECA insists that a waiting period apply after the assured has obtained an arbitration award or a judgment. It is said that the ECA can waive the "arbitration award/judgment" clause,[74] but under what circumstances is that available remains to be observed. It is therefore more worthwhile to explore how to

73 Cheng Lin, "Berne Union Academic Survey: The Legal Nature of Buyer Credit Insurance and Buyer Credit Guarantee", *The BUlletin (The Official Newsletter of the Berne Union)*, January 2020, 29 <https://www.berneunion.org/Articles/Details/489/January-BUlletin-Mega-Trends-and-Trade> accessed 1 February 2022.

74 The Hon Mrs Justice Geraldine Andrews & Richard Millett QC, *Law of Guarantees* (7th edn, Sweet & Maxwell 2015), [15-008].

address the harshness of the "arbitration award/judgment" clause by adjusting its contractual wording.

This research found that there are few ECI policies that include an assured-friendly "arbitration award/judgment" clause. For instance, Clause 13 of Atradius DSB's policy provides that:

> Advance indemnification in the event of a dispute
>
> (a) If a dispute arises between the Insured and the Borrower or a guarantor with regard to the Loan Agreement and
>
> (1) The Insured, in accordance with the provisions of the Loan Agreement or the rules of the law which otherwise apply, has instituted judicial or arbitration proceedings in order to resolve the dispute, and
>
> (2) Insurer is of the opinion, on the basis of the information known to it at that time, that the position of the Borrower or a guarantor is not well-founded,
>
> Insurer may pay an advance on any indemnification subject to such conditions as it may specify.
>
> (b) As soon as the dispute between the Insured and the Borrower has been resolved in the proceedings referred to in (a)(1) above, the calculation of indemnification shall be made on this basis and the advance must be repaid.

However, the approach above seems not welcomed in the industry, as most ECAs are unwilling to make advanced indemnification in case of a dispute between the assured and the buyer. Nevertheless, this research submits that the ECAs can at least address the harshness of the "arbitration award/judgment" clause in the following aspects:

Firstly, the term "dispute" should be clearly defined, and the scope of the "arbitration award/judgment" clause should be restricted. The buyer's refusal to pay can sometimes be evidently groundless. In such circumstances, the ECA should not rely on the "arbitration award/judgment" clause to refuse to indemnify the assured. Therefore, where a dispute arises between the assured and the buyer, the ECA must always make a basic and initial assessment by reviewing the evidence and supporting documents provided by the assured. The ECA should not refuse to pay without making any such assessment. If the buyer's reason for non-payment is evidently groundless, the ECA should indemnify the assured, regardless of such a "dispute". Clause 8.8.3 of Finnvera's policy provides a good example of restricting the scope of the "arbitration award/judgment" clause:[75]

> If there is a dispute … the payment obligation of the disputing party shall be confirmed before a decision on indemnification is made. Such payment

75 See also Clause 13 of Atradius DSB's policy.

> obligation shall be confirmed through legal proceedings or arbitration unless, in the reasonable opinion of Finnvera, the dispute is evidently groundless or otherwise invalid.

Secondly, the ECA should, according to the insured percentage of the policy, reimburse the legal cost the assured incurs in proving the loss by obtaining an arbitration award or a judgment. If the arbitration award or the judgment holds that the assured has breached the underlying contract and is not entitled to the buyer's payment, then, of course, the ECA does not need to reimburse the assured's legal cost. But if the assured proves to be entitled to the buyer's payment by taking the legal proceedings, the ECA should reimburse the assured's the legal cost because the assured has saved the ECA's efforts in the future subrogation and collection process. Naturally, a dispute does not always conclude that the buyer is liable for the entire loss that the assured suffered. Where the buyer is found liable for some part of the loss only, the ECA should be required to contribute to the assured's legal costs proportionately. For example, assume that the insured percentage is 95% of the total amount of the underlying export contract, and the total amount is £10,000. If the assured is held to only be entitled to a payment of £7,000 and the legal cost the assured incurs is £2,000, then the ECA should only pay the legal cost of £2,000 × 95% × (£7,000/£10,000) = £1,330.

Thirdly, as discussed above, the waiting period clause should not apply where the "arbitration award/judgment" clause applies. For instance, Clause 18 of Credendo's policy states that:

> If the Loss for which the Insured is requesting Compensation corresponds to disputed rights or if the Debtor claims to be entitled to exercise any set-off right, the Waiting Period shall expire on the day on which the decision of the competent court.

Fourthly, the "arbitration award/judgment" clause should be brought to the assured's attention at the contract formation stage of the ECI policy. Such clause falls outside the scope of s 11 of the IA 2015, and when the ECA draft such clause as a condition precedent to liability, it does not need to contract out of the IA 2015 in compliance with the transparency requirements under s 17 of the IA 2015. However, if such a clause is clearly explained to the assured before concluding the policy, it will be less likely to be regarded as "particularly onerous" by the English court.[76]

Based on the discussion above, this research proposes a model clause for the "arbitration award/judgment" clause to address the harshness of clauses of this type:

(1) If any dispute arises between the assured and the buyer relating to the sales contract, the assured must prove the existence and amount of its loss by

76 See *US Trading Ltd* [2010] Lloyd's Rep IR 505; *D&J Koskas* (1927) 27 Ll L Rep 59.

obtaining an arbitration award or a judgment that is final and binding, unless such dispute is evidently groundless in the opinion of [the ECA];

(2) The assured's compliance of Clause (1) is a condition precedent to [the ECA]'s liability under this policy;

(3) [The ECA] shall indemnify the assured once it has obtained such an arbitration award or a judgment under Clause (1), according to the amount ascertained by the arbitration award or the judgment and subject to the insured percentage and the maximum liability. For the avoidance of any doubt, the claim waiting period under this policy shall not run where this Clause applies;

(4) [The ECA] will reimburse the legal cost the assured incurs in performing Clause (1) *pro rata*, according to the insured percentage, provided that the arbitration award or the judgment has established that the assured is fully entitled to the buyer's payment under the sales contract. If the arbitration award or the judgment holds that the assured is only partially entitled to the buyer's payment, [the ECA] will contribute to the assured's legal cost *pro rata*, according to the insured percentage as well as the portion of the amount that the assured is entitled to under the sales contract.

The claim provisions in ECI that are common in other types of insurance policies

The general claim handling clause

English law requires that the insurer handle the claim within a reasonable time. Section 13A(1) of the Enterprise Act 2016 provides that it is an implied term that the insurer should indemnify the assured in a reasonable time. Section 13A further provides that "a reasonable time includes a reasonable time to investigate and assess the claim" and that what is reasonable depends on many factors such as "the type of insurance, the complexity of the claim … and the factors outside of the insurer's control". Article 8.1.1 of the FCA's ICOBS further provides that an insurer must "(1) handle claims promptly and fairly and (2) provide reasonable guidance to help a policyholder make a claim". Meanwhile, the assured should not delay in submitting its claim.[77] An insurance policy thus normally includes a general claim handling clause which clearly stipulates both parties' rights and obligations in the indemnification process.[78] That is also the case under ECI.

On the one hand, ECI polices always require the assured to submit the formal claim in a timely and proper manner. As explained above, the assured can file the claim as soon as the waiting period elapses, but it needs to do so without delay. For instance, Clause 5.1 of UKEF's policy states that the assured should make a claim within 12 months from the expiry of the policy. A sample policy

77 If the assured excessively delays in submitting the claim, the insurer will not be liable to cover the interest of its late payment. See *The Julia* [2005] Lloyd's Rep IR 365.

78 John Birds, *Modern Insurance Law* (10th edn, Sweet & Maxwell 2016) 280–5.

from an anonymous Berne Union member stipulates a shorter period, requiring the assured to submit the claim by no later than 45 days from the date of loss, i.e., the expiry date of the waiting period, by using the standard claim handling form and attaching the relevant evidence of loss. The assured's obligation to submit the claim promptly and properly can be stipulated as a condition precedent to the ECA's liability,[79] and if so, the assured's breach will discharge the ECA from liability, and s 11 of the IA 2015 cannot come to the assured's rescue.

On the other hand, ECI policies normally stipulate a specific timeframe for the ECA to handle the claim. The ECA usually needs some days to process the claim and assess the loss, and this period, ranging from 15 to 30 days from the receipt of the claim, is called the "claim handling period". After the expiry of the claim handling period, the ECA is obliged to indemnify the exporter without delay.[80] Such provisions are widely accepted by the industry and are codified in ss 25 and 28 of Directive 98/29/EC:

> The policyholder is entitled to indemnification at the end of the claim waiting period … provided that the conditions precedent to the insurance and the indemnification have been fulfilled, the claim is legally valid, and the policyholder has managed the risk with due diligence.
>
> The claim shall be paid without delay, at the latest, however, within one month of the end of the claim waiting period, provided that the insurer has been notified promptly of the occurrence of the claim and received all necessary information, documents, and evidence in order to establish the validity of the claim in good time.

The acceleration clause

ECI as "back-to-back indemnity" with the underlying loan agreement

In supplier or buyer credit transactions, an ECI policy is generally provided as a "back-to-back indemnity" with the underlying loan agreement. For instance, as will be discussed below, the policy in *Merrill Lynch International Bank Ltd (formerly Merrill Lynch Capital Markets Bank Ltd) v Winterthur Swiss Insurance Co*[81] "deliberately tracked the definitions" in the underlying loan agreement regarding the terms "Events of Default", "Bankruptcy" and, more importantly, "Early Termination" which concerned the assured's acceleration right.

79 For instance, an ECI policy may provide that the assured's observation of every stipulation under the policy is a condition precedent to the ECA's liability.

80 See, e.g., Clause 6.1 of Credendo's policy, Clause 12.1 of Finnvera's policy and Clause 12(c) of Atradius DSB's policy. Some policy may provide a one-month period from the receipt of the claim for the ECA to make the decision on indemnification, and one further month period thereafter for the ECA to pay out the claim. See Clause 9 of SERV's policy.

81 [2007] EWHC 893 (Comm).

The acceleration clause in the underlying loan agreement

To obtain an ECI cover, the bank under supplier/buyer credit transactions would typically ensure that it had an acceleration clause in the underlying loan agreement. For instance, Section 6 "Early Termination" of the loan agreement in *Merrill Lynch* provided that:[82]

> (a) Right to Terminate Following Event of Default
> If at any time an Event of Default with respect to a party (the "Defaulting Party") has occurred and is then continuing, the other party (the "Non-defaulting Party") may, by not more than 20 days' notice to the Defaulting Party specifying the relevant Event of Default, designate a day not earlier than the day such notice is effective as an Early Termination Date in respect of all outstanding Transactions.

Section 6(c) and (d) further stipulated the effect of "Early Termination" and the calculation method of all accelerated payments.

The acceleration provision in the ECI policy

Despite the acceleration clause in the underlying loan agreement, whether the insurer under ECI will indemnify the assured should it exercise its acceleration right depends on the policy wording. For instance, Clause 1(i)(c) of the ECI policy in *Merrill Lynch* provided that:[83]

> Upon the occurrence of a Bankruptcy Trigger Event, the Insurance shall promptly, upon becoming aware of the Bankruptcy Trigger Event, terminate the [the Loan Agreement] in accordance with the terms of Section 6 therefore. On or as soon as reasonably practicable following the occurrence of an Early Termination Date designated in accordance with Section 6(a) of the [Loan Agreement], the Insured shall provide to the Insurance Company a Notification of Loss.
>
> If the Insured does not terminate the [Loan Agreement] … then the Insurance Company shall not, under any circumstances and notwithstanding any other provision hereunder, be under the obligation to indemnify the Insured for the Defaulted Payment Amount.

Nevertheless, it should be noted that not every insurer under ECI is willing to indemnify the assured for losses in respect of the accelerated payments. For instance, Lloyd's *Performance Management – Supplemental Requirements & Guidance* states that:[84]

82 Ibid, [28].
83 Ibid, [24].
84 See Lloyd's of London (n 2) 44.

> Where policies provide for the insured to be indemnified for the non-payment of a financial obligation by the obligor where the obligation in question involves the obligor making a payment at a future date or a number of payments over time (for example the re-payment of a loan in instalments) then it will be usual for the insurance backing the obligation to pay out over time in accordance with the original payment schedule. Lloyd's may agree in appropriate cases to the inclusion of provisions for the making of accelerated payments at the sole election of the insured. As a general rule, however, underwriters should, in each case, have the opportunity to agree or decline to make the accelerated payments.

Worldwide, some ECI policies provide that the assured shall not, without the prior written consent of the ECA, exercise its debt acceleration right under the loan agreement.[85] Even if the policy does not forbid the assured to exercise the debt acceleration right, ECAs might provide that the assured's decision to declare acceleration shall not affect their obligation to indemnify only after the waiting period elapses. Some sample clauses were collected through the Berne Union Academic Survey:

> **Sample wording A (from an anonymous Berne Union member):**
> Any acceleration of amounts due under the Loan Agreement shall not give rise to a corresponding acceleration of the Insurer's liability under the policy, with indemnity to be paid in accordance with the original terms of the Loan Agreement. The Insurer may at its sole discretion pay amounts due to the Insured on an accelerated basis.
>
> **Sample wording B:**[86]
> Using his own criteria, the Insurer will decide upon the convenience to pay an indemnity for amounts of the principal sum which have not yet matured at the time that the Insured declares applicable the Acceleration Clause agreed in the Loan Agreement. This indemnity will in any case be paid if the Acceleration Clause is applied by the Insured at the request of the Insurer.
>
> **Sample wording C:**[87]
> Acceleration of maturity in the case of violation of the provisions of the Buyer credit, as agreed with the Borrower, shall not apply to the Insurer.

The notification and mitigation clause

The UKEF's sample clause

Prior to making the formal claim, the assured under ECI is obliged to notify the ECA of the probable loss and mitigate the loss. As with other types of insurance

85 See, e.g., Clause 10.6.1 of EGAP Czech's policy.
86 See Clause 21 of CESCE's policy.
87 See Clause 17 of HBOR's policy.

contracts, ECI policies also include a notification and mitigation clause. The assured under an ECI policy is always required to notify the ECA if it becomes aware of "any act, omission, event or circumstance which indicates that the buyer may not pay, or may be unable to pay".[88] Such notice given by the assured is called "notice of probable loss".[89] In addition to the notification, the assured should also mitigate the loss where appropriate. Clause 7 of the UKEF's policy provides a relatively comprehensive example of the notification and mitigation clause in ECI:

> 7.2 The Insured shall notify UKEF of any Relevant Event within 15 days of becoming aware of it, and … provide all available information relating to that Relevant Event in writing to UKEF.
>
> 7.3 The Insured shall notify UKEF immediately if the Buyer has failed to pay any part of the Sum Due under the Contract 30 days after its Due Date.
>
> 7.4 The Insured shall:
>
> (a) promptly take all practicable steps to prevent or minimise any loss covered by this Policy (and preserve its rights to take such steps in the future) including (i) enforcing security for the performance of the Buyer's obligations and (ii) any steps which may be required by UKEF; and
>
> (b) not enter into any compromise of any relevant claim against any person without the written consent of UKEF.
>
> 7.5 If the Insured fails to comply with any of Clauses 7.2–7.4 above then UKEF shall have no liability under this Policy in respect of a loss unless the Insured can show that such failure to comply could not have increased the risk of that loss taking place.

It appears that the UKEF has taken s 11 of the IA 2015 into consideration in drafting Clause 7 as conditions precedent to its liability. As has been discussed in Chapter 3 of this research, under s 11 of the IA 2015, if a term does not define the risk as a whole and would tend to reduce the risk of the loss of a particular kind, location, then the assured's breach of such term will not discharge the insurer's liability if the assured can prove that the breach could not have increased the risk of the loss which actually occurred in the circumstances in which it occurred. Accordingly, Clause 7.5 provides that the assured's breach of Clauses 7.2–7.4 will discharge the UKEF's liability unless the assured could prove that such breach could not have increased the risk of the loss taking place. Clauses 7.2–7.4 relates to the assured's notification and mitigation obligations. Clause 7.5 indicates that the UKEF believes that the notification and mitigation clause fall within the scope of s 11 of the IA 2015, which, however, is not correct. The IA 2015 "is not

88 See Clause 7.1 as well as the definition part of the UKEF's policy.

89 See, e.g., *Kazakstan Wool* [2000] CLC 822 and *ECGD v Davenport* [1983] 2 WLUK. See also Salcic (n 7) 166–7.

designed to have any effect on policy terms unrelated to the risk", and therefore notification and mitigation terms are not affected by the IA 2015.[90] Nevertheless, it is open to the UKEF to draft a more assured-friendly clause on notification and mitigation, although it might not be the true intention of the draftsman.

The notification and mitigation clause can also be stipulated as a condition precedent in the two policies from the anonymous Berne Union members that are governed by English law. As discussed in Chapter 3, these policies treat the assured's observations of every stipulation under the policy as conditions precedent to its liability and contract out of s 11 of the IA 2015 in a clear and unambiguous way. The assured's breach of the notification or mitigation obligation under these policies, therefore, will discharge the ECA from liability.

The duty to provide a "duly completed" notification of loss?

It might seem strange for the insurer to reject a claim on the ground of the assured's failure to provide a "detailed" notification of loss, notwithstanding that the assured has promptly provided a (less "detailed") one. In *Merrill Lynch*,[91] the abovementioned case reported in the pre-IA 2015 era, in addition to questioning whether a "Bankruptcy Trigger Event" had occurred (which has been discussed in Chapter 3), the insurer also alleged that the assured failed to provide a "duly completed" notification of loss, which constituted a breach of the condition precedent to liability under the policy. Clause 14 "Notification of Loss" of the policy provided that:[92]

> A notice in substantially the same form as the notice attached in Annex F, from the Insured to the Insurance Company (1) confirming the occurrence of a Trigger Event, (2) specifying any amount payable under Section 6(e) of the [Loan Agreement], (3) giving details of the relevant account to which any amount payable to it is to be paid, and (4) providing the Insurance Company with such other information about the Trigger Event that the Insurance Company may reasonably require, except that the Insured shall not be obligated to provide any information to the Insurance Company that it would not be obligated to deliver to the Counterparty in accordance with Section 6(d)(i) of the [Loan Agreement].

Clause 11(viii) stipulated that

> the due observance of the conditions, warranties and exclusions of this Policy by the Insured insofar as they relate to anything to be done or complied with by the Insured … shall be a condition precedent to any liability of the Insurance Company to make payment under this Policy.

90 Robert Merkin & Özlem Gürses, "Insurance Contracts after the Insurance Act 2015" [2016] 132 (3) LQR 445, 451.
91 [2007] EWHC 893 (Comm).
92 Ibid, [61].

A sample notification of loss form was attached in Annex F of the policy, requiring the assured to "insert details as appropriate".[93] Upon the occurrence of the "Bankruptcy Trigger Event", the assured promptly submitted a "Notification of Loss" form (using the template in Annex F) but informed the insurer of a recalculated total amount payable during their subsequent correspondence.

The court identified two interrelated issues to be decided: (i) whether assured's obligation to provide a "duly completed" Notification of Loss was a condition precedent to any liability of the insurer; and (ii) whether such an obligation was in fact fulfilled by the Bank. The case was decided for the purpose of a summary judgment under Pt 24 of the Civil Procedure Rules 1998 (SI 1998/3132), and thus Gloster J found it "neither necessary nor appropriate" to decide issue (i). Nevertheless, he proposed to "assume … but without deciding the point, or expressing any view on it" that due notification was a condition precedent of the insurer's liability.

Regarding issue (ii), Gloster J referred to *A/S Rendal v Arcos*[94] where Wright J held that sufficient notice would be given if the party receiving the notice was thereby able to meet the claim by preparing and obtaining appropriate evidence. Gloster J thus held that a precisely formulated claim giving full details was not required unless the particular contractual wording provided so. He then noted that notwithstanding the phrase "insert details as appropriate", the policy did not state "what precise details, or level of detail, were or was regarded as appropriate", and thus there was no reason why the insurer should escape liability. The judge held that the assured had supplied the insurer with enough information to inform it that an insured loss had occurred and thus had triggered the insurer's obligation to provide an indemnity. To reinforce his conclusion, the judge also said that Clause 14(4) of the policy envisaged that further information could be provided in response to reasonable requests by the insurer and did not need to be contained in the original notification of loss.

The fraudulent claim clause

In English law, the assured's duty not to make a fraudulent claim is entirely separate from the duty of utmost good faith,[95] which means that the insurer cannot avoid the policy *ab initio* because of the assured's fraudulent claim.[96] The IA 2015 codified the remedies for the assured's fraudulent claim. Sections 12(1) and (2) provide that in the case of a fraudulent claim, the insurer (a) is not liable to pay the claim; (b) may recover from the assured any payment in respect of the claim

93 Ibid, [63].

94 [1937] 58 Ll L Rep 287, 292 (Wright LJ).

95 See *Manifest Shipping Co Ltd v Uni-Polaris Insurance Co Ltd (The Star Sea)* [2001] UKHL 1, [2003] 1 AC 469; *K/S Merc Skandia XXXXII v Certain Lloyd's Underwriters (The Mercandian Continent)* [2001] EWCA Civ 1275, [2001] Lloyd's Rep IR 802; *Agapitos v Agnew (The Aegeon) (No 1)* [2002] EWCA Civ 247, [2003] QB 556.

96 *Axa General Insurance v Gottleib* [2005] EWCA Civ 112, [2005] 1 All ER (Comm) 445; *Versloot Dredging BV v HDI Gerling Industrie Versicherung Ag* [2016] UKSC 45, [2017] AC 1.

and (c) may by notice terminate the policy with effect from the time of the fraudulent act. If the insurer terminates the policy, it (a) may refuse all liability under the policy in respect of a relevant event occurring after the time of the fraudulent act and (b) need not return the premiums. Section 12(3) further clarified that termination under s 12(1) does not affect the rights and obligations of the parties with respect to a relevant event occurring before the time of the fraudulent act.

The IA 2015 does not define what constitutes a "fraudulent act", but that has been well defined by other legislation[97] and case law authorities. Mance LJ in *Agapitos v Agnew (The Aegeon) (No 1)*[98] concluded five classes of fraudulent claims, which include (1) the absence of loss, (2) exaggerated loss, (3) subsequent discovery that no/lesser loss had been suffered, (4) suppression of defence and (5) use of fraudulent means or devices to further a genuine claim. The Supreme Court in *Versloot Dredging BV v HDI Gerling Industrie Versicherung Ag*[99] denied category (5) and reclassified it as "collateral lies".

Accordingly, in drafting the fraudulent claim clause, ECAs normally do not define what a "fraudulent claim" is, but invariably provide for the remedies for the assured's fraudulent claim. S 12 of the IA 2015 is clearly taken into account by ECAs who choose English law as the applicable law to their policies in drafting the fraudulent claim clause. For instance, Clauses 5.3 and 5.4 of the UKEF's policy basically copies out the provisions in s 12(1)–(2) of the IA 2015, which means that under their policies, the assured's fraudulent claim will not have a retroactive effect. Lloyd's *Performance Management – Supplemental Requirements & Guidance* also states that "subject to any local legal or regulatory requirements, all policies must contain a clause, or clauses, to the effect that the insurer shall have at least the remedies available under the Insurance Act 2015 in relation to fraudulent misrepresentation and fraudulent claims".[100]

Meanwhile, it should be noted that some ECI policies may contract out of s 12 of the IA 2015. For instance, a sample wording from an anonymous Berne Union member read as follows:

> Clause 22 Fraud
>
> (1) Any fraudulent conduct in relation to this Policy, to any claim under it, or to any irrevocable letter of credit to which the Policy applies, on Your part will render the Policy voidable. In this event We may retain any premium paid and You will be liable to refund to Us any payment We may have made under the Policy…
> (2) Section 12 of the Insurance Act 2015 shall not apply to this Policy. If You make a fraudulent claim under this Policy our respective rights and obligations shall be as set out in Article 22(1) above.

97 The word "fraud" was defined by ss 2 and 3 of the Fraud Act 2006.
98 [2002] EWCA Civ 247.
99 [2016] UKSC 45.
100 Lloyd's of London (n 2) 44.

Clause 22(1) above indicates that if the assured engages in any fraudulent conduct, the ECA will not be liable for any claim affected by the fraud and the assured will have to refund any payment made by the ECA. Clause 22(1) clearly differs from s 12 of the IA 2015. By providing so, the ECA wishes to be entitled to (a) render the policy voidable *ab initio* instead of terminating the policy and (b) recover any payment inclusive but not limited to the payment in respect of the fraudulent claim. Clause 22(2) further states that s 12 of the IA 2015 shall not apply. Therefore, it is clear that the ECA here seeks to contract out of s 12. What needs to be scrutinised is whether it complies with the transparency requirement of s 17 of the IA 2015. Clause 22 includes "disadvantageous terms" which could put the assured in a worse position than under s 12, but the wording of Clause 22 is clear and unambiguous.[101] As long as the ECA takes sufficient steps to draw the assured's attention to such a clause, it can contract out of s 12.

The paragraphs above show that those ECAs who choose English law as the applicable law to their policies take the IA 2015 into account in drafting their fraudulent claim clause. The UKEF includes almost identical provisions as s 12(1)–(2) of the IA 2015, and the anonymous Berne Union member clearly contracts out of s 12 in its fraudulent clause. Both approaches indicate that these ECAs regard their ECI policies as contracts of insurance which should be read subject to the IA 2015.

Summary: the claim handling process of ECI and its legal nature

As has been discussed above, regarding the claim handling process, an ECI policy includes both peculiar terms which could prolong the indemnification process and other claim provisions that can be widely found in all types of insurance contracts. This chapter clarifies how the waiting period clause and the "arbitration award/judgment" clause operates prior to the indemnification in ECI, which can be illustrated in the diagrams below (see Figures 5.1 and 5.2). It argues that despite the controversies and perhaps the harshness of these two clauses, they do not contradict the principles of insurance law and do not indicate that ECI is not a contract of insurance. On the contrary, they are essential prerequisites for the assured to be indemnified and for the ECI to exercise the subrogation right. The waiting period clause helps the ECA to ascertain the loss, and the "arbitration award/judgment" clause ensures that the assured can prove its loss and that the ECA can subrogate into an undisputed right against the buyer. This chapter also scrutinises the claim provisions that are common in other types of insurance contracts, i.e., the general claim handling clause, the acceleration clause, the notification and mitigation clause and the fraudulent claim clause. In drafting these clauses, ECAs who chose the English law as the applicable law clearly took the IA 2015 into consideration, which indicates that they regard their ECI policies as

101 For the criteria for "disadvantageous terms" to be clear and unambiguous, see Chapter 3 of this work.

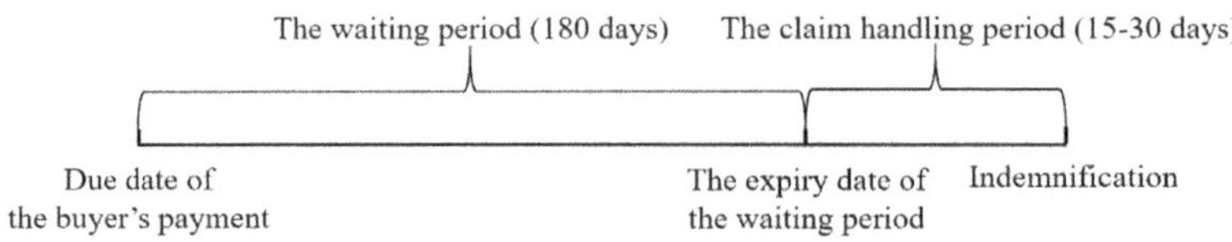

Figure 5.1 The ordinary claim handling process under ECI.

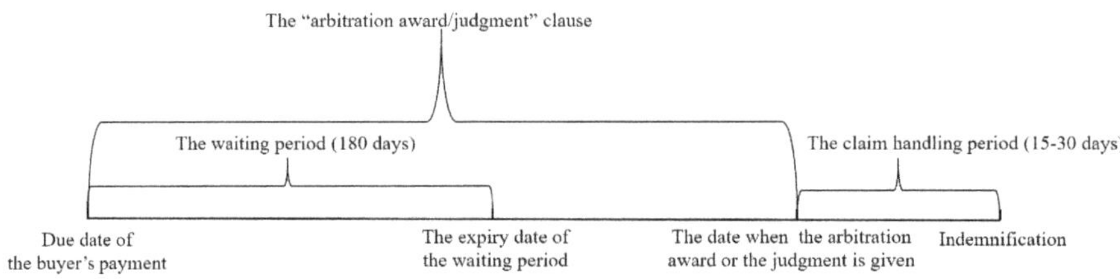

Figure 5.2 The claim handling process under ECI, where a dispute arises between the assured and the buyer.

contracts of insurance. In sum, although the claim handling process in ECI might be different from that in other types of insurance, that does not mean that ECI is not a contract of insurance.

The claim provisions in ECGs

Chapter 3 has demonstrated that an ECG, as a contract of guarantee, has many characteristics that distinguish itself from ECI: for example, an ECG is unconditional and on-demand. This means that in the claim handling process under an ECG, the ECA, as the surety, should pay to the creditor without delay once the debtor defaults in payment. The following paragraphs will examine whether this hypothesis is correct. Although there are very few ECAs around the world who provide ECGs, and none of their sample ECG contracts is available online, during the Berne Union Academic Survey, two anonymous Berne Union members kindly shared with the author copies of their standard ECG (buyer credit guarantee) contracts. In addition, another anonymous member did not attach its ECG contract (because it is not drafted in English and has not been officially translated) but contributed to the Survey by submitting its response with detailed comments. All these materials will be analysed below.

Do ECGs include a waiting period clause and an "arbitration award/judgment" clause?

Do ECGs contain a waiting period clause?

As is discussed above, ECAs invariably include a waiting period clause in their ECI policies in order to ascertain whether the foreign buyer defaults in payment.

Does an ECG contract also include a waiting period clause for a similar purpose? The Berne Union Academic Survey found that ECAs' approaches are different:

Anonymous Berne Union member A indicated that it does not apply a waiting period clause in its ECG covers because it regards an ECG as a guarantee which "should be honoured upon creditor's demand", but it has a 30-day claim handling period to process the claim and pay out.

Anonymous Berne Union member B does not include a waiting period clause in its ECG contract, either. Instead, Clause 1(a) of its standard term ECG contract stipulates a 180-day "Guarantee Claim Period" from the due date of the buyer's payment, and that the bank should file a formal claim within the "Guarantee Claim Period". In other words, the bank can make a claim as soon as the buyer fails to pay on the due date, and the ECA shall pay the bank within 14 business days after receipt of the claim. Clause 5 further provides that the ECA will pay to the bank both the "Guarantee Payment" (i.e., the principal amount of the contract between the bank and the buyer) and the "Guarantee Interest" which accrues in the period between the due date of the buyer's payment to the date when the ECA pays the bank, but such period should be no longer than the "Guarantee Claim Period". The "Guarantee Interest" rate shall be fixed by the sum of the LIBOR rate plus two percentage points. That means under this ECG contract, where the buyer fails to pay on the due date, the bank does not need to wait for 180 days before it can file a formal claim and, on the contrary, it has 180 days to make a claim. Clause 1(a) is very bank-friendly.

Meanwhile, anonymous Berne Union member C applies a waiting period clause in its ECG contract. Clause 5.1 of this contract provides that the "Default Payment Period" is 90 days from the due date of the buyer's payment, and that the ECA will pay to the bank on the expiry date of the "Default Payment Period" both the principal amount and the interest which accrues in the "Default Payment Period". Clause 5.2 further provides that the bank should notify the ECA of the amount of such interest payable no fewer than four business days before the expiry date of the "Default Payment Period". Clauses 5.1 and 5.2 indicates that although the ECA applies a waiting period, it does not apply any additional claim handling period to process and pay the claim. It has to pay the bank within the 90-day waiting period. It is submitted that the waiting period clause in this ECG contract does not indicate that the ECG is not a guarantee. In common law, under a contract of guarantee, the surety's liability arises when the principal debtor defaults in his obligations[102] and the purpose of the waiting period clause in the ECG is also to ascertain whether the buyer defaults in payment. It should be noted that Clauses 5.1 and 5.2 are not stipulated as a condition precedent to the ECA's liability.

Besides, ECG contracts in reported English cases[103] generally did not contain a waiting period clause, either. As was clarified by Edward-Stuart J in *Crown*

102 *Rawstone v Parr* (1827) 3 Russ 539, 38 ER 678; *W. R. Browne v Lee* (1827) 6 B&C 689, 108 ER 604; *Ex parte Gardom* (1808) 15 Ves Jr 286, 33 ER 762.

103 See, e.g., *Crown Aluminium Ltd v Northern and Western Insurance Co Ltd* [2011] EWHC 1352 (TCC); *Export Credits Guarantee Department v Universal Oil Products Co* [1983] 1 WLR 399.

Aluminium Ltd v Northern and Western Insurance Co Ltd,[104] the guarantor's liability under the ECG "would arise at the moment" that the buyer did not pay on the due date required by the underlying contract of sale.[105]

The paragraphs above show that ECAs tend not to include a waiting period clause under ECGs. Anonymous Berne Union members A and B do not apply a waiting period clause at all, and whilst anonymous Berne Union member C applies a waiting period, such a period is shorter than the waiting period in ECI policies and there is no additional claim handling period before it pays the bank. Moreover, anonymous Berne Union member B takes a very creditor-friendly approach by turning the waiting period into the "Guarantee Claim Period", during which the bank can file a formal claim. That means that the bank can either make a demand of the ECG as soon as the buyer fails to pay on the due date or wait for up to 180 days to ascertain whether such failure is temporary or not. Under its ECG contract, the right to verify the loss is conferred to the bank, and the ECA will pay the creditor bank as soon as it submits a claim. Such a creditor-friendly provision has not been found in any ECI policies.

Do ECGs contain an "arbitration award/judgment" clause?

This research found that none of the ECAs above includes the "arbitration award/judgment" clause in their ECG contracts. It might be argued that the "arbitration award/judgment" clause is not necessary under ECGs, which mostly covers the loan transaction between the bank and the buyer, because the possibility of a dispute between the bank and the buyer is rather low. However, as is explained above, over 70% of the ECI policies which insure the same loan transaction between the bank and the buyer still include an "arbitration award/judgment" clause even if the possibility of a dispute is low. Particularly, anonymous Berne Union members A and C provide both ECGs and ECI products, but they both indicated that they only include an "arbitration award/judgment" clause in their ECI policies. The absence of the "arbitration award/judgment" clause under ECGs suggests that an ECG is an unconditional and on-demand guarantee.[106]

The claim handling process in ECGs is not likely to be prolonged

Therefore, the claim handling process under ECGs is not likely to be prolonged as occurs under ECI. On the one hand, ECA tends to include no waiting period

104 [2011] EWHC 1352 (TCC).

105 Ibid, [64]. Of course, this general rule is subject to contractual wording. For instance, as has been discussed in Chapter 3, the guarantee clause in *Credit Lyonnais Bank Nederland NV (now Generale Bank Nederland NV) v Export Credits Guarantee Department* [1999] CLC 823, 827–8 stipulated that the ECA guaranteed payment to the bank of the face value of the bill of exchange which remained unpaid six months after the due date of payment.

106 "The distinction between the justified and unfair calling of an unconditional and on-demand guarantee is not significant for the bank since it must pay the foreign buyer regardless of the reason for calling". See Salcic (n 7) 92.

or, at least, a shorter waiting period in their ECG contracts. On the other hand, they do not include an "arbitration award/judgment" clause. Whilst anonymous Berne Union member C includes a waiting period, it does not have an additional claim handling period to process the claim. It has to pay the creditor bank by the expiry date of the 90-day waiting period. This means that under ECGs it will not take long for the bank to be paid after it makes a formal claim against the ECA: 12 business days for anonymous Berne Union member B's cover, 30 days for anonymous Berne Union member A's cover and in anonymous Berne Union member C's case, no longer than 90 days. In the meantime, as demonstrated above, under ECI it takes a waiting period of 180 days plus a claim handling period of 15–30 days before the assured gets indemnified. Therefore, the claim handling process under ECGs is invariably faster than under ECI, which indicates that an ECG is an unconditional and on-demand guarantee.

The general claim handling clause

Whilst ECI policies normally include a general claim handling clause which stipulates both the ECA's and the assured's obligations in the claim handling process, the general claim handling clause in ECG contracts only concerns the timeframe for the ECA to handle the claim and pay the guaranteed amount, without stipulating the steps which the creditor bank should follow in making a claim. For instance, the ECG contract in *Crown Aluminium* provided that:[107]

> In the event of any notice from the Trade Creditor to the Guarantor that demands payment and requires resolution of the default, the Trade Creditor agrees to allow the Guarantor a period of thirty (30) business days from the receipt of notice in which the claim must be settled.

In English law of guarantees, the surety's liability arises at the date of the principal debtor's default, but his obligation to pay to the creditor does not arise until the creditor makes a demand against him. The demand marks the time when the surety's liability can be enforced,[108] but generally, the creditor is not obliged to make a demand in specific ways (e.g., the demand should be made in writing or the demand should be made against the principal debtor first) in the absence of an express contractual provision.[109] Even where such a provision exists, it is usually construed as a purely procedural requirement rather than a condition precedent to the surety's liability.[110] This research found that ECG contracts do not include much requirement on the formalities of a "demand", which means that for the creditor bank, the way to make a claim is very flexible. It can do so by simply

107 [2011] EWHC 1352 (TCC), [19].
108 *Stimpson v Smith* [1999] 2 WLR 1292, 1304 (Tuckey LJ).
109 Andrews & Millett (n 74), [1-011], [7-005].
110 *Thomas v Nottingham Incorporated Football Club Ltd* [1972] Ch 596, 604 (Goff J).

submitting a "claim request form" to the ECA. Therefore, ECAs do not stipulate the general claim handling clause as a condition precedent to liability under ECG contracts, which again indicates the unconditional nature of ECGs.

The refund of payment clause

Although ECAs tend to pay the bank in a very speedy way under ECGs, they may also include a refund of payment clause if they subsequently discover that some of the conditions precedent to liability under the ECG contract are not fulfilled by the bank or if the bank enters into a restructuring agreement with the buyer. For instance, Clause 6 of anonymous Berne Union member B's ECG contract provides that after paying the creditor bank, the ECA is entitled to review the documentation about the guaranteed transaction and check whether all conditions precedent to liability under the ECGs are met. If the ECA finds that the bank did not comply with all the conditions precedent, then it is entitled, within 60 days after the "Guarantee Payment" is made, to require the bank to refund the "Guarantee Payment" as well as the interest which accrues from the date when the "Guarantee Payment" is made. Such interest will be fixed at the same rate as the "Guarantee Interest". Clause 9 also provides that after the "Guarantee Payment" is paid, if the bank, with the written consent of the ECA, reaches a restructuring agreement with the buyer regarding the guaranteed project, then the buyer is no longer regarded as defaulting in payment and thus the bank is obliged to refund the "Guarantee Payment" plus interest in the same manner as stipulated in Clause 6.

It is submitted that the refund of payment clause cannot deny that an ECG is unconditional and on-demand. On the one hand, the refund under Clause 6 is not very likely to happen. The conditions precedent to liability under this ECG contract only concern the bank's duties to (a) duly provide the loan, (b) provide the ECA with the supporting documentation of the loan and (c) exhaust all non-judicial efforts against the buyer if the buyer defaults in payment. That means that except for the obligation to make the loan to the debtor buyer, the bank is under no other substantial obligations under ECGs, and it is not difficult for the bank to fulfil the duties (b) and (c). Therefore, the possibility that the ECA exercises the right to request a refund is low. The bank will be most likely to keep the ECG payment it receives.

On the other hand, Clause 9 also has a rationale. The surety's liability is secondary under a contract of guarantee, and if the principal's debtor's liability is discharged, then the surety's liability will be discharged, too.[111] Under ECGs, if the bank enters into a restructuring agreement with the buyer, then the buyer is no longer deemed defaulting in payment, and thus its liability is discharged. The ECA will accordingly be no longer liable and is therefore entitled to claim the refund of the ECG payment.

111 *Scottish Amicable Heritable Securities Assn Ltd v Northern Assurance Co* (1883) 11 R (Ct Sess) 287, 303; *Dane v Mortgage Ins Corp Ltd* [1894] 1 QB 54, 61.

The notification and mitigation clause

ECAs tend to include a notification and mitigation clause in ECG contracts as they do in ECI contracts. For instance, the ECG contract in *Crown Aluminium* includes a notification clause (which has been discussed in Chapter 3) and a mitigation clause which provided that:[112]

> Following the resolution of any default demanded under this Guarantee, the Trade Creditor undertakes for the benefit of the Guarantor, to uphold the details of the Contract of Sale and all other security provided in direct proportion to the payments made by the Trade Debtor.

Edward-Stuart J commented that under this clause, the exporter was obliged to enforce its remedies under the contract for the benefit of the guarantor and not allow the buyer to "walk away from its obligations".[113] It thus seems that the notification and mitigation clause in ECG contracts is similar to its counterpart in ECI. However, the difference is that, as discussed in Chapter 3, ECAs do not draft the notification and mitigation clause as a condition precedent to liability under ECGs as they do under ECI. The rules regarding mere conditions in the law of guarantees are similar to the rules in insurance law. If the creditor's breach of a mere condition "strikes at the root of the contract", then the surety's liability will be discharged.[114] If not, the surety can only claim damages against the creditor, which reduces his liability *pro tanto*.[115] Therefore, if the creditor bank breaches its obligations under the notification and mitigation clause under an ECG, the ECA cannot be discharged of its liability but can only claim damages.

Summary: the claim provisions in ECGs and the legal nature of ECGs

The paragraphs above explored the claims provisions in ECGs. ECAs tend to apply no waiting period or at least a shorter waiting period than ECI before they pay the creditor under their ECG covers. Even where the waiting period clause is included in an ECG, that does not mean that the ECG is not a contract of guarantee because the ECA needs to ascertain whether the principal debtor defaults in payment or not. In particular, anonymous Berne Union member B's contract is a very typical contract of ECG, under which it does not include a 180-day waiting period but stipulates a "Guarantee Claim Period" of the same length during which the bank can file a claim. It is obliged to process the claim and pay the bank within 12 business days, but it includes a refund of payment clause as a safeguard of its right. Of course, the refund of payment clause is not likely to become operative. All those provisions show that the claim handling process under ECGs is very speedy.

112 [2011] EWHC 1352 (TCC), [19].

113 Ibid, [25]–[26].

114 See *Ankhar Pty Ltd v National Westminster Finance (Australia) Ltd* (1987) 162 CLR 549.

115 Andrews & Millett (n 74), [9-018].

Besides, none of the ECAs includes an "arbitration award/judgment" clause in their ECG contracts, which means that the claim handling process under ECGs will invariably be much shorter than that in ECI. Moreover, the claim provisions in ECG contracts, such as the general claim handling clause and the notification and mitigation clause, are not stipulated as conditions precedent to liability, which reflects the unconditional nature of ECGs.

A common framework for ECA-supported buyer credit transactions: LMA's Export Finance Buyer Credit Agreement

Background to the LMA project

The sections above demonstrate that under supplier/buyer credit transactions, it is always crucial for ECAs to keep the wording of the ECI/ECG contract consistent with that of the underlying loan agreement, as the ECI/ECG is usually provided as a "back-to-back" cover. In response to demand from the international credit risk market to provide a unified form of the loan agreement for ECA-supported buyer credit transactions, the Loan Market Association (LMA) launched a project to develop a model loan agreement for such transactions. As the outcome of the project, in 2018, the LMA issued the "Single Currency Term Buyer Credit Agreement for Use in Export Credit Agency Supported Finance Transactions" ("Export Finance Buyer Credit Agreement"). Whilst the nature of ECA-supported finance transactions was such that it would be very difficult to produce a document which was in any way "standard", the Export Finance Buyer Credit Agreement is regarded as a big step forward in promoting the efficiency of the market and a good starting point for the draftsman, as it provides a common framework for the parties involved in buyer credit transactions.[116] It has been produced in compliance with the OECD Arrangement on Officially Supported Export Credits ("the OECD Arrangement"). A copy of the user guide and full text of the Export Finance Buyer Credit Agreement was kindly shared by the LMA with the author for the purpose of this book.

A working party consisting of representatives from banks (including in-house lawyers), various European ECAs and major City law firms was established to consider the drafting of the Export Finance Buyer Credit Agreement. The Berne Union also participated in the project as an observer. The LMA emphasises that the Export Finance Buyer Credit Agreement is in a non-binding and recommended form, of which the intention is to be used as a starting point for negotiation only; individual parties are thus free to depart from its terms and should always satisfy themselves with the regulatory implications of its use. The LMA also states that the Export Finance Buyer Credit Agreement is not intended to interfere with the positions taken by ECAs in relation to documentation risk, a specific exclusion discussed in Chapter 3.[117]

116 See LMA, Users Guide to Single Currency Term Facility Agreement for Use in Export Finance Buyer Credit Transactions (20/03/2020), 1–3, available to LMA members via www.lma.eu.com.

117 Ibid.

Assumptions

The Export Finance Buyer Credit Agreement has been produced on the basis of the assumptions that:[118]

- It is to be governed by English law;
- There will be a single ECA providing either an ECI or ECG cover;
- The drawing mechanics are typical to an ECA buyer credit transaction including that: (a) the loan can be either directly paid to the exporter or reimbursed to the buyer, and (b) financing of any ECA premium is permitted and is capable of being financed via the proceeds of the initial loan rather than on a pro rata basis under each loan;
- There can be a separate role for an "Agent" who will act as the conduit between the lenders (i.e., the banks) and the ECA;
- The down payment under the export contract will be included as a condition precedent to initial utilisation of the loan;
- The ECI/ECG cover being provided by the ECA will be in respect of a designated percentage of the principal and contractual interest due under the Export Finance Buyer Credit Agreement;
- The parties have an option for floating interest or fixed interest;

Terms of payment

Down payment

The OECD Arrangement stipulates that

> the Participants shall require purchasers of goods and services which are the subject of official support to make down payments of a minimum of 15 per cent of the export contract value at or before the starting point of credit as defined in Annex XV.[119]

Some ECAs may have more stringent requirements in this respect. Therefore, Clause 1.1 of the Export Finance Buyer Credit Agreement provides that "Down Payment" means an amount equal to 15 per cent of the export contract value.[120]

ECA premium

Clauses 3.1 and 11.4 of the Export Finance Buyer Credit Agreement provide that the initial utilisation of the loan proceeds shall be advanced directly to the ECA in respect of the ECA premium so that the ECA is "on cover".[121]

118 Ibid, 3–4.
119 The OECD Agreement, s 10(a).
120 LMA, Single Currency Term Facility Agreement for Use in Export Finance Buyer Credit Transactions (20/03/2020), 7, available to LMA members via www.lma.eu.com.
121 LMA (n 116) 13.

Repayment date

The OECD Arrangement requires that other than in exceptional and duly justified circumstances (further details of which are contained in the OECD Arrangement), the first instalment of principal shall be repaid no later than six months after the starting point of credit, and principal and contractual interest shall be repaid in equal instalments no less frequently than every six months.[122] Therefore, Clause 1.1 of the Export Finance Buyer Credit Agreement defines the term "First Repayment Date" as the date falling six months after the starting point of credit and the term "Repayment Date" as (a) the First Repayment Date, (b) each date falling at six monthly intervals after the First Repayment Date, and (c) the Termination Date.[123] Clause 6 further provides a model clause for the parties to record the details of the repayment dates and respective repayment instalments.

Calculation of interest

Interest rate

As is explained above, ECAs normally cover both the principal and the contractual interest of the underlying loan transaction. With respect to the interest rate, the OECD Agreement stipulates that minimum interest rates shall apply to official financing support for export credits. Such minimum interest rates are known as the relevant Commercial Interest Reference Rates (CIRRs), which have been established for each currency of the Participants to the OECD Arrangement and are updated on the OECD's website on the 15th of each month. Accordingly, Clause 8 of the Export Finance Buyer Credit Agreement provides that the interest rate can be either a fixed rate or the aggregate of (a) "Margin" (which is to be agreed by the parties on a case-by-case basis) and (b) the applicable CIRR, LIBOR, EUROBOR or alternative "Benchmark Rate" (determined pursuant to Clause 10.1 and Schedule 11).[124]

Default interest

Clause 8.4 "Default Interest" provides that if the buyer fails to pay any amount payable under the loan agreement on its due date, interest shall accrue on the overdue amount from the due date up to the date of actual payment (both before and after judgment) at a rate that is to be determined by the parties.[125] The existence of such a clause in the loan agreement would reinforce this chapter's submission that the waiting period interest (i.e., the default interest) should be indemnified by ECAs under ECI.

122 The OECD Agreement, s 14(a)–(b).
123 LMA (n 120) 12, 14.
124 Ibid, 52.
125 Ibid, 53–4.

Events of default

Political and commercial events

Clause 22 "Events of Default"[126] provides a detailed list including (a) the non-payment by the buyer; (b) the insolvency of the buyer; (c) expropriation; (d) any foreign exchange law that affects the convertibility/transferability of the payment; (e) the termination, cancellation, suspension or revocation of any material business licence; and (f) political and economic risks, such as an act of war or hostilities, invasion, armed conflict or act of a foreign enemy, revolution, insurrection, insurgency or threat thereof occurs in or involving the parties' jurisdictions.

It thus can be seen that the "Events of Default" under the loan agreement read identical to the "insured risks" section under ECI policies discussed in Chapter 3 of this work. Such consistency would ensure that once an "Event of Default" occurs under the loan agreement, the bank is entitled to request prompt indemnification from the ECA.

The acceleration clause

Clause 22.22 "Acceleration" further stipulates a model acceleration clause as follows:[127]

> Acceleration
>
> On and at any time after the occurrence of an Event of Default [which is continuing] the Agent may, and shall if so directed by the Majority Lenders, by notice to the Borrower:
>
> (a) cancel each Available Commitment of each Lender whereupon each such Available Commitment shall immediately be cancelled and the Facility shall immediately cease to be available for further utilisation;
> (b) declare that all or part of the Loans, together with accrued interest, and all other amounts accrued or outstanding under the Finance Documents be immediately due and payable, whereupon they shall become immediately due and payable; and/or
> (c) declare that all or part of the Loans be payable on demand, whereupon they shall immediately become payable on demand by the Agent on the instructions of the Majority Lenders.

It should be noted that, as has been explained above, notwithstanding such an acceleration clause under the loan agreement, it is perfectly open to the ECA to stipulate terms under ECI/ECGs that are relevant to the ability of the bank to accelerate.

126 Ibid, 99–105.
127 Ibid, 105.

The Isabella clause

Clause 1.5 "Independence of the Finance Documents" contains a so-called "Isabella clause"[128] to ensure that the obligations of the buyers towards the banks are not prejudiced by matters related to the export contract or the exporter:[129]

> Each Obligor acknowledges that its obligations under the Finance Documents:
>
> (a) are independent and separate from the Export Contract and any other document or agreement (other than any Finance Document);
> (b) are not subject to, or dependent upon, the execution or performance by the Exporter or any other person of its obligations under the Export Contract or any other document, contract or arrangement related to it;
> (c) will not be affected or discharged by:
>
> (i) any matter affecting the Exporter, the Buyer or any other person or the Export Contract or any other document, contract or arrangement related to them;
> (ii) non-performance, breach, frustration or invalidity of, or the destruction, non-completion or non-functioning of any of the goods and services to be supplied, or rendered, under, the Export Contract or any other document, contract or arrangement related to it;
> (iii) any dispute under the Export Contract or any other document, contract or arrangement related to it, or any claim which the Buyer, the Exporter or any other person may have against, or consider that it has against, the Exporter or any other person under or in relation to the Export Contract or any other document, contract or arrangement related to it;
> (iv) any administration, bankruptcy, insolvency, liquidation or similar proceedings commenced against the Exporter or any other person party to the Export Contract, or being applicable to any transactions contemplated thereunder, or the Exporter or any other person party to the Export Contract or any transactions contemplated thereunder being insolvent; or
> (v) any unenforceability, illegality or invalidity of any obligation of the Exporter, the Buyer or any other person under the Export Contract or any other document, contract or arrangement related thereto.

The Isabella clause is common in buyer credit structures and is often required by ECAs. In light of the "arbitration award/judgment" clause discussed above, Berne

128 Salcic (n 7) 79.
129 LMA (n 120) 32.

Union members believe that given the existence of the Isabella clause, the possibility of a dispute between the bank and the buyer is not as high as that in the export contract between the exporter and the buyer, but they still tend to stipulate an "arbitration award/judgment" clause in their buyer credit insurance policies.[130]

The interrelationship between the Loan Agreement and the ECI/ECG contract

Clause 1.6 "Export Credit Agency Override" provides that:[131]

> (a) Notwithstanding anything to the contrary in any Finance Document, nothing in any Finance Document shall oblige any Finance Party to act (or omit to act) in a manner that is inconsistent with any requirement of [the ECA] … under or in connection with the [ECA Cover Document] and, in particular, each Finance Party shall:
>
> a. be authorised to take all such actions as [it] … may consider necessary to ensure that all requirements of [the ECA] under or in connection with the [ECA Cover Document] are complied with; and
>
> b. not be obliged to do anything if, in [its] … opinion, to do so could … result in a breach of any requirement of [the ECA] under or in connection with the [ECA Cover Document], or affect the validity of the [ECA Cover Document] …
>
> (b) Nothing in this Clause 1.6 shall affect the obligations of any Obligor under the Finance Documents.

The term "ECA Cover Document" here refers to the ECI/ECG contract. This clause is intended to ensure that the provisions of the loan agreement do not conflict with the ECI/ECG contract and that the banks are not obliged to do anything that conflicts with the ECI/ECG contract or the requirements of the ECA. Therefore, the existence of the acceleration clause and the Isabella clause does not affect the ECA's position under its ECI/ECG contract.

In addition, Clause 1.7 "Instructions from the Export Credit Agency" provides that:[132]

> The Parties acknowledge and agree that, in accordance with the terms of the [ECA Cover Document], [the ECA] may, at any time, instruct a Finance Party … to suspend or to cease to perform any or all of its obligations under this Agreement or any other Finance Document. That Finance Party will be required to comply with any such instruction. Each Party agrees that it will not hold any Finance Party responsible for complying with any such instruction.

130 See n 42 above.
131 LMA (n 120) 32–3.
132 Ibid, 33–4.

This clause is intended to protect the bank if they act in accordance with the instructions of the ECA. This can be particularly important given ECAs often have ongoing reporting and consent requirements under the terms of the ECI/ ECG contract.[133]

Conclusion

This chapter studied the claim handling process in ECI and ECGs by exploring the claim provisions in both types of contracts. It contributes to the overarching theme of this work by the following findings and arguments:

Firstly, what can be learned from the ECI claim provisions about the legal nature of ECI? An ECI policy normally contains two peculiar claim provisions that could prolong the indemnification process, i.e., the waiting period clause and the "arbitration award/judgment" clause. These two clauses might cause uncertainties to the parties and might be harsh to the assured. It is necessary to draft the waiting period clause and the "arbitration award/judgment" clause in a fairer way proposed by this chapter. However, despite all of these peculiarities and controversies, these two clauses do not contradict insurance law principles and do not indicate that ECI is not a contract of insurance. On the contrary, they are the prerequisites for the assured to be indemnified and the ECA to exercise the subrogation right. Moreover, ECI policies also share similar claim provisions with other types of insurance policies, including the general claim handling clause, the notification and mitigation clause and the fraudulent claim clause. The influence of the IA 2015 has been clearly seen in the claim provisions in ECI policies in the UK, which suggests that by drafting the policies, the ECA regarded ECI as a contract of insurance.

Secondly, what can be found from the ECG claim provisions about the legal nature of ECGs? ECG contracts tend to include no waiting period clause and no "arbitration award/judgment" clause, which means that the claim handling period in ECGs should be very speedy. Even where the ECA applies a waiting period under ECGs, it does not indicate that an ECG is not a guarantee, and the bank can still receive the money in a timelier way than under ECI. An ECG contract might include a refund of payment clause as a safeguard of the ECA's speedy payment, but the ECA is not likely to rely on such a clause to recover the ECG payment from the bank. Besides, the claim provisions in ECG contracts are not stipulated as conditions precedent to the ECAs' liability, which demonstrates that under an ECG, the conditions precedent only concern the creditor bank's duty to provide the loan and pay the guarantee fee. All of these characteristics demonstrate that an ECG is an unconditional and on-demand guarantee.

Thirdly, what are the differences between ECI and ECGs regarding the claim handling process? Because of the existence of the waiting period clause and "arbitration award/judgment" clause, the claim handling process in ECI will be

133 LMA (n 116) 14–5.

prolonged, and the same is not experienced in ECG. ECI and ECGs might share some similar claim provisions, such as the claim handling clause and the notification and mitigation clause, but those provisions are not stipulated as conditions precedent in ECGs as they are in ECI. In sum, the bank under ECGs will be paid much more quickly than under ECI. As the Berne Union members suggested in the Berne Union Academic Survey, an ECG is "better defined, less controvertible and timelier in the claims process" and is "easier for the bank to use".

References

Andrews, G & Millett, R, *Law of Guarantees* (7th edn, Sweet & Maxwell 2015)
Beale, H G, *Chitty on Contracts* (33rd edn, Sweet & Maxwell 2018)
Birds, J, *Modern Insurance Law* (10th edn, Sweet & Maxwell 2016)
Lomnicka, E, "Export Credit Guarantees" in M Bridge (ed) *Benjamin's Sales of Goods* (11th edn, Sweet & Maxwell 2020)
Merkin, R, *Colinvaux's Law of Insurance* (12th edn, Sweet & Maxwell 2019)
Merkin, R & Gürses, Ö, "Insurance Contracts after the Insurance Act 2015" (2016) 132 (3) LQR 445.
Salcic, Z, *Export Credit Insurance & Guarantees: A Practitioner's Guide* (Palgrave Macmillan 2014)

6 Subrogation and recoveries under ECI and ECGs

This chapter focuses on subrogation and recoveries under export credit insurance (ECI) and export credit guarantees (ECGs). The first part of this chapter explores subrogation and recoveries under ECI. It aims to establish that the subrogation process in ECI fully reflects the legal nature of ECI as insurance. It starts with the juridical basis of the subrogation right in ECI and discusses the export credit agency's (ECA) pre-indemnity right and the control of proceedings. It then explores the collection and allocation of recoveries under ECI and further analyses assignment as an alternative to subrogation. There have been several reported English ECI cases regarding every aspect of subrogation and recoveries, all of which are important to the development of the principle of subrogation in English insurance law. This part discusses all those cases in detail and shows that the English courts regarded ECI as insurance in deciding ECI disputes regarding subrogation and recoveries.

The second part studies subrogation and recoveries under ECGs. It argues that the common law principle of subrogation, which applies under ECI, should also fully apply to ECGs. It also shows that the subrogation provisions under ECGs and ECI are similar; hence the distinction between ECI and ECGs is insignificant regarding subrogation and recoveries. Furthermore, this part suggests that the English courts refer to English ECI cases as an analogy in deciding future ECG disputes regarding subrogation and recoveries. A conclusion is given at the end of this chapter.

In common with previous chapters, it is necessary here to explain the selection of the topics to be covered in this chapter. First, the control of proceedings clause is sometimes embedded in the notification, mitigation and consultation clause in an ECI policy. However, such a clause is related to the assured's obligation to preserve the ECA's subrogation right rather than its obligation to prevent or mitigate the loss. Therefore, the control of proceedings clause is discussed in this chapter rather than Chapter 5. Second, whilst the focus of this chapter is the ECA's subrogation right, all methods the ECA might adopt to collect debts will be discussed: (a) the assured effects recoveries against the buyer; (b) the ECA becomes subrogated into the assured's rights and collects debts in the assured's name; (c) the ECA takes assignment of the assured's right and collects recoveries in its own name, as an alternative to subrogation. All those approaches are relevant for the

DOI: 10.4324/b22864-6

complete understanding of the subrogation process in ECI and ECGs. Third, the subrogation clause in ECI normally includes three parts of provisions, i.e., the subrogation protection clause, the allocation of recoveries clause and the collection costs clause, but this chapter will only focus on the former two, since most ECAs will reimburse the collection costs the assured incurs, and there has not been any reported English ECI dispute on collection costs.[1]

Subrogation and recoveries under ECI

The juridical basis of the subrogation right in the context of ECI

The subrogation right of the insurer has been long recognised in the common law. There are two roles of subrogation. The "negative" role is to prevent the assured from recovering more than indemnity,[2] and the "positive" role is to ensure that the insurer can take over all of the rights of the assured.[3] Stemming from equity,[4] the right of subrogation takes effect by the operation of law rather than contractual provisions.[5]

The juridical basis of subrogation in the context of ECI was confirmed by the English court in *Re Miller, Gibb & Co*.[6] The assured exporter in that case was insured under an ECI policy against political risks such as currency control. In 1952, the assured exported goods to Brazil, but the transfer of the payment was prevented by Brazilian currency exchange regulations. It then made a claim against the ECA, and in the claim request form, the assured undertook to assign all its rights to the ECA and to pay to the ECA any future payments received from the buyer. In 1954 the ECA paid the claim, and the assured sent an instruction letter to its bank requiring the latter to hand any future payments from the buyer to the ECA. The assured was subsequently ordered to be wound up, and in 1956 the bank eventually received the buyer's payment. The ECA claimed to be subrogated into the assured's right for the payment, but the liquidator insisted

1 It is also well established in common law that the insured is entitled to deduct the costs of recovery from the third party before he is obliged to account to the insurer. See *Assicurazioni Generali di Trieste v Empress Assurance Co Ltd* [1907] 2 KB 814; *Hatch Mansfield & Co Ltd v Weingott* (1906) 22 TLR 366.

2 *Castellain vs Preston* (1883) 11 QBD 380, 387.

3 Ibid, 388; *Burnand v Rococanachi* (1882) 7 App Cas 333, 339.

4 See *Randal v Cockran* (1748) 1 Ves Sen 98, 27 ER 916; *Blaaupot v Da Costa* (1758) 1 Eden 130; *White v Dobinson* (1844) 14 Sim 273. Moreover, the House of Lords in *Napier and Ettrick (Lord) v Kershaw* [1993] 1 All ER 385 confirmed that the subrogation originated in the "plainest equity".

5 It should be noted that some authorities also recognised an implied term of the subrogation right in every insurance country. The subrogation right can also take effect by an express contractual provision. See, e.g., *Banque Keyser Ullmann SA v Skandia (UK) Insurance Co Ltd and Others* [1998] 1 All ER 737, 745. For a full discussion on the juridical basis of subrogation, see Robert Merkin, *Colinvaux's Law of Insurance* (12th edn, Sweet & Maxwell 2019), [12-005-007]; John Birds, Ben Lynch and Simon Paul, *MacGillivray on Insurance Law* (14th edn, London: Sweet & Maxwell, 2018), [24-013-020].

6 [1957] 1 WLR 703.

that he was entitled to keep the payment for the benefits of all the assured's creditors. Wynn-Parry J held that since the ECI contract is one of indemnity, then as a matter of law, the ECA, as the insurer, has the benefit of the right of subrogation "which is in its origin as an equitable doctrine". Had any payments from the buyer been received by the assured, the assured would have become the trustee for the ECA. The court further held that there was an equitable assignment by the assured to the ECA by virtue of its undertakings and its instructions. The ECA was therefore entitled to the payment.

Miller, Gibb confirms that the ECI policy is a contract of indemnity insurance under which the ECA is entitled to be subrogated into the assured's right by the operation of equity. Wynn-Parry J emphasised that the doctrine of subrogation applied by reason of the nature of the ECI contract rather than as a result of "any extreme term" in the policy.[7] The learned judge relied on many English insurance case authorities such as *Randal v Cockran*,[8] *Castellain v Preston*[9] and *King v Victoria Insurance Company Ltd*[10] to elaborate on the juridical basis of subrogation. Moreover, *Miller, Gibb* has been widely cited by many subsequent English insurance cases such as *Lord Napier and Ettrick v RF Kershaw Ltd*[11] and *Yorkshire Insurance Co Ltd v Nisbet Shipping Co Ltd*.[12] In particular, it has become the authority for many English ECI cases which will be discussed below. *Miller, Gibb* demonstrates that the juridical basis of subrogation under ECI is exactly the same as that under other types of insurance contracts.

The ECA's pre-indemnity right and the control of proceedings under ECI

Established principles in English insurance law

The common law has long established that the insurer's right of subrogation comes into effect only after it has indemnified the assured,[13] whereas the assured is obliged at all times to preserve and not to prejudice the insurer's subrogation right; otherwise, he will have broken the duty of good faith.[14] However, that does not mean that the insurer can always control the assured's proceedings prior to

7 Ibid, 709.
8 (1748) 1 Ves Sen 98, 27 ER 916.
9 (1883) 11 QBD 380, 387.
10 [1896] AC 250.
11 [1999] 1 WLR 756.
12 [1962] 2 QB 330.
13 In *Yorkshire Insurance v Nisbet*, Diplock J confirmed that "the principle is that the right of subrogation crystallises at the time of payment." See ibid, 335. See also *Santos Ltd v American Home Assurance Co* (1987) 4 ANZ Insurance Cases 60-795; *Rap Industries Pty Ltd v Royal Insurance Australia Ltd* (1988) 5 ANZ Insurance Cases 60-876; *Rathbone Brothers Plc v Novae Corporate Underwriting* [2013] EWHC 3457 (Comm), [2015] Lloyd's Rep IR 95.
14 *Napier v Hunter* [1993] 2 WLR 42; *Horwood v Land of Leather Ltd* [2010] EWHC 546 (Comm), 56–70, [2010] Lloyd's Rep IR 453; *Boag v Standard Marine Insurance Co Ltd* [1937] 2 KB 113.

indemnification. On the contrary, the English courts have confirmed that until the assured is indemnified and in the absence of anything to the contrary in the express policy wording, as a matter of law, the assured retains the exclusive right to control the proceedings against the third party.[15] One might question whether all those principles apply to ECI? Is the ECA, prior to indemnification, entitled to require the assured to commence legal proceedings against the buyer or, in a more unusual situation, to prevent the assured from doing so? If the ECA wishes to fully control the proceedings before indemnifying the assured, how clear and precise should the policy wording be? These issues will be addressed in the following paragraphs.

The ECA's right to control the assured's proceedings prior to indemnification?

In *AB Svensk ExportKredit v New Hampshire Insurance*,[16] the private credit insurer insured a bank under a buyer credit insurance policy against the default in payment by the borrower (i.e., the foreign buyer), who was an organ of the Iraqi government. The underlying transaction was a loan agreement, under which the borrower had to repay the loan to the bank in five instalments. Clause 10.01 of the loan agreement stated that the borrower's "default" occurred when it failed to pay on the due dates of any instalment. Clause 10.02 of the loan agreement was a "notice of acceleration" clause, providing that (a) should the borrower default in payment in respect of any instalment, the bank would be entitled to terminate the loan agreement, and (b) the entire loan, i.e., five instalments, plus all accrued interest, shall become due and payable upon the notice given by the bank. The policy, on the other hand, applied a waiting period of 120 days to each instalment after the "default" as defined in the loan agreement occurred.[17] Clause 2 of the policy provided that the "due date" bore the same meaning as under the loan agreement, and in the event of the acceleration the entire loan became due upon the notice of acceleration, the bank's right of acceleration would be effected only after prompt consultation with the insurer. Clause 4D of the policy, the key clause in that case, provided that the bank warranted and agreed:

> To use all reasonable measures to prevent or minimise Loss hereunder, to keep the Insurer fully informed of any material discussions and developments with the Borrower, and to take all reasonable steps to effect recoveries of any

---

See also Merkin (n 5), [12-019]. In the context of ECI, ECAs will normally reimburse the expenses the assured incurs in preserving their subrogation right. See, e.g., Clause 8.2(b) of UKEF's policy.

15 *Commercial Union Assurance Co v Lister* (1874) LR 9 Ch App 483; *Page v Scottish Insurance Corp Ltd* (1929) 33 Ll L Rep 134.

16 [1988] 3 WLUK 387.

17 It should be noted that the policy defines that the "loss" occurs on the due date of the borrower's payment rather than the expiry of the waiting period, which is different from the commercial practice in the industry nowadays, as discussed in Chapter 5.

amounts due, including if required by and, at the expense of the Insurer, the institution of legal proceedings against the Borrower.

The borrower failed to pay any of the instalments and, on the due date of the third instalment, the bank decided to exercise its acceleration right and commence legal proceedings against the borrower. However, the insurer, according to the opinions of its local advisers in Iraq, believed that to service a notice of acceleration or to start proceedings would "rock the boat and frustrate the recovery negotiations".[18] In other words, the insurer was afraid that the acceleration of debt would affect its future subrogation right. Therefore, although not asking for an injunction to restrain the service of the notice of acceleration, the insurer sought a judicial declaration that it was entitled to direct the assured as to the nature of the proceedings to be instituted against the borrower, to control the timing of such proceedings and to be kept fully informed of the progress of such proceedings. The insurer also sought an injunction to restrain the assured from starting any proceedings against the borrower without its consent. In claiming the declaration and injunction, the insurer heavily relied on Clause 4D of the policy and argued that the bank had breached this clause. By the time the dispute arose, the waiting period regarding any of the instalments had not passed, and the insurer had not indemnified the assured. Therefore, the issue in this case was whether, prior to indemnification, the ECA was entitled to control the assured's proceedings. In particular, did Clause 4D entitle the ECA to stop the assured from taking proceedings against the borrower?

Dillon LJ first confirmed that in the absence of express contractual wording, the assured owes no duty of care to the insurer in commencing legal proceedings against the third party. His lordship cited *Fraser v BN Furman (Productions) Ltd*[19] and clarified that the claim controlling provision in Clause 4D only obliged the assured not to act in bad faith or recklessly in taking reasonable precautions

18 *AB Svensk ExportKredit* [1988] 3 WLUK 387. The reason why the insurer sometimes wishes to debar the assured's proceedings against the debtor is well explained in Robert Merkin, *Colinvaux and Merkin's Insurance Contract Law* (Sweet & Maxwell 2021), [C-0552]:

> The insurer's paradox here is readily understandable. If it made payment to the assured, it would have subrogation rights against the borrower and the bank, which in its view would have to be exercised with care; whatever the outcome, it was plain that the insurer would be out of pocket for a lengthy period. However, if it did not make payment to the assured, and the assured set about suing the borrower and the bank in a fashion which offended them and led to a refusal to pay, the insurer would be obliged to make payment under the policy but would by that time have no worthwhile subrogation rights. The insurer's ideal solution was not to pay the assured, and to seek to restrain any precipitate legal proceedings by the assured so that some settlement could be negotiated gently with the Iraqi authorities. In those circumstances, the assured would not suffer any loss.

For a similar analysis, see *ABN AMRO Bank NV v Royal and Sun Alliance Insurance Plc* [2021] EWHC 442 (Comm), [800], [828], [832], [843] (Jacobs J).

19 [1967] 1 WLR 898, 905–6, (Diplock LJ).

to prevent or minimise the loss, and there was no evidence of any fraud or recklessness in the present case; on the contrary, the bank's decision to serve the notice of acceleration or to commence legal proceedings was perfectly reasonable to effect recoveries. His lordship also referred to *Morley v Moore*[20] and emphasised that whilst the insurer had the "absolute" right to require the assured to enforce his remedies against the third party, it had no right to prevent the assured from doing so in the absence of express provisions. The insurer's submission was therefore rejected by the court.

AB Svensk ExportKredit contributes to the development of the subrogation doctrine in insurance law in the following aspects. Firstly, it clarifies that the assured owes no duty of care to the insurer in taking legal actions against the third party, except that the assured should not act in bad faith or recklessly, which has been long established in English law.[21] Secondly, it illustrates the rather unusual situation where the insurer wishes to debar the proceedings by the assured against the third party. As Dillon LJ indicated, it is always open to the parties to include an express contractual provision as to "who is to have what degree of control over what steps are taken by way of avoidance of loss or recovery of money due under the policy", but in the absence of such provisions, the insurer is not entitled to intervene the assured's proceedings against the third party and, particularly, to require the assured to refrain from taking such proceedings. Clause 4D in that case, unfortunately, lacked such express stipulations. Thirdly, the court confirmed that ECI policy is indemnity insurance in its legal nature. Citing *Fraser*, Dillon LJ stated that whilst the insurance policy in *Fraser* was an employer liability policy that was not "the same type of insurance as the policy in the present case", *Fraser* was perfectly applicable as a case law authority. Moreover, his lordship emphasised that the rule established in *AB Svensk ExportKredit* applies "equally with other forms of insurance", which indicates that the court fully regarded ECI as insurance.

Stipulating a clear and precise control of proceedings clause in the ECI policy

AB Svensk ExportKredit shows the importance for the ECA to include a clear and precise control of proceedings clause if it wishes to fully control the assured's proceedings prior to indemnification. What needs to be further observed is whether ECI policies nowadays include such a clause and, if not, whether they should. This research studied the ECI policies collected through the Berne Union Academic Survey and found that ECAs take different approaches to draft provisions regarding this issue. Some ECAs only stipulate the ECAs' right to full control of proceeding after indemnification. For instance, Clause 8.2 of the UK Export Finance's (UKEF) policy provides that after being indemnified, the

20 [1936] 2 KB 359, 369 (Scott LJ).

21 See *Commercial Union Assurance Co v Lister* (1874) LRCH App 483.

assured shall "exercise or enforce or refrain from exercising or enforcing all relevant rights solely in accordance with the directions of UKEF and take all steps for this purpose as UKEF may require".[22] Some ECAs tend to require that the assured "at all times" follow their instructions in mitigating the loss and collecting recoveries. For instance, Clause 11.3 of Credendo's policy provides that the assured shall "comply at all times with the measures that Credendo deems appropriate to avoid the occurrence of a covered risk, limit its effects or maximise the recoveries under the Policy, such as … taking legal action against the Debtor".[23] Some ECAs include a more assured-friendly clause which allows the assured to control its legal actions to some extent. For instance, Clause 13 of Finnvera's policy provides that:

> 13.1 In the event that the Borrower … fails to pay any amount payable … the Guarantee Holder[24] shall, on its own initiative and without delay, initiate measures to collect the Guaranteed Receivables from the party liable for payment …
>
> 13.2 The Guarantee Holder shall consult with Finnvera regarding measures of collecting the Guaranteed Receivables in cases where … the collection or enforcement could lead to exceptionally high costs. However, the Guarantee Holder, without prior consulting with Finnvera, may initiate such collection and enforcement measures that need to be initiated urgently. Should the Guarantee Holder and Finnvera not be in agreement as to the collection and enforcement measures, Finnvera will make the decision, with reasonable consideration of the Guarantee Holder's interests.

It is submitted with due respect that none of the policies above is sufficiently clear for the ECA to fully control the proceedings. Firstly, some policies only provide that the ECA is entitled to such a right after indemnification and stipulate nothing about the pre-indemnification stage. Secondly, although some policies provide that both before and after indemnification, the assured should take legal action as instructed by the ECA, it remains unclear whether the ECA is entitled to prevent the assured from doing so. Thirdly, Clause 13 of Finnvera's policy is undoubtedly better drafted, but it may still cause some uncertainties: it allows the assured to initiate collection and enforcement measures if that needs to be done urgently, but what constitutes such an "urgent" situation? Furthermore, how reasonably should the ECA consider the assured's interest? If applying the decision in *AB Svensk ExportKredit* to the wording as seen in Clause 13, the court is still very likely

22 See also Clause 16.1 of ASHRA's policy, Clause 11(1) of EH Germany's policy and Clause 5.5 of EKN's policy.

23 See also Clause 7(a)–(c) of Atradius DSB's policy.

24 The Berne Union Academic Survey confirmed that Finnvera, as many European ECAs do, names its ECI cover as "Guarantee" and the assured "Guarantee Holder", whereas it actually regards its ECI policy as insurance.

to conclude that the ECA is not entitled to prevent the assured from taking legal actions against the buyer.

This research suggests that ECAs include a clear and precise control of proceedings clause that applies to both pre- and after-indemnification stages and emphasises the ECA's sole discretion on taking or refraining from taking legal actions against the buyer. A model control of proceedings clause is proposed as follows:

> The Insurer's Full Control of Proceedings
>
> Both prior to and after indemnification, the assured shall consult with the Insurer and take all reasonable steps to effect recoveries, including if required by the expense of the Insurer, the institution of legal proceedings against the Buyer. For the avoidance of doubt, all such steps, including commencing or refraining from commencing such legal proceedings, shall be taken solely in accordance with the directions of the Insurer. The Insurer shall contribute proportionately to all costs the assured incurs in effecting recoveries.

In addition, if ECAs do not wish to indemnify the assured should it exercise its acceleration right in the loan agreement as seen in *AB Svensk ExportKredit*, they should include an express provision to achieve that effect. For such sample wordings, see Chapter 5 of this work.

The collection of recoveries under ECI

The subrogation protection clause: general

After indemnifying the assured, the insurer will consider how to collect the debts against the buyer in order to make up for the loss it indemnifies the assured. That can be achieved in three ways: (1) the assured effects the recoveries; (2) the insurer exercises the subrogation right by stepping into the assured's shoes against the buyer. Both ways are conducted in the name of the assured; (3) alternatively, the insurer can take an assignment of the assured's right and sue in its own name.

Although the assured is required by law at all times to preserve the insurer's subrogation right, insurers normally include an express subrogation protection clause in their policies. This is also the case in ECI policies, where ECAs invariably have a subrogation clause that consists of three parts: (a) the subrogation protection clause that ensures that the ECA's subrogation right is well preserved by the assured and that the assured will take actions to collect debts if required by the ECA; (b) the allocation of recoveries clause that specifies how to allocate the recoveries between the assured and the ECA; and (c) the collection costs clause that provides whether and how the ECA would reimburse the collection costs the assured incurs in collecting the debts against the buyer.[25]

25 The Berne Union Academic Survey revealed that after indemnification, most ECAs would reimburse the collection costs the assured incurs in effecting recoveries against the buyer. See, e.g., Clause 9.1 of the UKEF's policy, Clause 1 of HBOR's policy and Clause 31.6 of NEXI's policy.

This section focuses on part (a), an example of which can be found in Clause 8 of the UKEF's policy:

> 8.1 Upon payment of any amount due to the Insured under this Policy, UKEF is subrogated to all Relevant Rights … These rights of subrogation shall be in addition and without prejudice to all rights and benefits to which UKEF is entitled under the general law of subrogation.
>
> 8.2 At all times after payment of any amount due to the Insured under this Policy, the Insured shall:
>
> (a) execute and deliver all instruments and papers and do whatever else is necessary to enable UKEF to exercise the Relevant Rights;
>
> (b) exercise or enforce or refrain from exercising or enforcing all Relevant Rights solely in accordance with the directions of UKEF and take all steps for this purpose as UKEF may require;
>
> (c) on request assign and transfer all Relevant Rights to UKEF, and execute and deliver to UKEF all such documents as UKEF may require for this purpose; and
>
> (d) authorise and permit UKEF, in the name of the Insured, to settle or compromise any claim which the Insured may have against the Buyer … in connection with the Contract or institute and conduct legal or arbitral proceedings in respect of any such claim.

Clause 8 indicates that the way of effecting recoveries in ECI is not different from that in other types of insurance. The recoveries can be collected by either the assured or the UKEF, at the latter's option.[26] The assured, if required, should also assign its rights to the UKEF. Clause 8.1 further provides that the UKEF's contractual subrogation rights shall be in addition and without prejudice to all rights and benefits that the UKEF is entitled to under the general law of subrogation, which shows that in drafting the subrogation protection clause, the UKEF is fully aware that is subrogation right takes effect by the operation of law, and that the UKEF regards its policy as insurance. It should be noted that Clause 8 is not stipulated as a condition precedent to liability; it thus should be regarded as a mere condition of which the remedies for breach are either termination or damages.[27]

It should be noted that such reimbursement of the collection costs is different from the reimbursement of the legal costs incurred under the "arbitration award/judgment" clause, as has been discussed in Chapter 5.

26 The Berne Union Academic Survey found that after indemnification, ECAs may prefer taking control of the proceedings against the buyer and effecting the recoveries by themselves. For instance, Clause 17.1 of CESCE's policy provides that:

> The Insurer shall undertake the management of the collection procedures, including the percentage not insured, even for amounts ancillary to the Loan, insured or not. The Insured undertakes to waive any right of action he may have against the Debtor arising from the Loan or collateral to the Debt, in relation with either unpaid instalments or those not yet due.

27 The difference between conditions precedent to liability and mere conditions is discussed in Chapter 3.

The subrogation protection clause in contractor–subcontractor transactions

Where the ECA insures the supplier of an exporter against the risks of non-payment by the buyer, it may insist that a tailored subrogation protection clause be embedded in the contract between the supplier (i.e., the subcontractor) and the exporter (i.e., the contractor). In *Simon Container Machinery Ltd v Emba Machinery AB*,[28] the exporter concluded an export contract with a buyer in Moscow. The exporter (hereinafter referred to as "the contractor") then reached an agreement with its supplier (hereinafter referred to as "the subcontractor") with regard to the supply of the goods. Both the contractor and the subcontractor arranged credit insurance against the risk of the non-payment by the buyer. The former was insured by the subscription market, whereas the latter was insured by the UKEF. The subcontractor, as required by the UKEF, inserted a clause in its supply agreement with the contractor which read as follows:

> Clause 4
> [The Contractor] agree that on the occurrence of a loss to take all steps which may be necessary or expedient or which [the Subcontractor] may at any time require to effect recoveries from [the End Buyer] including if so required the institution of legal proceedings in any country.

The total value of the export transaction was around £30 m, of which the contribution of the subcontractor in that case was worth some £11 m. The buyer defaulted in payment, and the contractor was partly indemnified by its insurers. In making a claim, the contractor included two invoices related to the goods supplied by the subcontractor. The subcontractor, relying on Clause 4, sought to recover from the contractor the amount it received from its insurers. The contractor argued that it was under no such duty on the true construction of Clause 4.

The court held that: (1) the term "loss" in Clause 4 should mean the loss for the purpose of the subcontractor's credit insurance, namely a non-receipt by the subcontractor of payment for goods shipped, of which the primary cause was likely to be the non-payment by the foreign buyer to the contractor; (2) although Clause 4 did not expressly set out any obligation on the contractor to pay, it was implicit that if any recovery was made, it should be paid to the subcontractor; (3) in order to give the subcontractor an effective cover, the UKEF had to insure not only to the risk of the contract not paying as obliged by the purchase order but also the risk of the foreign buyer not paying; (4) accordingly, the object of Clause 4 was to put the UKEF in no worse position than it would have been if the export contract was made directly between the subcontractor and the buyer. Therefore, Jack J held that the contractor was obliged to pay to the subcontractor and that the UKEF, having paid the subcontractor, was entitled to be subrogated into the subcontractor's right to receive that money.

28 [1998] 2 Lloyd's Rep 429.

Simon Container Machinery showed the importance of inserting an express subrogation protection clause not only in the ECI policy but also in the assured's contract with the contractor, if the assured is a subcontractor of the exporter. As Jack J commented, only in this way can the UKEF be put in "no worse position than it would have been" if the contact had been made between the subcontractor and the buyer.

The intergovernmental debt rescheduling clause

Subrogation in ECI may be conducted by the ECA's government (which is also the exporter or the bank's government) via an international debt rescheduling arrangement with the buyer's government. Accordingly, in addition to a general subrogation protection clause that stipulates the ECA's rights in the normal subrogation process, many ECI policies also include a specific clause requiring the assured to provide necessary assistance to ECA to collect debts in case of an intergovernmental debt rescheduling agreement (sometimes also referred to as "intergovernmental debt restructuring agreement"[29]). How such an arrangement operates will be fully illustrated below, whereas it is necessary here to cite a sample of the intergovernmental debt rescheduling clause under ECI. For instance, Finnvera, the ECA of Finland, in Clause 17 of its policy, provides that:

> Rescheduling of Debts between States
>
> The Policyholder shall, in respect of the Insured Receivables, authorise the Government of Finland and/or Finnvera to enter into agreements between States concerning payment arrangements, writing off and rescheduling of debts. The Policyholder shall co-operate in measures required to carry out such agreements. The conclusion of such an agreement does not diminish Finnvera's liability to pay indemnification.

Such an intergovernmental debt rescheduling clause can be widely found in many ECI policies.[30] This type of clause shows the peculiarities in the collection of debts under ECI, but it is simply an additional provision to the general subrogation protection clause, both of which aim to facilitate the ECA to exercise its subrogation rights.

The subrogation protection clause in the underlying export contract/loan agreement

In addition to the subrogation protection clause under ECI, ECAs usually ensure that a subrogation protection clause is also embedded in the underlying export

29 See, e.g., Clause 15 of KUKE's policy.

30 See, e.g., Clause 16.6 of ASHRA's policy, Clause 17 of Atradius DSB' policy, Clause 14 of EH Germany's policy, Clause 2.2 of EKN's policy, Clause 12 of SERV's policy, Clause 2.2.4 of CESCE's policy, Clause 18.3 of EGAP Czech's policy, Clause 15 of KUKE's policy and Clause 5.7 of OeKB's policy. However, ECI policies governed by English law seem not to have included such a clause.

contract/loan agreement. For instance, in the light of buyer credit transactions, Clause 22 of LMA's Export Finance Buyer Credit Agreement provides that:[31]

(a) Each Party acknowledges that [the ECA] will be subrogated to the rights of … the Lenders to the extent of any payment made by or on behalf of [the ECA] under the [ECA Cover Document].
(b) Nothing in any Finance Document shall prejudice the right of [the ECA] to be subrogated, pursuant to the [ECA Cover Document] or applicable law, to the rights of … any Lender under this Agreement and each other Finance Document.]

The allocation of recoveries under ECI

Established principles in English insurance law

Following the collection of debts against the buyer, whether such steps are taken by the assured or the ECA, one important and perhaps more complicated issue is how to allocate the recoveries between the parties. There have been some established principles regarding the allocation of recoveries between the assured and the insurer in English law. On the one hand, the insurer can recover up to the amount it has paid to the assured.[32] On the other hand, *Yorkshire Insurance*[33] established that if the sums recovered by the assured from the third party exceed the amounts paid by the insurer, for instance, as a result of currency fluctuations, the surplus belongs to the assured. However, the common law has not confirmed whether such rules regarding the allocation of the surplus equally apply where the recoveries are received by the insurer.[34] In the context of ECI, it seems straightforward that the ECA (or the private credit insurer) is entitled to recover the amount it has paid to the assured, and the assured is entitled to the uninsured percentage of the loss from the recoveries. Nevertheless, it should be noted that it is not uncommon in ECI that the recoveries collected exceed the amount of loss. That can be due to many reasons, such as the fluctuation of the currency rate, the rising of the buyer's stocks which are provided as a security for the assured, and the interest that accrues from the due date of payment and the actual payment day.[35] One might therefore raise the following questions regarding the allocation of surplus in ECI: (1) Are

31 LMA, Single Currency Term Facility Agreement for Use in Export Finance Buyer Credit Transactions (20/03/2020), 105, available to LMA members via www.lma.eu.com.

32 *Glen Line v Attorney-General* (1930) 6 Com Cas 1, 14.

33 [1962] 2 QB 330.

34 See *Lonrho Exports Ltd v Export Credits Guarantee Department* [1997] CLC 259, 274 (Lightman J) ("there is no authority or textbook affording guidance on this question").

35 Chapter 5 of this thesis has discussed the default interest, i.e., the waiting period interest in detail. Where an ECI policy covers the waiting period interest, the ECA is of course entitled to recover it because it is within the scope of indemnification. What this chapter seeks to discuss is whether the ECA is entitled to the "surplus" of recoveries, e.g., the default interest which it is not covered by the ECI policy but paid by the buyer during the collection of recoveries process.

the established rules in common law equally applicable to ECI? (2) Where the recoveries are obtained by the insurer, how will the surplus be allocated between the assured and the insurer, if there is any? (3) What if there is an express ECI term that contradicts the abovementioned principles? The following paragraphs will explore the answers by taking the relevant English ECI cases as examples.

Circumstances where the assured effects the recoveries

As is mentioned above, *Yorkshire Insurance* has established that where the assured receives the recoveries, the insurer can recover up to the amount it has paid to the assured and that any surplus belongs to the assured. However, are the parties allowed to include a contractual provision that contradicts that principle? Where there is an express policy term providing that any recoveries "in respect of a loss" to which the cover applies should be divided proportionately between the parties, can ECA be entitled to both the paid amount and the surplus pro rata? All these issues were fully discussed by the trial court, the Court of Appeal and the House of Lords in *L Lucas Ltd and another v Export Credits Guarantee Department*.[36] Clause 1 of the policy in that case, as the insuring clause, stipulated that the ECA shall pay the assured exporter 90% of the amount of the "loss" resulting from the occurrence of political events such as the prevention of or delay in the transfer of payment from the buyer's country to the UK. The export transaction was to be paid for in US dollars, and under Clauses 7 and 9, the amount of loss had to be ascertained on the expiry date of a waiting period of four months and be calculated at the buying rate of exchange in the London foreign exchange market on the date when the goods were exported. Clause 8 provided that the ECA should pay 90% of the insured loss. The key provision was Clause 17, which obliged the exporter to take all steps to effect recoveries if required by the ECA and provided that:

> Any sums recovered by the merchant or the guarantors[37] in respect of a loss to which this guarantee applies, after the date at which the loss is ascertained, whether from the buyer or any other source, shall … be divided between the guarantors and the merchant in the proportions of 90 and 10; The merchant shall pay all sums recovered to the guarantors forthwith upon their being received by him or any person on his behalf, the merchant hereby acknowledging and declaring that until such payment is made to the guarantors, he receives and holds such sums in trust for the guarantors.

The assured exported goods to the United Arab Republic (UAR) and suffered a loss caused by the exchange control restrictions in the UAR. The amount of loss

36 [1973] 1 WLR 914.

37 Throughout the policy, the exporter was named "the merchant", and the ECA was named "the guarantor". It should be noted although the ECI policy in that case was described as a "guarantee", the trial judge, the Court of Appeal and the House of Lords all regarded it as insurance.

was GBP 413,000 equivalent. The ECA paid 90% of the amount of loss, i.e., a sum of GBP 372,000. The assured effected recoveries and, as a result of the devaluation of sterling, it received GBP 443,032 from the buyer in total. The assured repaid the ECA the sum of indemnification (i.e., GBP 372,000) but refused to pay any more, whereas the ECA, relying on Clause 17, claimed that it was entitled to 90% of the total recoveries.

The issue in *Lucas* included two aspects: (1) Can the parties provide an express contractual provision that contradicts established principles of subrogation regarding the surplus? (2) If so, was the policy wording in the present case sufficient to have that effect? In other words, on the true construction of Clause 17, should (a) any sums recovered in respect of the "loss" only or (b) any sums recovered be divided proportionately between the parties?

The trial court held that the excess of recoveries at common law belonged beneficially to the exporter. Cooke J believed that the correct approach was to "consider the general law of insurance in relation to the principle of subrogation, disregarding for the moment any question of the particular terms of the particular policy, and then to construe the policy in the light of that principle". Heavily relying on *Yorkshire Insurance*, Cooke J concluded that in the absence of very express policy provisions, according to the general law of subrogation, the insurer is not entitled to any sums in excess of the amount it had paid to the assured. He held that Clause 17 of the policy in the present case was not sufficiently clear to lead to a different result.[38]

The Court of Appeal, however, reversed the trial decision. Megaw LJ clarified that in insurance policies it is open to the parties to introduce express terms which are at variance from or in conflict with the ordinary principles of subrogation. His lordship emphasised that:

> The correct approach is to consider the insurance policy by reference to its terms and, if, but only if, there should emerge some real doubt or ambiguity in the construction of the policy, would it be right to invoke the general principles of subrogation as a guide or controlling authority to the construction of the policy.[39]

Sir Gordon Willmer then took a closer look at the policy wording. He pointed out that the "loss" in Clause 17 referred to the "loss" defined in Clause 1 (i.e., the loss resulting from the prevention of or delay in transfer of payment by the buyer), which should be distinguished from the "amount of loss" under Clauses 7 and 9. Therefore, he believed that the ordinary meaning of Clause 17 was to ensure that all sums recovered, "whatever these might be", should be divided between

38 It should be noted that how Cooke J read Clause 17 and reached his conclusion seems not clear to the author, since the trial judgment seems not available online and was only summarised by Megaw LJ in the appeal judgment in a few paragraphs. See *Lucas* [1973] 1 WLR 914, 922.

39 Ibid.

the ECA and the assured. The Court of Appeal did not challenge the correctness of the decision in *Yorkshire Insurance*, and it held that Clause 17 was "precise" enough for the court to reach its conclusion.

The House of Lords agreed with the Court of Appeal that the correct approach in deciding the allocation of recoveries is to first refer to the policy wording, but it disagreed with the Court of Appeal's construction of the term "loss" under Clause 17. Lord Morris of Borth-Y-Gest held that the term "loss" in Clause 1 and the term "amount of loss" in Clauses 7 and 9 were interchangeable, and that the term "loss" was used to denote the sum of money which the assured did not receive at the time when he should have received it. His lordship clarified that "the loss is always a sum of money the amount of which is specified by the policy", and that the "loss" and the "amount of loss" are invariably interchangeable. His lordship further clarified that the prevention or the delay in payment was not the loss but was the event or occurrence which caused the loss, and the loss was the sum of GBP 413,000. Therefore, Clause 17 only obliged the assured to repay 90% of the amount of loss to the ECA, and once the recoveries exceeded the amount of the loss, Clause 17 "had no further application". Therefore, the House of Lords held that the ECA was not entitled to any of the surpluses.

Lucas makes the following contributions to the development of the rules regarding subrogation in insurance law. Firstly, both the Court of Appeal and the House of Lords confirmed that if there is an express contractual term which is at variance or in conflicts with the principles of subrogation regarding recoveries and, particularly, the rules regarding the allocation of surplus established in *Yorkshire Insurance*, such policy wording should prevail. Secondly, the House of Lords clarified that in an insurance policy, the term "loss" equals to "the amount of loss", and that a loss is always a specific sum of money. Thirdly, *Lucas* shows the importance of including a clear and precise provision if the ECA wishes to be entitled to the surplus. Clause 17 of the policy in that case provided that "any sums recovered … in respect of a loss" should be divided between the parties, which led to the House of Lord's conclusion that such sums only referred to the amount of the loss and no more. The phrase "in respect of a loss" was apparently redundant. If, on the contrary, the policy provides that "any sums recovered should be divided between the parties, even though such recovery would exceed the amount paid by the insurer", it might make a difference. Lastly, the courts in *Lucas* expressly confirmed that the ECI policy is a contract of insurance. Although the policy was described as a "guarantee", both the Court of Appeal and the House of Lord regarded it as insurance. Sir Gordon Willmer held that "although it is called a 'guarantee' … it amounts in substance to a contract of insurance."[40] Lord Morris of Borth-Y-Gest also stated that:[41]

40 Ibid, 925 (Sir Gordon Willmer).

41 *Lucas* [1974] 1 WLR 909, 914, 921 (Lord Morris of Borth-Y-Gest). It should be noted that Lord Simon of Glaisdale, in his concurring opinion, also concluded that the ECI policy in *Lucas* was a contract of indemnity insurance by relying on *Miller, Gibb*.

> The contract is called a guarantee … but it has many of the features of a contract of insurance … The document issued by the respondents in return for the payment of a premium would be more aptly described as a policy of insurance, a policy to indemnify the appellants against a percentage of a loss in sterling which might be sustained on the contracts covered by the policy from one of the specified causes.

Circumstances where the ECA effects the recoveries

The section above demonstrated the principles regarding the allocation of recoveries in ECI where the assured effects the recoveries. One might further question whether these rules apply where the ECA collects the debts and effects the recoveries after indemnifying the assured. What should be particularly taken into account is the Export and Guarantees Act 1991 ("the 1991 Act"), the statute that gives the UKEF the power to exercise the functions to facilitate export and investment on behalf of the Secretary of State. Art 14 of the 1991 Act provides that "any sums received by the Secretary of State by virtue of this Act shall be paid into the Consolidated Fund[42]". Does it indicate that the assured is not entitled to any surplus or that the assured is not entitled to even the uninsured percentage of the loss? What makes the issue more complicated is that the ECA sometimes collects the debt through a debt rescheduling arrangement under a bilateral treaty between the ECA's country, namely the exporter or the bank's country, and the buyer's country. Do those international elements affect the allocation of recoveries between the ECA and the assured?

The allocation of recoveries effected by the ECA under an intergovernmental debt rescheduling arrangement was thoroughly discussed in *Lonrho Exports Ltd v Export Credits Guarantee Department*.[43] In that case, the assured exporter under an ECI policy suffered a loss as a result of foreign exchange restrictions in Zambia, which was the buyer's country. In 1980, the assured, together with many other UK exporters who also insured their sales business in Zambia with the Export Credits Guarantee Department (ECGD), made individual claims against the ECGD. Their claims were duly processed and paid, and the ECGD was then given the mandate by those exporters, including the assured in this case, to recover debts due against the Zambian buyers and was required to repay these exporters part of the recoveries in proportion to their uninsured losses. Following a multilateral agreement to reschedule its debts, Zambia entered into a bilateral agreement with the UK government. In 1984, the Zambian government made a payment to the ECGD (hereinafter referred to as "the 1984 payment"). However,

42 According to Parliament's website, the term "Consolidated Fund" refers to the UK Government's general bank account at the Bank of England. Payments from this account must be authorised in advance by the House of Commons. The Government presents its "requests" to use this money in the form of Consolidated Fund Bills. See <https://www.parliament.uk/site-information/glossary/consolidated-fund/> accessed 1 February 2022.

43 [1997] CLC 259.

it was not until 1991 that the ECGD confirmed that the assured was one of the creditors eligible for the 1984 payment. The ECGD paid the assured the uninsured loss, but the assured claimed interest which accrued between 1984 and 1991, on the basis that the UKEF, as the insurer, held the money on trust for the assured.

Before turning to decide the legal issue, Lightman J spent lengthy paragraphs explaining the peculiarities of the debt rescheduling arrangement in the context of ECI,[44] which, for the purpose of this research, is worthwhile to be illustrated as follows. By 1983, Zambia's economy was in crisis. It lacked hard currency to pay all sorts of its foreign debts, including long, medium and even short-term debts. This gave rise to an urgent need for the rescheduling of its debts, and in particular, debts owed to foreign governments and debts insured by ECAs over the world. In order to do so, Zambia participated in discussions at the "Paris Club",[45] an informal grouping of wealthy creditor countries which meets monthly in Paris to discuss proposals brought by developed or most undeveloped countries wishing to reschedule debts payable in the hard currency where the debts are insured by ECAs of these creditor countries. Once recommendations for debt restructuring have been agreed, they are embedded in a multilateral agreement signed by the debtor country and the creditor countries. Such a multilateral agreement, as Lightman J pointed out, has no legal force in international law, and each creditor country has to negotiate a bilateral agreement with the debtor country, which sets out in detail the terms on which the debt is to be repaid. Such bilateral agreements, i.e., treaties, are binding in international law. For the UK at that time, such a bilateral agreement in respect of export credit debts was negotiated by the ECGD in its capacity as the representative of the Crown and was formally signed by an ambassador or high commissioner or some other official of the Foreign and Commonwealth Office. In May 1983, a multilateral agreement was made between the Zambian government and 12 creditor governments, including that of the UK, providing general principles for the rescheduling of Zambia's international long, medium and short-term debts. In order to conclude a bilateral agreement with Zambia, it was necessary for the ECGD to establish which UK nationals had claims that might fall within the scope of the multilateral agreement so that a list of creditors and the respective amounts owed could be agreed with Zambia. The ECGD contacted some 120 exporters, including the assured in this case, and the assured was included in the list of short-term creditors. In December 1983, the UK entered into a bilateral agreement with Zambia, which provided that the latter should repay the debts in several instalments. However, Zambia only made one single payment instalment in January 1984 and failed to pay the rest. The 1984 payment was considerably less than the total sum claimed by the UK creditors. The ECGD had to seek the agreement of the Zambian government to the allocation of the 1984 payment between (1) different categories of debts, i.e., long, medium and short term; (2) principal and interest; and (3) the amounts of the individual debts payable to the creditors.

44 Ibid, 259–71.
45 See <http://www.clubdeparis.org/en> accessed 1 February 2022.

It took the ECGD several years to confirm with the Zambian government which creditors were eligible for the 1984 payment, and the assured was finally paid the uninsured loss in 1991. Having set out this prolonged process, Lightman J commented that it was not open to the court to question or evaluate whether the ECGD delayed in allocating the 1984 payment because it was at all times for the Crown alone to decide the rules, the speed and the intensity of its activity in agreeing on the allocation of the 1984 payment, and the Crown had to exercise a delicate judgment in the foreign relation field.

The court then turned to the core issue in this case, i.e., whether the ECGD held the 1984 payment on trust for the assured. Lightman J approached the issue in three stages: (1) Whether, as a matter of law, the assured had a proprietary interest in the surplus of recoveries made by the ECGD: in other words, did the surplus belong to the assured? (2) Whether, under the terms of the ECI policy in the present case, the assured had such a proprietary interest? (3) If the answers to questions (1) and (2) were both affirmative, did the 1984 payment constitute a "recovery"?

For question (1), Lightman J pointed out that whilst there had been authorities confirming that where the assured obtained recoveries it would be entitled to the surplus,[46] there was no authority or textbook that provided guidance on the situation where the insurer obtained recoveries. Nevertheless, he decided that the principle in the former situation should equally apply in the latter, i.e., where the insurer obtained recoveries, it should also hold the surplus on trust for the assured.

For question (2), Lightman J read the allocation of recoveries clause in the ECI policy in the present case, which provided that all recoveries shall be divided proportionately between the ECGD and the assured, whether or not such recoveries exceed the amount of loss or not.[47] He held that such a clause would entitle the assured to a share of the surplus, namely the interest, as long as the 1984 payment constituted a "recovery" under the policy.

Question (3) became a critical issue to be determined before the court. Lightman J held that since the 1984 payment was an inter-state payment made by the Zambian government to the UK government, the Crown received it in its sovereign capacity as the sole and absolute property of the state. The bilateral agreement between Zambia and the UK did not confer any rights on the assured or other policyholders under the ECGD's ECI policies. Therefore, the 1984 payment did not include a "recovery" under the ECI policy and the assured was not entitled to the surplus.

Lonrho contributes to English insurance law in the following aspects. Firstly, it established that in the context of insurance contracts, as a general matter of law, where the insurer collects and receives recoveries, any surplus belongs to the assured. *Lonrho* demonstrated that the rules regarding the allocation of recoveries in situations where the assured effects recoveries also apply to situations where

46 See *Lord Napier and Ettrick v Hunter* [1993] AC 713.

47 The allocation of recoveries clause of the policy in *Lonrho* will be further discussed below.

the insurer obtains recoveries. Secondly, *Lonrho* confirmed that the abovementioned rules regarding the allocation of recoveries fully apply in ECI policies. It indicated that where the ECA exercises the subrogation right and collects the debts in the ordinary course other than the "Paris Club" approach in the present case, any uninsured percentage of loss as well as surplus should belong to the assured, subject to any express terms to the opposite effect. Notably, Lightman J rejected the ECGD's submission that since art 14 of the Export and Guarantees Act 1978 (which is the predecessor of art 14 of the 1991 Act) provides that any sums received shall be paid into the Consolidated Fund, any surplus recovered by the UKEF should belong to itself. He emphasised that "the identity and qualities of the insurer are surely quite irrelevant".[48] The learned judge pointed out that if a sum constitutes a "recovery" under an ECI policy, then the ECGD should either (a) if the sum has been paid into the Consolidated Fund, withdraw it and pay to the assured; or (b) if not yet paid in, seek to pay it directly to the assured, instead of paying it into the Consolidated Fund. Thirdly, *Lonrho* drew a complete picture of the "Paris Club" approach, i.e., the debt rescheduling arrangement under multilateral and bilateral treaties. It indicates that where the ECA negotiates debt rescheduling on behalf of the exporters via the Paris Club and collects the debts through an international treaty, the payment by the government of the buyer's country to that of the ECA (as well as the exporter)'s country is to be regarded as the absolute property of the State, rather than the recovery for the assured under a single ECI policy. The rationale is straightforward: through the normal subrogation process, the ECA collects the debts on behalf of the assured alone, but through the "Paris Club" approach, the ECA collects the debts on behalf of a massive group of creditors. How to distribute and allocate the payment by the buyer's government remains the sole decision of the ECA. Such payments will not constitute a "recovery" under a single policy unless and until distributed as such by the ECA.[49] The "Paris Club" approach to collecting debts is not uncommon in the ECI industry. *Lonrho* is informative to ECAs in respect of the allocation of recoveries where the ECA collect debts via the Paris Club. Lastly, Lightman J in *Lonrho*, in common with the English courts in *Lucas*, *AB Svensk ExportKredit* and *Miller Gibb*, confirmed that ECI is a contract of insurance.

The allocation of recoveries clause in ECI policies

The main objective of the sections above was, by reviewing *Lucas* and *Lonrho*, to establish that in determining the allocation of recoveries between the ECA and the

48 Lightman J held that art 14 does not prevent the sums received by the UKEF from being analysed or identified as "recoveries". Since arts 1 and 12 of the Export and Guarantees Act 1978 (which are arts 1 and 12 of the 1991 Act) confer upon the UKEF the power to conclude ECI contracts on such terms as it thinks fit, if the normal consequences of the allocation of recoveries were to be excluded, an express term to this effect in the ECI policy would be expected. See *Lonrho* [1997] CLC 259, 276–7.

49 Ibid, 259.

assured, the English courts regarded ECI as insurance, hence the wording of the allocation of recoveries clause was not the focus of discussion. Meanwhile, it is of equal significance to learn from the decisions in *Lucas* and *Lonrho* that in English insurance law, it is open to the parties to include an allocation of recoveries clause that is at variance with established law principles. *Lucas*, in particular, shows the importance for the ECA to include a very clear and precise allocation of recoveries clause if it wishes to be entitled to any surplus of the recoveries. This section therefore further scrutinises the wording of the allocation of recoveries clause used in ECI policies in both the past and the present.

Drafted in the 1960s, the allocation of recoveries clause in the policy in *Lucas* clearly influenced the drafting of the allocation of recoveries clause in later policies. For instance, the ECI policy in *Lonrho*, which was drafted in the 1970s, provided that:[50]

> All sums recovered by the Insurer relating to a contract in respect of which a claim has been paid, shall after receipt by the Insurer be divided between the Insurer and the Insured in the proportion in which the amount of loss ascertained … is borne by each of them respectively, whether or not such division results in the retention by the Insurer of a greater or lesser sum than the amount paid by the Insurer under this Guarantee[51] in connection with that amount of loss.

The allocation of recoveries clause in the policy in *Lonrho* was much better drafted. As Lightman J pointed out, this detailed clause was "designed to negate the application of the decision in *Lucas*".[52] There are two improvements in the allocation of recoveries clause in *Lonrho* over that in *Lucas*. First, the policy in *Lucas* provided that all sums recovered "in respect of a loss to which this guarantee applies" shall be divided proportionately between the ECA and the assured, whereas the policy in *Lonrho* provided that all sums recovered "relating to a contract in respect of which a claim has been paid" shall be divided between the parties. The latter's scope seems broader than the former's. Second, the policy in *Lonrho* further provided that such division should be carried out whether or not it results in the retention by the ECA of a greater or lesser sum than the amount paid under the policy. Therefore, if the ECA adopts an allocation of recoveries clause as seen in *Lonrho*, it would be proportionately entitled to the recoveries, whether such recoveries exceed the amount of loss or not.

There has been no reported English ECI dispute on the allocation of recoveries since the judgment of *Lonrho*. What needs further observation is whether ECAs and private insurers now tend to include a detailed allocation of recoveries clause as seen in *Lonrho*. As with previous chapters, by scrutinising the up-to-date ECI

50 Ibid, 275.
51 The term "Guarantee" here means insurance, as confirmed by the courts in *Lonrho*.
52 *Lonrho* [1997] CLC 259, 276.

policies collected via the Berne Union Academic Survey, this chapter finds the following tendencies in the current ECI industry.

Some ECAs and private insurers, especially those whose policies are governed by English law, take an assured-friendly approach regarding the allocation of recoveries clause. On the one hand, they define the term "recovery" narrowly. For instance, the UKEF provides that "recoveries" means "any sum recovered from any source which mitigates the loss sustained by the Insured". A sample wording from an anonymous Berne Union member also provides that "recoveries" means "any monies … received by the Insured … for the purpose of reducing a loss". Where a policy defines a recovery as one "mitigating" or "reducing" the loss, then, applying the final judgment in *Lucas*, one would easily come to the conclusion that the insurer is not entitled to any surplus. On the other hand, they clearly provide that all the remainder of recoveries should be returned to the assured. For instance, Clause 10.2 of the UKEF's policy provides that "UKEF shall retain the Insured Percentage of each Recovery received by it and shall pay the remainder to the Insured". A sample wording from an anonymous Berne Union member also provides that

> (a) the Insurer shall receive the Insured Percentage of all amounts recovered until the amount of the payment of the loss … have been fully reimbursed, and (b) all further amounts recovered shall be for the benefit of the Insured.

Some ECAs might provide that they are entitled to the amount they pay to the assured plus the default interest collected from the buyer pro rata, whilst all the rest of recoveries shall be returned to the assured.[53]

Other ECAs, on the other hand, tend to protect their own interest in terms of the allocation of any surplus of recoveries by stipulating clear policy provisions as seen in *Lonrho*. For instance, Clause 17.3 of Credendo's policy provides that "recoveries shall be shared regardless of the amounts recovered, without regard to, in particular, any foreign exchange gains or losses".[54] Such provisions would ensure that the insurer is entitled to its proportion in the recovery even if the amount falling to the insurer's share exceeds the amount of claim paid by it. Some ECAs may provide a limitation to their entitlement of the surplus. Clause 17.3 of ASHRA's policy provides that where the recoveries exceed the amount of loss, then it will be entitled to the surplus, until such surplus equals the interest which, based on LIBOR rate, accrues from the date of indemnification and to the date of the receipt of the recoveries. Whether limited or unlimited, the abovementioned clauses are clear enough for these ECAs to be entitled to the surplus of the recoveries.

It is submitted that both approaches are perfectly in line with the case law, as both include a very clear and detailed allocation of recoveries clause. What is

53 See, e.g., Clause 19 of EGAP Czech's policy.

54 See also Clause 24.2 of KUKE's policy, Clause 36.7 of NEXI's policy and Clause 17.3 of ODL's policy.

interesting is that credit insurers in the UK nowadays tend to include a modest allocation of recoveries clause rather than the clause as seen in *Lonrho* which would entitle the ECA to any surplus of the recoveries. The reason is perhaps that they wish to keep their policies more attractive to the assured in competition with their counterparts in the global market. Nevertheless, this research suggests that if an ECA wishes to be entitled to the pro rata share of any sums recovered from the third party including the surplus, it should include a clear and precise allocation of recoveries clause as seen in *Lonrho*.

The allocation of recoveries clause and the waiting period clause

Chapter 5 of this work has demonstrated that one of the peculiarities of ECI policies is that they invariably include a waiting period clause to the effect that the loss shall be deemed to occur on the expiry date of the waiting period rather than the due date of payment. Therefore, the expiry date of the waiting period is always the "date of (ascertainment of) loss" when the ECA becomes liable to indemnify the assured. The expiry date of the waiting period, as a cut-off point, is significant for the allocation of recoveries in that if any payment is received from the buyer before that date, it will go in the reduction of the loss; otherwise, it will be regarded as a recovery which should be divided between the ECA and the assured proportionately.

The scenario above was fully illustrated in *Kent Engineering & Foundry Ltd v Export Credits Guarantee Department*.[55] The ECI policy in that case provided a waiting period of six months after the due date of payment. The allocation of recoveries clause, which read highly identical to the allocation of recoveries clause in *Lonrho*, provided that all sums received from the buyer "after the date of ascertainment of loss" shall be divided between the ECA and the assured proportionately. The insured percentage was 90% under that policy, and accordingly, the credit limit was £62,500 × 90% = £56,250[56] for each particular buyer. The assured exporter suffered losses in respect of two consignments of goods to the same buyer: (1) in respect of the first consignment, the waiting period expired on May 3, 1979. The amount of loss was £49,895, 90% of which, being £44,906, was the amount the ECA was liable to pay; (2) in respect of the second consignment, the waiting period expired on August 1979. The amount of loss was £52,524, 90% of which was £47,271, but the ECA was only liable to pay, subject to the credit limit, £56,250 − £44,906 = £11,344.

The assured subsequently received three sums of payments from the buyer, namely: (1) on June 19, 1979, £17,584; (2) on September 18, 1979, £12,878; and (3) on June 5, 1980, £7,515. The total of these sums was £37,977. The assured

55 [1983] 2 Lloyd's Rep 556.

56 How the credit limit operates in ECI has been discussed in detail in Chapter 3 of this research, but it is necessary here to briefly reiterate how to use the credit limit: the ECA issues a credit limit to the assured regarding a particular buyer or transaction, but its liability is capped by the insured percentage, e.g., 90%, of that credit limit.

claimed that all these sums should go in the reduction of the losses. The ECA, on the other hand, argued that all these sums should be regarded as recoveries and be divided proportionately between the parties.

The different ways proposed by the parties to deal with these sums could lead to significantly different consequences. According to the assured's contention, all these three sums shall go in the reduction of the losses and be paid to the assured. That means that the total amount of losses indemnifiable would then be (£49,895 + £52,524) × 90% − £37,977 = £54,203, which fell below the credit limit, and thus the ECA shall pay in full. In that case, the assured would only bear uninsured 10% of the loss, which only amounted to (£49,895 + £52,524) × 10% = £10,242, and the ECA was entitled to no recoveries at all. However, if the ECA's approach was correct, then it should pay £44,906 + £11,344 = £56,250, but it can be allocated to 90% of the recoveries, i.e., 90% × £37,977 = £34,719. That means that the ECA would only bear the loss of £56,250 − £34,719 = £21,531, but the assured would bear the loss of £49,895 + £52,524 − £56,250 − £37,977 × 10% = £42,371.

Parker J, reading the allocation of recoveries clause in that case, held that such a clause in an insurance contract "has nothing whatever to do with the amount of loss". The judge pointed out that "such a clause merely regulated what was to happen with regards to post-loss receipts if there were any; it did not affect the amount of loss." The payments received after the date of loss, therefore, should not go in the reduction of the losses. Dealing with the three sums in question, the judge held that since the first sum was received after the date of the first loss, it became a recovery that should be proportionately divided between the parties "in accordance with ordinary insurance principles". The second and third sums, in the judge's opinion, were received after the second loss and should therefore be regarded as recoveries, too. The assured's submission was accordingly rejected.[57]

Kent Engineering & Foundry contributes to the English insurance law in the following aspects. Firstly, it clarifies that as a general insurance principle, the allocation of recoveries clause in an insurance policy has nothing to do with the amount of loss. It merely regulates post-loss receipts. Secondly, it illustrates how the allocation of recoveries clause operates with the waiting period clause in an ECI policy, a complex issue which reflects the peculiarities of ECI: where the payment is received from the buyer before the date of (ascertainment of) loss, i.e., the expiry date of the waiting period, then it should go in the reduction of the loss. Otherwise, it constitutes a recovery that should be divided between the ECA and the assured proportionately. Thirdly, *Kent Engineering & Foundry* confirmed that ECI is in its nature of an insurance policy. Parker J fully regarded the ECI cover in that case as insurance, and held that the ECA was subject to "ordinary insurance principles" and "ordinary principles of subrogation", in that it would be entitled to recoup itself to up to the amount of the claim out of the recoveries.[58]

57 *Kent Engineering & Foundry* [1983] 2 Lloyd's Rep 556, 559–60.
58 Ibid.

Assignment under ECI as the alternative to subrogation

The potential advantages of assignment over subrogation

Assignment in the context of ECI is of no difference from its counterpart in other types of insurance policies. In English law, subrogation does not create a fresh right but merely transfers a right of action.[59] Thus the essence of subrogation is that the insurer sues in the name of the assured. However, English law also allows the insurer to take an assignment of the assured's rights against a third party.[60] Assignment is said to be "probably rare" in the ordinary insurance business as the insurers prefer to use the name of the assured because of the consequent lack of publicity.[61] It also seems that in ECI, ECAs normally prefer to work through the assured to get repaid and assignment is generally used as the last resort.[62] However, assignment does have some advantages over subrogation. Firstly, if the insurer takes an assignment, it can sue the third party in its own name and receive the proceeds of the judgment.[63] Secondly, there will be no requirement that the assured be fully indemnified before the insurer can sue.[64] Thirdly, the insurer can "stand to profit from the assignment"[65] and keep everything they recover, including the surplus.[66] The House of Lords in *Lucas* confirmed that should the assured assign its rights to the insurer, the latter would have been entitled to receive and keep all sums including the surplus, a rule that was applicable to both ECI and all other types of insurance.[67]

Contractual assignment and equitable assignment

Whereas the right of subrogation arises as soon as indemnification is made, an assignment normally requires an agreement that the rights of the insured are to be assigned to the insurer.[68] ECI policies normally include an assignment provision stipulating that the assured should upon the request of the ECA assign its rights against the buyer to the ECA. The assignment provision is usually embedded in the subrogation protection clause[69] but is sometimes also included in the "notifica-

59 *Simpson & Co v Thomson* (1877) 3 App Cas 279 HL.

60 *Compania Colombiana de Seguros v Pacific Steam Navigation Co* [1965] 1 QB 101.

61 John Birds, *Modern Insurance Law* (10th edn, Sweet & Maxwell 2016) 344.

62 The Berne Union Academic Survey found that whether the ECA prefers subrogation or assignment depends on the jurisdiction in question. In civil law jurisdictions, ECAs normally take assignment (which is sometimes called "cession") of the assured's rights, whereas in common law countries, ECAs prefer subrogation to assignment.

63 *Central Insurance Co v Seacalf Shipping Corp* [1983] 2 Lloyd's Rep 25, 33–4.

64 See n 61 above.

65 Merkin (n 18), [C-0542].

66 The principle of *Yorkshire Insurance* will not apply simply because the cause of action is entirely the insurer's and the assured has forfeited all interest in it. See Birds (n 61) 345; Merkin (n 5), [12-009].

67 *Lucas* [1974] 1 WLR 909, 922.

68 See Birds and others (n 5), [24-011]; Merkin (n 5), [12-009].

69 See, e.g., Clause 8.2(c) of the UKEF's policy cited above. The assignment clause can also be found in the policies cited by the English courts in *Miller*, *Lucas*, *Lonrho* and *Euler Hermes*.

tion, mitigation and consultation" clause. For instance, in the UKEF's policy, the assignment provision is stipulated in both Clause 7 "Notification, Mitigation and Consultation" and Clause 8 "Subrogation". Clause 7.6 provides that:

> The Insured shall upon request assign to UKEF such rights as it has under the Contract, and to any Goods and/or Services and any documents and securities relating to the Contract. If the Insured fails to do so then UKEF shall have no liability under this Policy.

In the absence of an assignment of rights clause in the ECI policy, the English court may also establish an equitable assignment by taking the circumstances of the case into account. In *Miller, Gibb*,[70] the ECI policy itself did not include an assignment clause but, in the claim request form, the assured undertook to assign all its rights under the sales contract to the ECA, and it instructed its bank to hand any payments received from the buyer to the ECA. Relying on *Alexander v Steinhardt, Walker & Co*,[71] an insolvency case which established that an equitable assignment could be found in the letters from the creditor assignor to its debtor and to the assignee, Wynn-Parry J held that the assured's undertaking and instruction constituted such an equitable assignment.

Assignment and set-off

An ECI policy may stipulate an assignment clause together with a set-off clause. For instance, Clause 4 "Assignment" of the policy in *Merrill Lynch International Bank Ltd (formerly Merrill Lynch Capital Markets Bank Ltd) v Winterthur Swiss Insurance Co*,[72] provided that "upon irrevocable payment in full by [the Insurer]", there shall be a transfer or assignment of the assured bank's rights against the buyer in "any Loss Amount". Clause 6 of the policy addressed "set-off" in circumstances where, having paid the claim, the insurer sought recovery of the "Loss Amount" from the buyer under transferred or assigned rights and the buyer asserted a pre-existing set-off against the assured. As has been explained in previous chapters, on 17 July 2006, the assured in *Merrill Lynch* terminated the loan agreement upon the occurrence of a "Bankruptcy Trigger Event", claiming against the insurer that the "Loss Amount", via accelerated payments on early termination, totalled some €29.9 m. However, on 26 July 2006, the buyer paid an instalment of €8.9 m on the basis that it did not accept that the loan agreement had been terminated. The assured accepted that sum on the basis that it was a partial payment of the "Loss Amount" due on early termination. After its application in this way, the assured treated the "Loss Amount" as being €21 m.

The assured's entitlement to take this approach was disputed by the insurer, who claimed to be entitled to the benefit of this €8.9 m payment by setting off this

70 [1957] 1 WLR 703.

71 [1903] 2 KB 208.

72 [2007] EWHC 893 (Comm), [2007] 2 All ER (Comm) 846.

sum against its liability to the assured. It might seem difficult at first glance to tell what the benefit was, but inference can be made from the assured's submission that if it applied this payment in partial discharge of the total "Loss Amount", it should be entitled to the interest which accrued on this payment. For instance, if the insurer was held liable to indemnify the assured on 20 April 2007 (which was the date of the judgment), and the interest which accrued from the €8.9 m payment between July 2006 and April 2007 amounted to €0.1 m, then: (a) if the assured applied this payment in partial discharge of the total "Loss Amount", the insurer would be liable to pay €29.9 m – €8.9 m = €21 m; but (b) if the insurer was entitled to set off this payment plus interest against its total liability under the policy, then it should only pay €29.9 m – (€8.9 m + €0.1 m) = €20.9 m.

The insurer contended that although Clauses 4 and 6 of the policy did not apply to this situation (as it had not indemnified the assured), the assured's approach would be "contrary to the basic principles of indemnity underlying an insurance contract of this sort", namely ECI. The assured, on the other hand, argued that it was only upon indemnification by the insurer in full that it was obliged under Clause 4 to assign all rights and interests that it might have against the buyer. Gloster J held that whilst Clauses 4 and 6 were "arguably not directly applicable" to this situation, they "strongly support" the argument that the insurer was entitled to the benefit of the payment by the buyer – "certainly once the insurer had paid". The judge ruled that, in the absence of any express term in the policy addressing the position, the assured's approach would breach the principle of indemnity in insurance law.

Merrill Lynch is another example where the English court treated ECI as indemnity insurance. More importantly, it demonstrates the interrelationship between assignment and set-off under ECI, thereby again confirming the potential advantages of assignment over subrogation: the insurer could "stand to profit from the assignment" even prior to full indemnification.

Assignment and the jurisdiction clause of the underlying transaction

When arranging an assignment under ECI, insurers must be aware of the risk of any potential jurisdiction dispute of the underlying negotiable instruments to be assigned. In *China Export & Credit Insurance Corporation v Emerald Energy Resources Limited*[73] (*Sinosure v Emerald*), the exporter obtained an oil prospecting licence (licence number: OML 141) to explore and extract hydrocarbons in a coastal area of Nigeria and to sell the hydrocarbons so found and extracted. In order to raise funds to cover the extremely high costs of finding and extracting hydrocarbons, the exporter entered into a suite of four contracts (known collectively as the "Farm-In Agreements") with Sinosure, the ECA of China, by which Sinosure acquired a 38% interest in OML 141 in return for payment and certain funding commitments. Under the Farm-In Agreements, Sinosure was obliged to

73 [2018] EWHC 1503 (Comm), [2018] 10 WLUK 487.

raise money to cover the work programme on OML 141 and to provide technical services required for the exploration of it, and was entitled to its share of the "Net Revenue" which was defined as the proceeds from the sale of hydrocarbons. The Farm-In Agreements were all expressed to be governed by Nigerian law, and all contained an identical arbitration clause as follows:[74]

> Any dispute, controversy, or claim arising out of or in relation to or in connection with this Agreement, including without limitation any dispute as to the construction, validity, interpretation, enforceability, or breach of this Agreement, shall be exclusively and finally settled by arbitration … in London, England.

The exporter then engaged BGP, a company on Sinosure's recommendation, to provide 3D seismic data for the work programme. Sinosure issued an ECI policy to BGP in respect of the debt owed by the exporter to BGP ("the BGP Debt") which amounted to some US$66.5 m. However, when the BGP Debts were due, there were no funds available from hydrocarbon production to discharge the exporter's liability. To deal with this difficulty, the parties arranged the following refinancing package:

First, a bank agreed to provide a loan to the exporter in order to discharge its liability relating to the BGP Debts on the security of a promissory note issued by the exporter. The loan agreement provided that the lender could assign any of its rights to Sinosure without the consent of the exporter. The loan agreement was governed by English law and included a nonexclusive English jurisdiction clause.

Second, the exporter issued a promissory note ("the Note") to the bank in which it irrevocably and unconditionally promised to pay the BGP Debt. The Note stated that it constituted the exporter's "legal, valid and binding obligations enforceable in accordance with its terms" and that "all or any right, title and interest in this Promissory Note" was "freely transferable in whole to any person". The exporter also acknowledged that it did "not have and will not claim or exercise any set-off or counterclaim in respect of the Promissory Note". The Note was governed by English law and contained a non-exclusive jurisdiction clause (NEJC) which read as follows:

> This Promissory Note shall in all respects be governed by and construed in accordance with the laws of England. The issuer hereby submits to the non-exclusive jurisdiction of the English courts in respect of any legal action or proceedings arising out of or in connection with this Promissory Note.

Third, Sinosure issued an ECI policy to the bank providing coverage in respect of the latter's right to receive the proceeds of the Note. Article 15(1) of the policy provided that, once Sinosure had paid out under the policy, at Sinosure's request,

74 Ibid, [15].

the bank shall assign to Sinosure "all rights and interests under the Financing (including its security interest) in compliance with proper legal procedures".

The buyer subsequently defaulted in repaying the loan. Sinosure duly paid the bank under the policy and was transferred the Note which became payable. However, the exporter protested that under the Farm-In Agreements, Sinosure was only entitled to be paid on the Note out of "Net Revenue" (i.e., the net proceeds of production of hydrocarbons), and no such production had yet started. Sinosure, relying on the NEJC of the Note, commenced proceedings in England against the exporter, but the latter argued that the English court should stay the claim under s 9 of the Arbitration Act 1996 because the dispute under the Note was in connection with the Farm-In Agreements and thus governed by the arbitration clause. The exporter contended that the fact that the Note was not issued to Sinosure in the first place but only became actionable by Sinosure against it by virtue of the assignment from the bank weighed significantly against the proposition that the NEJC displaced the arbitration clause if a claim was brought on the Note in England.

Sir Richard Field clarified that the court's task was to determine whether the issue in the proceedings was a matter which under the arbitration agreement was to be referred to arbitration. He adopted the "commercially rational construction" approach articulated by Thomas LJ in *Deutsche Bank v Sebastian Holdings (No2)*[75] in construing potentially overlapping agreements on jurisdiction:

> There is no presumption that a jurisdiction (or arbitration) agreement in contract A, even if expressed in wide language, was intended to capture disputes under contract B; the question is entirely one of construction … In the final analysis, the question simply requires the careful and commercially-minded construction of the various agreements providing for the resolution of disputes, the point of departure being that agreements which appear to have been deliberately and professionally drafted are to be given effect so far as it is possible and commercially rational to do so, even where this may result in a degree of fragmentation in the resolution of disputes. It may be necessary to enquire under which of a number of inter-related contractual agreements a dispute actually arises; this may be answered by seeking to locate its centre of gravity…

Sir Field noted that the "commercially rational construction" approach was adopted and applied by Blair J in *PT Thiess Contractors Indonesia v PT Kaltim Prima Coal and Standard Chartered Bank*,[76] where there were two agreements in relation to a coal mining project: agreement A provided for the constructor's right to be remunerated at a rate per tonne of coal produced and how to review that rate periodically, whereas agreement B was concerned with the distribution of the cash proceeds of the sale of coal produced. The former included an arbitra-

75 [2011] 2 All ER 245, [39]–[49] (Thomas LJ).
76 [2011] EWHC 1842 (Comm).

tion clause, whilst the latter contained a non-exclusive jurisdiction clause. Blair J held that the claim under agreement B was "a discrete claim, related to, but distinct from, the underlying dispute" arising under agreement A, and that there is no reason why the parties cannot be taken to have intended that these claims are to be the subject of different jurisdiction clause: "it is possible and commercially rational to do so, even though this may result in a degree of fragmentation in the resolution of the dispute".[77]

Sir Field then dealt with the exporter's submission. He ruled that the exporter was contractually bound by the NECJ to submit to the jurisdiction of the English court by reason of the assignment of the Note by the assured to Sinosure, because the Note contained specific provisions to that effect. Moreover, the exporter fully appreciated when it issued the Note that the Note would be assigned to Sinosure once Sinosure had paid the bank under the policy. The judge confirmed that the wording of the NEJC was clear and unambiguous. Since Sinosure had commenced proceedings on the Note before the English court, the exporter was bound to submit to the jurisdiction of that court, which was "an obligation that manifestly involves an implicit promise not to seek to have the proceedings determined by a reference under the arbitration clause". He therefore concluded that the issue in this case is whether the exporter was liable in English law on Sinosure's claim on the Note, and this was not altered by the fact that the exporter intended to raise a Nigerian law issue by way of defence arising under the Farm-In Agreements which were "quite separate" from the Note.[78]

Following this decision, Sinosure further applied for summary judgment[79] on its claim for payment on the Note. Knowles J, referring to *Nova (Jersey) Knit Ltd v Kammgarn Spinnerei GmbH*,[80] clarified that unless there were exceptional circumstances, a court would grant summary judgment on a claim under a promissory note and would not allow a defendant to assert some sort of set-off or counterclaim. The judge held that the buyer had no real prospect of successfully defending the claim and there was no other compelling reason why the case should be disposed of at a trial; even if the buyer could assert some sort of set-off or counterclaim that fell within the limited exceptions to the court's practice of granting summary judgment, it would be prevented from doing so by the contractual clause in the Note which barred set-off. Accordingly, Sinosure was held entitled to payment under the Note plus the interest that had accrued on it.

Although Sinosure succeeded in its proceedings, *Sinosure v Emerald* demonstrates the importance for insurers under ECI to examine any possibility of

77 Ibid.

78 The exporter began proceedings in Nigeria seeking: (i) a declaration that the Note was null and void on the basis that it had been procured under "economic duress"; (ii) an injunction preventing Sinosure from bringing winding up proceedings against it; and (iii) an order restraining winding up proceedings before any Court of law in furtherance of the enforcement of the Note. However, these proceedings had not been served by the time of the judgment of *Sinosure v Emerald*. See ibid, [35].

79 *Sinosure v Emerald* [2018] EWHC 3740 (Comm).

80 [1977] 1 WLR 713.

jurisdiction disputes in relation to the underlying transaction when taking an assignment. It is suggested that insurers stipulate an exclusive jurisdiction clause or ensure that documents of the underlying transaction are subject to a unified arbitration/jurisdiction clause.

Summary

The sections above demonstrated that in all aspects of the subrogation process in ECI, the English courts consistently treated ECI policies as ordinary insurance in deciding subrogation disputes.[81] Moreover, the English ECI cases which have been discussed above largely contributed to the development of the principles regarding subrogation in English insurance law. Those cases have become or will undoubtedly serve as valuable case authorities for future ECI cases and all other types of insurance cases. Moreover, the judgments in all those cases influenced the drafting of subrogation-related clauses in ECI policies today. ECAs now tend to include a well-drafted control of proceedings clause, subrogation protection clause and allocation of recoveries clause. In drafting those clauses, ECAs regard their policies as insurance.

Subrogation and recoveries under ECGs

The legal basis of the subrogation right in the context of guarantees

As Diplock J pointed out in *Yorkshire Insurance*, "the doctrine of subrogation is not restricted to the law of insurance".[82] It has long been accepted in English law that subrogation in insurance law is grounded in the nature of a contract of indemnity and is not a doctrine peculiar to contracts of insurance.[83] The subrogation right also exists in English guarantee law.[84] As is the case in insurance, in guarantees the subrogation right is not a right deriving from the contract[85] but one stemming from the relationship of the surety and creditor. In other words, equity intervenes to assist the surety to take over all the creditor's rights in respect of the guaranteed debt.[86] Subrogation in guarantees can also be analysed from the

81 This view is widely supported by academia. See, e.g., Merkin (n 5), [24-073]; Birds (n 61) 345; Birds and others (n 5), [24-025].

82 [1962] 2 QB 330, 339.

83 *Simpson v Thomson* (1877) 3 App Cas 279, 284; *Castellain v Preston* (1883) 11 QBD 380, 394, 401–3; *Burnand v Rodocanachi* (1882) 7 App Cas 333, 339; *Morris v Ford Motor Co* [1973] QB 792.

84 *Craythorne v Swinburne* (1807) 14 Ves Jr 160, 162 (Sir Samuel Romilly); See also *Morgan v Seymour* (1638) 1 Rep Ch 120, 21 ER 525, *Ex p. Crisp* (1744) 1 Atk 133; *Aldrich v Cooper* (1803) 8 Ves Jr 382, 34 ER 1050; *Newton v Chorlton* (1853) 10 Hare 346, 61 ER 748; *Highbury Pension Fund Management Co v Zirfin Investments Ltd* [2013] EWCA Civ 1283, [2014] Ch 359.

85 *Yonge v Reynell* (1852) 9 Hare 809, 68 ER 744; *Duncan Fox & Co v North & South Wales Bank* (1880) LR 6 App Cas 1, 13 (Lord Selborne).

86 *Aldrich v Cooper* (1803) 8 Ves Jr 382, 384–9 (Lord Eldon LC), 34 ER 1050; *Nicholas v Ridley* [1904] 1 Ch 192; *Lord Harburton v Bennett* (1829) Beat 386. See also the Hon Mrs Justice Ger-

perspective of restitution under the doctrine of unjust enrichment. Such a doctrine operates to treat the security, which is discharged by the payment to the creditor, as if it were still available to the surety to assist him in recovering the amount he has paid in reduction or extinction of the principal debt.[87] Similar to insurance, the subrogation right in guarantees arises only after the surety has paid in full to the creditor the amount he guarantees.[88] The common law principle of subrogation in the context of guarantees was codified by s 5 of the Mercantile Law Amendment Act 1856, which provides that having made payment, a surety is subrogated to the rights of the creditor against the debtor.

All analysis above shows that in terms of subrogation, insurance and guarantee share highly similar characteristics. One might question whether the doctrine of subrogation has been confirmed in the context of ECGs. There has been no English case regarding subrogation in ECGs, whereas the doctrine of subrogation in ECGs was examined by the Scottish court in *Export Credits Guarantee Department v Turner*.[89] The facts in *Turner* were similar to that in *Miller, Gibb*: the ECGD issued a supplier credit guarantee facility to the bank who made advances to the exporter against goods exported to the foreign buyer. The ECGD and the exporter concluded a recourse agreement, Clause 3 of which read as below:

> The Exporter hereby acknowledges and declares that all sums received by the Exporter … in respect of any transaction which is the subject of a Guaranteed Advance shall … be received and held in trust by the Exporter for the Guarantor until the Exporter has made such repayment to the Bank or has paid to the Guarantor the amount of any demand made by the Guarantor in respect of that Guaranteed Advance.

The exporter then became insolvent and went into voluntary liquidation. A sum of £4,623, which was the subject of the guaranteed transaction, was received by the liquidator after liquidation from the buyer. The ECGD claimed that Clause 3 constituted a trust whereby the liquidator held the money received by the buyer as trustee for the ECGD and that the money should not be made available to the general body of creditors. The liquidator, on the other hand, argued that Clause 3 had not established a trust and that the ECGD should merely be listed as an ordinary creditor.

Two submissions were made by the ECGD. The core submission, which argued that Clause 3 constituted a trust, was rejected by the trial and appeal courts. Both courts held that the wording of Clause 3 was not sufficiently clear to achieve that effect.[90] A detailed analysis was made by Lord Justice-Clerk (Wheatley) of the

---

aldine Andrews & Richard Millett QC, *Law of Guarantees* (7th edn, Sweet & Maxwell 2015), [11-017].

87 *Banque Keyser* [1999] 1 AC 221. See also Andrews & Millett, ibid.

88 *Re Howe Ex p. Brett* (1871) LR6 Ch App 838, 841 (Mellish LJ).

89 1979 SC 286.

90 Due to space limitations, the legal elements of a trust are not the focus in this work. For details see ibid., 293–4 (Clerk Wheatley LJ).

appeal court, who pointed out that the subjects of a trust should be all the "debts" to be incurred by the exporter's buyers, rather than just "all sums" actually made by the buyers as stipulated in Clause 3. Therefore, his lordship held that Clause 3 created no effective trust but only a contractual obligation on the exporter, which did not bind the liquidator.

The subsidiary submission, which was made by the ECGD in the trial but subsequently abandoned in the appeal, was that the insurance principle of subrogation applied to the transaction in that case. The only case authority the ECGD referred to was *Miller, Gibb*, the ECI case regarding the juridical basis of subrogation which has been discussed above. However, that argument was regarded as "unsound" by the trial court. Lord Ordinary (Dunpark) clarified that the ECGD in that case did not pay the bank under an insurance policy "but as a guarantor". The judge further stated that the principle of subrogation "has never, so far as I am aware", been applied to guarantees. Given that the ECGD failed to submit further authorities which showed any good reason why the principle of subrogation should be extended to guarantees, the judge rejected the ECGD's subsidiary submission.[91]

This research argues that *Turner* is not sufficient to indicate that the principle of subrogation does not apply to ECGs. There are several reasons why the courts in *Turner* reached their conclusions. First of all, *Turner* is a Scottish case. All above-mentioned English guarantee case authorities about subrogation are not binding the Scottish courts but can only serve as persuasive authorities.[92] The Mercantile Law Amendment Act 1856 does not apply in Scotland, either.[93] Secondly, the ECGD in that case adopted the wrong legal tactics. It did not raise the argument of subrogation as the core submission but focused on the constitution of trust which was rejected by both the trial and appeal courts. Worse still was that in supporting its subsidiary submission, the ECGD only referred to *Miller, Gibb*, an ECI rather than ECG case, without citing any guarantee case authorities. The paragraphs above have shown that there have equally been plenty of English cases that established that the principle of subrogation applied to guarantees, but unfortunately, the counsel for the ECGD did not cite any of them before the court. Nevertheless, what can be learned from *Turner* is the importance of clarifying the legal nature of ECGs. Regarding the ECG as a contract of guarantee rather than an insurance policy, Lord Dunpark refused to rely on *Miller, Gibb*. Should the ECGD cite the correct guarantee case authorities, the decision in *Turner* might be different.

Notably, *Turner* was decided in the late 1970s, whereas in *Liberty Mutual Insurance Company (UK) Ltd & Another v HSBC Bank plc*,[94] a relatively recent case, the English court again confirmed that the principle of subrogation applied

91 Ibid, 291 (Lord Dunpark).

92 Abigail Bremner, "Civil Justice-Civil Courts and Tribunals", in *Scottish Parliament Information Centre Briefing*, SB 16/98 <https://archive2021.parliament.scot/ResearchBriefingsAndFactsheets/S5/SB_16-98_Civil_Justice_-_Civil_Courts_and_Tribunals.pdf> accessed 1 February 2022.

93 See the Mercantile Law Amendment Act 1856, s 17.

94 [2002] EWCA Civ 691, [2002] 5 WLUK 424.

to guarantees. In this case, the creditor (who was a bank) provided an admiralty bond to the debtor (who was a P&I club). The creditor took a fixed charge over all the debtor's book debts as a continuing security. A surety bond was issued by the surety (an insurance company that also run guarantee business) to support and secure the creditor's engagements. The surety bond, which was a contract of guarantee, included a clause (hereinafter referred to as "the separation clause") stating that "this agreement is separate from any other security or right of indemnity taken in respect of this guarantee from any person". Subsequently, the debtor became insolvent, and the creditor looked to the surety to recoup its losses under its engagements. The surety, prior to making payment under the surety bond, contended that once it paid in full, it should be entitled to be subrogated to the creditor's security under its fixed charge on the debtor's book debts. The creditor, however, argued that the separation clause excluded or at least postponed the surety's subrogation right. The creditor's submission seemed far-fetched, but prior to construing the separation clause in dispute, Rix LJ wrote substantial paragraphs on clarifying the nature of subrogation, which, in the learned judge's opinion, was a preliminary issue. His lordship stated that:[95]

> There was no dispute about the applicable principles of subrogation. It is a remedy, rather than a cause of action, founded in equity and natural justice not in contract, designed to prevent unjust enrichment … An insurer as well as a surety is entitled to the rights of subrogation when once he has paid the assured … Thus, subrogation provides to the surety or the insurer an equitable or proprietary interest in the creditor's rights against the debtor.

In addition to confirming the common law principle of subrogation in the context of guarantees, Rix LJ also referred to s 5 of the Mercantile Amendment Act 1856. Based on that position, his lordship held that clear words were required to remove the surety's right of subrogation. Given that subrogation was not expressly mentioned in the separation clause, his lordship "firmly concluded" that the surety's subrogation right remained intact.[96] Arden LJ, in her concurring opinion, added that the true intention of the separation clause should be that the proceeds of the surety bond should be kept separately in a security realisation account and not applied in reducing the amount due from the debtor until the creditor chose to apply those proceeds in this way.[97] However, since the separation clause failed to be so formulated, it could not have the effect of excluding or postponing the surety's subrogation right. Both judges thought that such clauses were "contrary to commercial reality" and could lead to "odd results": "if they have been agreed, so be it; but it is not easy to see how they are to be found in the clause's brief wording".[98]

95 Ibid, [43]–[46] (Rix LJ).
96 Ibid, 42, 58–60 (Rix LJ).
97 Ibid, 104 (Arden LJ).
98 Ibid, 61 (Rix LJ). For a similar examination of the principles of subrogation in the context of guarantees, see *Ibrahim v Barclays Bank Plc* [2011] EWHC 1897, [2013] Ch 400.

Liberty indicates that the judgment in *Turner* was incorrect: the surety's subrogation right stems from equity rather than being based on the contract. The surety need not create a trust to secure its subrogation right. On the contrary, subrogation is inherent in equity and natural justice, exclusion of or limitation on which requires clear words. It is therefore submitted that the ECA was entitled to the subrogation right against the debtor under ECGs, based on all abovementioned common law authorities as well as s 5 of the Mercantile Amendment Act 1856.

Although the legal basis of the ECA's subrogation right under ECGs now seems ascertained, further questions remain to be answered. First, how does the subrogation right operate under ECGs? Second, do ECG contracts share similar characteristics with ECI policies regarding subrogation and recoveries? Third, if so, what should the law be regarding subrogation and recoveries under ECGs? The following paragraphs will explore how the subrogation right operates under ECGs by reading the subrogation provisions in a sample ECG contract kindly shared by an anonymous Berne Union member during the Berne Union Academic Survey.

The subrogation provisions under ECGs

The subrogation protection clause

This research found that the sample ECG contract from the anonymous Berne Union member includes as detailed provisions regarding subrogation as ECI policies do. It stipulates a subrogation protection clause to ensure that the creditor will not prejudice the ECA's subrogation right. Clause 10 of the sample ECG contract provides that:

> Assignment and Subrogation of Lender's Rights Under the Financing
>
> In consideration of a Guarantee Payment by [the ECA] to Lender regarding a Financing (and pro-rata to the extent that the Guarantee Payment represents a portion of the obligations of Debtor under such Financing), immediately after a disbursement from [the ECA] to Lender of such Guarantee Payment …
>
> (a) Lender shall unconditionally and irrevocably transfer and assign to [the ECA] all of its right, title in or to, all claims of Lender against Debtor under such Financing,
> (b) [The ECA] shall be subrogated to such claims of the Lender against the Debtor (and any guarantors thereof) and
> (c) [The ECA] shall succeed to any liens held by the Lender against any assets of the Debtor or otherwise granted in respect of the Financing.
>
> The Financing Documents shall provide Lender with sufficient rights to transfer and assign to [the ECA] all of Lender's right, title in or to, all claims thereunder.

It appears that the subrogation protection clause under ECGs is highly identical to the subrogation protection clause under ECI discussed above. Under provisions such as Clause 10, the creditor is obliged to preserve the ECA's subrogation right.

The collection of recoveries clause

ECG contracts may also include a collection of recoveries clause stipulating that the creditor shall at the ECA's election either effect recoveries itself or authorise and assist the ECA to effect recoveries in its name. Meanwhile, some ECAs might emphasise that it is the creditor's sole duty to effect recoveries under ECGs. For instance, Clause 11(a) of the sample ECG contract from the anonymous Berne Union member provides that (1) the bank, as the creditor, should seek to collect debts from the debtor buyer, whether judicially, extra-judicially or by arbitration; (2) in particular, the bank should commence legal proceedings against the buyer within 60 days of the ECA's guarantee payment; (3) the bank should make regular reports to the ECA, every six months, on the progress of the collection proceedings; (4) if, after collection proceedings, the bank cannot recover the debts, it should provide evidence of such "non-recoverability" by submitting relevant documents including "an opinion of outside counsel ... confirming the extent of such non-recovery ..."; and (5) if the non-recovery of the debts is because of the bank's negligence or omission, then the bank should fully refund the ECA the guarantee payment plus interest.[99]

It is submitted that although such a detailed clause seems onerous to the bank, it merely specifies the bank's duty to collect recoveries. It cannot indicate that under ECGs the bank is under a heavier duty to effect recoveries than under ECI: the bank under the ECG cover is obliged to refund the ECG payment only if the non-recovery of debts is because of its negligence or omission.

The allocation of recoveries clause

ECG contracts also include an allocation of recoveries clause, just as ECI policies do. For instance, Clause 10 of the ECG contract from the anonymous Berne Union member provides that the bank should, deducting the collection costs it incurs, hold the recoveries in trust for the ECA:

> For the avoidance of doubt, if the Guaranteed Amount equals 100% percent of the amount of the Financing, [the ECA] shall retain all amounts recovered

99 Clause 11(c)(iii) provides that:

> In the event that recovery of some or all of the unpaid portion of a Financing...is not possible because (a) Lender did not commence a judicial, extra-judicial or arbitral proceeding in a timely manner, (b) Lender does not act with reasonable diligence in the course of such collection efforts or (c) there is a final adverse decision against Lender or [the ECA] because of a procedural right which has been barred or not timely exercised, to the extent such bar or failure to exercise has adversely impacted the outcome of the proceeding and is attributable exclusively to actions or inactions of Lender, Lender shall immediately reimburse [the ECA] the amount of the Guarantee Payment plus interest. Interest on such reimbursement shall accrue at the Financing Rate from the date such Guarantee Payment was made through the date the amount of the Guarantee Payment is returned; provided that interest shall be at the Default Rate to the extent reimbursement payment is not received within such five (5) Business Day period.

> under any such Financing to the extent that the Guaranteed Amount is less than the full amount of Debtor's obligations under the relevant Financing, then [the ECA] shall retain a pro rata portion of all amounts recovered under such Financing that correspond to the Guaranteed Amount.
>
> In the event that … Lender receives any payment, distribution or other property after such assignment which should have been paid or distributed to [the ECA], Lender shall hold such payment in trust for [the ECA] and
>
> (i) deduct the amount equal to Lender's out of pocket expenses (including reasonable attorneys' fees) incurred in connection with its attempts to collect payments from the Debtor and
> (ii) promptly pay or transfer the balance to [the ECA].

It is uncertain whether, by including an allocation of recoveries clause as above, the ECA will be entitled proportionately to both the recoveries up to the guaranteed amount and any surplus of the recoveries. Therefore, it is necessary to explore what the law should be regarding subrogation issues in ECG contracts.

What should the law be regarding subrogation and recoveries issues in ECG contracts?

The paragraphs above show that the subrogation provisions in ECGs are highly similar to that in ECI. However, whilst the English courts have fully elaborated the law on subrogation in ECI cases, there have been no reported English ECG cases confirming what the law should be regarding subrogation issues in ECGs. The lack of English case authorities on ECGs is due to the fact that ECG products are less common in the market than ECI covers. The Berne Union Academic Survey found that only 4 of the total 27 respondents members provide ECG products. However, that does not mean that ECGs are not as important to the export industry as ECI. On the contrary, an ECG is a very important type of export credit facilities product in the market because it is unconditional, on-demand and highly preferred by banks. The ECA sometimes issue both an ECG and an ECI cover to support one single transaction and an ECG is sometimes irreplaceable for some transactions, which will be discussed in Chapter 7. That said, despite the limited availability of ECG products, it is equally necessary to consider what should the law be regarding subrogation issues in ECG contracts.

This research submits that the well-established law on subrogation in English ECI cases can be referred to by the English courts in future ECG cases as a helpful analogy. Whilst the Scottish court in *Turner* held that the principle of subrogation did not apply to ECGs, its judgment was questionable. The English courts, in both early and recent guarantee cases, all held that the principle of subrogation fully applied to guarantee contracts. Moreover, the sections above show that the subrogation provisions in ECGs are highly similar to their counterparts in ECI policies. Therefore, whereas the difference between ECGs and ECI is important regarding issues such as the duty of fair presentation and claim settlement, there is no significant difference between these two types of products regarding subrogation. It is submitted that the English courts should establish the following rules regarding subrogation and recoveries in ECGs by referring to English ECI cases including *Miller, Gibb*, *AB Svensk ExportKredit*, *Lucas*, *Lonrho* and *Kent Engineering & Foundry*:

(1) The creditor, i.e., the bank, should at all times preserve the ECA's subrogation right. In the absence of clear and express wording in the ECG contract, the creditor has exclusive control of its proceedings against the debtor;
(2) The ECA and the creditor shall share pro rata the recoveries for the amount up to the guaranteed amount under the ECG cover. Any surplus of the recoveries, in the absence of clear and express wording to the contrary, belongs to the creditor;
(3) In case of an international debt rescheduling arrangement conducted by the ECA's government and the debtor's government, any payments received from the latter should be regarded as the State property of the ECA's country, unless the ECA, in the process of rescheduling, has specified that certain part of the payments constitutes the recoveries under the ECG cover.

Conclusion

This chapter explores the legal issues regarding subrogation and recoveries in ECI and ECGs and contributes to the overarching theme of this research in the following aspects:

On the one hand, English ECI cases regarding subrogation disputes, such as *Miller*, *Euler Hermes*, *AB Svensk ExportKredit*, *Lucas*, *Lonrho* and *Kent Engineering & Foundry*, confirm that ECI policies are contracts of insurance. In all those cases, the English courts, treating ECI as ordinary insurance, not only made their decisions relying on previous insurance law case authorities but also contributed to the developments of the principles of subrogation in English insurance law.

On the other hand, although there is no reported English ECG case concerning subrogation, English guarantee cases demonstrate that the juridical basis of subrogation in guarantees is the same as that in insurance. Moreover, subrogation provisions in ECG contracts show that the ECA's subrogation right operates in a very similar way to that in ECI. Therefore, the principle of subrogation should fully apply to ECG contracts, and the English courts can refer to the rules regarding subrogation and recoveries established in ECI cases as a helpful analogy in determining relevant ECG cases in the future.

It thus seems that the difference between ECI and ECGs is insignificant in terms of subrogation. As pointed out by the commentator, "it is not always necessary to determine whether the contract is one of insurance or guarantee as they share many characteristics, although they also have important differences".[100] It

100 Merkin (n 18), [A-004].

can be said that in terms of subrogation, ECI and ECGs share similar characteristics. Therefore, this research submits that the law regarding subrogation and recoveries should be the same in ECI and ECG contracts. The courts should refer to English ECI cases as an analogy when deciding subrogation issues in future ECG cases.

References

Andrews, G & Millett, R, *Law of Guarantees* (7th edn, Sweet & Maxwell 2015)
Birds, J, *Modern Insurance Law* (10th edn, Sweet & Maxwell 2016)
Birds, J, Lynch, B & Paul, S, *MacGillivray on Insurance Law* (14th edn, Sweet & Maxwell 2018)
Merkin, R, *Colinvaux and Merkin's Insurance Contract Law* (Sweet & Maxwell 2021)
Merkin, R, *Colinvaux's Law of Insurance* (12th edn, Sweet & Maxwell 2019)

7 Why ECAs provide ECGs in addition to ECI

The legal nature of ECI and ECGs as revealed in Chapters 2–6

Chapters 2–6 have made the following findings regarding the legal nature of export credit insurance (ECI) and export credit guarantees (ECGs):

- How are ECI and ECGs used in the export credit industry?

  Chapter 2 demonstrated that ECI is the mainstream product in the export credit industry, whereas some ECAs provide ECGs in addition to ECI. In terms of the "basic" cover, ECAs and private credit insurers always insure the exporter. In terms of supplier and buyer credit transactions, ECAs either insure or guarantee the bank.
- Are ECI and ECG contracts of insurance and guarantee in their legal nature? Do the principles of insurance law and guarantee law apply to them, respectively?

  Chapters 2–6 indicated that the answers should both be "yes". ECI is a contract of indemnity insurance, and an ECG is a contract of unconditional and on-demand guarantee. Chapter 2 showed that the formation process of ECI and ECGs is similar to that of general contracts of insurance and guarantee. Chapters 3–6 demonstrated that in English ECI cases regarding different issues such as the credit limit clause, the exclusion clause, the conditions precedent to liability, the duty of fair presentation, the claim handling process as well as subrogation and recoveries, the English courts all regarded ECI as a contract of insurance and all applied general principles of insurance law. In addition, Chapters 2–6 discussed various standard form ECI clauses drafted and revised by the UK Export Finance (UKEF) and anonymous Berne Union members in response to the enactment of the IA 2015, which indicates that in revising those clauses, they clearly take the IA 2015 into consideration. On the other hand, Chapters 2–6 also revealed that although there are fewer reported ECG cases, in those cases the English courts all regarded ECGs as ordinary contracts of guarantee, too.
- What are the differences between the legal characteristics of ECI and ECGs?

  The discussion throughout Chapters 2–6 pointed to a clear answer: from a contractual perspective, an ECG is a client-friendlier product and easier than

DOI: 10.4324/b22864-7

ECI for banks to use. Chapter 2 analysed that the formation process of supplier credit insurance could cause great difficulties to banks, whereas the formation of supplier credit guarantees is very straightforward. Chapter 3 showed that the assured under ECI is subject to a number of contractual limitations, such as the insuring clause, the exclusion of documentation risk as well as various types of conditions precedent and warranties. Those restrictions, however, are not seen in ECG contracts. An ECG is an unconditional and on-demand guarantee, under which the ECA, as the surety, merely guarantees to pay the bank should the principal debtor default in payment. Chapter 4 demonstrated that ECI is a contract of utmost good faith under which the bank is subject to the duty of fair presentation, whereas such a duty does not apply to ECGs. Chapter 5 discussed the waiting period clause and the "arbitration award/judgment" clause, the two peculiar clauses that could prolong the claim handling process of ECI, and again, such clauses are not seen in ECG contracts. Of course, ECI and ECGs share some similarities, especially in terms of subrogation and recoveries, an observation made in Chapter 6.

It thus becomes clear that an ECG has significant strengths over ECI regarding contractual terms, which makes an ECG a preferred product for banks. However, why do ECGs remain a relatively rare product in the market, and why do ECAs provide ECGs in addition to ECI? Based on the findings made by the previous chapters, this chapter aims to explore the answer from an empirical perspective.

Why do ECGs remain a less popular product?

It is first necessary to discuss why ECGs remain a less popular product. This research submits that several practical reasons explain such a state of affairs.

ECI works well in most circumstances

The Berne Union Academic Survey found that ECI seems to work well in most circumstances. On the one hand, Berne Union members indicated that there is no evidence that there are more claims rejected under ECI than under ECGs: they always handle the claim with due diligence and good faith under ECI as they do under ECGs.[1] In other words, they believed that they do not arbitrarily use the terms and conditions of an ECI policy as an unsubstantiated excuse to reject a claim. On the other hand, banks might not be really concerned about the differences between ECI and ECGs. For instance, as demonstrated in Chapter 3, the exclusion of the documentation risk is a peculiar clause in ECI, but some banks

1 Cheng Lin, "Berne Union Academic Survey: The Legal Nature of Buyer Credit Insurance and Buyer Credit Guarantee", *The BUlletin (The Official Newsletter of the Berne Union)*, January 2020, 31 <https://www.berneunion.org/Articles/Details/489/January-BUlletin-Mega-Trends-and-Trade> accessed 1 February 2022.

who took part in the Berne Union Academic Survey said that they were fine with such an exclusion. They believed that prudent banks would rarely suffer a loss due to the documentation risk.[2]

This research submits that that reason alone cannot fully explain why ECGs remain a less popular product. Indeed, ECI seems to work well in most circumstances, but the devil is always in the details. As demonstrated in the previous chapters, there are always significant differences between the contractual terms and legal characteristics of ECI and ECGs, ignorance of which could result in potential severe disputes. That has been evidenced by the fact that there have been far more reported English ECI cases than ECG cases. Banks, as the user of ECI and ECGs, might not be really concerned about whether an export facility is called "insurance" or a "guarantee" because they are not really aware of the differences between ECI and ECGs. However, one thing for sure is that they always prefer a contract that is easier to use: the "cleaner" the contract, the better.[3] Therefore, an ECG contract, due to its legal characteristics, is always friendlier to banks than ECI. The following paragraphs seek to further explore whether there are other factors that make ECGs a less popular type of product.

The costs for ECGs are higher than ECI

Consistent with the findings of this research, the respondents to the Berne Union Academic Survey agreed that ECGs are "better" than ECI in many aspects, but in the meantime, they also pointed out that ECGs are considerably more expensive.[4] Indeed, the premium rates for ECGs are generally higher than ECI, which has been evidenced by OECD's Agreement on Officially Supported Export Credits (OECD Agreement). According to art 29(b) of the OECD Agreement, all export credit facilities provided by the ECAs of the OECD members can be classified into three categories:

(a) "Below standard products", i.e., insurance products which do not cover the waiting period interest, and insurance products which cover the waiting period interest with an appropriate premium surcharge;
(b) "Standard products", i.e., insurance products which cover the waiting period interest without an appropriate premium surcharge; and
(c) "Above standard products", i.e., all guarantee products.

Under Annex IX of the OECD Agreement, different minimum premium rates (MPRs) shall apply to those three types of products respectively. The MPR for "above standard products", which are ECG products, is the highest among the three.[5]

2 Ibid.
3 Ibid.
4 Ibid, 27.
5 The formula for calculating the applicable MPR is provided in Annex IX of the OECD's Agreement.

That is an important reason why an ECG is a less common product. An ECG, indeed, is friendlier to banks than ECI, but turning the coin, it is more "burdensome" to ECAs. The commercial and political risks that an ECA undertakes are similar under ECI and ECGs. However, without the protection of a number of restrictions and exclusions on the coverage and conditions precedent to liability they would have under an ECI policy, ECAs are more likely to bear a loss under an ECG. That, of course, can be compensated by a higher premium of the ECG, but the higher premium adds to the costs of the bank.[6] Therefore, most ECAs choose to provide ECI covers only, and some ECAs provide ECGs mainly because they take the organisational form of an Eximbank (which is the abbreviation of "Export-Import Bank"), and according to the financial regulation in their countries, banks are not allowed to provide insurance products.[7] In other words, had they taken the form of an insurance company, they would probably have also chosen to provide ECI products.[8]

The processing time for underwriting an ECG cover is longer than ECI

In the Berne Union Academic Survey, some respondents also indicated that the processing time for underwriting an ECG cover is longer than ECI: since an ECG is not a contract *uberrimae fidei* and the documentation risk is borne by an ECG, the ECA needs to vet all the underlying documents.[9] By contrast, as seen in Chapter 2, most ECAs and private credit insurers have developed a standard procedure for an ECI contract to be concluded. The bank completes a standard proposal form, and the ECA/private credit insurer issues a standard term ECI policy. In export credit transactions, business efficacy matters. That is perhaps a reason why many banks are willing to choose ECI over ECGs.

The division of the global market by ECAs and private credit insurers

Another reason why ECGs are less popular lies in the current division of the global export credit market by ECAs and private credit insurers. Traditionally, private insurers were reluctant to take credit risks caused by certain political and commercial events.[10] However, due to the "development of more sophisti-

6 And this ultimately adds to the cost of the exporter (in supplier credit transactions) or the buyer (in buyer credit transactions), since banks normally shift the costs of premiums to them. See Zlatko Salcic, *Export Credit Insurance & Guarantees: A Practitioner's Guide* (Palgrave Macmillan 2014) 130. See also < https://www.gov.uk/guidance/export-working-capital-scheme-overview-and-how-to-apply> accessed 1 February 2022, where the UKEF states in the light of supplier credit guarantees that "the guaranteed lender pays us a guarantee fee; this is a proportion of the interest margin received from the UK exporter for providing the working capital facility".

7 See Delio E. Gianturco, *Export Credit Agencies: The Unsung Giants of International Trade and Finance* (Quorum 2001) 126–31.

8 Lin (n 1) 24.

9 Ibid, 25, 30, 31.

10 Private insurers were unwilling to take export credit risks because of the long payment terms of credits, the lack of experience in recovering losses in foreign jurisdictions, the difficulties in

cated models for risks analysis, the new techniques for database handling and the establishment of an international network",[11] they are now more and more active in the global market.[12] Nevertheless, they still prefer underwriting short-term risks rather than offering medium- and long-term covers.[13] As explained in Chapter 2, all short-term export credit facilities are provided to exporters in the form of ECI.[14] Therefore, private credit insurers normally provide ECI products only, especially short-term "basic" ECI covers.

In response to that tendency, there have been some international rules which require ECAs to avoid competing with private credit insurers. For instance, under art 5 of the OECD Agreement, ECAs of all OECD members are not allowed to provide ECI or ECGs with a duration of less than two years if the foreign buyer is from an EU or OECD member country. Moreover, under art 3.1(a) of WTO's Agreement on Subsidies and Countervailing Measures, ECAs of all WTO members can provide ECI and ECG covers only if the premium rates are adequate to cover the ECA's "long-term operating costs and losses of the programmes". The WTO and OECD rules have helped to "foster a level playing field for official support in order to encourage competition among exporters based on quality and price of goods and services exported rather than on the most favourable officially supported financial terms and conditions" and thereby prevented potential trade distortion and subsidies.[15]

In compliance with those rules, ECAs tend to play a complementary role in the market. For instance, for the exporter to be insured by the UKEF's "Export Insurance Policy", a "basic" ECI cover discussed in the previous chapters, the UKEF requires that (a) the exporter should demonstrate that it could not obtain an ECI cover from any private credit insurers, and (b) the export contract should be no less than two years, and the foreign buyer should be based outside the EU or other OECD countries.[16]

That said, a considerable portion of the current global export credit market is occupied by private credit insurers who provide ECI only. According to the "Berne Union 2020 State of the Industry Report", by the end of 2020, short-term export credit facilities took up 65% of the total outstanding amount insured/guaranteed by all types of products offered by the Berne Union members.[17] The public and private share (i.e., the share between ECAs and private credit insurers) of

---

assessing the financial standing of foreign buyers and the political developments in the world. See Salcic (n 6) 10.

11 Anders Grath, *The Handbook of International Trade and Finance* (Kogan Page 2008) 113.

12 Ibid, 112–6.

13 Salcic (n 6) 40.

14 See also ibid, 37.

15 The OECD Arrangement, art 1(ii).

16 See < https://www.gov.uk/guidance/export-insurance-policy> accessed 1 February 2022.

17 Berne Union, "2020 State of the Industry Report" (8 November 2021), 17 <https://www.berneunion.org/Articles/Details/606/2020-State-of-the-Industry-Report> accessed 1 February 2022.

those short-term facilities was 30% versus 70%.[18] In terms of the medium- and long-term export credit facilities which made up 25%[19] of the total outstanding commitments by the Berne Union members, the public and private share was 90% versus 10%. As can be evidenced by Appendix 2 of this work, the majority of those medium- and long-term facilities are also provided in the form of supplier/buyer credit insurance rather than supplier/buyer credit guarantees. Therefore, whether in short-term or medium- and long-term facilities, ECI products always prevail.

Why are ECGs still significant?

Despite all the factors that make ECGs less popular than ECI, from the perspective of the bank, an ECG is a client-friendlier product, without which some banks might be reluctant to finance the trade. Therefore, some sophisticated ECAs with good experience and portfolios tend to take a "compromised" approach: on the one hand, they provide ECI as the main product which is not as easy to use as an ECG but generally more affordable for banks; on the other hand, they offer ECGs as a tailored facility in certain transactions to cater to the needs of some banks. ECGs, therefore, still play an important role. The paragraphs below seek to illustrate how ECGs are used in supplier credit transactions and buyer credit transactions, respectively.

In supplier credit transactions: how is an ECG used as a "top-up" facility together with ECI?

An ECG can be used as a "top-up" facility together with ECI in supplier credit transactions to cater to the needs of the bank. In such a scenario, the ECA provides a "basic" ECI cover to the exporter and a supplier credit guarantee to the bank. As has been explained in Chapter 2, under a "basic" ECI cover, the ECA insures the exporter against the political and commercial risks, and under a supplier credit guarantee, where the bank purchases the negotiable instruments from the exporter, the ECA guarantees that the negotiable documents will be honoured. Since the bank here is guaranteed rather than insured by the ECA, it acquires a stronger form of security and is thus more willing to provide the finance.[20]

18 Ibid, 11.

19 Apart from short-term (65%) and medium and long-term (25%) export credit facilities, the remaining 10% of the total outstanding commitments consisted of overseas investment insurance and domestic credit insurance, which fall outside the scope of this research. See ibid.

20 Sometimes the exporter also assigns the "basic" ECI policy to the bank to access finance. However, Chapter 2 has demonstrated that such an arrangement must be made in a clear and unambiguous way, otherwise the bank might take the risk of not being recognised as the assured by the court. That said, an ECG cover directly issued to the bank from the outset is always the best form of security.

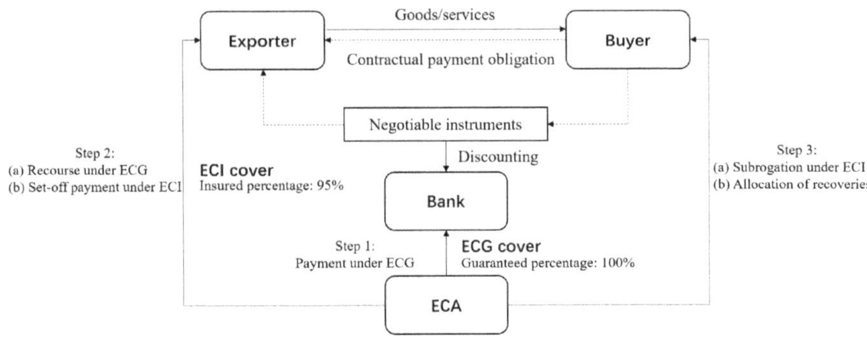

Figure 7.1 How an ECG is used together with ECI in supplier credit transactions

The supplier credit guarantee functions together with the "basic" ECI cover under a set-off arrangement which works in the following way:[21] under the "basic" ECI cover, the debtor is the buyer, and under the supplier credit guarantee, the debtor is the exporter. If the buyer fails to pay, then there will be two interrelated consequences: (a) the bank makes a claim under the ECG and (b) the exporter makes a claim under ECI. What the ECA will do is to (a) pay the bank under the ECG and (b) exercise its right of recourse against the exporter.[22] Since the exporter is the assured under ECI, it can, according to the set-off clause which is usually embedded in the ECI policy,[23] set off the debt against the payment under ECI. For instance, if the insured percentage under ECI is 95% and the guaranteed percentage under the ECG is 100%, then the ECA, after paying in full to the bank, can set off 95% of the amount of loss against the payment under ECI with the exporter. Then the ECA can be subrogated into the exporter's rights against the buyer under the ECI policy. After effecting recoveries, if there is any surplus available, the ECA can keep the 5% of uninsured loss as long as it includes an express allocation of recoveries clause to that effect in the ECI policy. How an ECG and ECI work under such a set-off arrangement is illustrated in Figure 7.1.

The pattern above is not uncommon in the industry and has been fully considered by the English courts in *Credit Lyonnais Bank Nederland NV (now Generale*

21 Cheng Lin, "Why Export Credit Agencies Provide Guarantees in addition to Insurance: A Contractual Perspective" [2021] (1) LMCLQ 149, 162–3. See also Eva Lomnicka, "Export Credit Guarantees", in Michael Bridge (ed.), *Benjamin's Sales of Goods* (11th edn, Sweet & Maxwell 2020), [25-034].

22 The exporter normally signs an agreement at the outset of the transaction giving the ECA such right of recourse. See *Export Credits Guarantee Department v Davenport (Shoes) Limited* [1983] 2 WLUK 36.

23 For instance, Clause 12.1 of the UKEF's "Export Insurance Policy" provides that "UKEF may at its option set off any amounts due to or from the Insured under this Policy or any other contracts."

Bank Nederland NV) v Export Credits Guarantee Department[24] and *Export Credits Guarantee Department v Davenport (Shoes) Limited*,[25] which both illustrated the reason why an ECG is used together with ECI in supplier credit transactions. The House of Lords in *Credit Lyonnais* recognised that ECGs "can be valuable to exporters who need to obtain immediate finance for their exports" and "would make it easier for exporters to obtain finance from their bankers by way of loan";[26] Ackner LJ in *ECGD v Davenport* also pointed out that ECGs and ECI, as two "interrelated schemes", could help exporters run their business more effectively and, particularly, the ECG cover would encourage the bank to finance the exporter's business. The learned judge also cited ECGD's pamphlet which explained the "combined effect" of ECI and ECGs:[27]

> Because the ECG is guaranteed to the bank as unconditional and for 100% of the value of the bills or notes, the exporter signs an agreement at the outset giving ECGD recourse, in the event of payment being made by the bank in excess of the amount due to the exporter under the credit insurance policy.

In buyer credit transactions: how is an ECG used as a standalone and tailored product to support transactions of a larger amount and a longer credit period?

Supplier credit facilities are not always suitable for exporters and banks. If a transaction involves more than just delivery of goods/services or covers a larger amount or a longer credit period, then supplier credit facilities are not compatible. Buyer credit facilities are the most compatible choice for such transactions.[28] For instance, if the exporter undertakes to complete a major project regarding the construction of infrastructures or factories, then the transaction cannot be sim-

24 [1999] CLC 823.

25 [1983] 2 WLUK 36.

26 *Credit Lyonnais* [1999] CLC 823, 859. For a similar analysis, see *Crown Aluminium Ltd v Northern and Western Insurance Co Ltd* [2011] EWHC 1352 (TCC), [14], where Edward-Stuart J clarified that the advantage of a supplier credit guarantee was that the buyer would be able to discount the bill of exchange so that it could pay its suppliers straight away whilst obtaining credit for a long period.

27 *ECGD v Davenport* [1983] 2 WLUK 36. In this case the ECA paid the bank under the ECG when the bills of exchange were due and then exercised the right of recourse against the exporter. The ECI policy provided a six-month waiting period and, when the buyers failed to pay on the due date, the exporter duly sent to the ECA a notice of probable loss. However, the exporter agreed to extend the due date without the ECA's prior written consent, thereby breaching Clause 17 of the ECI policy in this case. The ECA was thus held not liable to indemnify the exporter under ECI, and accordingly there was no payment under ECI that the exporter could set off against its debt to the ECA. The exporter was therefore held liable to reimburse the ECA.

28 ICISA, *A Guide to Trade Credit Insurance* (Anthem Press 2015) 141. In addition, some exporters in the UK prefer buyer credit guarantees to supplier credit guarantees because progress payments are available under the former but not the latter. See Lomnicka (n 21), [25-032], [25-035], [25-041].

ply invoiced by negotiable instruments used in supplier credit facilities. A loan agreement between the buyer and a lending bank, which sets out all the details of the loan, is then necessary, for which the ECA issues a buyer credit insurance or buyer credit guarantee cover to the bank.

The bank under a buyer credit transaction can either be insured or guaranteed but, as demonstrated above, because of its legal characteristics, an ECG cover will be preferred by the bank. Therefore, some ECAs provide a buyer credit guarantee cover to the bank as a standalone and tailored product to secure the bank's finance. In particular, a respondent to the Berne Union Academic Survey provides both buyer credit insurance and buyer credit guarantees. To explore the rationale behind their products, the author of this work interviewed a senior manager of this anonymous Berne Union member, whose response was as follows:

> We provide both types of cover to meet the banks' demand (financial guarantees are more similar to other banking products and easier to use, due to their irrevocable and unconditional nature). Nevertheless, it must be noted that guarantees are only provided on a case-by-case basis (e.g., aircraft sector), and the relevant pricing is usually higher compared to standard buyer credit insurance policies.

Therefore, an ECG is used as a tailored product to the specifications of the buyer. It is available on a case-by-case basis in certain transactions (e.g., aircraft sector) of a large sum of money and a longer credit period, whereas ECI can be issued on a standard basis for general transactions. That is why, as explained in Chapter 2, the UKEF requires that the eligible export transaction under its buyer credit guarantees must have a value of over £5m and a loan period of over two years. Moreover, the abovementioned "Export Refinance Facility", the add-on to the standard buyer credit guarantees, can cover non-sterling loans with values above £50m if the loans are intended to be refinanced through the debt capital markets (DCM) or other commercial loans.

A typical example of how ECGs can support buyer credit transactions is *Export Credits Guarantee Department v Universal Oil Products Co.*[29] The transaction in that case related to the design, construction and installation of an oil refinery in Newfoundland, which involved a huge sum of money: the bank provided a loan of £39m to the buyer (who paid that loan to the exporter), and the buyer had only to pay £1m guarantee fees for the UKEF's ECG cover. The exporter conceded that without the UKEF's ECG protection, there would be no other way for English exporters to obtain export finance in respect of such a large sum of money.[30] Another example of how an ECG could cover a larger sum of money than

29 [1983] 1 Lloyd's Rep 448. The core dispute in *Universal Oil* was about the effect of the penalty clause, which has been discussed in Chapter 3 of this research.

30 The lawyer for the exporter in the appeal of *Universal Oil* made the following statement about the significance of the UKEF's ECG products:

ECI was illustrated in *Crown Aluminium Ltd v Northern and Western Insurance Co Ltd*,[31] where the exporter's existing credit insurers were not willing to continue to insure the trade transactions when the buyer began placing orders of a much higher value than in previous years. The exporter, accordingly, indicated to the buyer that it was not prepared to continue making supplies on credit without the benefit of suitable insurance. To obtain an alternative financial risk product, the buyer through a broker found a guarantor who was willing to provide the exporter several ECG covers. Although *Crown Aluminium* concerned a "basic" transaction rather than a buyer credit transaction, it again demonstrates the capability of ECGs to cover a larger transaction than ECI.

One might question why ECAs are able to provide ECGs to cover a very large sum of money which private credit insurers cannot insure under ECI. That is because ECAs, as official financial institutions supported by the state, will not become insolvent,[32] so they will always be capable of paying a guarantee to support a buyer credit transaction no matter what the guarantee amount might be. Private credit insurers, however, are not capable of doing so; otherwise, they might become insolvent.

Therefore, ECGs can be very significant in supporting some buyer credit transactions. It should be noted that in buyer credit transactions, an ECG does not necessarily operate together with a "basic" ECI cover, because the exporter in a buyer credit transaction extends credit to the buyer[33] and the loan agreement is directly concluded between the buyer and the bank. A standalone ECG cover to the bank will be sufficient, and the exporter does not generally need a separate "basic" ECI cover.[34] That said, ECGs in buyer credit transactions are often used as a standalone product.

Concluding thoughts

This research examines the law of ECI and ECGs by exploring their legal nature and why ECAs provide ECGs in addition to ECI. An ECG is a client-friendlier product and easier than ECI for banks to use, in terms of almost every aspect of a contract such as the coverage of the facility, the exclusion of documentation risk, the conditions precedent to liability, the duty of fair presentation and the claim provisions. Banks prefer an ECG because of its unconditional and on-demand

---

> There is no other source for this sort of guarantee in respect of large sums of money … My Lord, *ex facie*, this is of significance, not merely domestically (in fact not domestically at all) but internationally, because it is an export guarantee and therefore it affects the export trade of this country.

31 [2011] EWHC 1352 (TCC), [7]-[18].

32 Salcic (n 6) 11.

33 Lomnicka (n 21), [25-001].

34 Of course, the exporter can apply for a "basic" ECI cover as a supplementary cover if it is exposed to the risk of not getting paid for sums not financed by the loan, such as termination payments. See Lomnicka (n 21), [25-036].

nature. Turning the coin, an ECG is more costly than ECI, which means it remains a less common product in the market. However, compared with ECI, ECG provides a stronger form of security to banks. ECGs can better cater to the needs of some banks by being used as a "top-up" facility in addition to ECI in supplier credit transactions and as a standalone and tailored cover in buyer credit transactions. Therefore, ECGs plays as a significant role as ECI does in international trade. Both enable exporters to widen access to finance: if the financial conditions of the exporter are good, then a "basic" ECI cover will be sufficient.[35] But if the exporter needs finance to maintain a healthy cash flow, then a supplier or buyer credit facility can encourage the bank to finance the trade.[36] If the bank insists on a guarantee rather than insurance to better secure its finance, then a supplier credit guarantee or a buyer credit guarantee cover will be critical for the exporter to gain the finance and conclude the trade deal. In particular, ECI and ECGs can cater to the different risk appetites of the banks: if the transaction involves a larger amount and a longer credit period, then an ECG is more suitable than ECI. That is the reason why ECAs provide ECGs in addition to ECI.

References

Andrews, G & Millett, R, *Law of Guarantees* (7th edn, Sweet & Maxwell 2015)

Grath, A, *The Handbook of International Trade and Finance* (Kogan Page 2008)

ICISA, *A Guide to Trade Credit Insurance* (Anthem Press 2015)

Lin, C, "Why Export Credit Agencies Provides Guarantees in addition to Insurance: A Contractual Perspective" (2021) 1 LMCLQ 149.

Lomnicka, E, "Export Credit Guarantees", in M Bridge (ed) *Benjamin's Sales of Goods* (11th edn, Sweet & Maxwell 2020)

Salcic, Z, *Export Credit Insurance & Guarantees: A Practitioner's Guide* (Palgrave Macmillan 2014)

35 Lin (n 21), 165.

36 For similar commentaries, see the Hon Mrs Justice Geraldine Andrews & Richard Millett QC, *Law of Guarantees* (7th edn, Sweet & Maxwell 2015), [15-002]; Lomnicka (n 21), [25-002].

Appendix 1: Special acknowledgements

Special acknowledgement to the Berne Union members who contributed to the outcomes of the Berne Union Academic Survey

ABGF (Brazil)
ASHRA (Israel)
BANCOMEXT (Mexico)
CHUBB (UK)
Credendo (Belgium)
Credit Oman (Oman)
DHAMAN (The Arab Investment & Export Credit Guarantee Corporation)
ECGC India (India)
ECGC Zimbabwe (Zimbabwe)
EKF (Denmark)
EKN (Sweden)
Euler Hermes Gov (Germany)
Eximbanka SR (Slovakia)
Finnvera (Finland)
HKECIC (Hong Kong)
ICIEC (Islamic Development Bank Group)
KREDEX (Estonia)
KSURE (Korea)
NZECO (New Zealand)
SACE (Italy)
SERV (Switzerland)
SID (Slovenia)
Sinosure (Mainland China)
Sovereign (Bermuda)
Turk Eximbank (Turkey)
UKEF (UK)

Special acknowledgement to the Loan Market Association

Whilst the Loan Market Association ("LMA") has consented to the quotation of, and referral to, parts of its documents for the purpose of this publication, it assumes no responsibility for any use to which its documents, or any extract from them, may be put. The views and options expressed in the publication are the views of the author and do not necessarily represent those of the LMA. Furthermore, the LMA cannot accept any responsibility or liability for any error or omission.

Appendix 2: How are ECI and ECGs used by the Berne Union members? – full list

Berne Union Member	*Organisational Type*	*Basic Cover*	*Supplier Credit Facility*	*Buyer Credit Facility*
AIG (USA)	Private credit insurer	Insurance	–	Insurance
AOFI (Serbia)	ECA	Insurance	–	–
ASEI (Indonesian)	ECA	Insurance	Insurance	Insurance
ASHRA (Israel)	ECA	Insurance	–	Insurance
ATI (Kenya)	Multilateral ECA (African countries)	Insurance	–	Insurance
Atradius DSB (Netherlands)	ECA	Insurance	Guarantee	Insurance
AXA XL (UK)	Private credit insurer	Insurance	–	Insurance
BAEZ (Bulgaria)	ECA	Insurance	–	–
Bancomext (Mexico)	ECA	Insurance	–	Guarantee
BECI (Botswana)	ECA	Insurance	–	–
BPIFrance (France)	ECA	Insurance	–	Insurance
CESCE (Spain)	ECA	Insurance	Insurance	Insurance
CHUBB (UK)	Private credit insurer	Insurance	–	Insurance
COSEC (Portugal)	ECA	Insurance	–	–
Credendo (Belgium)	ECA	Insurance	Insurance	Insurance
Credit Oman (Oman)	ECA	Insurance	–	–
DHAMAN (Kuwait)	ECA	Insurance	–	Insurance
ECGC India	ECA	Insurance	–	Insurance
ECGC Zimbabwe	ECA	Insurance	–	–
ECGE (Egypt)	ECA	Insurance	–	–
ECI (United Arabia Emirates)	ECA	Insurance	–	Insurance
ECIC SA (South Africa)	ECA	Insurance	–	Insurance
ECIO (Greece)	ECA	Insurance	–	Insurance
EDC (Canada)	ECA	Insurance	–	–
EGAP (Czech)	ECA	Insurance	Insurance	Insurance
EGFI (Iran)	ECA	Insurance	–	Guarantee
Euler Hermes Gov (Germany)	ECA	Insurance	Insurance	Insurance

(*Continued*)

Berne Union Member	*Organisational Type*	*Basic Cover*	*Supplier Credit Facility*	*Buyer Credit Facility*
EIAA (Armenia)	ECA	Insurance	–	Insurance
EKF (Denmark)	ECA	Insurance	Insurance	Insurance
EKN (Sweden)	ECA	Insurance	Insurance	Insurance
EXIAR (Russia)	ECA	Insurance	–	Insurance
Exim Hu (Hungary)	ECA	Insurance	Insurance	Insurance
Exim I (Indonesia)	ECA	Insurance	Guarantee	–
Exim J (Jamaica)	ECA	Insurance	–	–
EXIM M (Malaysia)	ECA	Insurance	Insurance	–
Exim R (Romania)	ECA	Insurance	–	Insurance
Eximbanka SR (Slovakia)	ECA	Insurance	Insurance	Insurance
Eximgarant (Belarus)	ECA	Insurance	–	Insurance
Eximbank Chinese Taipei	ECA	Insurance	–	–
Eximbank Thailand	ECA	Insurance	–	Insurance
Eximbank Turkey	ECA	Insurance	–	Guarantee
Eximbank USA	ECA	Insurance	–	Insurance
EFIC (Australia)	ECA	Insurance	–	Insurance
FCIA (USA)	ECA	Insurance	Insurance	Insurance
Finnvera (Finland)	ECA	Insurance	Insurance	Insurance
HBOR Croatia	ECA	Insurance	–	Insurance
HKEC (Hong Kong)	ECA	Insurance	–	–
IEIEC (Saudi Arabia)	Multilateral ECA (Arabian countries)	Insurance	–	Insurance
JLGC (Jordan)	ECA	Insurance	Insurance	–
KAZAKHEXPORT (Kazakhstan)	ECA	Insurance	–	–
Ksure (Korea)	ECA	Insurance	Insurance	Insurance
KUKE Poland	ECA	Insurance	–	Insurance
LCI (Lebanon)	ECA	Insurance	–	–
MBDP (Macedonia)	ECA	Insurance	–	–
NEXI Japan	ECA	Insurance	–	Insurance
NZECO (New Zealand)	ECA	Insurance	Insurance	Insurance
ODL Luxembourg	ECA	Insurance	–	Insurance
OeKB Austria	ECA	Insurance	–	Insurance
QDB (Qatar)	ECA	Insurance	–	–
SACE (Italy)	ECA	Insurance	–	Insurance; Guarantee
SEP (Saudi Arabia)	ECA	Insurance	–	Insurance
SERV (Switzerland)	ECA	Insurance	–	Insurance
SID (Slovenia)	ECA	Insurance	–	Insurance
Sinosure (China)	ECA	Insurance	–	Insurance
SLECIC (Sri Lanka)	ECA	Insurance	Guarantee	–
Sovereign (Bermuda)	Private credit insurer	–	–	Insurance
UKEF (UK)	ECA	Insurance	Guarantee	Guarantee

Appendix 3: The Berne Union members' standard ECI and ECG contracts available online

All websites below were last visited on 1 February 2022.[1]

1. ASHRA, "Buyer Credit Insurance Policy": https://www.ashra.gov.il/eng/_Uploads/dbsAttachedFiles/ASHRA_Buyers_Credit_Policy_English.pdf
2. Atradius DSB, "Buyer Credit Insurance Policy": https://atradiusdutchstatebusiness.nl/en/documents/370---44.314.02.e--buyercredit-370-13.pdf
3. CESCE, "Buyer Credit Insurance General Terms": https://www.cesce.es/documents/20122/6679082/CG_Credito_Comprador_EN.pdf/8f7d6957-4038-e582-4d84-c02b54f0090a?t=1642508581952
4. Credendo, "General Terms 2021 ECA" (for all types of ECI covers): https://credendo.com/sites/default/files/media/files/2021-08/2021%20General%20Terms%20ECA%20EN.pdf
5. EGAP Czech, "Buyer Credit Insurance General Terms": https://www.egap.cz/dokumenty//field/image/produkty/vpp-d-2014-en.pdf
6. EKN, "General Conditions, Export Credit Guarantee" for all types of ECI covers: https://www.ekn.se/globalassets/dokument/allmanna-villkor/eng/general-conditions-for-export-credit-guarantees.pdf
7. Euler Hermes Germany Government Section, "Buyer Credit Insurance General Terms & Conditions": https://www.agaportal.de/_Resources/Persistent/b22c1ca09d4c0fffd49cc5182ddc524751d95613/e_ab_fkg.pdf
8. Finnvera, "General Conditions for Buyer Credit Insurance": https://www.finnvera.fi/eng/products/export-credit-guarantees/buyer-credit-guarantee
9. HBOR, "General Terms and Conditions on Insurance of Buyer Credit": https://www.hbor.hr/wp-content/uploads/2017/02/General-Terms-and-Conditions-on-Insurance-of-Buyer-Credit-OU-KK-01-17.docx

1 It should be noted that the standard term ECI and ECG contracts provided by the Berne Union members are subject to regular updates. Readers are advised to check the official websites of the Berne Union members from time to time for the latest version of these contracts.

10. KUKE, "General terms and conditions of export credit insurance guaranteed by the State Treasury-Individual Policy-Buyer's Credit": https://api.kuke.pl/files/attachments/d9c39380-3038-11ec-9df6-00abcd082070/buyer-s-credit-general-terms-and-conditions.pdf
11. NEXI, "Policy Conditions for Buyer Credit Insurance": https://www.nexi.go.jp/en/img/pdf/policy_c01.pdf
12. ODL, "Overall Agreement General Terms" for all types of ECI covers: https://odl.lu/wp-content/uploads/2019/05/GB-Version_General_Terms_664-02_new.pdf
13. OEKB, "Buyer Credit Insurance General Conditions": https://www.oekb.at/dam/jcr:a4918dd5-eb78-4c15-bd97-4e3fbaff66b4/OeKB-GeneralBusinessConditions-BuyersCredits-G3G9.pdf
14. SERV, "Buyer Credit Insurance General Terms & Conditions": https://www.serv-ch.com/fileadmin/Files/PDF/online-schalter/agb_ab_1.1.16/AGB_Kaeuferkreditversicherung_e.pdf
15. UKEF, "Specimen Export Insurance Policy" for basic ECI covers: https://assets.publishing.service.gov.uk/government/uploads/system/uploads/attachment_data/file/1041653/Docs_Policy_EXIP_SingleContract_All_Risks.pdf
16. UKEF, "Supplier Credit standard terms and conditions" for supplier credit guarantees: https://assets.publishing.service.gov.uk/government/uploads/system/uploads/attachment_data/file/889491/supplier-credit-terms-and-conditions.odt

Appendix 4: Questionnaires in the proposal forms for ECI and ECGs

Please note that the following tables are created by the author. The links of the full versions of those proposal forms for ECI/ECGs are provided under each table.[1]

Part I: sample questionnaires in the proposal form for the UKEF's ECI cover

Appendix 4.1 The main contents of the "Export Insurance Policy Proposal Form"[2]

Parts	*Questions*
1. Exporter Details	Contact details and registration information
2. Nature of Business	Goods/services the exporter supplies
	Whether the exporter is a manufacturer or a distributor of goods
	Number of years exporting
	Number of employees
3. Turnover	The estimated annual turnover for the current financial year
	Last year's domestic/export turnover
	Previous years' domestic/export turnover
4. Credit Control and Collections	The employee responsible for credit management procedures
	How many days after the due date does it contact the buyers for payment
	When does it raise the invoices and check the buyer's payment profile
	How often does it update its credit information on the buyer
	Does it have an "all monies" retention of title clause in its standard terms and conditions of trade
	Details of the three largest bad debts in the past three years
5. Buyer Details	Contact details and registration information

(*Continued*)

1 It should be noted that these forms may be subject to regular updates. Readers are advised to visit the UKEF's website to access the latest version of them.

2 Full text available at <https://assets.publishing.service.gov.uk/government/uploads/system/uploads/attachment_data/file/898048/10489_UKEF_Export_Insurance_Proposal_Form_20200331-fillable.pdf> accessed 1 February 2022.

Parts	*Questions*
6. Trading Information	Trading history with the buyer Estimated annual turnover with the buyer Details of amounts outstanding with the buyer, any failure to pay by the buyer
7. Other Insurance Arrangements	Whether it has been unable to obtain cover from the private insurance market The reason for its not being able to obtain cover Whether it has in the past held credit insurance cover on the buyer Whether it currently has any credit insurance of trade finance facilities
8. Export Contract to be Insured	Goods/services to supply The final destination of the goods/services The percentage of UK content of the export contract Whether the payments are to be made by a letter of credit Whether the payments are to be secured Whether it is a member of a group of which other members have a material part in the negotiation of the export contract Whether it is a party to any consortium which is in connection with the performance of the export contract Whether it appoints a trade agent
9. Cover Requirement	Type of cover the exporter requires Period of cover required Whether pre-credit cover is required Terms and method of payment under the export contract
10. Broker Details	Whether the exporter wishes to appoint a broker If so, the broker's contact details

(Note: In this form "it" refers to the exporter)

Part II: sample questionnaires in the proposal form for the UKEF's ECG cover

Appendix 4.2 The main contents of the "Export Questionnaire Form"[3] under "Export Working Capital Scheme"

Parts	*Questions/Requirements*
1. Exporter Corporate Details	Contact details
	Nature of business
	Number of employees
	Annual turnover
	Net profit after tax
2. Exporter Business and Customer Base	Main products or services
	Number of foreign costumers and percentage of total business turnover
	Average contract value
	Typical credit terms accepted by buyers
	Committed orders for the next three years
3. Summary of Exporting Experience	Number of years exporting
	Typical terms of trade (e.g., open account, L/C)
	Lists of countries exported to
4. Exporter Capital Structure	Committed capital
	Details of any inter-company debt
	Director's loans and terms
	Dividend policy
5. Shareholder and Management	Individuals and organisations holding more than 5% of share capital
	Board of directors
	Key managers
6. Current Financial Facilities	Provider
	Type and purpose
	Amount and limit
	Amount drawn
	Expiry date
	Security and estimated value
7. Enclosures	Audited financial statements for the past three years
	Year to date management accounts
	Financial forecasts for the next three years

3 Full text available at < https://assets.publishing.service.gov.uk/government/uploads/system/uploads/attachment_data/file/578136/ukef-bss-ewcs-export-questionnaire.pdf>, accessed 1 February 2022.

Appendix 4.3 The main contents of the "Standalone Guarantee Application Form"[4] under "Export Working Capital Scheme"

Parts	*Questions*
For Completion by the Exporter	
1. Exporter Details	Full legal company name and registration number Date of current Exporter's Questionnaire Whether all information provided in the Exporter's Questionnaire is still correct and complete
2. Export Contract Details	Buyer and destination Price and payment Delivery schedule Goods/services to be supplied
3. Ancillary Information	Exporter's experience of performing the export contract Technical, operational or financial challenges in performing the contract Exporter's experience with the buyer Is the exporter performing the contract as part of a consortium or joint venture
4. Working Capital Facility to be Guaranteed	Facility to be guaranteed Anticipated drawdown schedule Repayment schedule Trade timeline
5. Trade Agents	Whether the exporter has appointed an agent Details of the services which the agent is providing The amount of any commission, fees or other remuneration The country where the fees are payable to the agent
For Completion by the Bank	
6. Bank Details	Registration details
7. Current Relationship with the Exporter	(1) Current facilities: Type, purpose, amount, the amount drawn, expiry date, security, covenants (2) Account history: Length of relationship with the exporter Whether the exporter is an exit/watch-list/work-out customer in the past 12 months Have there been any uncured payment defaults in the past 12 months Have there been any covenant breaches in the past 12 months
8. Matters Relating to the Working Capital Facility to be Guaranteed	(1) Facility details: Whether the details in section 4 are correct (2) Guarantee details: Whether the bank wishes UKEF's guarantee to extend beyond the anticipated expiry date Percentage of the maximum value of the facility which the bank wishes UKEF to guarantee (3) Margin, interest and fees in consideration of its providing the facility: Credit margin Interest rate and basis Commitment fee and other fees Intervals at which the credit margin is payable (4) Facility agreement provisions: Covenants Events of default Other relevant provisions including risk mitigants
9. Security for the Working Capital Facility	Whether the bank hold or will receive any related security The details of the type of security and entity providing it

4 Full text available at <https://assets.publishing.service.gov.uk/government/uploads/system/uploads/attachment_data/file/618142/EWCS-BSS-stand-alone-application-20170609.pdf> accessed 1 February 2022.

Index

For Product Safety Concerns and Information please contact our EU
representative GPSR@taylorandfrancis.com
Taylor & Francis Verlag GmbH, Kaufingerstraße 24, 80331 München, Germany

www.ingramcontent.com/pod-product-compliance
Ingram Content Group UK Ltd.
Pitfield, Milton Keynes, MK11 3LW, UK
UKHW021248190926
475569UK00002BA/56

* 9 7 8 1 0 3 2 2 6 2 9 3 2 *